PITT LATIN AMERICAN SERIES

DEMOCRACY
WITHOUT EQUITY

FAILURES OF
REFORM IN
BRAZIL

Kurt Weyland

University of Pittsburgh Press

Published by the University of Pittsburgh Press, Pittsburgh, Pa. 15260
Copyright © 1996, University of Pittsburgh Press
All rights reserved

Manufactured in the United States of America
Printed on acid-free paper

10 9 8 7 6 5 4 3 2 1

Weyland, Kurt Gerhard.
    Democracy without equity : failures of reform in Brazil / Kurt Weyland.
        p.   cm. — (Pitt Latin American series)
    Includes bibliographical references and index.
    ISBN 0-8229-3924-X (cl : alk. paper). — ISBN 0-8229-5583-0 (pb : alk.
paper)
        1. Income distribution—Brazil.   2. Democracy—Brazil.   3. Brazil—
Politics and government—20th century.   4. Equality—Brazil.   5. Brazil—
Economic policy.   6. Brazil—Social policy.   I. Title.   II. Series.
HC190.I5W49   1996
330.981'06—dc20   95-51823
                                                                                  CIP

A CIP catalogue record for this book is available from the British Library.

Eurospan, London

CONTENTS

ACRONYMS

ABH	Associação Brasileira de Hospitais
ABRASCO	Associação Brasileira de Pós-Graduação em Saúde Coletiva
AD	Acción Democrática
AEB	*Anuário Estatístico do Brasil*
AEF	*Anuário Econômico-Fiscal*
AEPS	*Anuário Estatístico da Previdência Social*
AMB	Associação Médica Brasileira
ANC	Assembléia Nacional Constituinte
ANPEC	Associação Nacional de Centros de Pós-Graduação em Economia
ARENA	Aliança Renovadora Nacional
ATF	*Arrecadação dos Tributos Federais*
BC	Banco Central
CD	Câmara dos Deputados
CE	*Conjuntura Econômica*
CEBES	Centro Brasileiro de Estudos de Saúde
CGT	Central Geral dos Trabalhadores
CGT	Confederação Geral dos Trabalhadores
CIESP	Centro das Indústrias do Estado de São Paulo
CIPLAN	Comissão Interministerial de Planejamento e Coordenação
CMB	Confederação das Misericórdias do Brasil
CMS	Conselho Municipal de Saúde
CN	Congresso Nacional
CNA	Confederação Nacional da Agricultura
CNC	Confederação Nacional do Comércio
CNI	Confederação Nacional da Indústria
CNRH	Centro Nacional de Recursos Humanos
CNRS	Comissão Nacional da Reforma Sanitária

COBAP	Confederação Brasileira de Aposentados e Pensionistas
CONASS	Conselho Nacional de Secretários de Saúde
CONTAG	Confederação Nacional dos Trabalhadores na Agricultura
CPC	Confederación de la Producción y del Comercio
CSPAS	Conselho Superior de Previdência e Assistência Social
CUT	Central Única dos Trabalhadores
CUT	Central Unitaria de Trabajadores de Chile
DANC.S	*Diário da Assembléia Nacional Constituinte. Suplemento*
DATAPREV	Empresa de Processamento de Dados da Previdência Social
DIEESE	Departamento Inter-Sindical de Estatística e Estudos Socio-Econômicos
EAP	Economically Active Population
FBH	Federação Brasileira de Hospitais
FCESP	Federação do Comércio do Estado de São Paulo
FEBRABAN	Federação Brasileira de Associações de Bancos
FENAESS	Federação Nacional dos Estabelecimentos de Serviços de Saúde
FGV	Fundação Getúlio Vargas
FI	Fórum Informal
FIESP	Federação das Indústrias do Estado de São Paulo
FIPE	Fundação Instituto de Pesquisas Econômicas
FIPREV	Fórum Intersindical Permanente em Defesa da Previdência Social
FS	Força Sindical
FSE	Fundo Social de Emergência
FUNAMES	Fundação Nacional de Assistência Médico-Social
FUNRURAL	Fundo de Assistência ao Trabalhador Rural
IAPAS	Instituto de Administração Financeira da Previdência e Assistência Social
IAPI	Instituto de Aposentadoria e Pensões dos Industriários
IBGE	Instituto Brasileiro de Geografia e Estatística
IDB	Interamerican Development Bank
IEDI	Instituto de Estudos para o Desenvolvimento Industrial
IESP	Instituto de Economia do Setor Público
IL	Instituto Liberal
IMS	Instituto de Medicina Social

INAMPS	Instituto Nacional de Assistência Médica da Previdência Social
INPES	Instituto de Pesquisas
INPS	Instituto Nacional de Previdência Social
INSS	Instituto Nacional do Seguro Social
IPEA	Instituto de Planejamento Econômico e Social / Instituto de Pesquisa Econômica Aplicada
IPLAN	Instituto de Planejamento
IPS	*Informe de Previdência Social*
IRPF	*Imposto de Renda—Pessoa Física*
IUPERJ	Instituto Universitário de Pesquisas do Rio de Janeiro
MDB	Movimento Democrático Brasileiro
MEFP	Ministério da Economia, Fazenda e Planejamento
MF	Ministério da Fazenda
MIC	Ministério da Indústria e do Comércio
MPAS	Ministério da Previdência e Assistência Social
MPS	Ministério da Previdência Social
MS	Ministério da Saúde
MST	Movimento dos Trabalhadores Rurais Sem Terra
MTPS	Ministério do Trabalho e da Previdência Social
NEPP	Núcleo de Estudos de Políticas Públicas
NESP	Núcleo de Estudos de Saúde Pública
PDS	Partido Democrático Social
PDT	Partido Democrático Trabalhista
PeD	*Previdência em Dados*
PFL	Partido da Frente Liberal
PIASS	Programa de Interiorização das Ações de Saúde e Saneamento
PL	Projeto de Lei
PMDB	Partido do Movimento Democrático Brasileiro
PNAD	*Pesquisa Nacional por Amostra de Domicílios*
PNBE	Pensamento Nacional das Bases Empresariais
PSDB	Partido da Social Democracia Brasileira
PSOE	Partido Socialista Obrero Español
PT	Partido dos Trabalhadores
SAS	Secretaria de Assistência Social
SE	Secretaria Executiva
SEE	Secretaria de Estudos Especiais

SEE	Sub-Secretaria de Estudos Especiais
SEPLAN	Secretaria de Planejamento da Presidência da República
SG	Secretaria-Geral
SGA	Secretaria-Geral Adjunta
SINPAS	Sistema Nacional de Previdência e Assistência Social
SMS	Secretaria Municipal de Saúde
SP	São Paulo
SPS	Secretaria de Previdência Social
SRF	Secretaria da Receita Federal
SUDS	Sistema Unificado e Descentralizado de Saúde
TCU	Tribunal de Contas da União
TNC	Trans-National Corporation
UBE	União Brasileira de Empresários
UCD	Unión de Centro Democrático
UERJ	Universidade Estadual do Rio de Janeiro
UFRJ	Universidade Federal do Rio de Janeiro
UnB	Universidade de Brasília
UNICAMP	Universidade Estadual de Campinas
USI	União Sindical Independente
USP	Universidade de São Paulo

Acknowledgments

I WOULD like to thank the many people who contributed to my research in a variety of ways, especially all those I interviewed, and the librarians, archivists, and public officials who gave me access to crucial documents. For help that went far beyond the call of duty, I am particularly indebted to Maria Luiza Abbott, Maria Emília Rocha Mello de Azevedo, Enil Boris Barragan, Murillo Villela Bastos, Mauro Sérgio Bogéa, Celecino de Carvalho Filho, Amélia Cohn, Hésio Cordeiro, Adriana and Jimir Doniak, José Saraiva Felipe, José Augusto Coelho Fernandes, David Fleischer, Sonia Fleury, Luiz Carlos Andrade Janot, Bruno Konder, Celso Barroso Leite, Luiz Antônio de Medeiros, Marcelo Vianna Estevão de Moraes, Francisco Eduardo Barreto de Oliveira, Sérgio Piola, José Rui Gonçalves Rosa, Amarílis Prado Sardenberg, José Antônio Schöntag, Eivany Antônio da Silva, Amaury Temporal, Nelson Torreão, and Luiz Viegas. I would also like to thank the Ribeiro family, especially Ruth Ribeiro and Roberto and Lúcia Brügger da Costa, for their hospitality and generosity.

I benefited enormously from suggestions on various draft chapters made by Edward Amadeo, John Arquilla, David Bartlett, Simon Collier, Martha Finnemore, Erwin Hargrove, Laura Rosselle Helvey, Harry Makler, Rose McDermott, Roy Nelson, Robert Packenham, Timothy Power, Ben Schneider, Catherine Shapiro, David Steiner, and Francisco Weffort. I am especially indebted to Barry Ames, Richard Fagen, Evelyne Huber, Wendy Hunter, Terry Karl, Scott Mainwaring, and Philippe Schmitter for commenting on the whole manuscript in different incarnations.

I gratefully acknowledge the generous financial support of the Tinker Foundation and the Center for Latin American Studies at Stanford University, the Joint Committee on Latin American and Caribbean Studies of the Social Science Research Council and the American Council of Learned Societies (and the William and Flora Hewlett Foundation), the Kellogg Institute at the University of Notre Dame, the University Research Council of Vanderbilt University, and the National Endowment for the Humanities.

To Wendy Hunter, who has expended enormous energy to help with this project since its early stages and who has enriched my life immeasurably, I owe more than words can express.

This book is dedicated to my parents, Else and Dr. Helmut Weyland, as a small gift of gratitude for all the support, guidance, and example they have provided me over the years.

DEMOCRACY

WITHOUT

EQUITY

1

Introduction

DOES DEMOCRACY lead to social equity? Do liberty and political equality allow the poor to improve their plight by extracting resources from the rich? Or is political democratization a purely formal change that does not bring about substantively democratic, equitable policy outcomes? Scholars and philosophers since the time of Plato and Aristotle have debated these questions. Divergent assumptions about this issue have contributed greatly to the major ideological cleavages of the nineteenth and twentieth centuries, especially to the longstanding intellectual and political debates among classic liberals, Marxists, and social democrats.

Classic liberals assumed that the establishment of full democracy would empower disadvantaged sectors of the population, who would press successfully for redistributive reform. Yet they feared that the poor majority would install a "class government" (Mill 1975, 279), oppress and despoil the better-off, or endanger the market economy the classic liberals advocated. They therefore rejected complete political equality.[1] Marxists, in contrast, claimed that the formal mechanisms of democracy could not at all ensure the elimination of rule by the dominant class, whose political power derived from its exclusive control over the means of production. Insisting that only profound redistribution could bring about a democracy in which equal citizen rights would be guaranteed, even Marxists who inherently

1

valued democracy called for social revolution (Luxemburg 1970, 51–59). Social democrats, finally, shared liberals' assumptions about the empowering and redistributive impact of democracy, but lauded it as decisive for eliminating unjustified privileges and overcoming widespread poverty. They pressed for democratization, which, in addition to its value as such, would give disadvantaged sectors sufficient political influence to gradually institute a new, more just society (Bernstein 1991, 140–60).

Many contemporary political scientists of diverse theoretical orientations also claim that democracy brings about equity-enhancing reform.[2] In their view, freedom and political equality give the poor a chance to advance their interests through collective action and to form political parties, interest associations, or social movements that can press successfully for social reform. In order to preempt mass mobilization, state officials themselves may enact measures to reduce inequality and poverty. Empirical analyses, however, yield contradictory results (Sirowy and Inkeles 1990, 143–50). The methodologically sounder, yet still problematic, studies disconfirm the expected equity-enhancing impact of democracy.[3]

The debate about this issue is highly relevant for the Third World, where democracy is still contested, social inequality is particularly profound, and poverty affects much of the population. Has the recent wave of transitions from (usually conservative) authoritarian rule led to equity-enhancing reforms? Has democratization brought about redistribution by allowing the poor to articulate their interests and needs, which have long been suppressed? One may not expect radical challenges to the existing socioeconomic order; but have gradual reforms been made?

My study addresses these questions by examining the equity-enhancing impact of the recent restoration of democracy in Brazil, a country with one of the most skewed income distributions in the world. Specifically, I investigate the processes and outcomes of decision making in the areas of tax and social security policy, which can have considerable redistributive impact (and which have therefore been central to European social democracy). To assess the difference that democratization made in Brazil, the study compares the authoritarian government of President Ernesto Geisel (1974–1979), which initiated the country's slow process of democratic transition, with the first three civilian governments after the military regime (1964–1985), headed by José Sarney (1985–1990), Fernando Collor de Mello (1990–1992), and Itamar Franco (1992–1994).

Many political forces in Brazil assumed that the return to democracy would bring about some redistributive reform. In the early to mid-1980s, the major opposition party called for greater social justice (PMDB 1982). Masses of peasants mobilized for agrarian reform. Workers embarked on a wave of strikes to recoup wage losses (Sandoval 1993, 171–84). Other poor and disadvantaged groups, organizing in mushrooming social movements, were eager to voice their pent-up demands. While not fearing a major threat to the socioeconomic order (Payne 1994, 94–102), business was concerned about the rise of populists, like the earlier firebrand Leonel Brizola, and the redistributive measures they might take.

Contrary to these expectations, democratization in Brazil thus far has brought about very little redistributive change. Agrarian reform has been blocked. The program to provide cheap housing for the poor, which had been diverted to subsidizing the middle class, has been stalled. Emergency measures to distribute food to the needy have been undermined by widespread corruption and political patronage. Taxation has not become more progressive. The social security system has done little to extend coverage and eliminate privileges, and the health care system is still distorted by its heavy emphasis on curative treatments. The recent extension of public medical care to all the poor simply completes a gradual policy initiated by the authoritarian regime. Only one poor sector has made a net gain in one issue area, namely the rural population, who were meagerly compensated for the blocked agrarian reform by better social security benefits.[4]

What accounts for the dearth of equity-enhancing reform in Brazil's new democracy? The frequent response that elites retained most of their enormous power throughout the transition to democracy (Alves 1988) leaves most of the question unanswered. This claim provides a more or less accurate description[5] but not an explanation for the persistence of elite dominance. It remains unclear why and how elites could hang on to their power, despite a profound revamping of the rules of the political game. Why could poorer strata, like workers and peasants, not take advantage of the new opportunities for political participation that the return to democracy opened up?

What, then, does account for the dearth of redistribution in post-authoritarian Brazil? This book assesses three main lines of explanation. First, problems in joining forces for collective action (Olson 1971) may keep the poor from making redistributive demands. Second, external dependency and the ensuing distortions in the class structure may make re-distribution impossible. Third, institutional obstacles may impede equity-enhancing reform.

This book emphasizes the importance of institutional structures, which set parameters for collective action and mediate the impact of socioeco-nomic variables. As the case studies that follow show, organizational frag-mentation in society and in the state has created crucial impediments to redistributive reform in Brazil's new democracy. Associations of narrow scope and personalist links to people of higher status have kept the poor divided and separated them from potential allies. Few, if any, encompassing interest associations and social movements or broad-based political parties have emerged through which the poor could successfully advance their interest in redistribution. Personalist networks and narrow associations have also helped corrode the internal unity of the state. "Bureaucratic politics" has undermined the state's capacity to impose equity-enhancing reform on reluctant elites.[6]

These organizational factors have arisen from the pattern of Brazil's so-cioeconomic and political development. Rapid industrialization has rested on close cooperation between the state and private business, has integrated only part of the populace into the formal economy, and has left the numer-ically substantial remainder marginalized. In addition to their divergent interests, various social strata differ greatly in the form and effectiveness of their organizations. The lower classes have been incorporated into narrow organizations that keep them apart from each other and divide them inter-nally. Unable to act as a united front, they have not been able to effectively use their only significant power capability, namely their large numbers.

In contrast, organizations of narrow scope have given socioeconomic elites close links of institutional access to the state through which they have brought their enormous resources to bear with particular effective-ness. They do not need encompassing collective action nearly as much as the poor. Organizational obstacles have thus decisively aggravated the difference in power capabilities between the poor and the elite and made it extremely difficult for the lower classes to reverse social inequality.

The close connections between state agencies and business groups have exacerbated centrifugal tendencies inside the state, which lacks internal cohesion. As a result, state officials face tremendous problems when they try to advance redistributive initiatives. They have often run into diffi-culties inside their own agencies, whose bureaucratic staff insist on maintaining established procedures and narrow organizational interests, and they have encountered fierce opposition by other agencies that jealously guard their "turf" against any encroachments. Rampant bureaucratic politics has prevented the Brazilian state from enacting redistributive reform against elite resistance. Thus, low organizational scope—that is, fragmentation in society and the state—has created tremendous obstacles both to bottom-up and top-down efforts for equity-enhancing change.

CONTRIBUTIONS OF THIS STUDY

This book addresses several important debates in political science. First of all, it focuses on the age-old, yet very acute, problem of the relationship between democracy and equity. As mentioned earlier, different assumptions and value judgments about this issue have given rise to major theories and ideologies with enormous historical consequences. By providing empirical findings and, especially, a theoretical explanation, this study may help put the future discussion about the achievements and limits of democratic reformism on a more solid basis. Depending on an ultimate value choice, the selection of political goals is, of course, beyond the scope of this study.[7] But knowledge about the chances and requirements for achieving certain goals can make decisions about political strategies more rational.

The democracy/equity issue is particularly relevant for Latin American countries like Brazil. Equity-enhancing reform has decisive implications for the inclusiveness (Dahl 1971, 4–9) and the long-term stability of democracy in the region. In countries with extreme inequalities, redistributive change is indispensable for effectively extending citizenship to the poor. As the basic principle underlying democracy (Schmitter 1983, 891–96), universal citizenship demands that all members of a political community have equal chances of being taken into consideration when public decisions are made (Dahl 1971, 2).

Social inequality endangers this principle in Latin America. Abject poverty forces many people to enter into clientelist bonds with elites who offer minimal benefits and protection in exchange for obedience and political support—that is, for an abdication of citizen rights (Hagopian 1986; Gay 1988; Schmidt et al. 1977). Many poor people hardly act autonomously in politics. Only benefits guaranteed by the state through redistributive measures can break the hold of clientelist patrons and set the poor free to effectively exercise their citizen rights. Thus, the success of equity-enhancing reform conditions how restricted and elitist democracy in the region will be.

The absence of such redistributive measures might even endanger the very survival of democracy in the long run. Social elites may use their captive support among the rural poor for anti-democratic ends, as happened in Germany and Japan in the first half of the twentieth century (Moore 1967, 426). Alternately, the disadvantaged may be available for mobilization by populists, and the resulting sudden and widespread "unrest" may scare elite groups into appealing to the military for protection.[8] If transitional risks are avoided,[9] for instance through a pact guaranteeing the basic interests of all groups involved (Jaguaribe et al. 1986, 1989), redistribution could prevent those looming dangers and bolster the long-term stability of a democratic regime (Karl 1990, 13). Thus, the impact of democratization on equity-enhancing reform may affect the survival and quality of democracy itself.

By analyzing the effect of democratization on redistribution, this study takes the recent discussion on regime transitions one step further. Up to now, researchers have mainly investigated the causes and conditions of regime change (O'Donnell, Schmitter, and Whitehead 1986; Diamond, Linz, and Lipset 1989; Huntington 1991; Przeworski 1991; Stepan 1989) but not its substantive impact. The few analyses of the impact have focused almost exclusively on specific economic issues, especially structural adjustment to the debt crisis (Stallings and Kaufman 1989; Nelson 1990; Haggard and Kaufman 1992). Whereas most prior analyses took democratization as the dependent variable, this book uses it as the independent variable. In this way, the study contributes to the longstanding debate on whether politics, and more specifically regime change, makes a difference for the substance of decision making (see esp. Dahl 1971, chaps. 2, 6).

The book helps to fill another gap in the literature on democratic transitions in Latin America, which has so far been clearly society-centered. Whereas numerous analyses have been made of the role of political parties, interest associations, and social movements in processes of democratization,[10] little attention has been devoted to the state.[11] This book is "bringing the state back in" (Evans, Rueschemeyer, and Skocpol 1985). By examining how public policy making is affected by democratization, this analysis pays special attention to the state in its interaction with society. The state has played a crucial role as an authority structure and actor; it has also been influenced by social groups, especially business. Therefore, an interactive approach to state-society relations is most appropriate for the analysis of regime change and its effects (Skocpol 1985, 19–20; see recently Migdal, Kohli, and Shue 1994).

Finally, this book addresses the current debate in political science among different paradigms, namely rational choice, socioeconomic approaches, and institutionalism. It tries to show the usefulness of a neo-statist/institutionalist approach,[12] which provides the necessary context for rational choice and socioeconomic arguments. The latter make important contributions but are inadequate in their explanations unless they 'are embedded in an institutionalist framework.

Rational choice tends to take actors, their interests, and the parameters of their actions simply as given. It can account for the impact of institutions but not for their emergence. The claim that institutions are the purposive creation of rational individuals (Alt and Shepsle 1990, 2) or efficient solutions to problems of contracting (Williamson 1985, 23–32) vastly over-estimates the flexibility and functionality of institutions and neglects the institutional constraints on institutional change. Rational-choice arguments need to be grounded in an institutionalist explanation.

Socioeconomic approaches, such as dependency theory, call attention to crucial socioeconomic structures. But they tend to overlook the fact that institutional factors mediate the impact of these structures and condition their very constitution. In many developing countries, the state helped create social classes and shaped their interests and power capabilities. Institutional patterns thus set crucial parameters for rational choice and the operation of socioeconomic variables. Institutionalism/neo-statism provides the basic framework for the other approaches.

CLARIFYING THE TERMS OF THIS STUDY

Democracy

The concept of democracy has been understood in a wide variety of ways. This book uses a minimalist, formal-procedural notion because it seeks to discover what impact these procedures have on substantive reform. Adding input or output features like broad citizen participation or equitable public policies would rule out the current investigation or condemn it to "discovering" tautologies. *Democracy* is therefore defined as a set of institutions that, in the context of guarantees for political freedom, permits the entire adult population to choose their leading decision makers in competitive, honest, regularly scheduled elections and to advance their interests and ideas through peaceful individual or collective action.[13] These procedures for political choice are designed to make the citizenry the ultimate authority for public decision making.

According to this procedural definition, Brazil's gradual return to democracy started in 1974. After 1985, except for the indirect election of President Sarney,[14] all electoral posts have been filled through direct competitive elections, and the rules of democracy have been observed with considerable (though not perfect) honesty. As a result, all office holders with political ambitions for the future have faced the need to prepare their (re-)election. This anticipation of voter sanctions constitutes the central mechanism for guaranteeing democratic accountability. The electoral imperative has been obvious to politicians since Brazil held elections for various offices in 1985, 1986, 1988, 1989, 1990, 1992, and 1994; many national office holders ran as candidates for regional or even municipal posts. As regards citizens, legal chances for individual and collective political participation have after 1985 been equal and open to all categories of society, and a wide variety of groups have advanced demands. For all these reasons, the period from March 1985 on can be classified as democratic.

Certainly, however, Brazilian democracy in the late 1980s was imperfect. Most important, only the 1988 constitution gave Congress influence over the budget,[15] and the first popular election of a president took place in late 1989. The preceding deviations from democratic principles limit the strength of the conclusions about the redistributive capacity of democracy that my analysis of the Sarney government can yield. The case studies show, however, that organizational obstacles that operated in the late 1980s have continued to impede equity-enhancing reform in the early 1990s. As this comparison suggests, the imperfect state of Brazilian democracy in the late 1980s did not have a decisive impact on the chances for redistributive change; it therefore does not undermine the main argument of my study.

The fact that Brazil returned to democracy fairly recently, however, limits the generalizability of my conclusions. Strictly speaking, the findings of this book can claim validity only for the first ten years of a new democracy. Whereas they can plausibly be applied to established democracies, this issue merits further research. The comparative analysis of the concluding chapter can only begin to address this question.

In this book, which analyzes the impact of a *transition to* democracy, references to "authoritarian rule" mean the conservative military regimes that prevailed in Latin America in the 1970s. O'Donnell's (1979) "bureaucratic-authoritarianism" is their prototype. Mobilizational regimes, like those of Cuba and Nicaragua (1979–1990) as well as Peru's reformist military regime (1968–1975), are excluded from the analysis presented in this book.

Redistribution

Following Lowi (1964, 691), *redistribution* is defined as any change in the shares that broad categories of people have in a society's material wealth.[16] By covering only measures that affect broad categories of people,[17] this notion excludes "doling out" particularistic benefits to specific individuals and small groups, which is classified as a distributive measure. This distinction has important implications for decision making. Since redistributive policies benefit broad categories of people, the drain of resources they create on the finite sum of national wealth or public revenue usually becomes an issue. By altering relative shares in national wealth, redistributive policies have a zero-sum character (at least in the short run). Some categories win; others necessarily lose. In contrast, distributive policies dispense particularistic benefits without sensitivity to the finite sum of national wealth or public revenue through which they are financed. They give to some without visibly taking away from others.

This study deals only with social redistribution, that is, with measures involving broad categories of people defined by socioeconomic characteristics. Other types of redistribution—for example, redistribution among different generations, races, or regions—will not be considered (except as proxy for social redistribution). Generalizing a concept of tax theory, the book calls redistribution progressive if it favors the poorer over the richer socioeconomic strata; the opposite is termed regressive.

This book analyzes redistributive policy making and policy outputs, such as the allocation of public spending to the rich or the poor. It does not focus on policy outcomes, such as the distribution of income in society, which is affected not only by policy outputs, but also by many important "confounding" factors, such as economic growth and inflation.

Institutions and Organizations

Institutions are clearly defined, fairly stable systems of formal or informal rules that are designed to govern individual action and social interaction and that are enforced by sanctioning mechanisms based ultimately on coercion or expulsion. Institutions of domination, whose rules claim universal validity in a given domain, especially the state, can draw on coercion; institutions whose rules claim validity only for their members, such as democratic political parties, rely on (the threat of) expulsion. Political institutions include constitutional regimes, the state and its bureaucratic apparatus, political parties, and clientelist networks. In contrast to institutions, social and cultural norms, such as the norm not to have children out of wedlock, demand compliance but are not necessarily backed up by coercive sanctioning mechanisms. Sociocultural norms that lack institutional support have to rely on the power of persuasion and social pressure; institutions rely—as a last resort—on physical force or on expulsion.

An organization is an institution that integrates a group of people and orients them toward common goals so that they operate to some extent as a collective actor.[18] An organization thus is an institution to which supra-individual interests can be imputed. As March and Olsen (1989, 18) affirm, "Whether it makes pragmatic theoretical sense to impute interests . . . to an institution is neither more nor less problematic, a priori, than whether it makes sense to impute them to an individual."[19] A state or a political party, for instance, usually has sufficient unity of purpose to be considered an actor in its own right. Similarly, a clientelist network that seeks to gain access to patronage counts as an informal organization. By contrast, a political regime such as democracy is not an actor pursuing interests, but a normative framework for actors.

This book focuses on political organizations, particularly the degree of their internal coherence and their extension or encompassingness. Despite considerable overlap, this focus diverges somewhat from that of scholars who stress the impact of constitutional structure and other formal regime rules (Immergut 1990; Huber, Ragin, and Stephens 1993, 719–22; Tsebelis 1994; see also Linz and Valenzuela 1994). The reasons are twofold. In Latin America, political practice often deviates from formal rules. I therefore pay considerable attention to informal institutions, such as clientelist networks. Also, in "politicized" regimes (Chalmers 1977; Power 1991), legal rules are usually less enduring than basic characteristics of organizations, which have a powerful tendency to perpetuate themselves and often remain unaffected by formal rule changes. For instance, Chile's parties retained their strong organization and program orientation despite the adoption of an open list system of proportional representation (Mainwaring 1991, 29), which is often invoked as a crucial reason for party weakness in Brazil. Since organizations have relative autonomy from and greater weight than formal rules, I place them at the core of my explanation.

The State

This book uses a political-institutional concept of the state. The state is defined as the territorially based institution that "successfully claims the monopoly of legitimate physical coercion for the execution of its orders."[20] For the purpose of this study, such a political-institutional concept is vastly preferable to notions that incorporate socioeconomic elements. Defining the state as a "pact of domination" among social classes (Cardoso 1979, 38–40; see also Poulantzas 1980) would a priori restrict the autonomy of the state from the class structure and predetermine the result of this study. A class-neutral definition of the state is essential for examining empirically the influence of different social categories on public policy making.[21]

RESEARCH DESIGN

Why Brazil?

For analyzing the impact of democratization on redistribution, it is necessary to study a country whose citizens have a need for and an interest in equity-enhancing change. The need is strong where inequality is high, poverty is extensive, and economic stagnation leaves the poor little hope of improving their standard of living without redistribution. If in such a society redistributive needs are expressed as demands and reform proposals, the interest in equity-enhancing reform can be assumed to be considerable.

Accordingly, an excellent case for analyzing the impact of democratization on redistribution is Brazil. The country has one of the most skewed distributions of income in the world. Toward the end of military rule, in 1983, the richest 10 percent of the population held 46.2 percent of the nation's wealth (World Bank, *WDR* 1992, 277). This proportion is very high in international comparison, even in the Latin American context. The corresponding figure for the United States is 25 percent (1985), 23.4 percent for West Germany (1984), 33.2 percent for Venezuela (1989), and 39.5 percent for Mexico (1984) (World Bank, *WDR* 1993, 297). At the other end of the social pyramid, the poorest 20 percent of Brazil's population had 2.4 percent of national wealth, compared to 4.7 percent in the United States, 6.8 percent in West Germany, 4.8 percent in Venezuela, and 4.1 percent in Mexico.

This unequal distribution of income entails for the majority of Brazilians a life of poverty and for many a subhuman existence in abject misery. In 1988, 29.1 percent of the working population earned up to one minimum wage (IBGE 1990, 81), which at the time was worth about forty dollars per month. People forced to live on such little income cannot even fulfill their basic needs. Malnutrition, abysmal housing, deficient sanitary conditions, and neglect of major health problems are widespread in a country that also offers all the amenities of a comfortable life to the privileged few.

Since 1980, economic growth has been slow in this extremely unequal society. In contrast to the period from 1965 to 1980, when the average annual growth rate of GDP reached 9 percent, in the first half of the 1980s the aggregate growth rate dropped to 1.3 percent. If the increase in population (2.3 percent per year) is taken into account, the country's wealth *declined* in per capita terms (World Bank, *WDR* 1987, 205, 255). This stagnation did not give the poor good reason to hope for "automatic" gains from economic development. Redistribution was one of the few available avenues for improving their condition.

The need for redistribution has been subjectively perceived, defined as a political problem, and articulated in many ways.[22] In the early 1980s, discontent with the military government's meager record on social equity was already widespread (Rochon and Mitchell 1989, 309). The reinstallation of civilian rule unleashed a wave of pent-up demands. Urban workers pressed for wage hikes in numerous strikes (Sandoval 1993, 171–84), and part of the rural population mobilized in favor of agrarian reform (Santos 1985, 283–86, 299–301). The National Confederation of Workers in Agriculture has for many years demanded progressive redistribution (CONTAG 1984, 1988, 1989). Government experts have elaborated and promoted numerous proposals for equity-enhancing reform (SEPLAN 1985; MPAS 1986b;

MPAS. SEE 1988a; Resende 1986; Rosa 1986; L. Silva 1986). Masses of people expressed their diffuse desire for redistribution by voting for a leftist candidate, Luís Inácio Lula da Silva, who almost won the 1989 presidential election.

Thus, there seems to be considerable interest in equity-enhancing change in Brazil.[23] Redistributive demands and reform attempts and the resulting negotiations and conflicts provide ample material for this study. As one of the best cases for analyzing the impact of democracy on redistribution, the Brazilian experience should have implications for other countries as well. The factors that have caused the dearth of equity-enhancing change in Brazil should also affect the chances for social reform in other nations.

Why Focus on Tax and Social Security Policy?

To analyze the impact of democratization on the *politics* of redistribution, it is useful to focus on issue areas that affect a wide range of classes and sectors. A sectoral measure, such as agrarian reform, would not be an appropriate object for this study. Issue areas that are much better suited are direct taxation and social security.[24] Social security policy can effect a compensatory redistribution that corrects perceived distortions in the primary distribution of wealth resulting from the socioeconomic system. By extracting financial contributions from certain socioeconomic strata and conceding benefits to others, the social security system can alter their shares in national wealth. As direct and indirect contributors or as beneficiaries, most social categories are affected by social security, which has a crucial impact on social stratification (Esping-Andersen 1990, chap. 3) and on citizenship (Marshall 1963).

Tax policy has a redistributive potential that was evident to political theorists from Marx (1971, 547) to Tocqueville (1955, 98–104). By placing the burden of extracting resources from society on certain socioeconomic strata, the state can alter the primary distribution of income. Direct taxation is a more interesting case for this study than indirect taxation. It is visible and therefore arouses more demands and conflicts. Decision making involves a broader range of actors, whose interests, power capabilities, and patterns of interaction can be analyzed. Democratization can be expected to affect the politics and policy of direct taxation much more than indirect taxation.

All of society is affected by direct taxation. The majority of the population benefits from the public provision of collective goods without contributing revenues through direct tax payments. Because of Brazil's extremely skewed income distribution, only a minority of all citizens has to pay direct taxes. This well-to-do minority is spread across the different sectors of economy and society and includes the classes with most socioeconomic weight and political influence. Business and the middle class are the main direct taxpayers, but even better-off workers have to deduct income taxes from their wages. For these reasons, direct taxation is an appropriate case for analyzing the politics of redistribution.

Besides their crucial impact on the economic well-being of a wide range of classes and sectors, social security and taxation deeply affect the political power of these social actors and the state. The neo-statist/institutionalist approach of this study sees redistribution not only as politics of allocation, but also as politics of domination (Krasner 1984, 224–25). Wealth is at stake but also, and often more important, so is political power.

Thus, taxation allows the state to monitor and direct its citizens and to extract political support through incentives and sanctions. Since public bureaucrats have considerable discretion in the application of tax rules, businesspeople who oppose state goals have to fear retaliation.[25] Limiting the state's political control is therefore a preeminent motive for business resistance to extensions of taxation. Social security affects the power of a particularly wide range of actors. By providing benefits to large numbers of people, reform initiators can build political support and eclipse rivals.[26] They can also strengthen the state's direct control over its citizens. Established patrons see their political command over their clientelist followers threatened, whereas the latter can gain more latitude for independent demand making. Thus, redistribution shifts political power among social classes and sectors and strengthens state control over society. The following analysis therefore sheds light on changes in power relations among crucial political actors.

To arrive at broadly applicable conclusions, this study investigates policy areas that diverge on a number of dimensions yet share the feature of organizational fragmentation. The lack of redistributive reform in these issue areas can therefore be attributed to this common characteristic.

Tax and social security policy differ considerably in the kinds of issues and the types of actors involved in decision making. Whereas direct taxation imposes costs on specific categories, its benefits are widely diffused. In contrast, social security directly benefits many people, but its costs are much harder to pinpoint.[27] As regards actors, the technically competent Finance Ministry (Ministério da Fazenda–MF)[28] and its Secretariat of Federal Revenue (Secretaria da Receita Federal—SRF) face opposition from powerful business groups in tax policy; other social categories rarely get involved. In social security policy, the Ministry of Social Insurance and Welfare (Ministério da Previdência e Assistência Social–MPAS)[29] deals with a broad range of social and political forces, especially business sectors, trade unions, pensioners, and party politicians.

Regardless of these differences in issue type and actors, organizational fragmentation prevails in both areas. As regards bureaucratic politics, the MF faces strong rivalry from the Ministry of Planning (Secretaria de Planejamento–SEPLAN), and the MPAS from the Ministry of Health (Ministério da Saúde–MS) and the semiautonomous social security agencies. As for fragmentation in society, none of the social and political forces that are affected by or participate in decision making are comprehensively organized. In both areas, this low organizational scope has posed great obstacles to equity-enhancing reform, as the case studies demonstrate. Given this underlying similarity, my findings should be valid regardless of the specificity of the issue area. At least for Brazil, they should have general applicability.

THE ARGUMENT

Chapter 2 presents the main theoretical argument of this book. First it outlines the ways in which democratization could, theoretically, bring about redistribution. Then it critically discusses competing explanations for the actual dearth of equity-enhancing reform in Brazil's new democracy. Rational-choice and socioeconomic arguments are found deficient; they need to be integrated into an institutionalist framework. I emphasize the importance of organizational scope. Redistributive reform, which needs broad-based support to overcome likely elite opposition, is extremely hard to effect where narrow, fragmented patterns of organization prevail in society and inside the state. Organizational fragmentation makes effective interest representation difficult for the poor, who would benefit from equity-enhancing reforms, and strengthens their elite opponents by giving them privileged access to decision makers.

Chapter 3 turns to the examination of the Brazilian case, showing that low organizational scope has prevailed in society and inside the state. This institutional fragmentation has persisted throughout both authoritarian and democratic rule. The discussion of the historical development of organizational patterns also lays the basis for the subsequent investigation of tax and social security policy by introducing the main actors that are involved in decision making.

Chapters 4 through 7 use the theoretical framework of chapter 2 for a comparative analysis of decision making in direct taxation and social security. To shed light on the special characteristics of policy making under democracy, chapter 4 examines—as a contrast case—the decision-making process at the beginning of the regime change, namely under the government of President Geisel (1974–1979).

Chapters 5 through 7 investigate decision making in the new democracy in direct taxation, social insurance, and health care. The analysis follows numerous reform initiatives through different stages of the policy-making process and shows how the advocates and beneficiaries of redistributive change were weakened and its opponents strengthened by the organizational obstacles discussed in chapter 2. Analyses of decision outputs confirm the dearth of redistributive change under democracy.

Chapter 8 draws conclusions from the empirical analysis and reassesses the theoretical ideas of chapter 2. It also discusses how much room my institutional constraint approach leaves for political leadership. Then I broaden my view beyond the case of Brazil and discuss how the findings of this book apply to other countries. This comparative analysis focuses on Latin America, but also extends to India, the United States, and Europe.

The case studies are based on ample written documentation collected during two years of field research in Brazil (July and August 1987; September 1988 through March 1990; May through July 1992; October 1994). A wealth of reform proposals, executive projects, legislative bills, congressional committee records, laws and decrees, as well as petitions, suggestions, and criticisms from interest associations made it possible to reconstruct policy making in detail. Two hundred seventy-five interviews with interest group representatives, politicians, and state officials yielded insights into the crucially important informal aspects of Brazilian politics. Finally, two months of field research in Chile (June to August 1993) provided a comparative perspective.

2

Explaining the Dearth of
Redistribution Under Democracy

WHAT ACCOUNTS for the lack of redistribution in post-authoritarian Brazil? What prevented the many equity-enhancing efforts of social groups, politicians, and government experts from coming to fruition? To address these questions, this chapter outlines first the mechanisms through which democratization could, theoretically, bring about greater social justice. Thereafter, it critically discusses rational-choice and socioeconomic explanations for the dearth of redistributive measures in Brazil. These explanations make important contributions, but they are deficient, especially because of their neglect of institutional factors.

The main theoretical argument of this study therefore embeds rational-choice and socioeconomic arguments in a neo-statist/institutionalist framework. I claim that organizational fragmentation poses crucial obstacles to redistributive reform in democracies like Brazil's. Established fragmented patterns of organization, such as pervasive clientelism, impede the emergence of encompassing interest associations, broad-based social movements, and minimally program-oriented catch-all parties that could effectively press for equity-enhancing reform. They also undermine the internal unity of the state, which, as a result, cannot impose redistribution against elite opposition. This fragmentation of society and the state systematically weakens the proponents and beneficiaries of equity-enhancing measures and strengthens their opponents.

POTENTIAL IMPACT OF DEMOCRACY ON REDISTRIBUTION

Democratization may induce redistribution in two different ways, namely through bottom-up pressure from a mobilized society or through top-down state initiatives. With bottom-up pressure, a transition to democracy, which removes authoritarian restrictions on political participation, allows the poor and disadvantaged to promote their interests and press for redistributive reform.[1] Such pressure may be channeled through three different organizational mechanisms that democratization opens up: (1) autonomous interest associations; (2) social movements; and (3) political parties. In addition, redistribution can be effected through (4) top-down reform, that is, through efforts by state officials trying to preempt bottom-up pressure and to increase their autonomy from established elites.

Pressure for Redistribution Through Interest Associations

Democratization may enable the poor and disadvantaged to press successfully for redistributive reform through autonomous interest associations, such as trade unions. Under authoritarian rule, interest associations of popular sectors are prohibited or heavily controlled. With the regime change, new, independent organizations may spring up, and the existing associations may gain autonomy and strength. The popular sectors can acquire a powerful independent voice. By joining forces on a sustained basis in interest associations, the poor can effectively promote their collective interests, including their demand for a greater share in national wealth.[2]

In this model of organized democracy,[3] the influence of associations depends on the socioeconomic and political weight of their members and the encompassingness (Olson 1982, 47–53) and cohesion of their organization. The more they can act as a broad united front, the better their chances of success. In order to guarantee coordinated action, interest associations develop strong bureaucratic organizations. They tend to pursue pragmatic goals, especially economic interests, not moral values and ideals. These characteristics set them apart from other mechanisms of bottom-up pressure, especially social movements.

Pressure for Redistribution Through Social Movements

Democratization may also lead to redistributive reform by stimulating the proliferation of social movements. When the suppression of political participation by authoritarian rulers ends, popular mobilization and organization are unleashed (O'Donnell and Schmitter 1986, chap. 5). Expressing democratic and egalitarian values and reasserting their collective identity as citizens, the poor and disadvantaged spontaneously form social movements and demand redistributive reform.

Broad-based mobilization allows the poor to take advantage of the multiple avenues of political participation that democratization opens up. Social movements may become central channels of popular participation in the new democracy. They are particularly apt to use mechanisms of direct democracy, such as local community councils and national plebiscites. In this model of participatory democracy,[4] social movements try to guarantee the human dignity and full citizenship of their members through sociopolitical reforms, especially redistributive change.

Pressure for Redistribution Through Political Parties

By making elections a decisive mechanism of political choice, democratization leads to the emergence of parties that compete for citizens' votes. If parties were allowed at all under authoritarian rule (as in Brazil), they were tightly controlled. But under democracy, parties are free to advance their promises and programs and to appeal to any social class for support.

Under these conditions, electoral competition may induce parties to advance the interests of the poor and disadvantaged, including their desire for redistribution. In Latin America, large numbers of poor people are eligible to vote. Striving for majorities, parties have a strong incentive to cater to their interests and promise redistributive reform.[5] If parties that pursue this strategy are elected to the government, they can translate bottom-up pressure for redistribution directly into authoritative action. Thus, partisan democracy may bring about equity-enhancing reform.[6]

Redistribution Through Autonomous State Initiatives

Democracy may also bring about redistribution through top-down reforms in a model of vicarious democracy. Public officials try to guarantee the state goal of sociopolitical stability after authoritarian controls on popular mobilization are eliminated. In order to preempt bottom-up pressure, they may try to reduce stark inequalities by "conceding" equity-enhancing reforms on their own. They may also effect redistribution in order to increase their autonomy from elites who enjoyed a privileged position under authoritarian rule but whose political weight was weakened by democratization.[7]

Bureaucratic commitment to universalist principles, which receives a boost from the assertion of political equality under democracy, may also prompt state officials to enact redistributive measures.[8] As a result of their professional socialization and their institutional responsibility for the "common good," public servants may resent the privileges of the rich, such as tax exemptions, and discriminations against the poor, such as their exclusion from social protection. In these ways, democratization may motivate state officials to impose redistributive reform on their own, independent of bottom-up pressure by social forces.

Relationships Among Different Equity-Enhancing Mechanisms

Although they embody distinct concepts of democracy, these mechanisms can be combined. One social force may apply different mechanisms in different decision-making arenas. For instance, labor movements in Europe have advanced their redistributive interests via trade unions in collective bargaining and via political parties in parliament (Stephens 1986, chap. 4). Various forces using different channels of bottom-up pressure can ally themselves and work for the same goals, as labor unions, catch-all parties, and middle-class social movements have done repeatedly in Europe—for example, in Norway (Olsen 1983, chap. 1; Rokkan 1966). Bottom-up pressure and top-down initiatives can also reinforce each other, as in the creation of welfare states in Europe (Kraus 1987, 207–14) or as in various countries' reactions to the Great Depression after 1929 (Weir and Skocpol 1985, 117–49). Whereas such combinations strengthen the redistributive impact of democratization, each one of the four mechanisms is, in principle, *sufficient* for bringing about equity-enhancing reform. Therefore, my explanation for the dearth of redistribution in Brazil's new democracy must point to impediments that have hindered all of these mechanisms.

OBSTACLES TO REDISTRIBUTION: RIVAL APPROACHES

Why has democracy not brought about greater equity in Brazil? What explains the frequent failures and meager outcomes of efforts at redistribution? Three approaches offer divergent explanations. Rational-choice arguments point to collective-action problems (Olson 1971), which hinder challenges by the poor masses to elite privileges. Second, the socioeconomic approach claims that the external dependency of Third World countries and the resulting skewed balance of domestic class forces impede redistribution. Third, the institutionalist approach argues that organizational fragmentation in society and the state poses the main obstacle to reform. Specifically, pervasive personalist links, a segmented structure of interest associations, and rampant bureaucratic politics are said to block the four equity-enhancing mechanisms of democracy.

This section assesses the usefulness of the first two explanations. Rational-choice and socioeconomic theories emphasize important causal factors. But they often err by simply taking these factors as given. They overlook the fact that institutional structures constitute the crucial context for rational-choice calculations and socioeconomic variables. The next section therefore elaborates an institutionalist framework for explaining the dearth of equity-enhancing reform in Brazil's new democracy.

Rational-Choice Arguments

Why do the many poor people not extract more benefits from the few rich?[9] Rational-choice explanations start from Olson's insight that collective action becomes ever more difficult as the number of potential actors increases (1971, 34–52). While smaller groups may reach binding agreements to cooperate, large numbers of actors face enormous problems in inducing their members to work toward a common goal. According to this logic, redistribution is rare in Brazil's new democracy because the mass of poor people are unable to band together in collective action. Therefore, they cannot compensate for elite control over enormous power capabilities and use their large numbers to press successfully for equity-enhancing reforms. In contrast, the narrow elite can easily organize to defend their privileges and employ their power capabilities effectively.[10]

Since a broad mass challenge is unlikely, and the elite do not need an encompassing defense organization, the elite tend to form narrow "distributional coalitions" that single-mindedly pursue their own special interests (Olson 1982, 41–47). These small, elite groups refuse to make sacrifices for the sake of general interests, such as the legitimacy of the established sociopolitical order. They insist on maintaining their privileges and oppose equity-enhancing efforts. The same logic applies to strategically placed non-elite groups, such as middle sectors or highly trained workers, whose distributional coalitions resist the extension of benefits they have already attained to the poor who are still excluded.

As regards different sectors of the poor, the rational-choice approach purports to explain the "urban bias" prevailing in many developing countries (Lipton 1977). Since the urban masses are concentrated, they are easier to organize and more threatening to elites than widely dispersed rural masses; therefore, they gain more benefits than the latter (Bates 1981, 87–95). Any concessions that elites may eventually be forced to make benefit the urban sector; the rural poor remain neglected.

The rational-choice approach provides powerful arguments. In its parsimony and rigor, however, it fails to account for important facts. First, the successes of European social democracy contradict the emphasis of rational-choice authors on the difficulties of collective action, including bottom-up pressure for redistribution. In several European countries, the poor (especially workers) *were* able to organize collectively, counterbalance the power of the rich, and effect social change (Stephens 1986, chaps. 4–5). As the small-group advantage of elites (Olson 1971, chap. 2) did not prevail, pressure from the poor led to gradual equity-enhancing reforms. The rational-choice explanation for the lack of redistribution is thus not universally true but depends on contextual factors.

Second, contrary to rational-choice expectations, the *rural* poor obtained some rare equity-enhancing gains in Brazil's new democracy, whereas most of the urban poor have seen their miserable situation unchanged (see chapter 6). The ruralites' success was due to insistent demand making by an encompassing organization, the National Confederation of Agricultural Workers (Confederação Nacional dos Trabalhadores na Agricultura—CONTAG), which did not have an urban counterpart. Under military rule, the state had helped incorporate the diverse sectors of the rural population into a single association in order to guarantee support in the countryside. With the regime change, CONTAG became more and more autonomous and forceful in making demands. Thus, an independent state initiative and its unintended consequences mitigated collective-action dilemmas and gave the rural poor more influence than the urban poor could muster.

This observation highlights a theoretical lacuna in rational-choice arguments. Authors like Olson apply a society-centered approach. The decisive actors in their accounts are social groups influencing the state. The state is depicted as the object of demands, not as an actor on its own initiative. Even where state officials are taken more seriously, their rule is seen as resting on the cost-benefit calculations of social actors and embodying a contract (North 1981, 21–32; Levi 1988, 11–12; Ames 1987, 11–16). Yet ample evidence contradicts this reactive, dependent image of the state. The state can have considerable autonomy, use coercion to reach its goals, and shape society (Evans, Rueschemeyer, Skocpol 1985; Nordlinger 1981; Skocpol 1979; Trimberger 1978; Krasner 1978, 1984). As the case of Brazil's rural poor shows, the state can affect the very constitution of collective social actors.

Many rational-choice arguments are limited by simply taking actors, their interests, and the contextual parameters of their actions as given.[11] Other theories depict the institutional framework of action as the product of rational-interest calculations made by individuals.[12] Yet these accounts overestimate the flexibility and adaptability of institutions. As chapter 3 shows for Brazil, organizational patterns constitute persistent constraints on action, rather than easily alterable products of choice (see, in general, Krasner 1984, 234–43).

Indeed, rational-choice theorists themselves have come to acknowledge important limitations of their approach. For instance, there is less instability in political outputs than these scholars expected—based on Arrow's (1963, 51–60) "impossibility theorem" (Shepsle 1986, 53–57; for Brazil, Ames and Nixon 1993, 16–18). Also, rational incentives alone cannot account for individuals' frequent compliance with rules and the resulting social order (North 1981, 45–47; Miller 1993: chaps. 4–7). Finally, game-theory models (of bargaining, for instance) often have different possible solutions (multiple equilibria) and thus fail to yield determinate explanations (Kreps 1990, 95–102; Myerson 1992, 67–68). Recognizing these theoretical problems, rational-choice authors have come to invoke supra-individual, holistic factors such as culture, ideology, and norms (North 1981, chap. 5; 1990, chap. 5; Miller 1993, chaps. 9–11), socioeconomic factors (Bates 1990, 48–49; Levi 1988, 34–36), and institutional structures (Shepsle 1986; also Geddes 1994, 11–13, 184–90).

The limitations of rational-choice arguments are thus clear. To reach a more comprehensive understanding, one needs to go beyond this approach and investigate the conditions under which its claims apply. Given their explanatory power, rational-choice theories should not be dismissed, but they have to be embedded in socioeconomic or institutional frameworks. What they lose in parsimony and elegance they gain in determinacy and empirical accuracy.[13] Thus, it is crucial to address the following questions: Under what conditions is collective action by the poor virtually impossible? Under what conditions can it emerge and counterbalance the resource advantage of elites?

Socioeconomic Approach

Can the socioeconomic approach, which invokes the concept of dependent capitalist development, give answers to these questions? By pointing to the differences between the First and Third World, it elucidates an important empirical problem of the rational-choice approach, namely the contrast between the successes of European social democracy and the dearth of redistribution in post-authoritarian Brazil and other Latin American countries. This approach stresses the limits on redistributive efforts set directly by Latin America's external dependency (subsection one) and by the balance of class forces skewed in favor of elites that this dependency has brought about (subsection two).

Role of External Dependency

The socioeconomic approach claims that external dependency hinders redistribution directly because Brazil has to attract foreign capital. Social reform that reduces the privileges of business in order to give to the poor would scare off investors. Not to endanger dependent development, the government must refrain from enacting equity-enhancing measures.[14] The threat of "exit" (Frieden 1991, chap. 1) gives foreign investors considerable political influence. Since they do not find an important market among the poor, they resist redistribution. Thus, the logic of dependent development and the political influence of foreign investors impose tight limits on equity-enhancing reform.

Brazil's external dependency has persisted despite longstanding efforts to overcome it. The country succeeded in building its domestic industry, but only at the price of accumulating an enormous foreign debt. Severe problems in servicing this debt have forced Brazil to undergo a number of tough adjustment and austerity programs. Under these conditions, redistribution is particularly unlikely. Without growth, there is no additional income to allocate to the poor. Since redistribution would imply an absolute loss for the rich, they are especially opposed to making any concessions. The recent efforts at economic restructuring, which try to make Brazilian industry internationally competitive and to bring the country back to financial solvency, have perpetuated these strict limitations on equity-enhancing reforms. To attain efficiency, costs have to be lowered by cutting taxes on business and limiting the rise of direct and indirect wages. Thus, it has remained virtually impossible to impose burdens on the rich in order to favor the poor (see in general Petras and Morley 1992, 12–18, 187–98).

The claims that Brazil's external dependency and the ensuing economic crises are decisive obstacles to redistribution look very plausible, particularly with respect to social security policy. In this area, the "need" to contain public spending has indeed hindered efforts to redistribute income to the poor, especially in the early 1990s (chapters 6 and 7). In tax policy, however, economic crises have had the opposite effect. The necessity to raise revenues has been a strong incentive for state officials to eliminate tax exemptions for elite sectors (chapter 5). Even in social security policy, financial limitations have prompted attacks on the perceived privileges of better-off strata (chapters 6 and 7). In fact, the IMF and the World Bank, the enforcers of economic constraints, have also pressed for such revenue-saving redistributive measures (World Bank 1989a, 1989b; interviews Ramos 1989, Barbosa 1992). Since the economic crises resulting from external dependency have been active incentives to equity-enhancing reform rather than being mere obstacles, they can hardly be considered the decisive cause for the dearth of redistribution in Brazil's new democracy.

Runaway inflation, another manifestation of Brazil's crisis, tends to exacerbate inequality in social income distribution but does not necessarily make redistributive policy outputs, the main focus of this study, more regressive. For instance, rising inflation can devalue the tax breaks conceded to privileged sectors and cause "bracket creep" in the income tax,[15] raising more resources from the better-off minority who pay personal income tax in Brazil. In general, the sophisticated indexation mechanisms developed in the country, which are capable of eliminating inflationary losses, turn the distribution of the costs (and benefits) from inflation into a political decision. Whose income, prices, or tax the government or Congress readjusts by what rate at what interval have decisive distributional consequences. Thus, the impact of inflation on social equity is not predetermined but depends on political processes.

The structural limitations imposed by external dependency are also not stringent. Since Brazil has important assets (such as a huge domestic market) that make it highly attractive to foreign capital, the costs of gradual equity-enhancing reform would probably not scare off investors. Remarkably, the military regime, which tried to attract transnational investment, did not bother to eliminate the tough tax rules that the preceding populist government had imposed on foreign investors (Pinto 1989, 376–78). Brazil has had much more latitude in policy making than the dependency argument postulates.

Under democracy, parliament has, in fact, overridden the financial restrictions set by external dependency and economic crisis and enacted drastic increases in social expenditures and taxes (chapter 6). Budgetary spending by the federal government—excluding public enterprises and other agencies of the indirect administration, and excluding debt service and financial operations—rose enormously from 4.25 percent of GDP in 1985 to 7.54 percent in 1990 (Mussi, Ohana, and Guedes 1992, table III-d). Government technocrats were shocked at this "imprudence," but lacked the political power to prevent it. Politicians were eager to further their careers through patronage spending to influential sectors of the middle and working class and did not take the limits imposed by external dependency and the acute economic crisis seriously.[16] They followed a narrow political logic and did not care about general interests and systemic needs.

As this episode suggests, the dependency argument suffers from a theoretical lacuna. It does not pay sufficient attention to the problem of agency. It postulates systemic limitations and assumes that they have to be observed. But what if there is no actor with enough power or incentive to execute the "necessities" imposed by dependency? Attending to systemic limitations involves a collective-action problem that is not automatically resolved. Postulating a systemic limitation is logically insufficient. The dependency argument has to be complemented by hypotheses on collective action and organization. In their absence, it cannot resolve the problems of the rational-choice approach.

Impact of the Domestic Class Structure

The argument invoking the impact of external dependency on the domestic class structure makes a more important contribution to explaining the dearth of redistribution in post-authoritarian Brazil. In this view, foreign investors and domestic business try to guarantee efficiency and cut research costs by relying on First World technology, which is capital-intensive and does not require many workers. The dearth of regular jobs keeps the working class small and forces much of the growing urban population to eke out a living through self-employment and odd jobs (Sunkel 1972, 527–29; Cardoso and Faletto 1979, chap. 6; Roberts 1978, chaps. 5–7).

Society is structurally heterogeneous because only part of the population is integrated into the formal economy; the rest of the population subsists on informal activities. The formal sector is, on average, significantly better-off than the marginals,[17] many of whom have low, irregular incomes and precarious access to public services. As the interests of these sectors diverge, they find it difficult to unify for collective action. This cleavage splits the "popular sectors"[18] and greatly reduces the pressure they can put on elites to reach redistributive reforms (De Janvry 1981, chaps. 1, 6, 8).

Since the poor in Latin America comprise not only workers but also a mass of marginals that has remained much larger than it was in earlier decades in the First World,[19] the same policy outputs have different outcomes. In Europe and the United States, a higher share of the poor came to work in the formal sector and could be reached by policies targeted toward it, such as social security programs based on employee contributions. In Latin America, the same policies, adopted under pressure from the formal sector and in imitation of European experiences, have had a less equitable impact because they often exclude the informal sector, which is unable to make direct contributions (Isuani 1985; Mesa-Lago 1991, 56–58). These policies have frequently increased inequality and deepened the gulf between the formal and informal sector (Mesa-Lago 1978, chap. 7; 1989, 13–15).

A prediction follows from this reasoning. Since the extension of benefit programs to the very poor in the informal sector would have to be subsidized by the formal sector, the formal sector, which includes the industrial working class, is not in favor of such equity-enhancing reforms. On the contrary, self-interest dictates that not only elites but even the parts of the popular sectors integrated in the modern economy oppose it.[20] Since the poor in the informal sector control very few power capabilities and since the social forces in the formal economy tend to unite against them, redistribution through inclusion should be unlikely. Indeed, the more sectors of the middle and working class are *included* into benefit programs, the larger and more powerful should be the alliance that tries to keep the poor marginals *excluded*. According to the logic of the class-structure argument, the extension of social programs should stop far before reaching universal coverage.

The class-structure argument points to a cleavage in Latin American societies that is crucial for understanding the difficulty of redistribution. The gulf between the formal and informal economy poses an additional obstacle to the collective action of the popular sectors that the rational-choice approach fails to take into account. This cleavage goes a long way in accounting for the different experiences of social-democratic Europe and contemporary Latin America and helps explain the dearth of equity-enhancing reform in post-authoritarian Brazil.

This argument, however, also needs qualification. The cleavage between the formal and informal sectors is decisive for understanding the unequal historical development of Latin American social programs and the contemporary resistance to their equalization and universalization. But the prediction of the diminishing impulse and final stop in the extension of coverage has not come true. On the contrary, there has been an ongoing move toward universalization, driven by a small nucleus of government experts (Rosenberg and Malloy 1978, 163–70; Malloy 1979, chaps. 4–5). These experts are motivated by individual career and overarching state interests; commitment to principles, reinforced by foreign models, has also played an important role. The class-structure argument invokes only socioeconomic factors and overlooks the impact of these political interests and principles.

Furthermore, the divisive political consequences of the cleavage between formal and informal sectors can be mitigated by organization. It is possible to unite both sectors in the same association. In Brazil, the state promoted such an organization in order to control the rural population. CONTAG, which maintained its unity, increased its autonomy, and intensified its demand making during the transition to democracy, has pressed hard for higher social benefits for the rural poor and reached some redistributive successes. Thus, organization can override the disarticulating impact of the class structure.

The socioeconomic approach underestimates the importance of organization. Since collective-action problems are not resolved automatically, organization plays a decisive role for the political influence of social categories. It conditions whether they act in coordination and mobilize their resources effectively. Organization is not just a reflection of social interests and cleavages but shapes social forces themselves. In Brazil, for example, important organizational structures with lasting effects were created by the state at the beginning of the push for industrialization, before the social forces of modern society had emerged. Business and labor grew as a result of the economic development guided through Getúlio Vargas's state corporatism (Schmitter 1971). The class structure cannot be taken as given, as the socioeconomic approach pretends. It has been shaped by institutions, especially the state, which the socioeconomic approach tends to misrepresent as tightly constrained, if not determined by class forces or systemic needs.[21]

INSTITUTIONALIST APPROACH

In order to fill the lacunae of rational-choice and socioeconomic theories, I propose an institutionalist explanation for the dearth of redistribution in Brazil's new democracy. I argue in the first subsection that the organizational fragmentation of the state and society has blocked most equity-enhancing reform. Fragmentation is defined as the coexistence of multiple independent organizations that successfully claim to represent (segments of) the same social stratum or the coexistence of fairly autonomous agencies inside a state lacking internal coordination. The second subsection distinguishes different degrees of organizational fragmentation, and subsection three explains the impact of their coexistence in the same polity. Subsection four accounts for the origins and persistence of organizational fragmentation, and the fifth subsection shows how it blocks the four mechanisms through which democratization could, theoretically, bring about equity-enhancing reform. Finally, I discuss why efforts at redistribution have been made, despite all these obstacles.

Importance of Organizational Fragmentation

The institutionalist approach argues that the organization of the state and society has a decisive impact on political action and policy making, including decisions on equity-enhancing reform. This approach pays special attention to the state as the most important political institution. Following Tocqueville (1955), Weber (1976), and Hintze (1975, 1981), it examines how the modern state with its bureaucratic apparatus was created and how it has shaped the organization of society (Tilly 1975, 1992; Skocpol 1979; Badie and Birnbaum 1983; Evans, Rueschemeyer, and Skocpol 1985; Migdal 1988; Badie 1992). State building often involved conflicts with preexisting institutional structures, such as feudal networks and peasant communities. In these struggles, state builders invoked national interests and universalist causes and depicted their rivals as narrow particularistic forces. Where the state was under strong military pressure from other powers, it tried hard and often managed to reduce fragmentation and forge a unified nation to mobilize all available resources (Hintze 1975; Tilly 1975, 1992; Skocpol 1979).

Where external military threats were low, however, as in much of the Third World, the state often reinforced the fragmentation of society in order to bolster its domination in a strategy of divide and rule.[22] With differential benefits and sanctions, it kept social forces divided. Since these narrow categories could not challenge the state head-on, they infiltrated its bureaucratic apparatus in order to influence at least the implementation of decisions. Where this penetration of the state by social groups proceeded unchecked by efforts at centralization designed to respond to external military threats, as in most of the Third World, it undermined central command and control inside the state apparatus. Divide-and-rule tactics thus backfired by inducing a welter of social forces to corrode the internal unity of the state (see esp. Migdal 1988, chaps. 6–7; also Sandbrook 1985, chaps. 5–6; Migdal, Kohli, and Shue 1994).

Redistributive change does not merely affect the allocation of economic resources but also the distribution of political power and basic relations of domination. In polities where society is fragmented and the state is internally divided, most reform projects are initiated by state officials and are efforts at state building. Their success would weaken particularistic elite sectors, strengthen poor categories who could provide countervailing power, and extend the state's penetration of society. The forces who resist reform, in turn, do not only try to preserve their economic privileges but also to maintain their political autonomy and check the advance of state power.

Why are the forces of resistance often successful? Why has equity-enhancing reform remained rare, even under democracy? Since efforts at redistribution usually face strong opposition from established elites, a broad coalition of support in society or determined, coherent state action would be necessary for success.[23] But in a fragmented society, the potential beneficiaries of redistribution cannot form a united front; change via bottom-up pressure is unlikely. And since the state is weakened by internal divisions, it cannot enact reforms on its own initiative. The organization of society and the state is therefore crucial for the success of equity-enhancing reforms. The narrower the scope of interest representation and policy making—in other words, the deeper the organizational fragmentation—the lower the chances for redistributive change.

Low organizational scope strengthens the opponents of equity-enhancing initiatives and weakens their proponents and potential beneficiaries in two ways. First, it skews the influence of different social strata by making their main power capabilities more or less useful.[24] Organizational fragmentation systematically distorts the transformation of political resources into actual power in favor of elites and to the detriment of the poor. It undermines the political usefulness of numbers, the only power capability of the poor masses. If the poor cannot act in a united front but are split into innumerable fragments, they have minimal influence.

At the same time, organizational fragmentation in society and the state gives elites who command power capabilities, such as economic weight, special access to and influence on decision making and implementation. When elites are narrowly organized, they focus on gaining special favors for themselves and establishing direct connections to decision makers, who have considerable independence inside a fragmented state. These privileged links allow elites to bring their power capabilities effectively to bear and block equity-enhancing initiatives that would impose costs on them.

Low organizational scope reduces the clout of elite groups, such as big business, much less than the power of the poor. Major entrepreneurs do not need broad-based organizations for exerting influence because they have considerable clout individually and through their narrow associations.[25] Their small groupings may have so much interest in the outcome and so much weight that they advance some of the collective goals of business as a whole (Olson 1971, 48–52, 143–47). Through its differential social impact, organizational fragmentation greatly amplifies the difference in political influence that elites and the poor derive from their unequal control over power capabilities.

Second, low organizational scope in society and the state favors the opponents of redistribution over its initiators, regardless of the constellation of class forces. In a fragmented polity, democratization brings about a dispersal of power. The presidency and the central state apparatus lose influence with the regime transition, whereas parliament, law courts, and municipal and state governments (in a federal system) gain autonomy and strength. Coordinating mechanisms that could facilitate consensual decision making, especially well-organized and program-oriented political parties, fail to arise in a fragmented society.

Because of this dispersal of power, numerous independent decision-making institutions are involved in the reform process. Their concurrent approval would be required for enacting equity-enhancing measures, which affect broad categories of people. The proponents of redistribution face a hard task: They have to sway all the relevant decision-making institutions. In contrast, for the opponents of equity-enhancing reform it is sufficient to gain support from only one of these institutions to block change.[26] Thus, in an organizationally fragmented society and state, the cards are stacked against redistributive change under democracy.

Three Levels of Organizational Scope

The institutionalist literature sees the state as vying for control both with organized groups and personal networks. Thus, there are three levels of organizational scope in society and the state, ranging from low to high: personalism, segmentalism, and universalism.[27] These categories constitute ideal types—useful for theoretical purposes, though never fully embodied in empirical reality (Weber 1973, 234–59).

The units of personalism are individuals or small primary groups, such as families. The units of segmentalism are organized social categories, especially of an economic-functional nature, or relatively autonomous agencies of the state. The scope of universalism is not restricted by personalistic considerations or functional boundaries. Universalist organizations in society, such as catch-all parties, try to attract a broad cross section of the population. As for the state, a unified bureaucratic apparatus acting impartially on institutional interests is the prototype of a universalist institution.

Organizations at these three levels differ radically. Personalist networks strive for particularistic favors and are held together by norms of reciprocity among specific people. Segmentalist associations advance the interests of more or less narrowly defined categories, especially economic sectors, for which they try to create special rules. Universalist organizations, in contrast, promote the interests of the whole citizenry, embody and advance principles of equal treatment, and combat personalist and segmentalist privileges and discriminations.

Personalism

Personalism forms networks based on particularistic exchange and affective ties. In any large-scale society, these networks tend to assume a pyramidal form. Hierarchy thus pervades personalism. Since it is in the interest of those higher up in the personalist pyramid to keep their followers divided, horizontal links are discouraged, if not suppressed. Only actors at the top of the hierarchy have enough clout to counteract this divide-and-rule strategy and engage in horizontal relations.

The most widespread variant of personalism is clientelism, defined as a system of personal relations between individuals of different status that is based on the unequal but reciprocal exchange of particularistic benefits and protection for obedience and support (Landé 1977, xx; Scott 1977, 124–25). Clientelism predominates in the middle and lower rungs of personalist pyramids. Most typically, politicians try to win electoral support by "doling out" favors, especially to poorer people who depend on such help.

Relations at the top of personalist pyramids, which nowadays link state officials to clientelist politicians and businesspeople, are less hierarchical than clientelism. Public officials do have a superior position. They embody the authority of the state and can apply sanctions. Their petitioners, however, have much higher influence and more advantages to offer than clients do. Business leaders control decisive contributions to government programs, especially investment capital—not to speak of the frequent bribes. They can obtain infinitely more benefits through personal relations than can people at the bottom of the pyramid.

Despite the difference in the balance of power, relations at both ends of the personalist pyramid have a disaggregating impact. Clients are exposed to divide-and-rule tactics, and businesspeople who ask state officials for particularistic favors compete with one another. By hindering collective action among clients and higher-status petitioners, personalism keeps organizational scope low.

Segmentalism

Segmentalism has an intermediate level of aggregation. In society, it comprises categories defined by common characteristics and interests, not small primary groups, like personalism. Its principal units in modern times are organizations of economic sectors or classes. In its less aggregated form, in which cleavages are numerous and deep, a welter of distinct interest associations press their narrowly defined, specific demands and rival with each other for public resources. Because of their restricted base in society, none of these associations has a rational interest in taking systemic goals into consideration. Unable to resolve this collective-action problem, they only pursue their own special advantage and act as "distributional coalitions" (Olson 1982, 41–47). But in European social democracies, such as Sweden, social forces are organized at a much higher scope, namely at the level of classes. Since the actions of such encompassing associations have a clear impact on the whole nation, which in turn affects their own interests, they tend to take systemic goals into account and adjust their demand making accordingly (Olson 1982, 47–53).

As segmentalism reaches from distributional coalitions to encompassing associations, it embodies a range of organizational scope. This variation makes a crucial difference for the chances of redistribution. Where a welter of narrow associations prevails, as in Brazil, the poor cannot act in a united fashion and press effectively for equity-enhancing change. In contrast, where the disadvantaged are organized in encompassing organizations, as in European social democracies, they can reach reform (Stephens 1986).

As for the state, segmentalism means that public agencies have a high level of independence from central coordination. Where the apex of the state is incapable of imposing clear functional differentiation and hierarchical control, the internal unity of the state is undermined by bureaucratic politics, that is, the conflictual pursuit of organizational self-interests by individual state agencies (Allison 1971, chap. 5). As agencies try to conquer resources and invade each others' turf, their attributions come to overlap. In these rivalries, overarching state interests, such as financial viability, easily remain unattended. State agencies locked in bureaucratic politics act in a similar way as distributional coalitions in society.

The concept of segmentalism points to organizational and behavioral similarities of narrow interest associations and autonomous state agencies. This affinity is reinforced by the frequent close links between interest associations and state agencies in different political settings, ranging from the interest-group liberalism of the United States (Lowi 1979) to the eroding corporatism of Brazil (see chapter 3). These connections increase the independence of state agencies from central control and keep social organization divided, fueling the pursuit of narrow interests both inside the state and in society.

Universalism

Universalism transcends the limits on organizational scope that define personalism and segmentalism. Seeing the whole citizenry as their constituency, universalist organizations apply the same standards and principles to everybody. Obviously, differential treatment is allowed and even called for if it is required to implement goals and rules valid for the whole population. But exceptions based on particularistic criteria, such as personal or sectoral preferences, are inadmissible.[28]

The prototype of a universalist organization is the state as depicted in European state theory: a centrally coordinated bureaucratic apparatus that pursues the "national interest" and impartially makes and applies rules valid for all of society (Weber 1976, 551–79, 815–21; Heller 1983, 225–79; Badie and Birnbaum 1983, chap. 7; overview in Dyson 1980, 208–51). Internal unity guarantees that the specialized state agencies cooperate to achieve overarching state interests. Not dominated by arbitrary rulers or sectoral interests, this highly institutionalized state (Huntington 1968, 12–24) takes the interests and needs of all its citizens fully into account and acts on principles such as equality before the law and nondiscrimination in political participation and public policy making.[29]

In society, the prime example of a universalist organization is a catch-all party that uses a program to appeal to the entire citizenry. To gain electoral support, it does not promise special favors to narrow sectors or personal networks but designs a plan for the country by aggregating the demands and needs of the population. The effort to obtain a majority under the rule of "one person, one vote" creates pressure toward universalism in modern democracies, as evidenced by the broadening appeal of many class parties in Europe (Kirchheimer 1964, 184–91; Przeworski and Sprague 1986, 40–52).

In Third World countries where personalism and segmentalism are deeply entrenched, universalism is often an aspiration rather than a reality. It gains support with modernization, but actual behavior often remains unchanged (Da Matta 1985). One of the major sources of universalist ideas is the First World. It provides models for underdeveloped countries that are actively promoted by governments and international organizations. Experts, whose professional training makes them receptive to universalist notions and open to intellectual innovation, are the foremost media of this diffusion of ideas (Badie 1992, 152–67; Finnemore 1992, chaps. 1, 5). They promote universalist principles in order to enhance their own influence in society and inside the state and to establish their predominance over competing claimants to political influence and power, such as electoral politicians and interest associations. Thus, they have a basic professional interest in advancing universalist ideas and principles.

Universalism is not monolithic but has two main variants: universalism of opportunities and universalism of results. The former, an individualist, liberal version, insists merely on equal starting chances for everyone. Legal discrimination and distinctions that are not based on achievement are illegitimate. The state has to uphold a neutral, impartial framework of rules and apply it without exception to all citizens. But within this framework, individuals may achieve vastly different outcomes, depending on resource endowments, effort, and luck. Resulting from free competition, this inequality of results is fully acceptable. As the only corrective action, all citizens are to be ensured a minimal livelihood (Hayek 1944, chap. 9; Friedman 1962, chap. 12).

The collectivist, social-democratic version, universalism of results, does not accept the high level of inequality that free initiative can bring about.

Since citizens are seen as parts of a community, they deserve a fair share in its wealth. Though absolute equality of results is impossible to achieve (especially without sacrificing economic efficiency and political liberty), vast inequalities have to be reduced. All citizens must be guaranteed a comfortable level of sustenance that permits them the full exercise of their rights. Otherwise, universalist principles remain a formalistic sham for the poor and an easy target for the power of the elite (Heimann 1980, 121–57; Esping-Andersen 1990, 65–69).

Despite their divergence, the two variants of universalism converge in their rejection of personal and sectoral privileges and discriminations that characterize personalism and segmentalism. In countries like Brazil, where many people are excluded from social citizenship, the contrast between universalism of any stripe and personalism and segmentalism is stark. Where poverty is deep and widespread, even the minimal social protection advocated by liberal universalism may mean equity-enhancing progress.[30]

Coexistence of Organizations of Different Scope

Organizations of various power and scope often coexist, especially in loosely integrated Third World countries in which the central state has always had to vie for control with personalist networks (Migdal 1988, chap. 2; Badie 1992, chap. 5), and segmentalism has grown with modernization. Whereas the formal economy has segmental organizations, the marginals in the informal sector often can advance their interests only through clientelism. Many of the poor are organized at the lowest level of scope and have the least organizational capacity to press for redistributive reforms, which would benefit them most. This organizational disadvantage creates a particularly strong obstacle to equity-enhancing change.

Segmentalism and personalism serve to suppress interests as well as represent them. But in the main variant of personalism, clientelism, the balance is much less favorable to interest representation than in segmentalism. The higher-status patrons may take care of the clients' basic personal needs but rarely advance their interests on broader issues, such as redistribution. Patrons acquire control over the clients' political rights and obtain a captive political base (Landé 1977, xxi, xxix; Cornelius 1977, 339, 344). They impede horizontal mobilization and organization among their clients. Patrons' domination is often comprehensive, covering all spheres of clients' lives, especially in the countryside.[31] The more patrons succeed in monopolizing their clients' political access, the more clientelism prevents poor marginals from advancing many of their interests.

Compared to clientelism, segmentalism serves more to represent interests and less to suppress them. Of course, segmentalism also has an inherent organizational bias that deflects interest articulation toward specific demands and inhibits the expression of universal interests (Olson 1986; Schmitter 1981, 169–70). To the extent that segmentalist associations succeed in their effort to reduce, if not eliminate, competition from other organizations, they limit their members' demand making.

The interest-suppressing impact of segmentalism is, however, not as strong as in clientelism. Segmentalism delimits social interest representation on a higher level of aggregation than clientelism. Segmentalist associations pursue a broader range of collective interests than clientelist networks. They also do not control the range of their constituents' needs and interests as comprehensively as many clientelist networks. They mainly represent professional interests and leave their constituents free to pursue their nonprofessional demands in other ways (Schmitter 1983, 923).

Segmentalism is thus more adequate than clientelism for advancing collective interests. This gives business and the working class an important organizational advantage over large parts of the marginal mass who have to rely on clientelism. In a structurally heterogeneous society like Brazil, low organizational scope poses a particular obstacle to redistribution because it is most extreme at the bottom of the social pyramid, whose power capabilities are already scarce. Organizational and socioeconomic disadvantages reinforce each other and make it difficult for the poor to press effectively for equity-enhancing reform.

The cumulation of low organizational scope and scant power capabilities at the bottom of the social pyramid is a main reason why Third World countries are unlikely to follow the lead of European social democracy.[32] Social democracy reached its successes through sustained bottom-up pressure by creating an encompassing trade-union movement and a political party appealing to ever wider segments of the working population (Stephens 1986; Przeworski 1985). The absence of pervasive clientelist networks and the integration of many poor people in the formal economy provided the organizational and socioeconomic preconditions for this achievement. In line with the logic of encompassing organization, European social democracy did not plead for special favors for certain sectors of the working class but advanced the interests and needs of all the poor. Its basic goal was the extension of rights and benefits to everyone. The popular sectors had their large numbers as their main power capability and favored the rule of "one person, one vote" (Rueschemeyer, Stephens, and Stephens 1992). Therefore, social-democratic demands coincided with universalist principles, based on the notion of equal citizenship (Esping-Andersen 1990, 65–77). For these historically specific reasons, encompassing organization, universalism, and redistributive reform went hand in hand in the social-democratic countries of Europe.

In the contemporary Third World, such congruence is rare. The gulf between the formal and informal economy, the confinement of many marginals to clientelist networks, and the limited scope of workers' organizations usually impede its repetition (Ascher 1984, 34, 40–41; Rosenberg and Malloy 1978, 159–63). Many marginals lack the organizational capacity to advance their redistributive demands effectively. Trade unions often have workers in the formal sector as their core constituency; they demand measures that provide special favors for their members and exclude or even hurt the large mass of poor in the informal sector. The more advantages workers gain, the less business tends to expand employment and the higher the barrier becomes against the integration of marginals. In closed, noncompetitive economies, employers may also pass on increased labor costs to consumers, making the poor in the informal economy pay for part of the benefits that workers in the formal sector obtain. Given profound differences in socioeconomic and organizational structure, trade unions, which promoted progressive redistribution in social-democratic Europe, often have the opposite impact—and goal—in the contemporary Third World. Thus, the contrast between social-democratic Europe and Brazil's new democracy confirms the importance of the institutional factors emphasized in this book.

Sources of Organizational Fragmentation

Where do the organizational patterns analyzed so far come from? What accounts for their preservation despite important economic, social, and political changes? These questions are central to an institutionalist explanation. Organizational patterns cannot be taken as given; their origins and, especially, their persistence over time need to be explained. The following account emphasizes institutionalist factors but draws on socioeconomic variables and rational-choice mechanisms as well.

Sociocultural, economic, and geopolitical factors help explain the *origins* of low organizational scope. Thus, the sociocultural heterogeneity of a country's population and strong regional differences in economic development provide important impulses to organizational fragmentation. Also, in late-late industrializing countries such as in Latin America, where the working class is a relatively small part of the population and the informal sector is large, organizational fragmentation tends to be more pronounced than in the earlier developers of Europe with their proportionally bigger (and often sectorally less divided) working class.[33] Since workers are the most readily organizable category and since powerful trade unions and labor parties have historically been crucial for inducing business and conservative parties to strengthen and extend their own organization, the comparatively small size of the working class makes it harder for Latin American countries to arrive at encompassing organization.[34]

The lack of serious military challenges also favors organizational fragmentation. In Continental Europe, frequent wars induced states to break personalist (feudal) structures and create space for encompassing organizations in their efforts to mobilize all their national potential (Tilly 1975, 1992). In contrast, the low threat of external attack in much of the contemporary Third World has permitted the emergence and survival of fragmented organizations that pursue their special interests without much regard for national goals.

Whereas all of these factors help account for the emergence of organizational fragmentation, institutional factors also had a crucial impact. Colonial states applied divide-and-rule tactics and kept social organization fragmented so as to bolster their domination.[35] After independence, the new rulers inherited the "overdeveloped" state apparatus (Alavi 1972) and pursued similar tactics. They built personalist networks to create loyal followings and split the opposition (Migdal 1988, chaps. 6–7). When socioeconomic modernization threatened to undermine these control mechanisms by creating new social classes, such as business and industrial labor, states tried to establish new structures of domination. The more autonomy the state enjoyed from society, the more it managed to impose state-corporatist patterns that kept the organizational scope of the newly emerging strata at low levels (Schmitter 1974; Stepan 1978, chap. 2). State-corporatism left especially the popular sectors divided. By impeding challenges to the established social order, it also reduced the need for elite groups like business to unite in defense of their interests (Schneider 1992, chap. 6). Thus, independent state action played an important role as a source of organizational fragmentation in society.

As for the *persistence* of fragmentation, low organizational scope has a strong tendency to perpetuate itself. Established organizational patterns create interests that—in line with rational-choice arguments—favor their continuation. The leaders of fragmented organizations do not want to sacrifice their autonomy and power by uniting, unless they face a strong threat to common goals. They prefer maintaining control of a narrow segment or primary group to running the risk of having to submit to another leader. For the followers, founding new, encompassing organizations poses a collective-action problem that the existence of fragmented organizations exacerbates greatly. They have to overcome the defensive reactions of established leaders, who will try to co-opt opposition forces pressing for encompassing organization. The opponents tend to accept the existing fragmented organization rather than risk remaining alone in their quest for more encompassing organization.

Socioeconomic and institutional factors reinforce these self-perpetuating tendencies in developing countries like Brazil. The gulf between the formal and informal economy creates a cleavage that is hard, though not impossible, to bridge. More important, the informal economy is internally heterogeneous. Many of its members are self-employed, directly competing against each other, or they work in odd jobs without legal protection (Infante and Klein 1991, 124–34; Portes and Schauffler 1993, 45–53). Their precarious situation and their variegated, even conflicting, interests make any encompassing organization difficult. Even the formal economy consists of a welter of separate sectors because late-late development advanced in a staged process and created few intersectoral linkages (Hirschman 1971, 91–93). Sectoral cleavages can create more commonality of interest between businesspeople and workers in each branch of industry than among workers as a class. Since the working class is not numerically strong enough to challenge the existing order and reach structural reforms, the tendency to pursue specific interests and organize on a narrow basis is reinforced.

Institutional factors, especially state intervention in the economy and society, have also kept the scope of organization low. State officials have used co-optation to impede threats to their power. The selective concession of particularistic benefits creates support and suppresses challenges by undermining the unity of discontents. Most types of state intervention in Latin America have embodied this divisive political logic.[36] Personalist networks and segmentalist organizations have, in turn, tried hard to establish direct links to the state in order to obtain specific benefits. Unable and unwilling to press broad demands, they have concentrated on extracting particularistic favors. In return, they have offered support to state officials in rivalries inside the ever expanding public bureaucracy.

Such outside alliances have strengthened the autonomy of state officials and agencies from central direction and control. As a result, bureaucratic politics has become rampant, undermining the internal unity of the state. Latin American presidents, despite their enormous formal powers, often cannot guarantee effective coordination inside the state. They can only pay sporadic attention to any issue and are frequently unable to ensure the implementation of their own decisions. Thus, large-scale state intervention helps much to maintain the low level of organizational scope both in society and inside the state. This explanation, which integrates rational-choice and socioeconomic arguments into an institutionalist framework, accounts for the self-perpetuating tendency of low organizational scope.

Operation of Organizational Obstacles to Redistribution

How does organizational fragmentation block the mechanisms through which democratization could, in theory, lead to equity-enhancing reform? My institutionalist explanation points to obstacles that block all four of these pathways: Personalism and segmentalism hinder the formation of *encompassing interest associations* and *social movements* that could mobilize bottom-up pressure for redistribution. They tend to impede the emergence of minimally disciplined and program-oriented *parties* through which the large mass of poor people could elect governments committed to equity-enhancing reform. Finally, bureaucratic politics inhibits top-down *state* initiatives to impose redistribution.

Absence of Encompassing Interest Associations and Social Movements

Divergences of socioeconomic interests and the coexistence of personalism and segmentalism fragment society. The popular sectors are divided by multiple cleavages. Above all, inclusion in the formal economy sets the working class apart from the marginal mass, who are excluded. The coexistence of personalism and segmentalism exacerbates the fragmentation of society, particularly among the popular sectors. The working class is organized in segmentalist associations, whereas many marginals can rely only on clientelism (that is, networks at the bottom of the personalist pyramid) for gaining access to the national political arena.[37] This difference in organizational pattern prevents the popular sectors from joining forces.

The coexistence of segmentalism and clientelism aggravates interest divergences between the working class and marginal mass. Segmentalist associations leave out much of the informal sector and demand special favors for their narrow constituencies in the formal sector. Fearing for its relative privileges, the working class is reluctant to support the extension of benefits to marginals (Ascher 1984, 34, 40–41; Rosenberg and Malloy 1978, 159–63). Exclusionary organizational patterns thus reinforce interest conflicts among the popular sectors. As already explained, clientelism and segmentalism also create internal cleavages within classes and sectors.

By fragmenting society deeply, clientelism and segmentalism inhibit the emergence of encompassing interest associations and social movements. They create and reinforce cleavages that deflect attention from broad collective goals and prevent social categories from joining forces. Induced to focus on narrow demands, which are easier to attain, and facing sanctions if they try to escape from the control of patrons and association leaders, members of the popular sectors are not ready to support organizations pressing for structural reform. By setting such "selective incentives" (Olson 1971), clientelism and segmentalism aggravate the problem of organizing broad-based collective action that could achieve redistribution through pressure from below.

Even democratization may not overcome this fragmentation, which has strong self-perpetuating tendencies. Certainly, in the context of diminished state control, reasserted values of citizenship and pent-up demands may lead to efforts to establish more encompassing associations and social movements. But these organizations are usually limited in their scope and weakened in their clout by divisions that democratization itself unleashes. By removing authoritarian restrictions on the diversity of ideas and values, a transition to democracy intensifies the expressed ideological divergences and fuels partisan conflict (O'Donnell and Schmitter 1986, 58, 61). These cleavages split newly emerging and old interest associations and social movements (Schmitter 1992, 432). Thus, in developing countries like Brazil, democratization is unlikely to bring about encompassing interest associations and social movements that could successfully mobilize bottom-up pressure for redistribution.

Absence of Universalist Political Parties

In contrast to personalism and segmentalism, universalism does not fragment social forces. On the contrary, it tries to unite them for collective action. Electoral competition under the rule of "one person, one vote" gives political parties a special incentive to embrace universalism. Parties that seek support from all citizens and advance programs that aggregate a broad range of interests have better chances of gaining a majority than those that are bound to certain clientelist networks, corporatist sectors, or social classes (Przeworski and Sprague 1986; Dix 1989, 32–33).

Pervasive personalism and segmentalism, however, impede the emergence of universalist parties. Segmentalism restricts the importance of parties, and personalism prevents them from acquiring minimal discipline and program orientation. Segmentalist associations establish direct contacts to the state. This undermines the aggregative role of parties. In late-late developing countries like Brazil, the social sectors included in segmentalist associations do not have a majority in the electorate. Therefore, it is in their interest to settle important matters through unintermediated links with the state, rather than having them decided in the electoral arena, where the many votes of the marginal mass count. Segmentalism allows them to press their narrow demands directly on the state instead of relying on parties. Since parties are excluded from important decisions on development and distribution, their political weight is reduced (Kaufman 1977, 114).

Since parties do not articulate the collective interests of social categories, many of them serve mainly as vehicles for politicians. Much of the "political class" pursues its self-interest in political survival without articulating and aggregating organized interests.[38] For obtaining support, these politicians rely on (in addition to populist rhetoric) large-scale clientelist networks. Their main goal is to control resources that they can dispense to their political base (Geddes 1994, chaps. 2–5). They are not interested in party programs and do not observe party discipline (Archer 1991, 9–16; Chalmers 1977a; Scott 1977, 141). Regardless of party affiliation, they need good relations with the government to maintain access to the patronage disbursed by the state. This disaggregative behavior undermines the discipline and program orientation of parties.[39]

These politicians can afford not to represent the interests of broad social categories because their clientelist supporters are particularly powerless and dispersed. According to the norm of reciprocity, the more resources clients command, the more they can induce patrons to represent their interests. The marginal mass commands very few resources and has low bargaining power. This allows clientelist politicians to disregard most interests of their political base (Scott and Kerkvliet 1977, 441–43).

Even under democracy, many conditions for party weakness persist. Enduring segmentalism restricts the importance of parties; clientelism continues to undermine their organization and program orientation. Indeed, newly arising parties are tempted to play by the established "rules of the game" and adopt the clientelist style of support building in order not to lose out against their clientelist competitors (O'Donnell 1988, 61–64, 77–82; Nunes 1984, 109, 111). As a result, their program orientation and organizational strength diminish. The presidential system of government that predominates in Latin America further undermines party discipline (Linz and Valenzuela 1994). As parliamentarians do not need to sustain the government or offer unified opposition, they are reluctant to follow any clear party program and focus instead on distributing patronage to their voters.

In sum, segmentalism and personalism sharply limit the organizational discipline and program orientation of political parties and prevent them from serving as effective channels for bottom-up pressure for redistribution. The weakness of the organizations that could best embody universalist principles consolidates the fragmentation of society.

Lack of Internal Unity in the State

In many Third World countries, the state, like society, is fragmented. Massive interventionism in the economy and society, which is typical of late-late development, has led to a mushrooming of state agencies. To overcome the weakness of domestic business, the state has created a host of public enterprises and numerous agencies for fostering, protecting, and regulating private production. This institutional proliferation makes it difficult for the presidency to maintain direction and control.

Segmentalism and clientelism, which were often created or sustained by the state,[40] have reinforced these control problems by giving social groups direct access to public officials and agencies. The very importance of the interventionist state has induced segmentalist associations to capture many public agencies (Rueschemeyer and Evans 1985, 60). As explained earlier, the fragmentation of social organization makes such infiltration particularly rewarding. Using their privileged access, business groups lobby for the formation of state agencies designed to provide them with favors. They penetrate existing agencies and bend their activities to serve private sector interests. Such outside links increase the autonomy of state agencies from the presidency. Segmentalism thus exacerbates the command and control problems inside the state and fuels bureaucratic politics.

Clientelism also fragments the state. In order to use public benefits for patronage purposes, clientelist politicians try to have their followers appointed to state positions. They even press for the creation of new posts and agencies. Government leaders often grant these requests so as to guarantee support. Clientelist interference in recruitment fuels the cancerous growth of the state apparatus, establishes outside loyalties, and undermines professional cohesion and hierarchical command inside the public bureaucracy (Migdal 1988, chaps. 6–7; Grindle 1977).

Democratization keeps the unity of the state low. The regime change strengthens parliament relative to the executive branch, especially in presidential systems of government. This allows state agencies to undermine central command and control through lobbying in Congress. Moreover, as clientelism persists and democratization gives previously excluded partisan forces and ideological currents voice and influence, a more diverse set of actors can make patronage appointments. The political and ideological diversity of public officials grows, and the state's internal cohesion diminishes. Finally, in federal systems democratization increases the autonomy and strength of the local and regional governments vis-à-vis the national government, where power was concentrated under authoritarian rule.

This lack of internal unity impedes the state from imposing top-down reform on reluctant elites. Bureaucratic politics makes it difficult to formulate, enact, and implement coherent redistributive policies (Rueschemeyer and Evans 1985, 53–55). Thus, segmentalism and personalism block all four mechanisms through which democratization could lead to greater equity.

Impulses Toward Redistribution

Does this institutionalist explanation leave any room for redistribution? Where do the equity-enhancing impulses in Brazil's new democracy come from? As mentioned in the introduction, numerous reform efforts have been undertaken since 1985. What accounts for these progressive tendencies? Can they ever prevail over the organizational obstacles emphasized so far?

The weakest and most episodic but broadest-based impulses toward social change are unleashed in occasional outbursts of popular mobilization, as in Brazil's presidential campaign of 1989, when the socialist Luís Inácio Lula da Silva won 47 percent of the valid vote. Electoral competition even among weak and nonprogrammatic parties can tap into a diffuse and unarticulated desire among the popular sectors for an improvement in their life chances. This desire may on occasion sweep progressive candidates into office, as it almost did in Brazil. But moderates, or conservatives using populist tactics, usually find more support, especially among the poorest strata. Also, such waves of mobilization are sporadic and ebb quickly. They rarely provide the basis for effective reform, which requires sustained efforts.

More promising as protagonists of redistribution are the rare interest associations of larger scope. Even in a fragmented polity, state initiatives under authoritarian rule may promote islands of more encompassing organization (such as CONTAG in Brazil). Although the state often squelches threats from below by imposing a divisive form of state corporatism, it may rely on inclusionary corporatism when a sector of the poor who have previously been inactive start to mobilize (Stepan 1978, chap. 3). Since this sector does not pose a high threat, the state may try to co-opt it with inducements (Collier and Collier 1979), promoting an encompassing organization and fostering its growth.

During the transition to democracy, this association may draw on its organizational advantages to maintain its internal unity. At the same time, it may gain independence from state control and embark on ever more forceful demand making (Maybury-Lewis 1991, chap. 2). Since the association's broad scope induces it to focus on structural issues, it may mobilize bottom-up pressure for redistribution. Whether such an organization is successful in its equity-enhancing efforts depends, however, on overcoming the numerous obstacles that the fragmentation of society and state create during the decision-making process.

In a polity of low organizational scope, such equity-enhancing pressure from below is a rare exception. Segmentalism and personalism make most social forces focus on narrow interests not on broad-based redistributive change. Most reform initiatives are started by professionals and experts who promote universalist principles. Aiming at elite privileges and discriminations against the poor, experts inside the state try to assert their independence from social elites, preempt bottom-up pressure, and give every citizen equal status. By trying to increase state autonomy, combat particularistic forces, and maintain internal stability, they pursue basic state interests. In this effort at state building, they further their own career goals in gaining power and status by invoking universalist norms acquired in their professional socialization and reinforced by the international diffusion of ideas (Badie 1992, 152–67; Heclo 1974; Rosenberg and Malloy 1978; Ascher 1989, 420, 463–64). The lack of encompassing or universalist organizations in civil society makes even academic experts and party politicians who favor redistribution try to obtain an institutional position in the state from which they can launch reform initiatives.

In a fragmented polity, these state-centered universalist initiatives run into countless obstacles, as the following case studies show. These impediments are difficult, yet not impossible to overcome. Skillful leadership can achieve redistribution, mainly in certain types of crisis. One of the most propitious situations arises when temporary mass mobilization makes the electoral victory of a left-wing candidate possible. But when this outcome is averted by a moderate politician, the winner may then be able to coax the established elites, who are indebted to him or her for keeping the left out of power, into accepting some redistribution in order to buy off growing discontent and to prevent mass unrest in the future.[41]

Thus, my institutionalist argument is not deterministic but leaves some room for equity-enhancing successes. However, in a fragmented society and state such successes are infrequent. The cards are clearly stacked against redistributive reform.

CONCLUSION

To explain the dearth of redistribution in Brazil's new democracy, this chapter has embedded rational-choice and socioeconomic arguments in an institutionalist framework. Rational choice contributes powerful explanations of political actions but tends to take their institutional context simply as given. Socioeconomic factors affect the constitution, interest definition, and resources of political actors, but organizational structures mediate their impact. I therefore stress institutional factors and argue that persistent patterns of social and state organization create crucial impediments to equity-enhancing reform. My argument does not deny the possibility of redistribution under democracy, but it claims that in fragmented polities such change is difficult to effect and has little impact.

3

Organizational Fragmentation

in Brazil

CHAPTERS 3 through 7 apply the theoretical framework of this book to the Brazilian case in three steps. This chapter examines the organization of state and society. It shows that a high level of fragmentation emerged in Brazil's polity and that it has persisted in the new democracy. This finding provides the "antecedent condition" for using the theoretical argument of chapter 2 to explain the dearth of redistribution in postauthoritarian Brazil. Chapter 4 investigates the decision-making process in tax and social security policy under authoritarian rule, and in this way establishes the baseline for assessing the impact of democratization. Chapters 5 through 7 analyze policy making in direct taxation, social insurance, and health care under democracy; they demonstrate how organizational obstacles have blocked equity-enhancing impulses.

Since the institutionalist approach emphasizes historical development, this chapter first explores the origins of organizational fragmentation in Brazil and its maintenance until the onset of democratization in the late 1970s.[1] I stress the paradoxical effects of autonomous state action, which fragmented society in an effort at applying divide-and-rule tactics but ended up undermining the cohesion and power of the state itself. In order to control society, the state imposed narrow segmentalism on business and labor in the 1930s and 1940s and sustained the personalism enveloping the urban and rural poor. While the organizational fragmentation of society impeded challenges to state authority, it induced social groups to seek special favors, penetrate the state apparatus, undermine its internal unity, and limit its capacity for autonomous action. Thus, the state also became deeply divided.

This chapter shows that the transition to democracy did not overcome the fragmentation of society and state. Social interest organization is still split by old sectoral and regional cleavages or new political-ideological tensions; few encompassing associations or social movements have been formed. Political parties have not gained in organizational discipline and program orientation, and the unity of the state has further diminished with the dispersion of power under democracy. Organizational fragmentation thus continues to prevail in Brazil's polity.

ORIGINS OF ORGANIZATIONAL FRAGMENTATION IN BRAZIL

Development of Brazil's Class Structure

Organizational patterns are influenced (but not determined) by a country's socioeconomic development. Brazil has experienced late-late development.[2] From the 1930s on, a strong, autonomous state promoted import-substitution industrialization. It guided development through incentives and restrictions, undertook many productive activities, and guaranteed a stable sociopolitical framework by maintaining control over society, even during the democratic interlude of 1945 to 1964 (Schmitter 1973).

State-led development has deeply influenced Brazil's class structure, making the popular sectors internally diverse and giving business a privileged position. The state has assigned priority to rapid economic development and paid minimal attention to its social effects, such as increasing inequality. The military regime promoted industrialization forcefully but kept the majority of the population excluded from many benefits of development. The poor made absolute gains (Skidmore 1988, 286–87; Fox 1990) but remained at very low income levels. Better-off sectors gained much more in absolute and relative terms (Hasenbalg and Silva 1987, 78–80). Thus, the distribution of income became even more skewed.

Brazil's industrialization has been capital and technology intensive and has not used the abundant supply of cheap, unskilled labor. The industrial working class has remained small. In 1985, only 16.3 percent of the economically active population (EAP) were employed in the manufacturing industry (IBGE 1990, 42). Workers and employees in the formal sector of the economy (about 38 percent of the EAP) and professionals, shopkeepers, and businesspeople (about 10 percent) coexisted with urban marginals who lacked regular employment and people in the informal sector (approximately 28 percent of the EAP) (Cacciamali 1991, 139; IBGE 1990, 42). Another 24 percent were rural poor (subsistence peasants, seasonal laborers).[3]

The size of these different strata in Brazil is quite close to the Latin American average, but there is considerable variation inside the region (Portes 1985, 20–23). In Argentina, Chile, and Uruguay, formal workers and employees comprised close to 60 percent of the EAP in the early 1970s, but the deindustrializing policies pursued by their military regimes have probably lowered this share since then. In the poorer countries of the Central Andes and Central America, in contrast, the urban informal sector and the rural poor had especially large shares. In a region of such diversity, Brazil is clearly not an outlier.

In Brazil, as in other Latin American countries, the distinct categories of the popular sectors are also internally diverse. Workers are employed in firms of different size in different sectors of the economy. The marginal mass is even more disparate. Its members survive on variegated activities such as street-vending, repairs, and other occasional jobs. They often stand in direct competition with each other. Finally, the rural poor comprise various categories with different degrees of access to land (such as landless laborers and smallholders). Thus, late-late development has divided Brazil's popular sectors into distinct, internally heterogeneous categories. The class structure is fragmented, especially at the large bottom of the social pyramid.

Private business, in contrast, has enjoyed a privileged position. Because the state has considered entrepreneurs essential contributors to the urgent goal of economic development, it has greatly fostered the emergence and growth of domestic business by offering innumerable incentives and safeguards (O'Donnell 1978; Evans 1982). It has been responsive to specific business interests and provided support against challenges from other strata, especially the working class.

Fragmentation of Social Interest Organization

The cleavages in the class structure helped the state promote types of segmentalism and personalism, namely state corporatism and clientelism. Through these divide-and-rule tactics, the state tried to bolster its dominance over society. The authoritarian regime of Getúlio Vargas (1930–1945) coaxed business and urban labor into narrow state-corporatist associations.[4] The high level of state interventionism induced many sectors of society to seek limited favors and form narrow segmentalist organizations (Schneider 1992, chap. 6). Through the distribution of patronage, the state has also sustained clientelist networks, enveloping particularly the poor. As a result of these state actions, all strata in Brazilian society have had a fragmented organization. Encompassing interest associations and broad-based social movements have been rare.

Fragmentation of Business

Brazilian business has not had an encompassing association that could advance its collective interests as a class (Diniz 1989; Guimarães 1977). Vargas's state corporatism organized business along the lines of its main segments. There have been separate national confederations for industry (Confederação Nacional da Indústria—CNI), commerce (Confederação Nacional do Comércio—CNC), agriculture (Confederação Nacional da Agricultura—CNA), and so forth. Among the corresponding federations at the state level, the Federation of Industries of São Paulo (Federação das Indústrias do Estado de São Paulo—FIESP) is most important. Federations are composed of sectoral associations that comprise businesspeople from the same branch of activity.

In recent decades, businesspeople have founded numerous sectoral organizations outside the state-corporatist structure. These associations have been free of state control and have given the private sector an open avenue for interest articulation. But their organizational scope has also been narrow; they have a sectoral basis or duplicate state-corporatist associations. Like the latter, they have tried to establish close connections to public agencies in order to extract special favors from the highly interventionist state. The rise of these independent associations did not revamp the segmentalist framework of Brazilian business organization (Diniz and Boschi 1979). Thus, the "capitalist class" has been fragmented along sectoral lines.

Regional divergences, stemming from the concentration of industry and finance in the state of São Paulo, have also created tensions, especially inside corporatist associations. São Paulo's state federation of industry (FIESP) has not seen its enormous economic weight reflected inside its national confederation (CNI). Since FIESP has just one vote among more than twenty state federations, which are mainly from the backward Northeast, it has felt its modern orientation inadequately represented. It has established its own direct channels to the state and parliament, undermining CNI's authority to speak for industry as a whole.

As a result of its fragmentation,[5] business has not had a hegemonic vocation (Cardoso 1964, 1986; Leff 1968; Schmitter 1971). Even the most powerful associations, such as FIESP, have rarely advanced comprehensive programs. Rather, they have reacted to state initiatives. Where business organizations made general demands, as on the reduction of state interventionism, they have not had the organizational capacity to impose these proposals on their own members, whose individual interests have favored continued state intervention for their particular firm.

In other Latin American countries, in contrast, business has had more organizational unity and advanced overarching interests. Chilean entrepreneurs, for instance, used their encompassing association, the Confederación de la Producción y del Comercio, to design and promote political and economic projects both vis-à-vis the military government in the mid-1980s and the advancing democratic opposition at the end of the decade (Silva 1992; Feliú 1988). Similarly, FEDECAMARAS, the business peak association in Venezuela, propagated a comprehensive change in the country's development model (Becker 1990) though its effective influence on policy making was more limited (Gil 1977, 152; Salgado 1987). These contrast cases suggest that business in Latin America is not necessarily as fragmented as in Brazil.

Heterogeneity of the Middle Class

The Brazilian middle class has been especially heterogeneous in socioeconomic and organizational terms. While parts of the old independent middle class have survived modernization, the expansion of state interventionism since the 1930s has swelled the number of public employees, and economic development has led to the emergence of new groups of professionals. The middle class has had many corporatist councils with the authority to uphold a profession's norms. Innumerable non-official associations have pursued the interests of specific categories with considerable clout and success (Schmitter 1971, 203–04; Boschi 1987, chap. 5). But the middle class has lacked any overarching association that would represent its common interests.

Sectors of the middle class also have important internal cleavages, as the following example of medical doctors shows. This category has undergone considerable socioeconomic change. While most doctors used to be independent practitioners, more and more of them have taken employment in hospitals or medical firms. Their interest organizations have therefore comprised both liberal professionals and salaried employees. This divergence has led to tensions and conflicts. For a long time, the Brazilian Medical Association (Associação Médica Brasileira—AMB) was dominated by a group defining doctors as liberal practitioners. Trying to limit state control, it forcefully espoused economic liberalism. In the mid-1970s, however, a "renovation movement" formed that represented medical doctors as salaried employees. Acting like a trade union, it challenged the established leadership and took over several member organizations in major cities (Campos 1988a, 87–137). This case demonstrates the socioeconomic diversity of the middle class and the organizational splits in its midst.

Fragmentation of Labor

Organized labor was once the stratum of Brazilian society that was most strictly controlled. State corporatism tamed the pursuit of working-class interests for the sake of economic development and social stability. Peak organizations open to all workers were outlawed. The creation of separate union associations for different economic sectors kept the working class divided. National confederations for industrial workers, commerce employees, and so on, have existed side by side. State-level federations for different subsectors and local unions restricted to narrow areas have consolidated the fragmentation of labor organization (Erickson 1977, chap. 3).

In contrast to business, which was allowed to form autonomous associations outside the corporatist framework, the state insisted on the representational monopoly of the corporatist unions. For each category of workers, only one union has been allowed in each territorial unit. Since these units have been delimited narrowly, small local unions have proliferated, and the labor movement has had a highly fragmented foundation. All workers have had to pay dues to the union in charge of their economic activity. Guaranteed funding and lack of competition induced many labor leaders not to display much militancy. Tight state control over union bosses impeded autonomous demand making by workers. After government supervision eroded after the late 1950s, the post-1964 military regime reinforced state corporatism (Schmitter 1973; Mericle 1977). Thus, corporatism kept union organization fragmented and hampered the articulation of working-class interests.

In contrast to the divided structure of urban unionism, rural labor has had an organization that integrates both the formal sector and rural marginals. The National Confederation of Workers in Agriculture, Confederação Nacional dos Trabalhadores na Agricultura, or CONTAG, was formed in 1963 as a result of widespread rural mobilization. In a strategy of inclusionary corporatism, the authoritarian regime supported CONTAG and promoted unionization in the countryside in order to establish firm control. Acquiring organizational strength in the 1970s, CONTAG used the transition to democracy to increase its independence from state supervision and embark on more forceful demand making (Santos 1985, 284–86, 299–301; Maybury-Lewis 1991, chap. 2). Thus, an independent state initiative overcame an organizational gulf in the countryside that has remained deep in urban areas.

Heterogeneity of the Marginal Mass

The rural poor who do not participate in CONTAG and the mass of urban marginals have not had any overarching organization. The variety of their productive activities has ruled out associations based on their class interests. The social movements that started to spring up among urban marginals in the 1970s have been based on residential issues (property rights to lots and public services). They have mostly been delimited by neighborhood (Durham 1984; Boschi 1987; Mainwaring 1987). Before the late 1970s, mobilization for overarching interests was rare. Organizational fragmentation clearly prevailed among marginals.

Since most urban marginals and the rural poor outside CONTAG have had little capacity for broad-based organization, it has been very common and useful for them, in their desperate situation, to enter into clientelist connections.[6] Patrons of higher status can at least provide them with a minimum of protection and benefits. Large parts of these strata have asked paternalistic benefactors for favors and offered obedience and political support in return (Hagopian 1986, 264–75; Mainwaring 1987; Gay 1988). Through carrot and stick, patrons have often controlled the interest articulation and political activities of their clients, especially in the countryside. By fostering vertical cooperation and horizontal competition, clientelism has kept many urban marginals and rural poor organizationally divided.

In conclusion, specific types of segmentalism and personalism, namely state corporatism and clientelism, fragmented Brazilian society. Until the late 1970s, they prevented encompassing interest associations and broad-based social movements from emerging.

Weakness of Political Parties

Segmentalism and personalism have kept Brazil's parties weak and prevented them from advancing universalism. Segmentalism has restricted the importance of parties, and clientelism has undermined their programmatic orientation. Parties that tried to integrate large numbers of citizens were founded with the democratic transition of 1945. Yet existing institutions of interest representation and policy making that were already firmly established kept parties from assuming the role of aggregating social interests.

Policy making was centralized in the state (Souza 1983). Major social categories, especially the private sector, had input through segmentalist and personalist links to public agencies. Businesspeople preferred these avenues of interest representation, which gave them privileged, direct access to decision making (Leff 1968, chap. 7; Schmitter 1971, chaps. 10–13; Martins 1985, 194). Entrepreneurs neglected parties, which could not reliably cater to business interests because they had to appeal to various social strata to achieve a majority. Organized labor also had close links to some state agencies (Erickson 1977; Malloy 1979, 99–105). Since the interests of major strata were articulated through alternative channels, parties did not participate much in important decisions, especially on crucial issues of economic development.

As a matter of fact, parties did not arise as mouthpieces for social strata. Instead, two of the three major parties of the post-1945 period were founded by the outgoing dictator, Getúlio Vargas, who wanted to preserve his influence under democracy (Souza 1983). These parties, created to provide support for a political leader without restricting his freedom of maneuver, were organized as clientelist machines. The third party, arising in opposition to the authoritarian regime, officially denounced clientelism but succumbed to the temptation of using patronage in order to have any success in the clientelist game of Brazilian party politics (Nunes 1984, 101–09; Geddes 1994, 84–86). For these reasons, the programmatic commitment of all major parties was low and their organization weak.

These parties were incapable of channeling the sociopolitical mobilization of the late 1950s and early 1960s. The challenge of mass participation further diminished their internal unity and organizational cohesion. Intraparty factionalism and trans-party alliances grew (Santos 1986).

The post-1964 authoritarian regime further weakened parties. It outlawed the existing organizations and created by fiat two new parties, namely the Alliance for National Renovation (Aliança Renovadora Nacional—ARENA) as the government party and the Brazilian Democratic Movement (Movimento Democrático Brasileiro—MDB) as the official opposition party. To retain a facade of legitimacy, the military rulers allowed these artificial creations to compete in legislative elections. But they excluded parties for a long time from decision making, which was entrusted to the public technobureaucracy (Hagopian 1986, 189–98, 209–24). The military regime also instituted "bifrontal corporatism" (O'Donnell 1977, 64–79). While it suppressed the associational demand making of the popular sectors, it enhanced the privileged access of private business through corporatist and personalist avenues. Business therefore continued to neglect parties.

By excluding parties from social interest representation, the military regime directed politicians even more toward pure political survival based on clientelism. From the mid-1970s on, it used ARENA for doling out particularistic benefits in order to guarantee political support against MDB advances. For example, the Geisel government delegated to ARENA politicians the nomination of the agents who distributed social security benefits in rural areas (interview Corrêa 1990; in general, Cammack 1982; Hagopian 1986). By reinforcing corporatism and clientelism and by interfering frequently and arbitrarily in the party system and the electoral rules, the military regime further weakened Brazil's parties (Alves 1985, 212–30).

Lack of State Cohesion

The preceding discussion has shown that the state fragmented Brazilian society. It imposed corporatism on business and labor and maintained clientelism, and its concentration of power kept political parties weak. However, the fragmentation of society backfired and corroded the internal unity of the state. Too weak to confront the state, narrow social groups have tried to gain special favors by establishing close segmentalist or personalist links to public agencies and officials. This welter of outside connections has undermined state cohesion. Central control and coordination have diminished and, increasingly, different state agencies perform overlapping tasks. While late-late development has also strained the unity of the state, segmentalism and personalism in society have greatly aggravated the problem.

During the nineteenth century, the Brazilian state had considerable institutional stability and strength vis-à-vis society, a legacy from the colonial past (Schwartzman 1982). Using its autonomy to promote late-late development, it has since the 1930s taken on a wide range of responsibilities. An extensive para-state sector of independent agencies, public enterprises, and foundations has performed varied social, economic, and cultural tasks. To assure the flexibility it needed to achieve goals efficiently, this "indirect administration" has enjoyed considerable latitude. This autonomy has undermined central policy coordination, planning, and budgeting and has diminished the internal cohesion of the state (Martins 1985, chap. 2; Geddes 1986, 338–41; Rezende 1987).

Segmentalism and personalism have exacerbated these control problems. By impeding broad-based, powerful collective action, they induced interest organizations to petition public agencies for special privileges. Business groups, in particular, forged close links to state officials and bureaus. These segmentalist or personalist connections have induced public agencies to cater to the interests of their partners in society, who, in turn, have given them support in bureaucratic rivalries. This collusion has weakened the responsiveness of state officials to central commands and has diminished state cohesion (Abranches 1978; Barzelay 1986; Lima and Abranches 1987).

Connections between state agencies and business groups have assumed three different forms. First, many bureaus have consulted frequently with business associations. Knowing they will interact for a long time, public agencies and business groups have tried to avoid conflicts and put their cooperation on an institutional basis. Thus, segmentalism has regularized the access of business to the state. Second, in a more informal way, important business leaders have established personalist links to state officials. Through these "bureaucratic rings" they have obtained privileges that have not been conceded to the rest of their sector (Cardoso 1975, 181–84; 203–07; Boschi 1979, 163–74; Santos and Paixão 1989, 237–43). Finally, and least predictably, entrepreneurs have in several cases been appointed to state positions. All these particularistic connections of state officials and agencies to business have corroded the internal command structure of the state and diminished the effectiveness of state action.[7]

Clientelism has also fragmented the state. Many politicians have tried to obtain patronage resources by influencing appointments to state positions. Even the military regime, which initially restricted clientelism for the sake of state building, ended by using it to bolster the predominance of ARENA (Cammack 1982; Hagopian 1986). As clientelist politicians nominated their followers to public posts, innumerable outside links have undermined the unity of the state. Pervasive clientelism has multiplied task overlaps inside the state. Top government officials have created new posts or agencies in order to be able to make more clientelist appointments. This generation of patronage resources has disregarded functional needs, bloated the state apparatus, and diminished its cohesion and efficiency (Abranches 1985, 55–67; Magalhães 1988, 10–20).

Ironically, clientelism has induced government leaders to increase task overlaps even when they wanted to ensure efficient state action. Concerned about losing political support, presidents often considered it too costly to combat the clientelist penetration of existing state agencies. In order to execute a program, they created a new agency staffed with competent officials (Nunes 1984, 133–47). These efforts to bypass hubs of clientelism fueled the proliferation of state agencies with overlapping attributions and stimulated conflicts over bureaucratic turf. Since the new competent agencies were shielded from pernicious political influences, they gained a level of independence from political control that has allowed them to cooperate closely with sectoral business groups (Nunes 1984, 174–75; Abranches 1978). Thus, efforts to reduce clientelist corrosion have exposed the state to the fragmenting impact of segmentalism.

For all these reasons, the Brazilian state has become deeply fragmented

(Lima and Abranches 1987; Barzelay 1986, 95–98, 104–16; Daland 1981, 225–29). Public agencies have mushroomed. While the American state had twenty-eight top agencies, sixty-five lower-level agencies, and sixty-four boards and committees (Sloan 1984, 134), the Brazilian state had twenty-seven top agencies, about three hundred lower-level agencies, one hundred interministerial councils, and 560 public enterprises.[8] With the sheer growth and increasing complexity of the state apparatus, the finance and planning ministries and the presidency have become less and less capable of imposing internal unity (Rezende 1987). For a long time, the government did not even know how many agencies the Brazilian state had nor how many officials it employed (SEPLAN. SRH 1989, 3). The absence of a unified budget and of effective financial control undermined attempts at central supervision. Task overlaps have multiplied. The finance ministry, for example, had twenty-five offices involved in price control in the late 1980s.[9] As a result, bureaucratic infighting has been endemic.

The lack of institutional cohesion impeded efforts to pursue basic state interests like financial viability. President Geisel (1974–1979) attempted but failed to overcome the problem by centralizing power. He could control only top decisions, but rampant bureaucratic politics undermined their implementation.[10]

Thus, while the Brazilian state had fragmented society, the unintended consequences of this divide-and-rule strategy soon came to haunt it. Since narrow social groups and networks could not put pressure on the state head-on, they tried to advance their specific interests by penetrating the state apparatus itself. Innumerable outside links undermined command and control inside the state, already strained by expanding state interventionism. State initiatives and their paradoxical outcomes brought about a profound fragmentation of society and the state in Brazil.

IMPACT OF DEMOCRATIZATION

The institutionalist approach posits that the fragmentation of society and state will persist despite Brazil's gradual process of democratization. Three reasons support this expectation of continuity. First, late-late development continues to have a divisive effect, since the organizational preconditions for changing the exclusionary development model through political reform are not fulfilled. Second, established organizational patterns are highly capable of self-perpetuation. Segmentalism and personalism create interests that favor their own maintenance and undermine challenges. Third, the return of democracy creates new cleavages and splits social categories and organizations along new ideological and partisan lines.

As the following analysis shows, organizational scope has indeed remained low in Brazil's polity. There were attempts to give the organization of society and the state a more encompassing scope and greater cohesion, but for the reasons just mentioned they were mostly blocked. Very few, if any, encompassing interest associations, broad-based social movements, and program-oriented parties have emerged, and the institutional unity of the state has diminished further.

Impact of Late-Late Development

Democratization has so far not alleviated the exclusionary and fragmenting effects of Brazil's economic development. Inequality in income distribution has increased (IBGE 1990, 75; Oliveira 1993, 32–33). The marginal mass has not been integrated into the formal economy through an extension of employment. The informal sector, which is mainly poor, has maintained its share in the population (IBGE 1990, 42; IBGE 1992, tables 3.14, 3.21).

Temporarily, one economic program of the post-1985 government did spread the benefits of development more broadly. The Cruzado Plan of 1986 tried to stop chronic inflation through a price freeze and by interrupting the reindexation mechanisms that kept inflation from falling. Many poorer people benefited from temporary stabilization, which eliminated the inflationary corrosion of wages, salaries, and pensions. They also gained from an initial wage increase decreed by the government. In addition, the resulting consumer boom led to an expansion of employment and a further rise of wages. The Cruzado Plan particularly favored the poorer sectors of the working class and provided marginals with jobs in the formal economy or greater demand for their products and services (Camargo and Ramos 1988, 28–35, 45–61).

The overheating economy, however, soon fueled renewed inflationary pressures and greatly reduced Brazil's export surplus by stimulating do-

mestic consumption. Since the government postponed necessary correc-
tions in order to win the congressional and gubernatorial elections of fall
1986 (Sardenberg 1987, chaps. 12–13), these disequilibria quickly worsened. Despite the imposition of belated restrictions, the situation became
so unsustainable that the government had to give in to mounting business
pressure to rapidly lift the price freeze (Baer and Beckerman 1989). Inflation skyrocketed immediately. The failure of the Cruzado Plan quickly
reversed its redistributive effect. As real wages plummeted and unemployment soared, the marginal masses could not preserve their gains (Camargo
and Ramos 1988, 60–69).

An important reason for this reversal was the political weakness of the
popular sectors. Their organizational fragmentation prevented them from
exercising countervailing power against private business and the state.
They could not provide sustained support for the enforcement of price
controls and, above all, achieve a negotiated incomes policy through which
business and the state would have borne part of the cost of economic
stabilization (Singer 1987, 112, 126–30, 136). A circular pattern of causa-
tion was at work. Weakened in part by the exclusionary features of late-late
development, the popular sectors lacked a broadly encompassing association or social movement to press effectively for a reorientation of Brazil's
development model, which would in turn have made it easier for them to
strengthen their organization. This vicious circle has helped preserve unequal socioeconomic patterns that reinforce organizational fragmentation.

In addition to this sociostructural reason for continuity, segmentalism
and personalism have strong self-perpetuating tendencies, and democratization has created new cleavages and sources of fragmentation. As a
result, low organizational scope has persisted throughout Brazil's polity.

Organizational Continuities in Brazilian Society

Persistent Business Fragmentation

The self-perpetuating tendencies of segmentalism have been clearly at
work among private business. Sectoral associations, even the corporatist
organizations, survived the regime change and were not replaced by encompassing associations.[11] Despite occasional challenges and rare defeats,
many top business leaders retained their influence during the democra-

tization process.[12] Usually, they have not even faced challenges in internal associational elections, and when they have, as in FIESP, the corporatist structure of their organization allowed them to beat the opposition easily.[13]

Democratization, while not revamping the segmentalist organization of business, changed it through addition. Reacting to threats from labor and left-leaning forces in the Constituent Assembly (1987–1988), business associations created several organizations that encompassed many different sectors and tried to stimulate and coordinate their participation in politics (Dreifuss 1989, 49–92). The very variety of these organizations shows, however, that business did not reach organizational unity.

Only one of the new encompassing organizations temporarily acquired political importance, namely the Brazilian Union of Entrepreneurs (União Brasileira de Empresários—UBE). UBE was founded by the corporatist confederations and independent entrepreneurial associations. It was quite active in the Constituent Assembly but suffered from constant internal divergences. Its coordinating capacity was always limited, and it went into hibernation with the promulgation of the new constitution in late 1988 (interviews Branco 1989, Bornhausen 1992, Coelho 1992). It did not displace other business associations or interfere in the personalist and segmentalist links of business groups with the state, which have remained crucially important.

Attempts to coordinate demand making by business were also made in São Paulo. In 1987, associations like FIESP created an Informal Forum (Fórum Informal—FI), which has tried to unify the state's powerful business community. But as a state-level body, FI cannot speak for all of Brazilian business. Indeed, FI's formation was meant to counterbalance UBE, which—contrary to FIESP's initial hopes—was dominated by national-level associations.[14] Through FI, modern entrepreneurs from São Paulo asserted their weight and independence. FI organized one important fraction of business more cohesively, but increased the divergence between this fraction and the rest. Neither FI nor UBE have therefore served as the protagonist of united class action by Brazilian business.

As segmentalism has survived the regime transition, business has also retained numerous personalist links to the state. Although democratization has opened up avenues of interest articulation at higher levels of aggregation (for example, political parties), it has not eliminated bureaucratic rings.[15] Business leaders have continued to consider these connections useful for pursuing their specific interests. Public opinion has not acquired the strength to cut these links, which undermine the separation of public and private spheres, a basic principle of democracy (O'Donnell 1988, 64–67).

Altogether, the established fragmented patterns of business organization have proven very resilient. Democratization has also unleashed new cleavages inside the private sector. By boosting the principle of political equality, it has increased the importance of the large numbers of small and medium-sized firms vis-à-vis the economic weight of the few big enterprises. This has induced small- and medium-scale entrepreneurs to protest against the domination of associations by "big business." They have revitalized old organizations and formed new ones, especially a loosely organized movement called Pensamento Nacional das Bases Empresariais (PNBE).[16] PNBE has challenged the established "oligarchy" in FIESP and criticized its close links to government and the state as an impediment to the forceful pursuit of business interests. PNBE has advanced universalist principles, condemned corporatist business organization, and demanded complete freedom of association.[17]

The incipient universalism of PNBE and other small-business associations has, however, been far from breaking the dogged insistence of other business associations on segmentalism and corporatism. By stimulating new movements without revamping old organizations, democratization has created additional cleavages within the capitalist class. The new gulfs have counteracted the impulse that the regime change has given for enhancing the coordination of business associations. For all these reasons, democratization has not enhanced the encompassingness and cohesion of business organization. Brazil's private sector has not achieved greater internal ("class") unity (Payne 1994).

In contrast, business in other Latin American countries has achieved greater organizational cohesion. Responding to the uncertainty inherent in democratic rule, especially in a crisis-ridden country, Peruvian entrepreneurs formed an encompassing peak association in 1984, which gained considerable strength in the second half of the decade (Durand 1993, 93–94, 112–14, 126–31, 161–77). Established business peak associations in Chile, Mexico, Venezuela, Bolivia, and Nicaragua have preserved their unity and advanced overarching interests vis-à-vis democratic and authoritarian governments (Silva 1992; Tirado 1992; Becker 1990; Conaghan, Malloy, and Abugattás 1990; Spalding 1994).

Persistent Dispersion of the Middle Class

Democratization has not led to the formation of broad organizations for Brazil's middle class. Its enormous socioeconomic diversity ruled out an encompassing class association and made even less far-reaching efforts difficult. The middle class has not faced a threat from another social category or the state that would induce it to create an overarching defense organization. The established sectoral associations have proven quite successful in advancing the specific interests of their constituents (Boschi 1987, chap. 5).

Middle-class associations have been divided internally by sociostructural differences and ideological tensions among their constituents. In the Brazilian Medical Association, for example, these divergences erupted into open conflict after 1978. Two currents were vying for control. One (re)presented doctors as liberal professionals, the other as salaried employees. In 1981, the trade-unionist current defeated the entrenched liberal leadership, only to lose against its rejuvenated version in 1983 (Campos 1988a, chap. 3). But local-level associations in major urban centers, where many doctors are dependently employed, have remained under the control of the more left-leaning current. As this case suggests, the different sectors of Brazil's fragmented middle class are internally divided by socioeconomic and ideological rifts.

During the transition to democracy, members of the middle class created innumerable social movements, such as neighborhood associations in major cities (Boschi 1987, chap. 4) and organizations that advance environmentalist or feminist causes or fight racial or sexual discrimination. These movements have been kept apart by their single-issue orientation and have not drawn a significant following in other social classes.[18] Therefore, they have not provided the organizational bond for unifying large numbers of people across class and other cleavages.

Continued Fragmentation of the Labor Movement

Similar to business, counteracting organizational tendencies have affected labor. As a result of democratization, more encompassing trade-union associations above the official corporatist framework have emerged. But many features of corporatism have persisted (Rodrigues 1990b, 65–72; Boito 1991), and the new peak associations have been kept apart by strong ideological rivalries. The aggregating effect of democratization has remained rather limited.

The labor associations created by state corporatism have survived. The pyramids of separate local unions, state-level federations, and national confederations were not substituted by new unions organized at a higher level of aggregation. Several features of state corporatism were enshrined in the 1988 constitution. The new charter preserved the obligatory union contribution by all workers, which gives labor leaders guaranteed funding and thus enhances their autonomy from union members.[19] Unions still have monopoly representation in their territorial domain, and their base organizations remain restricted to small areas.[20] These corporatist characteristics continue to fragment and weaken the union movement. Conservative labor leaders have supported the maintenance of corporatist features in order to guarantee their own established position.[21] These remnants of corporatism have sustained union leaders with a personal stake in their perpetuation. They have also depoliticized union members (Cohen 1989; Mettenheim 1990, 38–39) and thus weakened challenges to the established organizational structure.

Democratization has, however, eroded other important aspects of state corporatism, especially government control. Unions and their leaders are now protected against state interference, which the military regime had used to emasculate the workers' movement by imposing conservative labor leaders, for example. The government does not meddle any more in internal union affairs. This autonomy from state control has allowed some powerful unions to advance far-reaching demands.

Overarching union associations have been founded and represent the most important organizational change that democracy has brought in Brazil. The creation of more encompassing associations is a big step beyond the fragmenting state-corporatist framework. Unions have been brought together from different sectors that had once been forced into separate corporatist confederations. Broader-based organizations can now articulate labor interests at a higher level of aggregation and can muster wider backing.

But democratization has created new cleavages inside the workers' movement. Several overarching associations coexist and are kept apart by ideological and partisan divergences that the regime change has fueled. The socialist Workers' Singular Peak Association (Central Única dos Trabalhadores—CUT) competes with the initially moderate but ever more left-leaning General Workers Confederation (Confederação Geral dos

Trabalhadores—CGT), the moderate Union Force (Força Sindical—FS), and the moribund conservative Independent Union Association (União Sindical Independente—USI) (Rodrigues 1991, 33–42). While CUT has a close connection to the socialist Workers' Party (Partido dos Trabalhadores—PT), CGT has not allied itself with any specific party but accepts partisan activities in its midst. In contrast, the new FS—and an old CGT splinter—is dominated by an avowedly non-ideological, economistic current ("unionism of results"), which has insisted on the separation of partisan and union activities (CGT 1989, 4–5; interview Medeiros 1989; see Keck 1989, 279–82; 1992, chap. 7; Rodrigues and Cardoso 1993, chap. 5).

Because of differences in their regional and sectoral strongholds, these peak associations take divergent positions on corporatism. CUT, which has its base in advanced economic sectors of major urban centers and some mobilized regions of the countryside (Rodrigues 1990a, 41–43, 113–17), represents the most modern wing of the labor movement. Managing to mobilize workers autonomously, it rejects the corporatist structure. In contrast, CGT included as member organizations the corporatist confederations, which have a broader base in regional and sectoral terms than CUT and extend to the more backward wing of the labor movement (CGT 1986, 14–17). Similarly, FS finds most support among weaker unions of the old corporatist structure (Rodrigues and Cardoso 1993, 40–41, 69, 73). Since many member unions of CGT and FS lack the mobilizational capacity of CUT unions, they fear to be weakened by the elimination of corporatism. They more or less openly support corporatist features like the compulsory collection of union dues from all workers.[22] Thus, corporatism continues to split the labor movement.

While CUT, CGT, and FS have occasionally cooperated, strong rivalry and fierce competition have prevailed. Concerned about the advances of CUT in the union movement, CGT and now FS have tried to design strategies of defense and counterattack. The Brazilian labor movement is far from forming an overarching association that could speak for the whole working class.[23] By opening up new cleavages, democratization has made it more difficult to achieve this goal.

In contrast to the splits in the urban labor movement, CONTAG has preserved its internal unity. The "initial incorporation" of a stratum has lasting effects by creating deep-seated loyalties and by giving the existing associations a competitive advantage over new, rival associations (Collier

1982). CONTAG retained its members' commitment by using its corporatist organization to press for the interests of rural workers ever more forcefully (Santos 1985, 284–86, 299–301; Stralen 1989). For a long time, its leaders avoided getting involved in ideological battles (Keck 1989, 273–79; Senhor 1 April 1986, 35–36). Although CONTAG has its strongest support among wage laborers, like the sugarcane cutters of Pernambuco, it covers the whole country and has members from different sectors and types of rural labor. Comprising both the formal and informal sector, it is the most encompassing organization in Brazilian society.

But CONTAG has faced competition from an organization founded in the late 1970s, namely the Movement of Landless Rural Workers (Movimento dos Trabalhadores Rurais Sem Terra—MST). The MST pursues a more radical strategy, especially on the crucial question of agrarian reform, and has close links to CUT and the socialist PT (Maybury-Lewis 1990, 12–13). It has found support mainly in the south of Brazil and is much weaker in the rest of the country. Thus, it has not been able to challenge the position of CONTAG as the principal representative of rural labor.

While not overcoming their fragmentation, trade unions have extended their reach by helping organizations of "policy takers" to form. Above all, retired workers from the formal sector of the economy have united in order to advance the interests of better-off pensioners.[24] They have used their ample time, organizational experience, and support from unions to build a network of very active associations. As their peak organization, the Brazilian Confederation of Pensioners (Confederação Brasileira de Aposentados e Pensionistas—COBAP) has gained representation on several government bodies. Thus, the labor movement has expanded into new areas of interest representation.

In several other Latin American democracies, labor organization is also quite fragmented. In Peru and Colombia, different peak associations compete, divided mainly along partisan lines (Hartlyn 1988, 183–87; Stephens 1983, 65–78). Argentine labor long had a single peak association, the Confederación General del Trabajo, but it suffered from internecine factional infighting (McGuire 1992) and split in the early 1990s. Only in Chile and Venezuela have workers maintained a high degree of unity as one peak association, the Central Unitaria de Trabajadores and the Confederación de Trabajadores de Venezuela, has clearly predominated in representing workers' interests (Frías 1993; McCoy 1989).

Persistent Fragmentation of the Marginal Mass

On a low level of interest aggregation, democratization has also had contradictory effects on the organization of the marginal mass. While new interest associations and social movements have been created, they have often been hampered by ideological and partisan cleavages. Indeed, clientelism has retained a hold on considerable parts of the urban and rural poor. For these reasons, the marginal mass has remained highly fragmented.

Democratization has allowed marginals to organize. Social movements and neighborhood associations have mushroomed from the mid-1970s on. But most of the new organizations concentrate on problems affecting their local community. Since the extension of public services is among their top priorities, their hopes are set on state action. State agencies have often used their command over resources for patronage and control. By raising the state's responsiveness to some needs of marginals, democratization has furthered this clientelist cooptation, a process that began at the end of military rule and has continued in the new democracy (Mainwaring 1987, 135–39, 147, 151–54; Boschi 1987, 154; Jacobi 1989, 114–23, 133–34, 138–59; Boschi 1990, 217–18).

Thus, marginals remain susceptible to divide-and-rule tactics and personalist domination.[25] Although socioeconomic modernization has slowly weakened the hold of clientelism, especially in urban centers, patrons have retained considerable control. Democratic competition has done little to strengthen the bargaining power of clients. In fact, it has bolstered clientelism by inducing most of Brazil's parties to rely on the distribution of patronage for electoral purposes. Clientelism has reinforced the narrow interest definition of marginals and impeded their autonomous horizontal organization. They can escape its hold during short episodes of mobilization (for example, in the presidential campaign of 1989), but they can rarely sustain collective demand making. Lacking a realistic alternative, they are easily lured back into clientelism. For all these reasons, the marginal mass has not founded overarching associations that could represent it before the central state.[26] Outside organizers, especially from the Catholic church, have succeeded mainly on the local level. Efforts to give these local movements an effective voice in policy making, especially through popular councils, seem to have had little success (Assies 1994, 92).

Democratization has also led to new splits within the marginal mass, especially along partisan lines. In Brazil, party allegiance often depends on clientelist calculations of access to patronage. Since the regime change has given a broader spectrum of parties a chance to gain power on the local and regional level and to use it to dispense benefits, divergences among marginals over which party they should support have intensified (Mainwaring 1989, 186–90; Cardoso 1988, 374–77). All these obstacles have kept most of the poor politically subordinate and have impeded their autonomous encompassing organization.

In other Latin American countries, the poor are equally fragmented and weak. In Peru, where in the 1980s social movements mushroomed, clientelism has retained its hold on many members of the informal sector (Stokes 1991, 76–82), and efforts to create more autonomous organizations (Stokes 1991, 76–82) failed at least on the national level, as the implosion of the leftist party alliance Izquierda Unida shows. In Chile, social movements have failed under the new democracy to maintain the mobilizational momentum developed under authoritarian rule (Oxhorn 1994, 57–65); they have not formed a strong national-level organization. In Mexico, popular movements have tended "to fall squarely into the logic of clientelism" (Hellman 1994, 127), and even in Venezuela, a competitive democracy, clientelism has maintained a strong hold on the poor (Hanes de Acevedo 1991). Thus, fragmentation of the urban and rural poor is a phenomenon all across Latin America.

Altogether, democratization in Brazil has had a double-edged impact on the organization of society. By removing restrictions on associational rights and by stimulating conflict, it has prompted the formation of a few more encompassing business and labor organizations. But the regime change has also intensified ideological and party-political rifts and strengthened small entrepreneurs vis-à-vis big business. Thus, it has created new cleavages within and among interest associations and social movements. Above all, segmentalism and personalism, especially longstanding corporatist and clientelist structures, have proven quite durable. For these reasons, democratization has not overcome the organizational fragmentation of Brazilian society.

Continued Weakness of Political Parties

With rare exceptions, democratization has not prompted Brazil's parties to acquire firmer organization and program commitment. To the contrary, parties have become even more fluid in recent years. Several new parties have emerged, especially through splits away from the opposition front against the military regime, which became the Party of the Brazilian Democratic Movement (Partido do Movimento Democrático Brasileiro—PMDB).[27] The movement of politicians in and out of parties has assumed enormous proportions. Party loyalty has remained low. In their effort to attract new followers, few parties champion ideological principles or specific programs (Mainwaring 1992–93).

In a vicious circle, the very weakness of parties has induced powerful interest groups, especially from business, to continue pressing their demands directly on the state. They rely on parties and politicians only as supplements, as an additional line of defense for their interests. For this reason, parties are not recognized by state officials as representatives of social categories. Both interest groups and public servants prefer to deal with each other directly (interviews Branco 1989, Cunha 1992, Solimeo 1989, Szajman 1992, Carvalho 1987, Rodrigues 1989, Silva 1989). Parties have not assumed an aggregative role, which could mitigate the organizational fragmentation of Brazilian society.

Rather than representing collective interests and advancing programs, parties have competed for votes through populist rhetoric and by distributing patronage. Many politicians continue to rely heavily on clientelism (O'Donnell 1988, 78–82; Ames and Nixon 1993, 14–15, 24–25; Ames 1994). In its self-perpetuating dynamic, clientelism has extended its reach. As soon as the opposition PMDB assumed government powers, it attracted clientelist politicians who had been allied with the military regime. They now joined the new government party so as to preserve their access to patronage (Hagopian 1986, 372–74). Even previous opposition politicians were tempted to adopt clientelist tactics in order not to lose out in electoral competition.[28]

Since clientelist politicians want latitude for maneuver, they enshrined in laws or in the constitution rules that prevent parties from acquiring programmatic commitment and organizational discipline (Mainwaring 1994, 2–9). For instance, in the open-list system for proportional elections, citizens with their votes (not rank-orders elaborated by party organizations) determine the chances of different candidates from the same party to win a legislative mandate. Since contending candidates have to distinguish themselves from competitors from their own party, they are not committed to a common party program. They owe their mandate to their own political base, not the party organization, which has therefore little hold over them. The open-list system thus has helped to keep Brazilian parties weak (Mainwaring 1992–93, 702–07; Power 1991, 91–92).

As a result of these deficiencies, interest groups have become ever more frustrated with clientelist politicians. Business leaders, in particular, want to use Congress, which has gained importance with democratization, as an additional avenue for articulating their interests. To gain influence over parties, they have made increasing efforts at lobbying, and more and more business leaders have joined parties and run for electoral office.[29] In these ways, they have tried to transform parties into more reliable channels for advancing their interests.

But the opposite effect has also occurred. Businesspeople have been drawn into politics and pulled away from the task of interest representation. When other entrepreneurs notice their political ambitions, they are less likely to trust them as reliable spokespersons.[30] Furthermore, businesspeople support and run for quite different parties. Since there is no socioeconomic basis for these divergent political preferences, no party will end up as the mouthpiece of sectoral interests—not to speak of business as a whole. Thus, the recent influx of businesspeople has not eliminated the organizational fluidity and low program commitment of Brazilian parties.

As the main exception, the Workers' Party (Partido dos Trabalhadores—PT) has established a new type of party organization in Brazil (Meneguello 1989; Keck 1992). It has an unusual level of programmatic commitment and a firm (though limited) base in society through its symbiosis with CUT and close connections to social movements. By appealing to both the working class and the marginal mass, it tries to bridge the gulf between the formal and informal sectors. If it broadens its appeal and adopts a social-democratic position, it could mitigate the organizational fragmentation of the popular sectors and become the germ of a universalist party, inducing competing parties to strengthen their own organization. But this potential is far from being realized, and the PT has up to now had scant political influence. Based on temporary mass mobilization and coalitions with center-left parties, it gained a surprising 47 percent of the valid votes in the second round of the 1989 presidential election. In Congress, however, it only had a minuscule delegation of 3 to 7 percent; the 1994 election increased its share of seats to just 10 percent.[31]

Except for the PT and some minor left-wing parties, democracy has not enhanced the institutional strength and program orientation of Brazil's parties. Segmentalism still restricts their importance as broad channels of interest articulation, and clientelism continues to be their main organizational basis. Parties of this type can hardly press effectively for redistributive reform.

Similar problems affect parties in other Latin American countries, though often to a lesser extent. Bolivia, Ecuador, and Peru have parties that are as uninstitutionalized as Brazil's, and Argentina's parties suffer from organizational weaknesses and increasing electoral volatility. Colombia's and Uruguay's parties have firm roots in society but are based mainly on clientelism. Only in Venezuela, Costa Rica, and Chile are parties well organized and more programmatically oriented (Mainwaring and Scully 1995, 6–21; Coppedge 1992, 12–13; see also Dix 1992). Thus, party weakness, while especially pronounced in Brazil, is not foreign to the region.

Persistent Lack of State Cohesion

Democratization has not increased central control nor reduced task overlaps inside the state apparatus. It has stimulated attempts to raise state cohesion but also unleashed dispersive tendencies. As the latter were stronger, the state has grown even less cohesive.

The governments of Presidents João Figueiredo (1979–1985) and José Sarney (1985–1990) tried to impose greater control on state agencies, for example, by creating a special bureau for supervising the welter of public enterprises. Most important, they gradually unified the federal budget. Under military rule, the government had operated with four different budgets. As only one of them needed congressional approval, the executive branch, and individual agencies within it, had enjoyed enormous financial latitude. Unifying the budget should strengthen parliamentary and government control and curb autonomous spending by state agencies.[32]

The Sarney government also made several attempts to reorganize and streamline the state apparatus. All these efforts were blocked or greatly watered down by resistance from public bureaucrats, clientelist politicians, and segmental interest groups.[33] Even budget unification has not had the expected controlling effect. Financial discipline has been undermined by the increased political weight of Congress, where state officials can lobby on behalf of their agencies and subvert the restrictions set by the ministries of finance and planning.[34] Thus, by giving state agencies a forum of appeal against government directives, democratization has exacerbated the internal disunity of the Brazilian state.

Innumerable segmentalist and personalist connections between the state and interest groups continue to fragment the state. Indeed, democratization has fueled partisan competition for patronage. State agencies that were staffed by meritocratic recruitment under military rule have been penetrated by clientelist networks under democracy.[35] The regime change has given a broader range of political forces the right to nominate their followers to state positions.[36] For these reasons, the public bureaucracy has acquired a more diverse composition and an enormous variety of outside links, which make it even more difficult to direct and control (SEPLAN. SRH 1989). The "divided Leviathan" of authoritarian rule (Abranches 1978) has become a Gulliver tied down by innumerable particularistic bonds.

Democratization has also reinvigorated Brazilian federalism. Authoritarian rulers centralized coercive powers and financial resources in the national executive and restricted the autonomy of states and municipalities. The regime change restrained imposition by the central government, reinstituted direct elections for state governors, and increased the share of states and municipalities in public revenues. Many state governors now have considerable independence and clout vis-à-vis the central government.[37] Their control over patronage gives them a hold over representatives from their state in parliament (Novaes 1994, 118). They can even affect the central government's composition by indicating followers for top posts, including ministers.

President Fernando Collor's (1990–1992) administrative reform did not overcome the command and control problems inside the state. He reorganized the public bureaucracy and concentrated power at the apex. Collor incorporated several ministries into the presidency and unified others. He also tried to extinguish agencies, sell public enterprises, and lay off superfluous state officials. These reforms raised state cohesion at the top and tamed longstanding rivalries among ministries. But bureaucratic politics continued to rage inside the new agencies, and the effort to make the state leaner ran into persistent opposition. Public officials and interest groups contested the privatization of state enterprises and the dismissal of personnel. The administrative reform was undermined in the implementation phase.[38] In fact, President Itamar Franco (1992–1994) reversed part of Collor's ministerial reorganization and pursued administrative reform with less zeal.

Fragmentation has plagued the state in both issue areas under investigation, although less in tax than in social security policy. The MF has had primary responsibility for taxation, but SEPLAN, the Ministry of Industry and Commerce (Ministério da Indústria e do Comércio—MIC), and the Ministry of Agriculture (Ministério da Agricultura) have also had some influence. Collor's administrative reform reduced rivalries by uniting MF, SEPLAN, and MIC into a Ministry of the Economy, Finance, and Planning (Ministério da Economia, Fazenda e Planejamento—MEFP), but President Franco recreated the old ministries. Inside the MF, the SRF (Secretariat of Federal Revenue) has jealously guarded its autonomy and control over tax policy, even against the apex of the MF. President Collor's appointees tried to undermine the SRF's esprit de corps and to marginalize the agency in policy making, but they were only partly successful and provoked considerable resistance. Under President Franco, the SRF regained its earlier status.

Overlapping obligations have been even more widespread in social security policy. MPAS/MPS has needed the approval of MF and SEPLAN for its budgeting, and it used to share responsibilities in health care with the Health Ministry (Ministério da Saúde—MS). The unclear delimitation of turf made rivalries endemic. President Collor divided tasks up more clearly by transferring health care from the MPAS to the MS, but incessant battles erupted over each ministry's share in the government's "social budget." Also, in contrast to the MF, the MPAS/MPS has not had its own executive apparatus. Social security has been administered by two to four para-state agencies with considerable autonomy. Since ministerial supervision has not been well defined,[39] wrangling over influence has been interminable. The MPAS/MPS has had difficulty in getting its plans enacted.

Thus, the Brazilian state has remained deeply fragmented. Central coordination and control have been exceedingly difficult. Frequent attempts at administrative reform have largely failed; rather than guaranteeing its internal unity, they have been badly executed and have disorganized the state apparatus even more.

The lack of analyses of state structures makes a systematic comparison with other Latin American countries impossible. Impressionistic evidence suggests, however, that organizational fragmentation and bureaucratic infighting plague many states in the region, especially in the area of social policy (Mesa-Lago 1994, 76–79; Isuani and Tenti 1989, 23–24). Also, the clientelist and segmentalist penetration of the public bureaucracy has corroded state capacity in several nations, especially Peru and Argentina (O'Donnell 1993, 1358–61). Countries such as Chile, where a powerful agency, the Secretaría General de la Presidencia, coordinates state action (Rehren 1993, 24–27), are exceptions. As in Brazil, many states in the region thus seem deeply fragmented.

CONCLUSION: DISPERSAL OF POWER IN BRAZIL'S POLITY

Brazil's transition to democracy has not enhanced the encompassing scope and cohesion of major interest organizations, social movements, political parties, and the state. By weakening the state vis-à-vis society, it has led to a dispersal of power. Under authoritarian rule, the state imposed its will and used the fragmentation of society to reduce challenges to its predominance. By diminishing state control without bringing about encompassing or universalist organizations in civil society, democratization has made it difficult to arrive at authoritative decisions, especially on conflictive issues such as redistribution.

Democratization has undermined the once overwhelming power of the state apparatus. The reaffirmation of civil rights and constitutional guarantees has restricted presidential autocracy. Law courts have gained autonomy; they are now willing to intercede against abuses of executive power. In recent years, the supreme court has declared several executive acts unconstitutional. The new constitution created legal instruments with which individuals and organizations can defend their rights against the state (Article 5).

Parliament has gradually gained political weight, and the 1988 constitution has further augmented its power. The substitution of the "decree-law," through which the president could legislate with little impediment from Congress, by the "provisional measure," which retains validity only if explicitly approved by parliament, gave congressional influence a boost. The executive can still draw on superior expertise, but—to the consternation of government *técnicos*—clientelist politicians often care little about the technical quality or long-term impact of their decisions.[40]

The state has also been weakened vis-à-vis interest groups. Corporatist controls over interest organizations have eroded. With the reassertion and extension of civil and associational rights, society has gained a degree of independence from the state that it had never enjoyed before. Business sectors, middle-class groups, and labor unions can now put pressure on the state—not necessarily with success, but mostly without risk of repression. The defensive capacity and veto power of these interest organizations has been augmented considerably.

As the state has lost its predominance over civil society, no organizations or institutions have emerged that could coordinate the diverse forces and power centers in Brazil's polity. The primary candidates for fulfilling this "function" are political parties. But Brazil's fluid and disorganized parties do not serve for aggregating collective interests and for designing and executing policy programs. This has made it very hard for Congress to arrive at authoritative decisions and fill the vacuum left by the weakening of the state apparatus. For example, the elaboration of the new constitution took much more time than planned, and it has never been fully regulated. Brazil's parties and parliament have fallen far short of fulfilling their coordinating role.

Thus, democratization has led to a dispersal of power. It has weakened the state without generating new mechanisms for political coordination. In line with the institutionalist argument of chapter 2, segmentalism and personalism have persisted throughout the regime change. Since democratization has unleashed new ideological and partisan cleavages, it has not brought about encompassing interest associations or social movements, more disciplined, program-oriented parties, or a cohesive state. For these reasons, all of the organizational mechanisms through which democracy could bring about equity-enhancing reform have failed to emerge.

4

Redistributive Policy Making
Under Authoritarian Rule

WHY HAS democratization not enhanced the chances for equity-enhancing change in Brazil? An investigation of redistributive policy making under democracy is decisive for answering the main question of this book. But before undertaking this task in chapters 5–7, I will establish a point of reference in this chapter by examining decision making under military rule. To show what a difference the transition to democracy made, policy making under authoritarian and democratic rule needs to be compared. This chapter therefore analyzes the government of President Ernesto Geisel (1974–1979), which was clearly authoritarian but which initiated the slow return to democracy.[1]

Can the institutionalist approach applied in this book provide some theoretical guidance for examining redistributive policy making under the military regime? By implication, it considers social reform during bureaucratic-authoritarian rule as possible, though not very likely. Some organizational obstacles to equity-enhancing change are diminished but do not disappear. Above all, the state can gain more institutional cohesion by centralizing authority at the top. It can enhance its autonomy and capacity by reducing personalist and segmentalist connections to social groups. Policy making may be determined by state-building technocrats with a universalist orientation who resent the privileges of the elite and discriminations against the poor and follow the model of socially advanced developed countries. Military regimes may also launch equity-enhancing initiatives in order to create support among the popular sectors and preempt bottom-up pressure, especially at the beginning of a transition to democracy. Thus, bureaucratic-authoritarian rulers may promote some compensatory redistribution.

Yet while their impact is reduced, several organizational obstacles to equity-enhancing reform remain in effect. Divisions within the state and the access often enjoyed by elites, especially business leaders and conservative politicians, can seriously obstruct attempts at social change. Clientelism becomes a powerful impediment when the transition to democracy begins and the authoritarian government uses patronage to retain support.

Although they have a higher capacity for enacting equity-enhancing reforms, authoritarian rulers may not want to use their power in this way because of conflicting goals. Bureaucratic-authoritarian regimes assign top priority to rapid economic development. This preference, which does not simply reflect business interests or the needs of the capitalist system, sets clear limits to redistribution. Because of this goal conflict, the reform initiators themselves tend to proceed cautiously. For these reasons, authoritarian rulers usually enact at best limited equity-enhancing reforms.

POLITICS OF DIRECT TAXATION

Development of Brazil's Tax System

Nineteenth-century Brazil collected almost all its tax revenues from indirect levies, but various taxes on different kinds of income were gradually introduced. A general income tax that integrated these levies was created in 1922, but it did not cover all types of income. Sectoral privileges and exemptions were common. Elites used their direct access to the state to demand and defend such favors. Because of segmentalist influences, Brazil's income tax never embodied the universalist principle of equal treatment of all income types (Bulhões 1948, 10–12). The application of tax rules provided another opening for favoritism. Friends of state officials could expect leniency, and some taxpayers managed to reduce their obligations through "gifts" to tax collectors. Private business and liberal professionals, in particular, took advantage of the available privileges and loopholes. Thus, tax laws were heavily corroded by segmentalist and personalist favors and exceptions.

The revenue reductions and resource needs caused by World War II led the authoritarian government of Getúlio Vargas to augment the income tax greatly in the mid-1940s (Fundação Getúlio Vargas 1966, 31–34). Deficient administration and weak enforcement of tax rules allowed the democratic governments from 1946 to 1964 to increase top tax rates further and make the income tax nominally quite progressive. Since powerful groups had an easy escape from these obligations, they did not strongly resist their enactment. As a result of these exit options, which rendered "voice" unnecessary (Hirschman 1970), the progressive income tax rules yielded meager revenues (Shoup 1965, 19–25).

Only the military regime improved the administration and enforcement of tax laws. Using its high level of autonomy after coming to power, it imposed some sacrifices even on its elite allies in order to stabilize the economy and enable the state to promote rapid development. Income tax revenues grew considerably (F. A. Oliveira 1981, 57–58, 120–24). Acting on state interests, authoritarian rulers effected some progressive redistribution through taxation (while hurting poorer sectors much more with tough stabilization measures, which forced wages down and reduced employment).

Over time, however, the military regime applied taxation more and more to provide incentives for economic development. While sectorally differentiated indirect taxes were the best instrument for this purpose, the income tax was also used. For example, the capital market was favored by exemptions for several types of investment, and the Geisel government lowered the tax burden on agriculture. These incentives were meant to stimulate important sectors temporarily, but under pressure from business they soon acquired permanency and proliferated across sectors. As a result, they lost their capacity to direct private investment and turned from steering mechanisms to mere handouts (F. A. Oliveira 1981, 125–29; Varsano 1982).

Since business enjoyed numerous tax breaks, the burden of the income tax fell mainly on sectors of the middle class and better-off workers. The dependently employed were unable to evade their obligations because they could not use most tax incentives and because part of their income tax was withheld at the source—that is, automatically deducted from their salary or wage. The income tax therefore had a much less equitable burden than its progressive nominal rates suggested. In contrast to indirect taxes, however, which absorbed a much higher proportion of the poor's low incomes than of the wealth of the rich, the income tax was progressive because the large mass of poor people was exempt (Eris et al. 1983, 127–28). Because of Brazil's highly unequal distribution of income, only about 13.5 percent of the economically active population had to pay income tax in 1976 (Dias 1984, 212).

Goals of the Geisel Government in Tax Policy

In the early 1970s, national and international criticism of the regressive social effects of the military regime's exclusionary development strategy intensified. The Geisel government promised to reduce extreme inequality and widespread poverty, which were embarrassing to a country claiming great-power status. It also wanted to transform the authoritarian regime into a limited, guided "democracy" in which conservative forces would be in control. To preempt any mass mobilization from the left, some reform measures seemed in order. Thus, maintaining political power was a crucial goal of President Geisel's equity-enhancing efforts.

As one step, the government announced its intention to make the tax system more equitable. Given the high concentration of income, this meant imposing more of the tax burden on the privileged strata. Direct taxes should be augmented at the expense of regressive indirect taxes, progressivity of the income tax should rise, and it should be extended to exempt types of income, especially capital gains. These goals, proclaimed by the finance minister, Mário Henrique Simonsen (Simonsen 1977, 28–34), were shared by most officials of the Secretariat of Federal Revenue (Secretaria da Receita Federal—SRF), the bureau inside the finance ministry (MF) which was in charge of taxation. The universalist professional orientation of SRF officials and their institutional mission to guarantee state revenues made them resent the tax privileges enjoyed by the rich.[2] But since Brazil was not facing severe budget problems and since foreign loans were easily available, these equity considerations were not reinforced by a strong state need for fiscal revenues, which could have prompted serious efforts to reduce the tax privileges of the rich.

Also, Simonsen wanted to use taxation as an instrument for making economic policy (Simonsen 1975). Brazil's development strategy assigned the domestic private sector an important role (Evans 1982), and the government faced business attacks on the high level of state intervention in the economy (Cruz 1984). Therefore, Simonsen planned to strengthen and guide the private sector through tax incentives. This "privatizing" orientation, which reflected the minister's close links to business,[3] was not shared by most SRF officials, who were trained to focus on fiscal concerns. Commitment to their agency's organizational interests also made them reluctant to have tax policy, which they claimed as their own domain, subordinated to development policy.[4]

These differences in background and goals affected decision making. Despite the concentration of power under authoritarian rule, the state apparatus was not fully unified. Minister Simonsen faced some opposition from SRF technocrats and other state agencies. Under the military regime, the public bureaucracy was the main site of policy making and interest conflict. Business groups were the only social stratum with significant (mainly defensive) influence. The following analysis shows how universalist impulses to make the tax system more progressive were held in check by conflicting government goals and by opposition from segmentalist forces inside and outside the state.

Changes in the Personal Income Tax

The progressivity of the personal income tax is determined by its effective rates and the extent to which it covers various types of income. Effective tax rates depend on nominal tax rates and on adjustments for the devaluation of money in Brazil's inflationary economy.[5] In all these dimensions, the Geisel government effected at most modest redistribution. Administrative problems, stressed by the SRF, and (anticipated) opposition from the private sector impeded farther-reaching change.

Nominal tax rates, which went up to 50 percent, were already quite progressive in 1974. The MF considered further raising the income tax on the rich and moving the sharpest increase in progressivity away from the lower end of the income scale. Since it saw such changes as technical, it did not consult with interest organizations. Only some tax lawyers voiced concerns, but did not exert much influence. Nevertheless, the frequent changes, including a new tax rate of 55 percent, did little to advance the cause of social equity (Dias 1984, 94–99, 123–29). Under Simonsen's guidance, the MF feared the exit options of the rich, such as tax evasion and capital flight, and increased their tax burden only slightly.

Manipulating income tax adjustments for inflation neutralized the redistributive effect brought by changes in nominal tax rates. In order to reduce consumer demand and control inflation, the MF readjusted income brackets at a rate below the general price index. The "bracket creep"[6] resulting from this subterfuge hurt especially taxpayers with lower incomes because the progressivity of tax rates rose most steeply at the bottom of the income scale. Under the Geisel government, this regressive increase in the tax burden was counterbalanced by changes in nominal tax rates. But with the sharp rise of inflation under its successor, the readjustment of the income tax below the real rate of inflation resulted in greater inequity (Dias 1984, 101–07).

Another mechanism to cope with the constant devaluation of money aggravated the unfair burden on lower- and middle-class taxpayers. In order to stop the erosion of revenues by inflation, the MF tried to collect tax as soon as income appeared. Such a "system of current bases," implemented through withholding taxes, was easy to impose on employees and workers; employers simply deducted tax from their wages and salaries. Businesspeople, liberal professionals and recipients of capital gains, however, were much harder to subject to immediate tax payments because their income flow was difficult to predict and to control.

These administrative problems, acknowledged by the SRF, together with opposition from some business associations made the MF proceed much more cautiously than planned (interviews Freire 1990, Lima 1990, A. Oliveira 1990, Coelho 1990). Many types of income remained exempt from the system of current bases. Only in the recession of the early 1980s, when the state urgently needed higher revenues, were capital gains in the financial market made subject to tax withholding at the source—but at proportional, not progressive, rates (Longo 1986, 26–28). Better-off people, who received most income of this kind, thus continued to have their tax obligations eroded by inflation. In contrast, the Geisel government raised the withholding tax on the dependently employed, who did not have much power and organizational capacity for defending their interests under authoritarian rule. Thus, the incomplete system of current bases put lower-

and middle-class taxpayers at an ever greater disadvantage and exacerbated inequality.

Opposition from the private sector also hindered the extension of the income tax to types of income that had so far been taxed very leniently, such as capital gains. In order to guarantee revenues and improve equity, the SRF promoted this universalist goal. It tried to eliminate segmentalist privileges and impose a fairer tax burden on the rich, who received most of these types of income. The SRF therefore proposed to subject capital gains to the general norms of the progressive income tax. This far-reaching plan was also meant to strengthen the MF's bargaining position with the strongest and best-organized social segment, namely business.[7]

Even under the Geisel government, which concentrated decision making in its own hands and seemed distant from social interests, the MF consulted regularly with the private sector over issues of taxation. Business was a decisive partner in the government's drive for rapid economic development, and Simonsen and his top aides had close links to private firms. For these reasons, they granted entrepreneurs considerable input in public decision making, both through associational and personal channels (interviews Coelho 1990, Freire 1990, A. Oliveira 1990, Simonsen 1988, Solimeo 1989).

This private-public consultation filtered out the SRF's farther-reaching tax proposals. Resistance from business made the government often take the easy way out, namely relying on readily available foreign loans, rather than raising revenues through politically costly tax increases. The MF also feared tax evasion and capital flight. All these considerations made it extend the income tax only cautiously. In several small steps, it increased the burden on real estate operations and capital gains in the financial market. Through these moderate progressive changes, it reduced some segmentalist privileges, but did not eliminate them; many others remained untouched. Wages and salaries continued to bear a much higher tax burden than the forms of income that the rich received disproportionately.

Changes in the Corporate Income Tax

Given its importance for President Geisel's development goals, the private sector had particular influence on corporate taxation. In the mid-

1970s, business and conservative voices in the media came to attack the "statization" of Brazil's economy (Cruz 1984). Interestingly, however, this campaign did not demand a reduction in the private sector's tax burden, which was nominally quite high. One reason was that the wealth of tax incentives allowed bigger firms to escape from taxation (FIESP and CIESP 1975, 24–37; Varsano 1982). Also, the organizational fragmentation of business hindered the defense of its overarching interests, and the Geisel government refused to consult with the private sector on basic guidelines of economic policy. Corporatist associations like FIESP, whose leaders were selected under government influence *(Relatório Reservado*, 29 January 1979, 1), assumed a conciliatory stance and pointed to the benefits of Brazil's high level of taxation (De Nigris 1975). Thus, the technocratic mode of decision making and the corporatist organization of business contributed to this "non-demand making." While exerting much influence on sectoral measures, the private sector did not control overarching government policy.

On more specific decisions, however, business leaders had considerable say. In 1977, the MF tried to overhaul the corporate income tax in order to strengthen the domestic private sector. It wanted to facilitate mergers, give national firms greater economies of scale, and make them competitive with transnational corporations. In line with his privatizing orientation, Minister Simonsen asked a lawyer to elaborate the new tax code. The resulting project was very favorable to the private sector; it contained "everything that businessmen [had] always demanded."[8] The MF distributed the draft law to business associations, which asked for even more favors. It assumed that ample consultation with the private sector made a congressional debate of the reform unnecessary—a striking indication of the prevailing corporatist mode of policy making.

President Geisel, however, refused to enact this generous proposal, which was too complicated for him to assess. Also, SRF *técnicos* advised him strongly against "gifts" to private business, which would reduce government revenues. Geisel therefore decreed only a few provisions of the project in late 1977. Yet the SRF continued its opposition even to these alterations. Criticizing loopholes opened by the 1977 decree-law, it convinced the president in 1978 to eliminate major reform provisions (especially on mergers) through which enterprises could evade taxation. Business and tax consultants protested in vain.[9] Thus, the bureaucratic apparatus of the SRF safeguarded the fiscal goals and political control interests of the state and checked the privatizing tendency of the finance minister and the corporatist influence of business.

Decision Making and Policy Outputs in Direct Taxation

Under the Geisel government, decision making in direct taxation was quite technocratic. State officials determined the basic guidelines of tax policy. They advanced several redistributive projects, but with little forcefulness because foreign loans were easily available to substitute for fiscal revenues. The state's concern for economic development also restrained equity-enhancing reforms. Of course, this concern took the weight and exit options of private business into account, and top MF officials were close to business and consulted with it extensively. But SRF technocrats provided a counterweight and safeguarded state interests.

The MF started most changes in direct taxation. The private sector had little policy initiative, but considerable power for defending its interests. Associational and informal links to the state allowed business sectors to blunt the bite of reforms. The MF and SRF often consulted with business and took its suggestions and criticisms seriously.[10] But where they anticipated opposition, they made tough initial proposals so that a compromise would lead to an acceptable result. Neither side was ever "defeated." As the MF and SRF implanted gradual reforms, they hoped for more success in the future.

State officials also consulted extensively with tax lawyers and consultants. In their technocratic approach, they took expert knowledge—even without "real" power—seriously. While these specialists claimed to be independent, most of them worked for business and defended its interests. But on issues that were not of immediate concern to the private sector, like the personal income tax, some assumed an independent position.

Except for business, no other stratum had voice or influence. Trade unions were under strict government control until 1978, and after their resurgence they focused on immediate issues like wages and on the authoritarian character of political rule, not on tax policy. Political parties and Congress played a minimal role in tax policy. The government enacted most changes through decree laws, and its official party made sure that parliament never voted them down. Until late 1977, the constitution imposed by the military regime was interpreted as prohibiting congressional initiatives on tax matters. This understanding changed with political liberalization (Rosas 1978), but Congress still lacked the technical expertise and political power to assume a leading role in tax policy.

What outputs did this technocratic decision making have? Overall, the redistributive performance of the Geisel government in taxation was unimpressive. Changes in the structure of the personal income tax canceled out in their equity-enhancing impact, yet the weight of this progressive tax par excellence in state revenues increased. As for the effective rates of the personal income tax, progressivity rose from 1974 to 1979 (Gerheim 1982, 20–33; see Dias 1984, 128–39). In contrast, the extension of the personal income tax did not compensate for the increased withholding on wages and salaries. The share of labor income among all income types reported for tax purposes rose from 84.4 percent in 1974 to 91.2 percent in 1979.[11]

However, the shares of different taxes in federal revenues changed in an equity-enhancing direction. From 1973 to 1979, the share of the personal income tax grew from 13.1 percent to about 20.2 percent. Since at the same time the most important indirect tax fell from 41.7 percent to 30.1 percent, this change was clearly progressive. How did reforms in the corporate income tax affect this picture? In Brazil, business passes most of this tax on to consumers through higher prices (Contador 1976, 153–65). This burden shift turns the corporate income tax into a regressive indirect levy.[12] From 1973 to 1979, its share in federal tax revenues grew from 9.6 percent to about 17.1 percent.[13] But since this increase came at the expense of indirect taxes, it did not have a regressive effect.

In sum, the Geisel government made the effective rates of the personal income tax more progressive and augmented its importance in public finances. Reforms in direct taxation did, overall, improve vertical equity, as richer taxpayers now bore more of the burden. However, the increased withholding from the dependently employed diminished horizontal equity as people earning the same amounts of income but from other sources (such as capital gains) continued to pay very low taxes. Altogether, the MF effected limited redistribution in taxation.

Thus, the greater emphasis of the Geisel government on social goals gave the universalist orientation of the SRF more space and led to some equity-enhancing tax reform. However, the priority assigned to economic development, which strengthened the position of business, set definite limits to redistributive change. Whereas entrepreneurs defended their interests with considerable success, this goal conflict was debated and decided mainly inside the state apparatus.

Development of Brazil's Social Security System

Brazil's public social security system dates from the 1920s when the state preempted bottom-up pressure from fairly powerful sectors of the newly emerging working class by conceding social protection (Malloy 1979, chap. 2). Initially, old-age pensions and medical care were granted only to strategically placed workers in the public sector (for example, railroad workers), but the authoritarian regime of Getúlio Vargas (1930–1945) used these "inducements" (Collier and Collier 1979) to include more and more sectors of labor into a state-corporatist system. In exchange for social benefits, they submitted to state control, which guaranteed their contribution to a crucial regime goal, rapid economic development. As state corporatism kept organized labor fragmented, social protection varied greatly by professional category. The various sectors of labor had their own separate pension schemes. Brazil's social security system was never based on the principle of universal citizenship but always full of segmentalist privileges and discriminations (Santos 1987). Thus, it shared some basic features with the corporatist/statist system prevailing in European countries such as Germany and France (Esping-Andersen 1990, 58–61).

In addition to different entitlements for those included, vast sectors of the population were left out. Following the Bismarckian model, social security was financed largely by contributions from workers and employers, not by general tax revenues. As inclusion depended on a regular, steady source of income (and official labor registration), the informal sector, which was most in need of social protection, remained excluded. Since employers passed on large parts of their social security contributions to prices, the poor were taxed as consumers without receiving benefits in return. Thus, the social security system favored better-off strata of the popular sectors; the poorest groups were left out and had to carry part of the burden. By raising the cost of labor in the formal sector, the system even reinforced the entry barriers for marginals (Bacha, Mata, Modenesi 1972).

From the 1940s on, experts in state positions, especially those administering the pension scheme for industrial workers (Instituto de Aposentadoria e Pensões dos Industriários—IAPI), tried to reduce these inequities. These IAPI technocrats were inspired by European models, especially Britain's Beveridge Report, which called for equalizing and universalizing social protection, at least by guaranteeing minimal livelihood to every citizen (Leite 1973, 15–19). This universalist tendency was held in check by doctrinal commitment to the contributive principle, which made benefits dependent on the payment of social security taxes, and by concern for the financial viability of the system. It seemed exceedingly difficult, above all, to cover the large mass of poor people who had few resources to contribute.

The reform-oriented technocrats therefore centered their efforts for a long time on eliminating the differences among those already included. They had difficulty achieving progress under democracy (1946–1964), which gave the more privileged groups ample opportunity for defending their special rights. After fifteen years of effort, formal entitlements for workers and employees were finally standardized in 1960—but better-off groups further improved their privileged access to social benefits and services of superior quality. Only the post-1964 military regime gave the universalist technocrats enough power to consolidate the 1960 reform by unifying the separate, sectoral social security schemes (1966–1967) (Malloy 1979, chaps. 4–5). But this measure also did not eliminate the great differences in effective social protection among workers and employees. In addition, public servants and military personnel retained their highly privileged systems of social protection, and the poor in the informal sector remained excluded. Despite the advance of universalism, segmentalist differentiation continued to pervade the social security system.

The military regime enacted another important reform in the early 1970s, when Brazil's "economic miracle" provided resources for extending social protection into the informal sector. The repressive government of General Emílio Médici (1969–1974) worried about swelling rural-urban migration and wanted to control the rural population in order to guarantee political support and prevent any mobilization by opposition forces. In a strategy of inclusionary corporatism, it created a social security scheme for agricultural laborers (FUNRURAL) and entrusted its administration to rural unions and the National Confederation of Workers in Agriculture (CONTAG), whose growth it promoted with incentives.

Since most rural laborers were dirt-poor, they could not pay the same social security taxes as the urban sector. Therefore, they were guaranteed a (truly) minimal entitlement independent of direct contributions. The urban sector shouldered most of the financial burden. This reform, enacted as an autonomous state initiative during the most repressive phase of military rule, was the most important redistributive change ever made in Brazilian social security. Besides its direct equity-enhancing impact, it set aside the contributive principle on which Brazil's social security system had always been based (Santos 1987, 83–85). This reform seemed to open the door for the inclusion of all marginals and the effective universalization of social protection.

Goals of the Geisel Government in Social Security

When President Geisel assumed power, some significant advances had been made in the reform of the social security system, but many problems of privilege, discrimination, and exclusion remained. The greater priority that Geisel assigned to social development led to further equity-enhancing efforts. Since the government did not want to change Brazil's economic model, it saw compensatory measures of social protection as especially important. Such programs would consolidate sociopolitical stability, prevent mass mobilization, strengthen the government party ARENA, and aid in gradual, cautious political liberalization (Nascimento e Silva 1975; see also Ames 1987, chap. 4, esp. 147–54). Thus, the state interest and government goal of bolstering existing structures of political domination was a preeminent motive of redistributive efforts in social security.

Luiz Gonzaga do Nascimento e Silva, who headed the newly created Ministry of Social Insurance and Welfare (MPAS), nominated as top aides a close-knit group of former IAPI technocrats who now gained an opportunity to advance their universalist goals. They wanted to equalize and extend social protection gradually, reduce privileges, and make social security taxes fairer but maintain the financial viability of the system. They tried to reduce the corporatist features of Brazil's social security system and put it on a more universalist basis (compare Esping-Andersen 1990, chap. 3). In these efforts, they saw organized interest groups, which advanced narrow segmentalist demands, as obstacles. They insisted on a technocratic mode of policy making, which the authoritarian regime made feasible. Thus, state officials, not social forces, initiated equity-enhancing efforts in social security (as in tax) policy.

Policy of Social Insurance

Extension of Coverage

Extending coverage was the main equity-enhancing goal pursued by MPAS technocrats in the area of social insurance, that is, of transfer payments like old-age pensions and sickness pay.[14] By the early 1970s, the formal sector of the urban economy was largely covered. But the rural poor enjoyed only minimal protection, and most city dwellers who lived off informal activities remained excluded from contributive social insurance. The MPAS estimated the number of these marginals as between 10 and 25 million persons, about 10–25 percent of the population.[15]

The inclusion of the informal sector faced an obstacle in the contributive principle underlying Brazil's social security system, which linked benefits to paying social security taxes. Most urban marginals had incomes that were too low or irregular to pay such taxes. The military regime had bent the contributive principle when creating FUNRURAL, but most former IAPI technocrats viewed this scheme as a temporary exception until the monetization of the rural economy permitted the collection of regular social security taxes. They were reluctant to soften the contributive principle further and undermine the actuarial soundness of the system.[16] Therefore, they promoted the extension of coverage only halfheartedly.

The MPAS decided to grant minimal social protection only to old or disabled urban residents who had contributed to the social security system for a certain time, yet not long enough to gain full entitlements. This reform was too limited to entail much redistribution. It was designed inside the MPAS bureaucracy, without consultation with society. Particularly, the new beneficiaries—and the many millions still excluded—had no organizational capacity to advance their interests.

With this reform, the limits of bending the contributive principle were reached. Any further extension of coverage required new sources of funding. The MPAS hoped to include in the long run all those unable to pay social security taxes, such as the marginal urban dwellers (Nascimento e Silva 1974, 155). Other categories would have to pay for this equity-enhancing reform, either by shouldering higher social security taxes or by accepting cuts in their own benefits. Since the poor lacked the organizational strength to press for the extension of coverage, however, the MPAS pursued these ideas only in a lukewarm way. As the proposals for revamping social security expenditures and revenues did not make headway, resource constraints ruled out universal social protection.

Efforts to Eliminate Privileges

An extension of coverage could be financed by cutting disproportionally high benefits for better-off recipients. In this vein, some MPAS technocrats wanted to phase out the time-of-service pension. In Brazil, not only do old age and disability constitute a right to a retirement pension, but also the documented completion of thirty or thirty-five years of work. Many Brazilians go to work at an early age and are therefore eligible for retirement in their late forties. But only people with steady jobs in the formal sector can prove their time of service. Most time-of-service pensions are thus granted to better-off workers and employees at an early age (Azevedo and Oliveira 1986, 159–60), whereas the large masses of poor people have to work until they become old or disabled.

Granting pensions to people in their late forties seemed a costly privilege. A minimum-age qualification was thus enacted until pressure from organized labor led to its elimination under the populist government of the early 1960s. Since the social security system was not under financial strain, the military regime did not reimpose the age limit. But under President Geisel, the exploding cost of health care (to be discussed) created the danger of deficits. Therefore, the MPAS's Secretariat of Accounting proposed in 1978 reintroducing an age limit.[17] But other MPAS technocrats objected successfully, claiming that the time-of-service pension was a "national and popular aspiration" and that financial problems were not severe enough to require a restriction (F. L. Oliveira 1978; interview L. Velloso 1990). These arguments took the resurgence of the labor movement into account, which had been made possible by the political liberalization promoted by the Geisel government. Thus, the gradual regime change hindered the reduction of privileges, which could have helped to finance the further extension of social security coverage.

Debates on Social Security Taxes

Government technocrats also considered changing the financial basis of the social security system. Traditionally, it had been sustained largely by a deduction from wages and salaries and a tax on the payroll of firms. Specialists linked to the planning ministry (SEPLAN) criticized this financial scheme because it imposed a high burden on labor-intensive sectors of the economy and worsened the severe problem of underemployment (Bacha, Mata, and Modenesi 1972). As an alternative, SEPLAN proposed a tax on firms' gross receipts or on value added, which would burden capital-intensive sectors more. It advocated a reform in order to create employment and promote domestic business, which was more strongly represented in labor-intensive sectors. But the MF offered resistance. It feared that the change would fuel inflation because entrepreneurs would transfer the burden of a social security tax on gross receipts or value added to consumers via higher prices.

The MPAS took an ambivalent position. It considered new taxes necessary for financing the extension of social security to those who could not pay direct contributions. But it feared revenue losses because the new taxes would be much harder to collect than the payroll tax. Everything considered, it preferred the established system (interviews Nascimento e Silva 1990, F. L. Oliveira 1990; SEPLAN 1979, 10; Leite 1981, 116–17).

Private business joined the debate. Labor-intensive sectors, which would benefit, strongly supported a change, whereas capital-intensive sectors opposed it (interviews Corrêa 1990, J. Velloso 1990). While the division of business reinforced the impasse, the divergences between different state agencies were decisive. The involvement of SEPLAN and MF made the MPAS suspect that a change would diminish its cherished control over the huge social security budget, and this made it even more wary (SEPLAN 1979, 24). Years of debate brought no practical results. Thus, state fragmentation and bureaucratic politics blocked reform. Under the Geisel government, redistributive reform was primarily blocked by the divergent goals of different state agencies and officials.

Decision Making and Policy Outputs in Social Insurance

In the policy of social insurance, state officials clearly were the decisive actors. They initiated equity-enhancing reforms and made decisions based

on their own goals and principles, with minimal "interference" from organized interests and Congress. Only in exceptional cases did they respond
to demands, particularly from rural unions. Most obstacles to reform arose
from state officials' own conflicting goals and norms, such as their commitment to the contributive principle, and from rivalry with other state agencies. Their main redistributive achievement was to extend minimal coverage to some of the urban poor. This reform was important for the target
group but modest in light of Brazil's enormous social problems and of the
goal of universalization the MPAS had initially announced.

Health Care Policy

As in social insurance, extending coverage was the MPAS's main progressive goal in the area of medical assistance. Many millions of Brazilians,
especially poorer people, were legally excluded from public health care, and
even people with full entitlements had to wait in long lines for medical
services. Given President Geisel's emphasis on social development, the
MPAS now tried to satisfy this unfulfilled demand. The government declared a commitment to better health care to forestall disaffection, guarantee political stability, and create support for the military regime and
ARENA (Nascimento 1975).

The dominant group in the MPAS, however, the former IAPI technocrats, wanted to get involved in health care as little as possible. The
insurance principle, which ties benefits to contributions, could not be
strictly applied because medical services were provided according to need
rather than the amount of social security taxes paid (J. Oliveira 1983,
30–47). As a result, it was difficult to subject the provision of medical
services to the accounting rules of an insurance system (interview Bastos
1990).

Therefore, the former IAPI technocrats responded only to expressed
demands and did not actively identify unfulfilled health needs. They neglected preventive measures and concentrated on curing those who had
already become sick. Rather than having the social security administration
provide medical services, they preferred contracting doctors and hospitals,
which treated social security recipients and were paid by the public administration.[18] The former IAPI technocrats believed in the higher efficiency
of the private sector and therefore considered such contracting cheaper

than building public facilities. Reinhold Stephanes, president (1974–1978) of the huge National Institute of Social Insurance (Instituto Nacional de Previdência Social—INPS), which administered social security for most of the urban population, had an even stronger preference for the private sector.[19] Since he was dealing directly with medical business, he became quite sensitive to its interests.

The doctrinal viewpoints of the former IAPI technocrats and the INPS president shaped policy making on health care under the Geisel government. In response to growing demand, they wanted to expand the provision of medical services as fast as possible. But this strategy led to financial and equity problems, which prompted some other state officials to propose redistributive reforms. The resulting debates and conflicts led only to meager equity-enhancing efforts and achievements.

Increasing Privatization of Health Care

Closer Public-Private Cooperation

To satisfy the demand for health care, the MPAS and INPS advocated greater cooperation with the private sector. The health business had grown enormously since the mid-1960s, stimulated by increased out-contracting by the social security administration. The MPAS and INPS decided to extend these contracts further, rather than build new public facilities. Health business interests praised this plan, but public officials did not act in order to please the private sector. A congruence of interests and principles made both sides agree independently. They consulted only on how to implement their common goals (interviews Nascimento e Silva 1990, Stephanes 1989, Ferreira 1989, Mansur 1990).

In 1974, the former IAPI technocrats liberalized the rules for private-public cooperation and attenuated state control (INPS 1975b, 6–13, 106). This made it easier for the public sector to contract private hospitals and doctors for services. The government also provided cheap credit for expanding the private health sector (Braga and Paula 1986, 125–32). In a more progressive vein, the MPAS extended social security coverage. In emergencies, anybody—insured or not—would be treated by public or contracted private providers at the expense of the INPS. This rule opened the door to health care for previously excluded urban marginals. Since private hospitals were interested in treating as many patients as possible, the number of "emergency" cases grew beyond all expectations (INPS 1975b, 24, 65–68, 110–12).

While MPAS, INPS, and medical business interests agreed on the parameters of their cooperation, they diverged on specific issues, such as remuneration for private contractees. In these conflicts, the state determined outcomes, based on technocratic calculations, and made few concessions to the Brazilian Hospital Federation (Federação Brasileira de Hospitais—FBH). Thus, MPAS remained in control. While it needed the private hospitals for its strategy of extending medical services, they in turn depended on the patients of the social security system. But despite its limited political power, medical business reaped enormous economic benefits from the expansion of health care.

Achievements and Problems

Closer public-private cooperation led to a virtual explosion of medical services. From 1973 to 1978, hospital treatments increased from 4.7 million to 9.7 million (INAMPS 1979b, 172), and doctors' visits from 54 million to 145 million (INAMPS 1979a, 136, 159). Medical business greatly extended its role in Brazil's health system. The number of hospital treatments and doctor's visits it provided to urban social security recipients grew by 78.8 percent and 342 percent, whereas public services rose only by 14.6 percent and 30.3 percent (INPS 1975a, 106–07, 112–16, 136; INAMPS 1979a, 16–18, 24–27, 39, 120–24).

This rapid expansion soon created problems. Expenditures exploded, undermining the financial equilibrium of the social security system. Public spending on health care rose by 32 percent in 1975 and by 36 percent in 1976 (Braga and Paula 1986, 100), much faster than revenues. Medical business abused the lax rules and performed many superfluous treatments or simply over billed the INPS (Mello 1977, 121–212; MPAS 1979, 27–28, 46). The deep inequality in the regional and social distribution of medical services persisted. The gap in health care between the developed Southeast and South and the impoverished rest of Brazil remained, and so did the gulf between urban and rural residents (INAMPS 1979b, 172–74; INAMPS 1979a, 136, 159). As the drastic expansion of hospital treatments shows, a lot of funds were spent on complicated treatments for relatively few, often well-to-do people, while many poor Brazilians did not receive cheap, simple health care to satisfy their most basic needs.

Efforts to Reform the Health Care System

Reform Impulses

A few experts in the MPAS, INPS, and the Ministry of Health (MS) responded to these problems with proposals to correct the privatizing model. Trained in social medicine, they did not share the former IAPI technocrats' preference for simply curing the sick. They advocated fighting the (often social) causes of illness. They focused on unfulfilled medical needs, especially of the poor, not only on expressed demands. These progressive technocrats invoked President Geisel's promise to pay more attention to social development. Their main goal was to universalize health care. While they conceded that people paying social security taxes receive priority in medical service provision, they planned to extend preventive measures and basic care to the uninsured poor. In the long run, they wanted to eliminate the different treatment of these categories (MPAS 1975a; 1975b; MPAS.SEE 1975).

The progressive technocrats wanted to reach these goals by strengthening the public sector. The state should allocate more resources for preventive measures and basic medicine. In order to diminish the distortions stemming from the heavy reliance on the profit-seeking private sector, the state should intensify its control and direction and give nonprofit hospitals preference. In this way, it could guarantee better access to health care for the poor whose needs the privatizing model neglected. In order to bring medical services closer to the users, their provision should be decentralized to the municipal and state level (MPAS 1975b, 41–44, 52–58; MPAS.SEE 1975, 26–46).

The former IAPI technocrats and the INPS president, however, defended their privatizing health care model and accepted only piecemeal reforms. Since they were clearly dominant inside the state apparatus, they succeeded in scaling down the impulse for equity-enhancing change to a mere administrative reform.

Reorganization of the Social Security System

For years, the MPAS had discussed a reorganization of the health care system, which was divided among several agencies. INPS was responsible for most of the urban population, FUNRURAL for ruralites, and a third agency for public employees. The former IAPI technocrats planned to concentrate health care for both the urban and rural population in a single new agency, which would work with more efficiency, and put INPS in charge of social insurance for both urban and rural recipients. Administrative unification would also clear the way for later efforts at extending coverage and reducing inequalities among different social categories (Leite 1978, 326–29). However, financial problems, commitment to the contributive principle, and resistance from privileged "policy takers" blocked immediate steps toward universalization, which the progressive technocrats advocated.

Although accepting some reform goals as a long-term program, the former IAPI technocrats and the INPS president resisted all ideas to use the new health care agency for reversing the privatization of medical services by strengthening the public sector (interviews Bastos 1990, F. L. Oliveira 1990, Mansur 1990). Many proposals of the progressive technocrats were disregarded. Rather than overhauling Brazil's inequitable health care system, the MPAS enacted only the administrative reform. It reorganized agencies that were defined by social target group along functional lines, putting INPS in charge of social insurance, extinguishing FUNRURAL as an independent agency, and creating the National Institute for Medical Assistance in Social Insurance (Instituto Nacional de Assistência Médica da Previdência Social—INAMPS) to administer health care.

The reform left the relationship between the public and private sectors virtually unchanged. Charging that some MPAS officials wanted to "statize" health care, hospital associations, especially FBH, wanted to participate in reform elaboration, but Minister Nascimento denied this demand. FBH criticized especially that INAMPS would have the right to intervene in contracted hospitals in order to guarantee the provision of medical services. It feared that this provision would endanger its autonomy and boost state power. The MPAS reassured the private sector that it would not apply its coercive power but retained the right of intervention and thus kept the threat alive.[20] Despite this disagreement, the close cooperation and cordial relationship between the private and public sectors were maintained.

Few other political forces participated in the reform debate. Rural labor unions opposed the extinction of FUNRURAL, which the state had allowed them to help administer. Using social security benefits as "selective incentives" to build their organizations (see in general, Olson 1971, 132–35), rural unions had mushroomed in the 1970s (Santos 1985, 284–86,

299–301). They now feared that the elimination of FUNRURAL would cut their lifeline as INPS and INAMPS would extend their bureaucratic apparatus to the countryside. Coordinated by CONTAG, they strongly resisted the reform (interview Silva 1990).

Many politicians also saw the reform as a political threat. ARENA depended on support from rural regions for maintaining its majority despite the MDB's advance in urban centers. In order to guarantee votes, the government party used the social security system for distributing patronage. FUNRURAL was the most important instrument of clientelist party politics. The government allowed ARENA to nominate the "representatives" who distributed social security benefits in regions where the public administration did not have outposts. After an electoral debacle in 1974, ARENA had pressed the government to extend this system and used it successfully for the 1976 municipal election (MPAS. FUNRURAL 1978, table 52; MPAS 1978a, 15; interview Corrêa 1990).

ARENA feared that the extinction of FUNRURAL would rob it of a powerful electoral asset and offered extraordinarily strong resistance.[21] Many former IAPI technocrats did, in fact, abhor the clientelist "representation" system, which contradicted their universalist principles by linking the concession of benefits to particularistic considerations. However, financial constraints and ARENA's opposition blocked the extension of the INPS and INAMPS bureaucracy into the countryside. Minister Nascimento promised ARENA and CONTAG to maintain the contracting of rural unions and clientelist agents. In this unprecedented conflict, conservative politicians helped limit the latitude of government technocrats whose universalist goals endangered their clientelist strategies of political survival. Since the government depended on electoral support for the slow regime liberalization, the MPAS had to leave clientelism and inclusionary corporatism in the countryside intact. Thus, specifically political interests sparked the strongest and most effective resistance to this equity-enhancing effort.

A Rare Reform Success

The preceding analysis shows that most reform proposals of the few progressive technocrats in the social security administration were blocked. However, their call for greater attention to preventive measures, which benefit the poor more than the prevailing emphasis on curing the sick, did have some success. The Geisel government set up a program to bring sanitary and basic medical facilities to rural communities in the poor Northeast (Programa de Interiorização das Ações de Saúde e Saneamento—PIASS). In this region, many basic health needs remained unfulfilled. The deficit in public services fueled rural-urban migration and created the risk of discontent. As low profit chances kept medical business out of the region, the responsibility for mitigating the problem fell to the public sector.

Certainly, the former IAPI technocrats resisted a transfer of funds from curative medicine, administered by the MPAS, to preventive measures, for which the MS was responsible. The MS had a meager budget and needed help from the MPAS, which controlled the huge revenues from social security taxes (Braga and Paula 1986, 91–109). Defending their basic doctrine and bureaucratic interests, MPAS officials insisted on the insurance principle and argued that social security contributions could not be deviated to benefit the still excluded poor through preventive measures.[22] It took constant pressure by the MS and by politicians from the Northeast to have PIASS enacted and to extract funds from the reluctant MPAS.

In addition to bureaucratic politics, pervasive clientelism hindered the implementation of PIASS. Patronage politics reduced the quality of the program, as incompetent personnel were hired. The clientelist calculation that services for individuals would create more political support than benefits for whole communities led to the neglect of important sanitary measures, such as sewage disposal (Lopes 1981, 15–17, 32–36; Pellegrini et al. 1979, 15–18; Teixeira, Silvany, and Saho 1979, 20–25, 32–37).

Despite these problems, PIASS had a redistributive impact. It gave millions of poor people access for the first time to basic medical services and sanitary facilities.[23] This program for a very poor region in which the privatizing model of MPAS and INPS was inapplicable was one of the few successes of the Geisel government in realizing the progressive goals it had proclaimed.

Decision Making and Policy Outputs in Health Care

In contrast to social insurance, in the area of health care, state officials faced the organized demand making of powerful social sectors, such as private hospital owners. Nevertheless, the MPAS initiated all important reforms and determined their basic outlook. The former IAPI technocrats acted on principles they had held for decades. Their goals were congruent with the interests of the private health sector, which therefore gained enormous benefits from their measures. But these reforms were not taken as a result of pressure from medical business interests, which had little say in decision making and focused mainly on program implementation to undermine control efforts and obtain special benefits.

While medical business did not have much influence on goal formulation, state officials took business interests into account. With the privatization of health care, the MPAS depended ever more on its private contractees. But this dependency stemmed directly from the goals and principles of state officials, and health business in turn depended on the patients of the social security system. The MPAS also counted on its coercive powers to deter open threats from private hospitals. Whereas both sides were willing to compromise, the MPAS retained the upper hand, as its frequent refusals to raise the remuneration for the private contractees suggest.

Other strata played only a minor role in decision making. With their resurgence in 1978, some urban unions attacked the delegation of health care to business firms but could not reach a change. Rural unions were unable to block the extinction of FUNRURAL, but retained much of their influence in rural social security. Many social movements springing up in urban centers paid considerable attention to health issues on the local level, but, lacking an overarching organization, they did not have the least impact on national policy making.

Members of Congress presented numerous bills providing benefits to specific, often privileged categories, but legal restrictions and the submission of ARENA to the government prevented their approval. Parliamentarians acted independently only in the rare case where their own political survival in the clientelist game of Brazilian party politics seemed at stake. In the conflict over the creation of INAMPS, they were able to safeguard their political interests, although the MPAS pushed through its crucial reorganization goals.

Did the Geisel government effect redistribution in health care? The expansion of medical services did enhance equity by giving some of the poor access to health care, but the MPAS's privatizing model had a high opportunity cost. As critics charged correctly, the government could have done much more for the poor with the available funds. Health care spending was ever more severely mistargeted (World Bank 1988, 3–5, 11–21), concentrating on expensive curative treatments and neglecting cheap basic care and preventive measures. The increased reliance on private contractees consolidated this distortion and made its correction more difficult by strengthening privileged sectors such as medical business.

Nevertheless, the health policy of the Geisel government did bring about some redistribution. PIASS clearly enhanced equity. This program used general budget funds and social security taxes, to which the middle class and urban workers contributed more, to attend to basic health needs of the destitute. While not designed to reduce inequality, the overall expansion of medical services also helped many poor people. Since better-off categories paid more in social security taxes than they used through medical services (Roriz 1980), the health care system had a redistributive net impact. Therefore, the growth of medical services disproportionally favored poor people. This redistributive effect was probably not neutralized by the frequent overcharging and fraud by private hospitals, which diverted public funds destined partly for the poor to privileged groups. Altogether, despite its sub-optimal strategy, the Geisel government improved social equity in health care.

CONCLUSION: REDISTRIBUTIVE DECISION MAKING UNDER MILITARY RULE

Decision making under authoritarian rule was characterized by the conflictual coexistence of technocracy, bureaucratic politics, bifrontal corporatism (O'Donnell 1977), and clientelism. Experts in state positions technocratically determined the basic guidelines of policy making and initiated almost all of the efforts at change. They promoted some equity-enhancing reforms, but their own conflicting goals created important impediments. Whereas their universalist principles and concerns about the sociopolitical consequences of growing inequality made them pursue redistribution, their commitment to stimulating economic development and their strong privatizing attitudes set limits. Bureaucratic politics posed further obstacles, especially in social security, where the state apparatus was highly fragmented. Policy coordination, which was required for redistributive success, especially in health care, was very difficult to achieve. Equity-enhancing initiatives of one agency were inhibited by other agencies, which saw their organizational interests endangered.

The influence of social forces was shaped by bifrontal corporatism, which excluded urban labor unions but gave business sectors considerable chances for defending their interests. Their organizational fragmentation and the reluctance of the Geisel government to consult on basic decisions made business sectors oppose mainly those equity-enhancing reforms that affected their specific interests. Their resistance created additional impediments to redistribution, but their influence was never alone decisive. In contrast, bifrontal corporatism did not give urban unions any role in policy making. Even rural unions, which the authoritarian regime fostered in a strategy of inclusionary corporatism, had very limited influence.

In addition to facing opposition from other public agencies and business sectors, state officials saw the execution of reform programs corroded by innumerable personalist links. Since politicians did not have a say in substantive choices under the authoritarian regime, they tried mainly to gain patronage. Only when a technocratic proposal threatened to undermine their clientelist base did they challenge the government. Normally, they merely intervened in program implementation in order to channel particularistic benefits to their followers and withhold them from their enemies. Businesspeople also used connections to state officials in order to obtain special favors. All this personalist interference siphoned off public funds, corroded universalist reform rules, and undermined efforts at control and redistribution.

Despite all of these obstacles, the Geisel government enacted some modest equity-enhancing reforms in direct taxation and social security. It augmented the progressivity of the personal income tax and increased its weight in tax revenues, and it took some measures to expand social insurance and health care for the poor. Certainly, at the same time it improved social security benefits for privileged groups, and its reforms were much too limited to combat the enormous problems of poverty and inequality head-on. Earlier military governments had aggravated these problems through their economic and social policies, but they had also effected some important redistributive reforms, such as the enforcement of the progressive income tax after the mid-1960s and the extension of social security to the countryside from 1971 on.

Thus, authoritarian governments did bring about some limited compensatory redistribution. Civil society is not the only source of equity-enhancing impulses. Rather, the autonomous interests of government bureaucrats, public agencies, and the state can motivate reform. Under the Brazilian military regime, the goal to guarantee sociopolitical stability and preempt discontent prompted equity-enhancing efforts. The universalist principles of public technocrats, who enjoyed much latitude for decision making, reinforced these impulses. However, several organizational obstacles, especially bureaucratic politics, bifrontal corporatism favoring business groups, and clientelist interference in program implementation, set tight limits to redistributive reform.

This finding sets the baseline for assessing the new democracy. Has the civilian regime achieved more equity-enhancing improvements than its authoritarian predecessor?

5

The Politics of Taxation

in the New Democracy

How DID the transition to democracy affect the chances for equity-enhancing reform in direct taxation? As this chapter shows, the regime change did, indeed, stimulate numerous redistributive initiatives, but they were blocked, greatly watered down, or soon reversed. Where did equity-enhancing impulses arise? What impeded their success?

In line with the institutionalist approach, bottom-up pressure for redistributive tax reform has remained weak in Brazil. Political parties have too scant a programmatic orientation to campaign with the promise of imposing a higher tax burden on the rich. Brazil lacks broadly encompassing interest associations that would demand higher social spending financed by progressive taxes and other general improvements, rather than simply insisting on special benefits, such as wage hikes, for their members. The most important redistributive impulses have come from experts. Under military rule, public technocrats had already pursued some equity-enhancing reforms; they now saw the advent of democracy as an opportunity to gain further support for their goals. More important, with the accession of the opposition PMDB to the government in 1985, progressive experts in society were nominated to state positions, from which they promoted redistributive goals.

Why did these many attempts to increase social equity in Brazil have so little success? The following analysis points to organizational obstacles, which stem especially from segmentalism in state and society. First of all, bureaucratic politics filtered out many reform initiatives. More conservative technocrats defended existing rules and procedures, and ministries with sectoral responsibilities, such as agriculture, protected "their" sectors from higher taxation. Even more important, business leaders tried to defend their economic resources and political power and used segmentalist associations or personalist links to the state to block reforms. Parliament provided another arena for segmentalist business groups and state agencies to protect their special interests. The weakness of parties and the absence of encompassing associations representing the popular sectors, which could have served as countervailing forces, robbed progressive experts of allies. The few equity-enhancing reforms that passed this maze of obstacles were corroded in the implementation phase by personalist links of businesspeople to the public administration.

REFORM IMPULSES

At the end of military rule, a broad consensus had emerged among experts that Brazil's tax system needed profound reform (Longo 1984, 1986; Moreira et al. 1984; Rebouças 1984; Serra 1983). In addition to decentralizing tax authority from the federal to the state and municipal governments, specialists proposed numerous equity-enhancing measures. They wanted to shift the burden of taxation from regressive indirect taxes to progressive direct taxes. The corporate income tax, which was passed on to consumers via higher prices and thus became an indirect tax, should be paid by the individuals who received income from profits (that is, dividends). The reform-minded experts maintained that personal income tax, which tapped mainly salaries and wages, should apply to all types of income, including capital gains. The welter of tax breaks for sectors such as agriculture should be cut. Some specialists also proposed a new tax on property.

Those advancing progressive tax reforms promoted their goals by using the channels for participation opened up by the regime change. In addition to seeking positions inside the state apparatus, they advanced reform projects through government study commissions, advice to leading congressmen, and influence on the PMDB's "program." Some officials of the Finance Ministry (MF) lobbied secretly in Congress against a conservative project of the MF's own Secretariat of Federal Revenue (SRF).[1] Thus, progressive experts made many efforts to reform Brazil's inequitable tax system.

Interestingly, the reform projects gained a strong impulse from the fiscal crisis of the Brazilian state. The new civilian administration faced much graver economic problems than the Geisel government had. Brazil could barely service its external debt and was emerging from its deepest recession in decades. While the crisis imposed severe costs on many strata, especially the poor, it did not stop inflation, which reduced state revenues by devaluing effective tax payments. The huge debt aggravated the fiscal problems. The public sector had contracted a large share of the foreign debt and had taken over obligations from the private sector. Debt service intensified the drain on state resources (Alves 1987; M. T. Silva 1988). Despite the fiscal crisis, the state kept renouncing a large amount of revenues. In the 1960s and 1970s it had extended more and more tax incentives to the private sector (Varsano 1982; Villela 1989); in the 1980s, it proved difficult to take back these gifts. For all these reasons, gross and net tax revenues had fallen considerably as a percentage of GNP, and the public deficit was growing.

By posing grave challenges to basic state interests and the institutional mission of the SRF, the fiscal crisis reinforced progressive reform efforts. The elimination of tax privileges for the rich, which the Geisel government had pursued with little zeal, acquired urgency because it could yield much-needed resources for the state. The SRF believed that a fairer distribution of the tax burden was essential for discouraging widespread tax evasion (interview Hülse 1989; see in general Peters 1991, 173). Universalist ideas and organizational interests became firmly wedded. By forcing the SRF to give absolute priority to the state's revenue needs, the fiscal crisis also impeded the use of tax policy to stimulate economic development. As a result, the arguments that business usually invoked against higher taxes became less persuasive. In fact, the MF claimed that the recuperation of the state's financial capacity through higher taxes was crucial for spurring economic development through public investment.[2]

Powerful international actors provided additional impetus for reform. The IMF frequently pressed the Brazilian government to reduce the public deficit. As spending cuts proved politically infeasible, this pressure strengthened attempts to eliminate tax privileges. While the IMF rarely demanded specific tax measures, the World Bank elaborated detailed proposals to raise revenues and make Brazil's tax system more progressive (interviews Calabi 1989, Ramos 1989, Barbosa 1992, Bogéa 1994; World Bank 1989b). Thus, the fiscal crisis of the state created urgent revenue needs and strong external pressure that reinforced efforts to raise the tax burden on the rich. External dependency and the resulting economic crises and foreign influences spurred equity-enhancing reform, rather than impeding it. This interesting finding contradicts the dependency explanation for the dearth of redistribution under democracy.

REFORM EFFORTS AND THEIR FAILURE: AN OVERVIEW

The impulse to reform led to equity-enhancing efforts of two types. The reformers tried to restructure tax rates so as to put a higher burden on the rich and to extend progressive taxation to business sectors that had so far enjoyed more lenient treatment. However, these proposals ran into strong opposition. Public bureaucrats defended established rules and procedures, and segmental business associations combated tax reform because it would impose costs on entrepreneurs and increase state control over their activities. As the reformers could not marshal much popular or partisan support in Brazil's fragmented polity, they were regularly defeated.

My analysis focuses on the five main reform projects designed under the new democracy. First, in late 1985 the MF tried to raise tax rates and extend them to income types received by privileged groups. These proposals were blocked by bureaucratic and entrepreneurial resistance or undermined in the implementation phase. Second, in an attempt to restore the state's capacity for promoting development, the MF undertook in late 1987 a bold effort to subject all income types to the progressive income tax while lowering tax rates slightly. Weak party support, determined resistance from business interests, and personalist influences on President Sarney doomed this equity-enhancing reform. Third, the MF learned from its defeats and proposed in 1988 to slash tax rates but make more income types fully taxable. Since this plan was neutral in terms of revenue and equity, it passed. By hampering its implementation, however, business groups obtained favors and turned the change regressive.

Fourth, since the fiscal crisis continued to worsen, President Collor used his strong support in early 1990 to raise revenues by all means possible. Yet only some of these changes improved equity, whereas others had a regressive impact. Also, some progressive proposals were blocked by clientelist and segmentalist resistance. Since Collor's initial success alleviated the fiscal crisis only briefly, his government designed in 1991 a fifth proposal to overhaul the tax system. This plan revived old projects and designed new schemes to increase revenues. However, segmentalist opposition from inside and outside the state has impeded a comprehensive reform, attempted several times between early 1991 and late 1994. In sum, efforts at equity-enhancing tax reform have been regularly defeated by resistance from public bureaucrats and segmentalist business associations.

REFORMERS IN POWER: THE FIRST FAILURE

At the beginning of the civilian government, continuity prevailed in the MF. President-elect Tancredo Neves appointed as finance minister his nephew Francisco Dornelles, a conservative technocrat who had headed the SRF under the last authoritarian administration. Dornelles was skeptical about progressive tax reform and tried to raise state revenues through technical tricks that the military regime had regularly used, burdening mainly the middle and lower class. Under democracy, however, political parties defended the "little people" and pressed President José Sarney, who had assumed office after Neves's sudden illness and subsequent death, to veto Dornelles's proposal. Weakened by this embarrassing defeat, Dornelles faced growing attacks from the main government party, the PMDB, on his restrictive fiscal policies. President Sarney also favored economic expansion as a way to strengthen his weak political position. Increasingly isolated, Dornelles resigned in August 1985.

Reform-minded forces now came to prevail in the MF. President Sarney appointed a friend, Dílson Funaro, to head the ministry. An entrepreneur from São Paulo, Funaro had been vice-president of FIESP and was a PMDB supporter.[3] Funaro nominated as top aides some experts who were linked to the PMDB and shared his plan to reorient Brazil's development strategy. Rejecting the austerity policies adopted in the crisis of the early 1980s, Funaro and his advisers wanted to stimulate growth by expanding the domestic market. In their view, production should focus more on the needs of the poor, who would gain purchasing power through income redistribution. Inward-oriented industrialization would spread the benefits of development more widely without antagonizing business, which would profit from renewed growth (Cruz 1988, 267–71).

Since equity-enhancing reform was crucial for this development strategy, Funaro and his aides planned a change in the tax system to relieve the middle and lower classes and impose a higher burden on the rich. They considered a wide range of measures, such as eliminating tax privileges for agriculture and capital gains. But several projects ran into difficulties. Landowners were already up in arms (often literally) out of fear of agrarian reform, for which masses of landless laborers and poor peasants were pressing. After consultations with parliament, the MF therefore shelved the universalist project to eliminate the generous tax deductions that recipients of agricultural income could use.

SRF technocrats objected to the plan to subject capital gains, which benefited mainly the rich, to the progressive income tax (interview Belluzzo 1989; also interview Patury 1989). Their claim that only the existing system could be enforced, which withheld capital gains taxes at the source at a flat rate, was technically weak.[4] The defense of established procedures and resentment of the "interference" of Funaro's aides into the SRF's policy-making domain were the main motives for this resistance.[5] Thus bureaucratic politics blocked the equity-enhancing project.[6]

The MF also kept the shift in the income tax burden from the less well-to-do to the better-off lower than planned. After Dornelles's defeat, Funaro listened to politicians, who anticipated discontent in the middle class. In addition, the SRF worried about a revenue loss. While many less well-off taxpayers were dependently employed and therefore subject to source withholding, which was easy to enforce, better-off sectors received much of their income from sources that were difficult to control. The danger of widespread tax evasion by the rich made the SRF warn against a progressive shift in the tax burden, which was therefore watered down. Thus, bureaucratic resistance and anticipated opposition from society considerably weakened the effort at redistribution.

But for the sake of his development project, Funaro insisted on some equity-enhancing reforms, especially a reformulation of the "system of current bases." The military regime had instituted this system so imperfectly that it imposed an unfair burden on the dependently employed. They were subject to ever more excessive source withholding, which the SRF did not refund until a year after the annual tax return was due. Thus, year after year the SRF extracted big interest-free loans from middle- and lower-class taxpayers. In contrast, the rich received much income from sources not subject to withholding, escaped this compulsory loan, and had their tax eroded by inflation. Funaro tried to end this discrimination by slashing source withholding and mandating the inflationary readjustment of all tax obligations (MF. SRF 1985). This change was aimed to enhance fairness, increase consumer purchasing power, and expand the domestic market.

Drawing on his links to PMDB politicians and on the superior technical knowledge of the MF, Funaro found support for this reform in parliament (interview Patury 1989). Exceptionally, he managed to forge a support base, despite the weakness of Brazil's political parties. He countered opposition from business associations through populist appeals to social justice. Congress approved the equity-enhancing reform in late 1985. But its implementation faltered with the heterodox stabilization program (Cruzado Plan) of early 1986. Since the MF hoped to extinguish inflation, it abolished the readjustment of tax obligations, thus undermining the "system of current bases." When inflation began to rise again, the rich regained their privilege because the devaluation of money corroded their taxes, which were due only with the annual tax return.

The reduction of tax withholding and the price stabilization and wage increase of the Cruzado Plan fueled a consumer boom that undermined the economic stabilization achieved temporarily. Starting in late 1986, inflation returned with a vengeance, and the government's inept efforts at adjusting its economic strategy fueled social unrest and sharp protests from business. The government's economic problems and political weakness led to Funaro's resignation in April 1987. Thus, this effort to reorient Brazil's development strategy and make the tax system more equitable ended in failure. After bureaucratic resistance and anticipated opposition from social segments had watered down the reform, the government's inept strategy of economic stabilization undermined its implementation.

REFORMERS IN POWER: THE SECOND FAILURE

The PMDB forced President Sarney to nominate as finance minister another PMDB-affiliated businessman and academic, Luiz Carlos Bresser Pereira. This gave reform-minded experts a second chance. Pointing to the worsening economic crisis, Bresser and his progressive aides called for profound fiscal reform in order to restore the state's capacity to push ahead Brazil's economic development. They claimed public investment was necessary for economic recovery and growth (MF 1987). Trying to make this state-led development strategy financially viable, they proposed to cut ineffective public spending and to increase revenues through an equity-enhancing tax reform. Bresser's economic plan and definition of state interests coincided with his universalist commitment to fair burden sharing.

The new finance minister and his aides considered many equity-enhancing tax measures, based on old SRF projects and their own innovative ideas. Since efforts to raise tax rates ran into growing opposition in public opinion and among politicians, they focused on extending progressive taxation to all types of income, especially capital gains, which were tax-exempt or taxed only at a flat rate. These projects could have boosted state revenues and eliminated regressive tax privileges. By including dividends in this plan, the MF also tried to reduce the weight of the corporate income tax, which was largely transferred to consumers via higher prices and thus turned into a regressive indirect tax. Enterprise profits that were not reinvested would be subject to lower corporate income tax, but those who received these profits via dividends should have to pay the full personal income tax (MF 1987; interviews Mesquita 1988, 1989; see Rosa 1986). This shift in the tax burden would reduce an inequity in Brazil's tax system, which has relied much more on the corporate income tax (relative to the personal income tax) than other countries (Longo 1984, 85–91, 103).

Bresser and his aides also planned to limit the generous tax deductions for agricultural income, which reduced revenues without reaching their purpose of stimulating investment. The SRF supported this change in order to close a gaping loophole; many rich people evaded taxes by ascribing much of their income to the rural property they owned. Furthermore, Bresser and his advisers proposed a new tax on property in order to extract much-needed revenues from the rich. A property tax could also make the capital gains tax more effective by discouraging accounting tricks.[7]

Interestingly, most of these redistributive proposals did not face direct resistance from the bureaucratic apparatus of the SRF. Bresser had nominated as SRF secretary a highly respected former agency official who shared most of his views, Antônio de Mesquita. Conservative technocrats, who preferred more cautious tax changes and who had opposed several of

Funaro's plans, therefore could not block Bresser's project through "technical" arguments. But it seems that some of them, who had links to conservative congressmen such as former Minister Dornelles, leaked the plans in order to arouse opposition in parliament and public opinion.[8] Thus, the weakness of hierarchical control inside the MF, an aspect of state fragmentation, continued to hinder equity-enhancing tax reform.

Since Bresser and his aides expected business to oppose their redistributive projects, they avoided consultation, which would force them to make concessions. They also foresaw much resistance in Congress, where conservative forces were gaining the upper hand. As the PMDB had become deeply divided and party discipline had disappeared, the reformers could not count on solid backing. The finance minister therefore asked President Sarney to enact the reform by decree-law (interview Bresser 1989), a procedure the military regime had introduced to marginalize parliament. Bresser's attempt to enhance equity by using this authoritarian means makes the dilemma of democratic reformism in Brazil glaringly obvious.

Parliamentarians protested, and business leaders were outraged about the tax reform. They worried not only about economic losses, but also about the control over their activities that the state would gain through the new tax measures, especially the property tax. Since Bresser tried to deny them access to policy making, they voiced their opposition via public opinion and, above all, through personalist links to top state officials. The president's friends among the business elite exerted strong influence. This pressure made Sarney back away from many of Bresser's proposals. Business opposition and lack of presidential support blocked most equity-enhancing measures (interviews Bresser 1989, Mesquita 1989, Bornhausen 1989, Branco 1989; see Bresser 1988, 23–25; Varsano 1988). Bresser quit in late 1987, and the progressive experts in the MF left with him.

The defeat of this wide-ranging reform effort demonstrates the multiplicity of organizational obstacles to redistribution. After Funaro had faced bureaucratic politics and segmentalist business influence as main impediments, Bresser deliberately tried to avoid these problems, yet the weakness of party support and the personal connections of entrepreneurs to top state officials brought down his bold equity-enhancing plan. Thus, a maze of organizational obstacles blocked redistributive change in the new democracy.

CONSERVATIVE RESURGENCE

With the reformers' failure, the technobureaucracy of the MF came back to power. The new finance minister, Maílson da Nóbrega, was a conservative career official whom the PMDB had vetoed for top posts in 1985 because of his links to the military regime. Determined not to offend the powerful forces that had won out over Bresser, Nóbrega made further concessions to specific business sectors, which used their reestablished associational access to the MF to combat the few tax changes Bresser had succeeded in enacting.

During his whole tenure, Nóbrega proceeded very cautiously in his efforts to mitigate the state's fiscal crisis. This political context made attractive neo-liberal plans that claimed a cut in tax rates would diminish tax evasion and *increase* revenue. Based on this hope, an academic, Paulo Rabello de Castro, captivated President Sarney with the proposal of a flat rate for the personal income tax (Castro 1987). Many SRF technocrats viewed this radical proposal with great skepticism, but some top officials embraced a more moderate plan, which collapsed the high rates of the personal income tax (up to 45 percent) into three brackets of 0 percent, 10 percent, and 25 percent.[9] In compensation, most exemptions and deductions would be eliminated, and all types of income would become subject to the (now much less) progressive rates of the personal income tax. This change, strongly inspired by the U.S. tax reform of 1986, would be distributionally neutral and increase or at least guarantee state revenues.

The reform plan found much support in public opinion and among interest associations. But opposition from business sectors blocked or watered down some important changes, such as the extension of the income tax to profits in the stock exchange and elimination of tax privileges for agriculture (interviews Hülse 1989, Salaro 1989). More important, business sectors and politicians impeded a revamping of the corporate income tax by strenuously resisting the elimination of tax incentives. Congress enacted the rest of the project with few changes in late 1988 (CD.PL 1.064/88).

By slashing income tax rates (while eliminating loopholes), the reform made it very hard to use taxation for large-scale redistribution. It limited the importance that the progressive tax par excellence could have in Brazil's tax system. Raising tax rates has become politically inviable (interview Rebouças 1989). In fact, the purported distributional neutrality of the reform, always questionable, was further undermined when the attorney general, a friend of President Sarney's with close links to business, created legal obstacles to the taxation of capital gains. This move blocked the equal tax treatment of all types of income, one of the main universalist attractions of the reform.

As a result of such concessions, the 1988 law did not resolve the fiscal crisis, which the new constitution of late 1988 made even worse. Frequent personnel turnover and a technocratic style averse to political bargaining had limited the MF's influence in the Constituent Assembly, which had convened in early 1987 (interview Lopes 1989). States and municipalities had used their patronage-based hold over parliamentarians to reach a drastic decentralization of tax revenues (without an equivalent transfer of state tasks). The federal government's share in income tax revenues was scheduled to decline from 67 percent in 1988 to 53 percent in 1993 (Piscitelli 1988, 76). This resource transfer aggravated the fiscal crisis of the central state.

Since the federal government urgently needed higher revenues, SEPLAN revived in early 1989 several redistributive projects, such as eliminating tax privileges for agriculture, creating a property tax, and instituting a 35 percent rate in the personal income tax. While the World Bank supported several of these plans (World Bank 1989b), the SRF resented SEPLAN "interference" in its policy-making domain and dragged its feet on the 35 percent rate and the property tax (interview E. Silva 1989). Also, segmentalist business organizations and President Sarney's conservative friends used their associational and personalist access to lobby against a reform. At the end of his term, Sarney refused to incur the political cost of imposing higher taxes on elite groups, only to have his successor benefit from the revenue gain (interview Vasconcelos 1989). The self-interest of a president without a firm party organization that could have encouraged him to pursue longer-term goals, prevented Sarney from caring for basic state interests and induced him to shelve the reform plan.

Altogether, the numerous redistributive efforts that experts initiated under the Sarney government met with very little success. Most attempts to universalize the income tax were blocked, and the limited success that was achieved in 1988 came at the expense of slashing tax rates. Bureaucratic resistance, the opposition of segmentalist business associations, and personal influences of entrepreneurs and politicians on top state officials posed enormous obstacles to equity-enhancing change.

PRESIDENT COLLOR'S EMERGENCY MEASURES

When Fernando Collor de Mello assumed the presidency in early 1990, Brazil was on the verge of hyperinflation. Collor saw economic stabilization as an urgent goal. After the immobilism of the Sarney government, he could count on considerable support. He invoked the 35 million votes he had won in Brazil's first democratic election for president in twenty-nine years. Conservative forces, such as business, were indebted to him for defeating the left. Collor augmented his power by reorganizing the state apparatus and strengthening the presidency. This increase in state cohesion allowed him to override intra-bureaucratic opposition and, for some time, reduce the access that business sectors had to decision making.

Collor used this extraordinary opportunity to design a wide array of drastic stabilization measures, including important tax reforms. In order to avoid concessions, his team refused to consult with powerful business associations like FIESP (Bornhausen 1991, 13; interviews Eris 1992, Kandir 1992, Solimeo 1992). On coming to office, Collor decreed several tax measures the MF had tried in vain to enact under the Sarney government. He eliminated the tax privileges for agriculture and transactions in the stock exchange, imposed a hefty one-time tax on financial applications, and proposed a property tax. The support of conservative forces for Collor and the widespread willingness to contribute to his effort at economic stabilization led Congress to approve many of these drastic measures. The unique political constellation that emerged after Collor assumed power made some redistribution possible.

For the new government, however, economic stabilization, not social equity, was the main priority. In its drive to raise revenues at all cost, it greatly increased some indirect taxes, thereby reinforcing regressive features in Brazil's tax system. Also, even the new president faced obstacles. After sounding out public opinion and the SRF, his economic team backed away from the idea to create a 35 percent rate in the personal income tax. Similarly, Collor's project for a property tax proposed rather low rates. Since these proposals could not generate revenues fast enough to mitigate the urgent fiscal crisis, the new team gave in to anticipated opposition.

Furthermore, the quick failure of Collor's stabilization plan diminished his political standing. Since the president had never gained a firm support base among Brazil's fluid political parties, which could have bolstered him despite this fall in popularity (Weyland 1993, 8–11), his latitude in decision making shrank. Thus, he was unable to effect further tax reforms. Under strong pressure from business associations, Congress never approved the tax on property. Also, the government could not complete its agricultural tax reform by revamping the rural property tax (compare L. Silva 1986, 53–54). Many of Collor's conservative allies in Congress, worried about their clientelist base in the countryside, rejected such a change, and parliament voted down the project (interview Kandir 1992; *Istoé Senhor*, 16 January 1991, 15–16). Clientelist and segmentalist opposition to equity-enhancing change thus quickly reasserted itself.

Collor's window of opportunity closed fast. He soon faced the same resistance to his redistributive proposals as the Sarney government. As the persisting economic crisis revealed that the government could not perform magic, Collor had to seek allies. His brash economy minister, Zélia Cardoso de Mello, who kept business at bay, had to quit in May 1991. Her successor, Marcílio Marques Moreira, a conservative diplomat with close links to domestic and international finance, courted entrepreneurs in order to reduce their opposition to the government. Expanding on earlier efforts, the economy ministry formed a consultative commission with 144 top entrepreneurs and created "sectoral chambers" for joint decision making by the government, business, and, in some cases, labor (CEC 1992; interviews Werneck 1992, Fernandes 1992). These neo-corporatist institutions improved the access of business segments to the state that the Collor government had tried before to limit. As a result, the president's power was further diminished. The old obstacles to equity-enhancing reform had crept in again.

EFFORTS AT STRUCTURAL REFORM

Since President Collor's stabilization efforts had failed, severe fiscal problems persisted. Starting in early 1991, experts in the economy ministry proposed an overhaul of public finances, including the tax system. They wanted to create or augment property taxes, revamp indirect taxes, and reverse part of the revenue gains that states and municipalities had reached at the expense of the federal government in the 1988 constitution. They planned to strengthen the SRF's enforcement powers and soften legal safeguards for taxpayers, which should be subject to closer supervision (Collor 1991, 26–30, 125–26; MEFP 1991; MEFP. SEPE 1991; interviews Barbosa 1992, Eris 1992, Kandir 1992).

The IMF supported many proposals out of concern for Brazil's public deficit. Yet they aroused enormous domestic opposition. States and municipalities insisted on their revenue shares and blocked any reversal through their patronage-based influence in Congress. Entrepreneurs used their links to the state to oppose any increase in the tax burden and defend the existing restrictions on the state's tax authority. They could also count on the growing aversion to tax increases in public opinion and Congress. As opposition parties insisted on dividing the project into separate reform packages, the government lost the chance to win quick approval for comprehensive change. Facing strong pressure from the government, but also from the opponents of the reform, parliament kept delaying a decision (CD 1992; interview Moreira 1995).

This passive resistance spurred the government to resume its reform effort in early 1992. By then, business had come to assume a more active role in tax policy, reacting to the opening of Brazil's economy that Collor had decreed. Facing the threat of international competition, entrepreneurs wanted to reduce the tax burden. In Brazil's closed, oligopolistic economy, they had commonly transferred most of the corporate income tax and various social contributions to consumers via higher prices (Contador 1976, 153–65). This burden shift, which reduced competitiveness, became unsustainable with trade liberalization. Since business was unwilling to pay corporate taxes out of its own pockets, it demanded their reduction. The tax burden should shift from production to consumption, or to individual income, as FIESP proposed in an unrealistic plan.[10]

Thus, Collor's trade liberalization reforms induced business to abandon its purely defensive stance on tax issues. The government responded to business pressure and to the failure of its own efforts to raise taxes by asking experts from society to elaborate the tax reform it sought. In early 1992, a commission of specialists (many with links to the private sector)[11] started to design a blueprint, embracing numerous elements of the government's original plan. After long consultations with business and state governments, it called for a redivision of tax authority and revenues to benefit the federal government without imposing an absolute cost on municipalities and states. This plan required an increase in revenues. In a regressive vein, the commission proposed to extend the personal income tax to less well-off categories and to raise or create excise taxes. It also called for a tax on all financial transactions and a tax on enterprise assets. The reduction of public spending, especially by revamping social security, should guarantee fiscal equilibrium (MEFP.Comissão 1992; Mattos 1993; interviews Mattos 1992, Longo 1992).

Although the commission followed much of the government's initial project, some plans reflected social pressures. For example, an academic, Marcos Cintra de Albuquerque, had proposed the tax on financial transactions as a miraculous cure for the fiscal crisis (Albuquerque 1991). He claimed that the large volume of financial operations in the Brazilian economy made a very low levy sufficient to guarantee state revenues. Many citizens and associations of small business wanted to scrap Brazil's complicated tax system and pay only this one, simple tax. Since the idea found support in Congress (Rocha 1992), the reform commission tried to preempt a radical change with an unforeseeable impact by "testing" the tax on financial transactions as an additional revenue source.

The commission's plan faced strong opposition, however. States and cities insisted on their revenue sources. They used the growing weakness of the Collor government, which was accused of corruption, to extract concessions. Many segments of business saw the need for fiscal adjustment, but as organizational fragmentation exacerbated problems of collective action, they refused to make sacrifices. The private sector was internally divided and unable to come up with an alternative to the commission's project (interviews Fernandes 1992, Delfim 1992), but it resisted several proposals. Associations like FIESP assailed the tax on enterprise assets, claiming it would discourage investment. Bankers attacked the tax on financial transactions as a threat to a functioning banking system. Since growing demands for his impeachment left President Collor in a very precarious position (Weyland 1993, 16–23), he vetoed any raise in the personal income tax that could trigger middle-class protest.

Thus, after some early successes, the Collor government soon faced obstacles to its tax policy similar to those experienced by its predecessor. Segmentalist business influence and personalist machinations crept up again as crucial impediments to redistributive reform (interview Collor 1995). In fact, economic liberalization reinforced the resistance of business to higher taxes. Concern for enhancing international competitiveness induced the government to take the private sector's needs and interests more seriously. Collor's reorientation of Brazil's development strategy (and not just the "objective" requirements of capitalism) created new barriers to equity-enhancing measures and counterbalanced the state interest in raising revenues by reducing the tax privileges of the rich.

Being politically as weak as President Sarney (Weyland 1993, 29), former vice-president Itamar Franco was unable to resolve this impasse and restore the state's fiscal health. After Collor's removal from office in late 1992, Franco enjoyed only a brief honeymoon. His government lacked a firm base of support. Many parties had representatives in the cabinet, but few offered the president reliable backing. As a modified version of the 1992 tax plan that the government submitted to parliament (MF. SRF 1992) continued to face strong resistance from business and from states and municipalities (interview Bogéa 1994), Congress postponed its decision on the core of the reform project once again and enacted only a few emergency measures in late 1992, especially a temporary tax on financial transactions. Persistent opposition even undermined the implementation of these very limited changes, perpetuating the severe fiscal crisis.

Franco's fourth finance minister, Fernando Henrique Cardoso (May 1993–April 1994), revived the tax reform project in order to take advantage of a seemingly golden opportunity. The constitutional revision scheduled to begin in October 1993 lowered the vote share required to alter the 1988 charter and thus seemed to facilitate the profound changes in the tax system sought by the MF. Through a sympathetic senator, Cardoso therefore submitted the government's proposals to Congress, which acted part-time as revising body (Blay 1993, esp. n° 13873).

However, organizational obstacles, particularly party weakness, once again blocked any lasting change. State governors and city mayors continued to resist a reduction in their tax revenues, and they used their command over patronage to mobilize strong support in Congress. The major business associations arrived at an unusually consensual position on tax reform, although some important divergences persisted.[12] Yet while the government tried to raise the tax burden, business, supported by conservative parties, wanted to reduce it.

Most important, the major parties' lack of organizational discipline undermined the whole effort at constitutional revision. Since the upcoming elections of late 1994 induced parliamentarians to campaign in their home districts, government and party leaders were rarely able to guarantee the quorum required for altering the constitution. A corruption scandal involving powerful members of Congress, which originated in the lack of accountability and rampant clientelism of Brazilian parties, further diverted attention from the reform debate. Since the government could not count on its supporters in parliament, persistent obstruction by the left to defend the "social conquests" of the 1988 charter succeeded in blocking most of the constitutional revision.

Seeing the opportunity for profound tax reform evaporate, Minister Cardoso designed in late 1993 a temporary plan to eliminate the budget deficit predicted for 1994. He wanted to augment the federal government's disposable resources by raising all taxes and social contributions during 1994 and 1995 by 5 percent, by limiting the constitutional revenue transfers to states and municipalities, and by reducing mandated social spending (Blay 1993, n° 13899). In order to attract political support, Cardoso called this crucial element of his economic stabilization program Social Emergency Fund (Fundo Social de Emergência—FSE). Business and rightist parties, however, opposed increases in enterprise taxes whereas left-leaning parliamentarians objected to raises in regressive indirect levies. States and municipalities defended their revenues, and clientelist politicians resisted reductions in social expenditures in order to retain patronage, which was crucial for the elections of late 1994. Even agencies of the federal government tried to undermine planned spending cuts.

As a result of this widespread opposition, the government and Congress in lengthy negotiations remodeled the FSE completely and kept losses for states and municipalities and for most of private business to a minimum.[13] Yet the middle class temporarily has to pay higher personal income taxes (Lei n° 8.848), and banks and landowners have to shoulder a heavier tax burden. These equity-enhancing changes, whose impact will be minor,[14] passed in Congress because some of them seemed attractive to the left, because conservative and centrist forces hoped to proceed with the constitutional revision, and because they wanted to preserve minimal governability so as not to boost the prospects of success by Workers' Party (PT) leader Luís Inácio Lula da Silva in the upcoming presidential election. Thus, in this pre-electoral situation—as after Collor's electoral victory of 1989—the threat from the left made limited and temporary reform possible.

A permanent revamping of the tax system, however, remained infeasible throughout 1994. In Brazil's weak party system, the electoral campaign prevented parliamentarians from debating serious policy issues and from approving unpopular measures, such as tax raises. Even after his stunning first-round victory, president-elect Cardoso refrained from using his popular mandate to push for reform before assuming office. Above all, any effort to reduce the states' tax revenues would have hurt his favorite candidates in the second round of gubernatorial elections.

In sum, President Collor's initial strength evaporated so quickly and President Franco's honeymoon ended so fast that they were unable to effect profound tax reform and resolve the fiscal crisis of the state in part by imposing a higher burden on the rich. Organizational fragmentation in the state and in society posed enormous obstacles. Widespread though rarely coordinated business opposition, operating more and more through Congress, blocked many changes. Party weakness deprived the government of reliable support. Revived federalism created further impediments as state governors used their patronage-based control over parliamentarians to defend their increased revenue shares. As a result, a string of efforts at revamping the tax system failed.

POLICY OUTPUTS IN DIRECT TAXATION

An analysis of policy outputs confirms that the new democracy has not improved social equity through the tax system. In principle, redistributive changes could occur in several ways, especially by placing greater emphasis on direct rather than indirect taxes; by imposing a higher direct tax burden on capital rather than labor; and by instituting more progressive rates for the personal income tax.

Has the weight of direct taxes increased under the civilian regime while the burden of indirect taxes has diminished? Indirect taxes are paid by all consumers at the same rate. Since the poor spend a much higher share of their income on consumption than the rich, indirect taxes in Brazil are regressive.[15] The personal income tax, in contrast, is the progressive tax par excellence because its rates can increase with the income level and burden the rich disproportionately. Thus, increasing the proportion of state revenues coming from direct taxes and lowering the share coming from indirect taxes could enhance social equity.

An assessment of the Brazilian tax system faces two complications. First, the corporate income tax is effectively an indirect tax because busi-

Table 5.1 Share of Progressive Income Tax in Federal Revenues
(in percent)

	1984	1985	1986	1987	1988	1989	1990	1991	1992
Fiscal Revenues	21.6	27.5	21.3	19.8	21.7	28.1	20.9	21.9	19.8
Tax Revenues	26.5	33.0	26.7	26.3	29.3	43.5	31.4	35.1	30.9

Source: Computed from MF. SRF 1993, 11.

Note: Progressive income tax comprises the personal income tax paid in the annual declaration and the shares of the withholding tax on labor and capital income (*rendimentos do trabalho* and *rendimentos de capital*).

ness firms seem to transfer most of this burden to consumers via higher prices.[16] Second, the very concept of *tax* is not clearly defined. Since the late 1980s, the Brazilian state has tried to evade legal and political limitations on its taxation powers and to avoid mandatory transfers of tax revenues to states and municipalities by raising social contributions and using part of the resources for fiscal spending. In fact, the government has deliberately shifted the source of revenue from taxes to social contributions; in late 1988, it lowered the corporate income tax when it created a new social contribution that has virtually the same tax base. Therefore, table 5.1 uses two bases of comparison: tax revenues narrowly defined and general fiscal revenues.

If general fiscal revenues are considered—the more valid denominator—democratization has not led to a redistributive shift of the tax burden from indirect to direct taxes. Compared to the last days of the military government, the relative weight of direct taxation has even diminished slightly. Only if one considers traditional tax revenues can it be said that the progressive income tax increased its revenue share significantly. These ambiguous findings suggest at best a modest equity-enhancing improvement under the new democracy. Yet several regressive changes more than compensate for this uncertain trend.

Brazil's income tax has always imposed a much higher burden on income from labor (that is, wages and salaries) than on income generated by capital (Longo 1984, 10; Dias 1986, 68–75). To reduce this kind of discrimination and to raise revenues, in the early 1980s the MF imposed withholding taxes on more and more types of capital gains. As a result, revenues from the withholding tax came in growing proportion from capital, whereas the share from labor fell. This shift in the tax burden, which experts praised as progressive (Longo 1986, 23–27), prevailed for only the first two years of

Table 5.2 Burden of the Withholding Tax
(ratio of revenues from labor over revenues from capital)

1984	1985	1986	1987	1988	1989	1990	1991	1992
.93	.62	.57	2.15	1.06	1.23	2.00	2.74	1.24

Source: Computed from MF. SRF 1993, 11.

Table 5.3 Taxable Share of All Income Declared in Tax Returns
(in percent)

1983	1984	1985	1986	1987	1988	1989
58.8	54.1	54.3	58.7	56.4	42.3	44.0

Sources: Giffoni and Villela 1987, 30–31; MF. IRPF 1986, 165, 219; MF. IRPF 1987, chaps. 3.1, 3.7; MF. IRPF 1988, chaps. 3.1, 3.7; MF. IRPF 1989: chaps. 3.1, 3.7; MF. IRPF 1990: chaps. 1.1; 2.1–3.

Note: The date refers to the base year, not the year income tax returns were filed.

the new democracy (table 5.2), whereupon this equity-enhancing trend was radically reversed. Revenue shares from the taxation of wages and salaries increased greatly, while revenues from capital gains taxes plummeted. As the relative tax burden on the capital market *decreased*, a regressive change took place under democracy.

As the personal income tax with its progressive rates has continued to burden mainly wages and salaries, other income types, particularly capital gains, have remained nontaxable or have been taxed only proportionately at the source. Has the new democracy extended the reach of the progressive income tax? As table 5.3 shows, the opposite has happened. Under democracy, even more income has remained tax-exempt or taxable only at flat rates. As the data for 1989—the last year available—suggests, even the 1988 reform did not achieve its goal to extend the reach of progressive taxation (Afonso et al. 1988, 3–4; World Bank 1989b, 18–19).

Finally, has the rate structure of the personal income tax become more progressive under the new democracy? This question is not easy to answer because inflation creates important distortions in Brazil's tax system that make it necessary to correct the data for calculating effective tax rates.[17] The value of the income on which tax is assessed has to be adjusted for inflation.[18]

To assess the impact of democratization, fiscal year 1984 (tax return of 1985) is the best base of comparison. The last available data is from fiscal

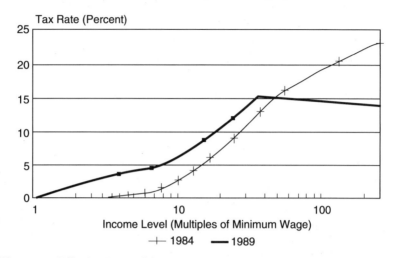

Figure 5.1 Effective Rates of the Personal Income Tax

Source: Computed from MF. IRPF 1985, 23, 32, 41, 50, 59, 68; MF. IRPF 1990, chaps. 1.1, 2.1–7; minimum wage data from CE 43 (1) (January 1989), 29; CE 44 (1) (January 1990), 50.

year 1989 (tax return of 1990). As figure 5.1 shows, the income tax in 1984 was clearly progressive. The rich paid a much larger share of their income in taxes than the less well-off. By 1989, the rate structure had become significantly less progressive. People at lower income levels, such as the working and middle classes, now paid income tax at substantially higher rates. The relative tax burden on the richest strata, by contrast, had greatly diminished owing to the slashing of tax rates in the 1988 reform. This comparison reveals another regressive change under the new democracy.

All this data suggests that democratization has not furthered the redistribution of income through the tax system. The weight of direct taxes in federal revenues has not clearly increased, and the rates of the income tax have become more regressive. The burden of the withholding tax shouldered by labor rather than capital has grown, and the share of income subject to progressive taxation has diminished. As a result, the tax burden on the rich has remained rather light.

CONCLUSION

Democratization has not improved the chances for equity-enhancing tax reform. The most striking finding of the preceding analysis is the high degree of continuity in decision making between authoritarian and democratic rule. Technocracy, bureaucratic politics, segmentalist resistance, and personalist interference characterize tax policy under both regimes. As a result, very few redistributive changes have been effected.

Almost all equity-enhancing projects were initiated by state officials and designed by experts in state positions; demands from interest organizations or political parties did not initiate any significant reform. These efforts embodied universalist principles, but the state's interest in higher revenues made them urgent given the grave fiscal crisis. The IMF and the World Bank reinforced this concern with the public deficit. Funaro, Bresser, and their expert aides also wanted to give the state the capacity to spur economic growth through public investments. Thus, state interests, as interpreted by public officials with universalist orientations, demanded the elimination of tax privileges for the rich and provided the basic impetus for equity-enhancing efforts.

The most important reform initiators, Ministers Funaro and Bresser and their aides, were newly recruited officials linked to the PMDB. But none of them was a party functionary or an electoral politician, and they acted quite independently of their party. They did not follow political guidelines,[19] but instead made decisions as experts and paid attention to politicians only in order to "sell" their projects.

Interest associations did not initiate any redistributive tax reform. The labor movement proclaimed progressive goals on taxation (Moreira et al. 1984, 150–51; DIEESE 1987) but did nothing to reach them, and the MF never tried to mobilize its support. In Brazil's inflationary economy, immediate issues such as wages absorbed unions' energies. The remnants of corporatism in labor organization have reinforced the focus on the special interests of union members and a neglect of general issues like progressive taxation, which European social democracy had made one of its banners.

Before the early 1990s, business associations did not initiate tax reforms either, not to speak of presenting concrete projects. Even the U.S.-inspired overhaul of the personal income tax in 1988 was proposed by an academic specialist, not by the private sector. Business merely reacted (negatively) to the projects elaborated by the SRF. Even after Collor's liberal reforms induced business associations to assume a more active role, their projects have been elaborated or influenced by experts who try to find support for their own ideas.[20] Also, various sectors of business have advanced quite different proposals, weakening each other's influence (FCESP 1992; FIPE

1993; IEDI 1991; PNBE 1992; Ponte 1992, 1993; *Propostas* 1993; Rezende 1992; interviews Fernandes 1992, Reis 1994, Zockun 1992).

As the continuing fragmentation of business has prevented agreement on specific reform proposals that go beyond the vague general principles elaborated for the constitutional revision, the corporatist "division of labor" between the public and private sectors has largely persisted. The state has taken care of general issues, whereas business associations have defended particular interests. The private sector also did not capture top state positions. Funaro and Bresser did not act as its agents. While they had entrepreneurial backgrounds and links to the private sector, they were not indicated by business associations and soon antagonized them by their decisions.

Important redistributive reforms were initiated mainly by experts newly recruited to state positions. They came with a general orientation, but they did not have a clearly defined program nor a source of technical knowledge outside the state. They often drew on earlier SRF projects and collaborated with the established technobureaucracy. This need for advice created the first filter for their redistributive ideas. With seemingly technical arguments, old-time state officials watered down or blocked several equity-enhancing plans. The aversion of SRF bureaucrats to interference by the newly appointed "outsiders" in their sphere of responsibility fueled this resistance.

While the SRF was skeptical toward daring reform ideas, it did advocate cautious equity-enhancing measures. Its basic concern was to increase state revenues (not to improve social justice), and it had learned in long years of consultation that it could press business only to a certain extent. Within these limits, it promoted redistribution, especially the reduction of tax privileges for the rich. After Bresser's defeat, for example, the SRF continued to pursue many of his goals, though in a watered-down version.

All these reform attempts faced determined opposition from the private sector. As the fiscal crisis deepened and the SRF made ever more desperate efforts to increase state revenues, business grew stubborn. It combated all tax reform as merely a trick for raising revenues or strengthening state control and demanded spending cuts instead. The economic weight of business and its established access to policy making induced the MF to take this resistance seriously. In fact, economic development, promoted by the state, had increased the weight of the private sector since the Geisel government.

Less openly, but as pervasively as under military rule, the MF consulted with business associations, especially from industry and finance.[21] In these contacts, MF officials often made concessions and sometimes withdrew their proposals. But as the fiscal crisis intensified, they became more determined to press on with their revised projects despite business resistance. When the MF tried to avoid opposition by skipping consultation, business leaders used their associational and personal links to President Sarney to block the planned changes. While President Collor's high degree of initial autonomy provided a temporary opening for some revenue-raising reforms, both of a redistributive and a regressive nature, this window of opportunity closed fast, and business associations reasserted their "rights" of consultation.

In addition, business leaders used personalist connections to lower-ranking state officials to obtain special favors in the implementation of tax rules. This interference hampered SRF efforts to control taxpayers more strictly and favored mainly the rich.[22] Business firms also employed tax consultants,[23] who helped them find loopholes to diminish their tax burden. These consultants influenced the SRF on the regulation of tax laws but played a lesser role than under military rule in formulating tax policy.

While there were many continuities in the decision-making process between authoritarian and democratic rule, important changes did occur. Above all, Congress gradually gained more influence. The 1988 constitution, which made the president's powers of legislation subject to parliamentary approval, boosted its importance. Reacting to this shift in power, business associations have paid more attention to Congress and intensified their lobby. Being used to technical discussions behind closed doors, this new tactic has not been easy for them to adopt (interviews Branco 1989, Rosar 1990). They now have to consider political criteria and public appeal, which provide different kinds of influence than pure economic weight. For example, small businesspeople have sometimes been more successful in parliament than powerful exporters or the financial sector.

The ascendance of Congress has made the links of segmentalist associations to the state less important in relative terms. But business organizations have merely added congressional lobbying to their repertoire of influence. They continue to regard direct contacts with the executive branch as the most effective way of interest articulation (interviews Bornhausen 1989, Branco 1989, O. Corrêa 1989, Rosar 1990). Also, since the members of Congress they lobby belong to parties without programmatic orientation, private sector interests are not aggregated in parliament. Congress has simply become another channel for the articulation of segmentalist business interests.

The demise of segmentalism is therefore not imminent. The rise of parliament's authority has not eclipsed this obstacle to redistributive reform but added another filter. Pervasive clientelism and the weakness of parties have given conservative interests a very strong representation in Congress, both via elections and via lobbying. In contrast, the popular sectors have had a disproportionately low number of champions in parliament, and their organizational deficits and limited resources have impeded persistent lobbying. For these reasons, the ascendance of parliament has not improved the chances for equity-enhancing measures in direct taxation.

Thus, strong obstacles to redistributive change have persisted under democracy. The recruitment of progressive officials to top state positions and pressing fiscal problems led to stronger *efforts* to reduce tax privileges for the rich. But the return of democracy weakened the state vis-à-vis society and diminished the *opportunities* for these state efforts to succeed. Since the initiators of reform could not draw on support from disciplined parties or powerful popular sector associations, opposition by business organizations, which now use multiple points of access to influence decision making, has been very hard to overcome.

The findings of this chapter and comparison with the tax policy of the Geisel government suggest that democratization has not improved the chances for redistribution. Bureaucratic politics, segmentalist influences, and personalist interference have created a series of obstacles and jointly impeded equity-enhancing reform even under democracy, except in extraordinary circumstances, such as the early months of the Collor government.

6

Politics of Social Insurance
in the New Democracy

Has democratization improved the chances for redistributive change in social insurance? Since this issue affects the interests of vast strata of Brazilian society, one might expect bottom-up pressure for reform. Encompassing trade unions, in particular, may call for better social protection, rather than demanding only wage hikes with their inflationary impact. Political parties may aggregate these demands into a platform appealing to the poor in order to win a majority. By unleashing such pressures, the advent of democracy could bring about a push for equity-enhancing reform.

State officials may promote top-down reforms so as to preempt such bottom-up challenges, assert their autonomy from established elites, and extend state control over society. The demise of authoritarian rule may broaden recruitment to the state and give progressive experts and politicians the opportunity to launch redistributive projects. Democratization boosts the principle of citizenship (Marshall 1963), which bolsters such universalist efforts. In all these ways, the regime change may prompt equity-enhancing impulses.

The new democracy did, indeed, elaborate several redistributive programs for social security (Comissão para o Plano de Governo 1985; SEPLAN 1985; MPAS.SPO 1985, 1986). Who started these reform efforts? Were bottom-up pressures or top-down initiatives more important?

Why did these progressive attempts not come to fruition? What blocked their success?

REFORM IMPULSES IN SOCIAL INSURANCE

As in taxation, experts had long demanded a revamping of social insurance, which was considered crucial for maintaining sociopolitical order (interviews Dain 1987, Carvalho 1989). Universalist principles and state interests gave rise to these proposals. When the recession of the early 1980s created financial deficits, specialists started to worry about the long-term viability of the social security system (Azevedo 1984; Rezende 1984; Coutinho 1986). As a remedy, they wanted to cut costly privileges and excessive favors. In social provision, criticism centered on the "time-of-service" pension. Experts had long charged that these pensions benefited mainly the better-off while costing enormous amounts of money contributed in part by the poor (Leite 1981, 73, 100–01; Azevedo 1984, 10–13, 27–30; Oliveira et al. 1985, 135–42; see recently Oliveira, Beltrão, and Maniero 1993). To keep the system from going bankrupt, experts also called for combating widespread fraud and the unjustified concession of benefits for purposes of political patronage.

Universalist principles, which international organizations promoted with much effort, reinforced these economic calculations and state interests. Time-of-service pensions appeared as unjustified privileges, given the unmet basic needs of the poor for social protection. In 1985, about 28 percent of the economically active population remained excluded from full social insurance,[1] and most of the rural population (another 24 percent) received only minuscule benefits. Experts with their universalist values condemned these inequities. In their view, democracy demanded that everybody be guaranteed basic well-being. They invoked the concept of citizenship (Marshall 1963) to justify their reform efforts (Cordeiro 1985; Dain 1988, xviii; interview P. Silva 1987). Making coverage universal would also help the state maintain sociopolitical stability and preempt mass mobilization.

Thus, state (and career) interests and universalist principles prompted redistributive efforts to curb privileges and fraud and extend coverage to the poor. Expert proposals gained strong impetus and support from MPAS ministers Waldir Pires (March 1985–February 1986), Raphael de Almeida

Magalhães (until October 1987), and Renato Archer (until July 1988). These politicians with long party careers belonged to the center-left wing of the PMDB. Trying to raise their party's electoral appeal and personally committed to social equity, they promoted redistribution. They appointed many progressive experts to state positions and shielded their initiatives from the ever more conservative orientation of the Sarney government after 1987.

Partisan considerations thus reinforced equity-enhancing efforts in social security, which (in contrast to taxation) directly benefited masses of voters. However, redistributive attempts had started much earlier and reached some successes under military rule (chapter 4), and the reformist experts kept their state posts and continued promoting their plans even after the center-left wing of the PMDB lost the MPAS in mid-1988. Thus, partisan forces had only limited importance as an impulse for equity-enhancing reform. How successful were these redistributive efforts?

EARLY REFORM EFFORTS

In the negotiations that president-elect Tancredo Neves held with his diverse support base over the division of spoils, the center-left wing of the PMDB won the MPAS. Minister Pires nominated a number of progressive experts to top positions. These appointments strengthened reformist forces inside the state apparatus, which had found it difficult to promote redistributive reform under the military regime.

When Pires assumed office, social security was in crisis. The danger of deficits reinforced doubts in its financial viability and prompted calls from business for privatization, especially of health care (CNI 1984, 11–13). Pervasive fraud, exposed by the press, further discredited the system. While Pires combated these acute problems with emergency measures, he asked the progressive experts to prepare a wide-ranging reform (Pires 1986, 35–54; interview Pires 1989). Since the minister and the newly recruited experts wanted to go beyond the limited measures recommended by the last authoritarian government (MPAS 1984) and since they did not have special expertise in the issue area, the elaboration of these projects took time.

Interestingly, the MPAS faced few demands from society for equity-enhancing change. Only CONTAG put sufficient pressure on the state to start a reform. Strengthened by inclusionary corporatism and gaining autonomy with democratization, rural unions had for years demanded improvements in their meager social security system. Workers in the formal sector of agriculture wanted access to the full gamut of benefits in return for paying direct social security taxes. The poor who could not afford such taxes wanted their minimal benefits doubled (CONTAG 1979, 1984).

In response to rising mobilization in the countryside, Pires convoked a corporatist commission with representatives of rural labor, landowners, and the state in 1985. Business agreed to better benefits for labor but rejected a raise in taxes. Facing this corporatist opposition, CONTAG made important concessions. In return for improvements for salaried workers, it shelved its demand for a full equalization of rural and urban social security (see MPAS 1986b, 405–12, 605; interview M. Oliveira 1990). The MPAS submitted this compromise proposal to the president (MPAS.SG 1986; interview Pires 1989).

Shortly thereafter, Pires left office and the project was shelved. Minister Magalhães followed the advice of progressive MPAS experts, who planned a universalist overhaul of social insurance and disliked a special project for the rural sector. Magalhães preferred such a comprehensive reform in order to strengthen the PMDB and raise his own political clout. Thus, the only pressure from society for redistributive change did not produce a reform.

Urban marginals did not even demand inclusion in the social security system. They lacked an encompassing organization like CONTAG that could advance their interest in social protection. Urban social movements never initiated any reforms in social insurance; such reforms were launched by party politicians and experts in state positions.

THE REFORM PROJECT

The plan of a comprehensive reform of social insurance soon took shape. The main redistributive goal was to extend coverage to the whole population. For this purpose, the system should be stripped of its remaining corporatist restrictions, derived from occupational distinctions (Santos 1987, chap. 5), and be based on universal citizenship.[2] The progressive experts therefore wanted to make enrollment independent of state-administered labor registration. In the 1980s, more than one-third of all non-agricultural

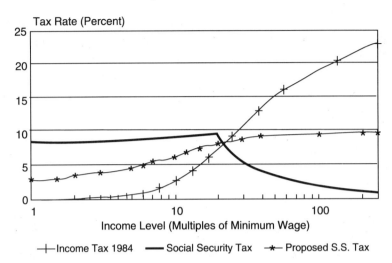

Figure 6.1 Comparison of Income and Social Security Tax Rates

Source: Computed from MF. IRPF 1985, 23, 32, 41, 50, 59, 68; Dain 1988, 167; and MPAS 1986b, 30.

workers and employees and about 80 percent of rural laborers were not officially registered (IBGE 1990, 45), and another 23 percent of the economically active population worked on their own account, usually in the informal sector (IBGE 1990, 42). Many of these people were not enrolled in contributive social insurance, which covered only 48 percent of the EAP in 1985.[3] De-linking social insurance from labor registration would allow these mostly poor people to acquire full entitlements. Any citizen should be eligible for complete coverage, regardless of occupation (MPAS 1986b, 371, 400–01, 787–88; Dain 1989, 41–42).

The reform initiators wanted to facilitate the enrollment of these poor people by making social security taxes more progressive. Compared to the personal income tax, the individual social insurance contribution and the payroll tax, the financial basis of the system, put an unfair burden on the poor (figure 6.1). Even workers earning just the minimum wage had 8.5 percent of their low income deducted. The self-employed poor had to pay twice this rate; it was thus no wonder that few of them enrolled. The reform-minded experts planned to slash social security taxes on the poor so that they could join the system (MPAS 1986b, 30, 305, 371, 389–90, 401, 693).

To compensate for revenue losses, the progressive specialists proposed to create new types of social security taxes, for example, on firm profits, agricultural income, and individual wealth.[4] They also wanted to limit expenditures by curbing privileges and therefore proposed a minimal age requirement for time-of-service pensions in order to prevent people from obtaining this costly benefit at a young age (MPAS 1986b, 98–101, 109–10, 389–92, 785–86, 1034). The reform-minded experts planned to use some of the savings and new revenues for improving the meager benefits of FUNRURAL and the welfare pension conceded to people without full social security entitlements (MPAS 1986b, 389–92, 400, 1010). These measures should help the poorest categories who could not even afford the proposed lower social security taxes.

This anti-corporatist, universalist project outlined a profound redistributive reform. It softened the contributive principle on which Brazil's social security system had always been based. De-linking contributions and benefits was decisive for universalizing coverage because most of the poor had low contributive capacity (MPAS 1986b, 305–12; Dain 1989, 2–5). Experts in state positions designed the project, but they drew on support from party politicians turned ministers. The return to democracy provided impetus to redistributive reform (yet several proposals had already been advanced under authoritarian rule). How did this plan fare in the decision-making process?

INTRA-BUREAUCRATIC DEBATES ON THE REFORM PLAN

The reform initiators faced resistance from the bureaucratic apparatus of the MPAS. Lacking experience in social insurance, they relied on the advice of holdovers from the military regime and of retired IAPI technocrats. Wary of major change, these old-time specialists defended basic features of the established system and blocked some farther-reaching reform ideas. Having built Brazil's social security system on the basis of the occupational structure, they considered its separation from labor registration infeasible. How could social security taxes be secured and entitlements be delimited for people without registered employment? Having to rely on the old-timers' expertise, the newly recruited reformers gave up this important proposal (interviews Dain 1990, M. Oliveira 1990). This retreat compromised the basic universalist goal of the reform.

The old-time specialists also questioned the diversification of social security taxes. They regarded the individual contribution and the payroll tax as a satisfactory financial base and considered profound change risky because the yield of new contributions, which would be difficult to collect, was unforeseeable (MPAS 1986b, 355–56, 457, 911). The individual contribution and the payroll tax embodied the contributive principle; this facilitated actuarial calculations and helped ensure financial viability in the long run. Responding to these pragmatic concerns, the reform-minded experts assured that individual contributions and payroll taxes would remain the backbone of social security finances (MPAS 1986b, 29–30, 356, 691). Since the middle class resisted higher taxes, this position limited the possibility for lowering social security taxes on the poor and for universalizing coverage.

Thus, old-time bureaucratic specialists defended established rules and procedures and moderated the redistributive impetus of the newly recruited experts. Their pragmatic objections persuaded the reformist novices that some proposals for profound change were not easy to enact. This opposition nipped in the bud several innovative ideas of great equity-enhancing potential.

CONSULTATION WITH INTEREST ASSOCIATIONS

To gain support for their project, the reform-minded experts engaged in extensive debates with affected interests. The MPAS created two consultative commissions with officials from social security agencies and other ministries, retired bureaucratic specialists, academic experts, and representatives of business, labor, and pensioners' associations (MPAS 1986b, 40; MPAS.CSPAS 1987b, 2). Yet only interest associations with national-level organizations could participate in these consultations. Whereas CONTAG spoke for the rural poor, urban marginals, who lacked an encompassing organization, were not represented. Their absence, a result of their deficient organization, weakened the advocates of redistribution and universalization of coverage (MPAS 1986b, 650).

The reform-minded experts invited organizations with divergent interests in order to assume the role of mediators and advance their own plan. Interest associations would neutralize each other's resistance. For example, whereas labor would oppose restrictions of the time-of-service pension, business was expected to support this proposal in order to limit social spending (see CNI 1984, 14–17). The backing of important interest associations would make it easier to gain approval of the reform in parliament. In their technocratic approach, the reformist experts distrusted political parties as representatives of social interests and doubted their technical capacity and interest in serious policy debates. They tried to sway Congress with a project the affected interests had already sanctioned. The effort to predetermine parliamentary decisions was understandable, given the weakness of Brazil's parties, but it perpetuated the problem by marginalizing parties from policy making.

The strategy of the reform-minded experts did not succeed, however. Business flatly rejected the equity-enhancing reform plan as unrealistic and too costly (CNI and CNC 1987). Urban workers and pensioners feared the universalization of coverage would curtail their own benefits and questioned the reduction of social security taxes for the poor. They strongly attacked curbs on privileges, especially the time-of-service pension (MPAS 1986b, 106, 312, 374–79, 467, 620, 644, 700, 912; MPAS.CSPAS 1987a; interviews Dain 1987, Carvalho 1989, Fernandes 1989, Viegas 1990), and demanded reforms that would favor better-off categories. They insisted especially on changes in benefit calculation to correct the substantial losses that inflation had brought for benefits of higher value.[5] Urban unions and pensioners showed little solidarity with the poor marginals. The organizational fragmentation of the popular sectors hindered redistributive reform, inducing better-off segments to pursue narrow self-interests while excluding marginals from consultation.

In contrast, CONTAG and the Movement of Landless Rural Workers (MST), which encompassed both the formal and informal sector, supported redistribution by demanding higher benefits for the rural poor (MPAS 1986b, 12, 266–67; 409–12, 609–17, 1010–12; interview J. Silva 1990). But CONTAG, in particular, focused more on extending the contributive urban system to the countryside, which interested mainly better-off rural workers (MPAS 1986b, 11–12). Even this encompassing organization did not assign priority to the needs of its most destitute members.

Opposition from business, urban workers, and pensioners did not block the reform project. The MPAS simply disregarded some outcomes of the debates and insisted, for example, on an age requirement for time-of-service pensions for the better-off (MPAS 1986b, 13–14; MPAS 1987b, art. 27). But resistance from interest associations foiled the MPAS's plan to obtain support for later stages of the decision-making process. Indeed, the demands of workers and pensioners for additional benefits, some of which the MPAS accepted (MPAS 1987b, art. 13), neutralized much of the redistributive thrust of the project as better-off sectors would receive considerable gains. These demands also raised resource needs and, given business opposition to higher social security taxes, reduced the chance for enacting the reform.

INTER-BUREAUCRATIC DISCUSSIONS

When Minister Magalhães submitted the modified reform project to the presidency, MF and SEPLAN offered fierce resistance because they doubted its financial viability. The proposal would reduce revenues by lowering the tax burden on the poor and raise spending, for example, by eliminating inflationary losses in calculating benefits. Yet curbing privileges through an age requirement for time-of-service pensions would cut expenditures only in the long run, and the yield of the new social security taxes was difficult to determine (interviews Luna 1989, Magalhães 1988, Mazzoli 1989; F. E. Oliveira 1987, 72, 74).

MF and SEPLAN tried to impose financial discipline on the MPAS, which the grave fiscal and debt crisis seemed to require. By enforcing these economic constraints, they also pursued a longstanding organizational interest, namely to get the huge social security budget under their control. Giving in to this resistance, Magalhães shelved some major redistributive proposals, especially the progressive restructuring of social security taxes. This retreat hindered the planned universalization of coverage and made improvements in the rural social security system much harder to achieve.[6] Despite this important concession, MF and SEPLAN persisted in their opposition. Therefore, President Sarney refused to act on the remainder of the reform in late 1986, as Magalhães demanded, but shifted responsibility to the Constituent Assembly.

DELIBERATIONS OF THE CONSTITUENT ASSEMBLY

The Constituent Assembly (Assembléia Nacional Constituinte—ANC) did not just want to lay down procedural rules but also planned to make substantive decisions on a wide range of issues. The MPAS therefore submitted its remaining reform project and developed a very active lobby. It called for the universalization of social security coverage, improvements in FUNRURAL benefits and the welfare pension, the admission of rural workers to contributive social provision, an age threshold for the time-of-service pension, and the diversification of social security taxes (DANC.S No. 97, 18 July 1987, 109–26; interview Azevedo 1989).

These proposals faced opposition from interest associations, which had open access to the ANC. Lacking firm organization and program orientation, most political parties did not guide their members, leaving them susceptible to group pressures. Thus, the ANC served as an additional forum for segmentalist organizations. The interest of politicians in increasing social expenditures, which could be used for patronage,[7] reinforced their willingness to give in to demands for special favors. This generosity to well-organized, better-off segments undermined redistribution.

Business associations had the defensive interest to forestall new social security taxes that they could not easily transfer to consumers via higher prices. Out of many initial proposals, the ANC indeed created only two taxes on firms' profits and gross receipts, which were commonly passed on to consumers. Under pressure from business, which feared the inflationary potential of these new taxes, conservative politicians opposed them, but lost out to colleagues who wanted to expand social spending (Azeredo 1987, 20–32, 39–40; Dain 1988, 96; interviews Azevedo 1989, Gabriel 1989, Scalco 1989). Focusing on its immediate interests, however, business left to state agencies the fight for overarching concerns it shared, such as containing the public deficit by reducing privileges in social benefits.

Urban unions and pensioners also challenged the MPAS plan. They attacked restrictions on benefits for better-off recipients, called for changes in benefit calculation to eliminate losses from inflation, and demanded additional favors. As a safeguard against technocratic manipulation, they insisted on the minimum wage as the index for readjusting benefits (DANC.S No. 96, 17 July 1987, 177–82; DANC.S No. 98, 19 July 1987, 96–98; interview Viegas 1990). Many politicians were happy to grant these demands, which the MPAS opposed strongly because they favored better-off categories, undermined redistribution, and were hard to finance. Some proposals could even hurt the poor. The (re)calculation of benefits based on the minimum wage could prompt the government to keep the minimum wage low so as to limit spending increases; this would aggravate the plight of the working poor (MPAS.SGA 1987, 5–13; MPAS.SEE 1988b, 3; interviews Azevedo 1989; Carvalho 1989). Yet many of these arguments fell on deaf ears. Most members of Congress wanted to increase social spending in order to appear popular and create patronage resources. Therefore, they approved the time-of-service pension without an age requirement and added several new favors for the better-off, especially the (re)calculation of benefits to eliminate losses from inflation.

In a more progressive vein, CONTAG reiterated its old demands for equalizing rural and urban social insurance and for drastic improvements for the rural poor (interview Scalco 1989). The ANC accepted these proposals and mandated some equity-enhancing measures. It stipulated that no income-substituting benefit could be worth less than the minimum wage. This measure helped rural recipients most, whose benefits had been fixed at one half the minimum wage. The ANC also lowered the pension age for rural workers by five years, compared to the urban population, a special benefit favoring mainly poor people. Finally, it extended the welfare pension (created in 1974) and promised all the elderly and handicapped poor—regardless of social security contributions—monthly payments worth a minimum wage. This provision embodied the universalist goal of guaranteeing every citizen's basic livelihood.[8] These reforms passed with the support of conservatives who wanted to appease CONTAG after having rejected its main demand for agrarian reform.

Thus, CONTAG's pressure had some equity-enhancing success. But the ANC also granted new favors to better-off strata and enabled business to transfer the cost of all these new expenditures in a regressive way to consumers. By creating new benefits *and* new tax burdens for most categories, the ANC did not *re*allocate income. Driven by the self-interest of politicians without strong party organizations, it mainly increased the mass of patronage. In sum, clientelist politicians and segmentalist associations took most of the remaining redistributive impulse out of the social security reform.

ELABORATION OF THE NEW LAWS ON SOCIAL INSURANCE

Despite key defeats, the reform-minded experts did not capitulate. They hoped to advance their goals through the law that was required for putting the constitutional rules into practice. In late 1988, they proposed to restrict time-of-service pensions, de-link the inflationary readjustment of benefits from the minimum wage, facilitate the extension of social security coverage, and implement the increase in the minimum benefit value (MPAS.SEE 1988a, 18–22, 27, 54–57, 84–85). Consulted in the elaboration phase, pensioners and trade unions objected to these proposals. The new MPAS head, Jáder Barbalho (July 1988–March 1990), was responsive to their demands. After the PMDB's center-left wing had finally quit the ever more conservative Sarney government in July 1988, the president had nominated this clientelist politician. Openly using patronage for political goals, Barbalho was unwilling to antagonize urban labor with unpopular redistributive proposals and changed the new bill to please unions (MPAS. SAS 1989a; interview Silva 1990).

Bureaucratic politics undermined the remaining reform plan. In order to alleviate the fiscal crisis and reach an agreement with the IMF, MF and SEPLAN had started to divert social security funds to cover other expenditures (IAPAS 1990, 20). They therefore blocked the MPAS's plan to lower social security taxes for the poor in order to enable them to join the system. The government's bill kept the unfair individual contribution virtually unchanged (CD.PL 2570/89, 15). As a result, many urban marginals would continue to be excluded, and most ruralites would remain confined to limited benefits and not be able to take advantage of the extension of contributive social insurance to the countryside that the new constitution mandated.

Since the MPAS tried to mobilize support in Congress for its bureaucratic struggles with MF and SEPLAN, its capacity to combat the generosity of parliamentarians toward segmentalist interests diminished. The divisions among state agencies gave Congress the latitude to add to the government's bill several new favors, mostly for better-off categories (CD. Comissão de Saúde 1989b). Lobbying most actively, pensioners reached considerable gains.[9] Above all, the committee on social security determined that benefits be readjusted in real terms by the same 3 percent per month as the minimum wage. This norm helped only the minority of retirees whose pension exceeded the minimum wage. Once again, the clout of segmentalist associations in Congress counteracted redistributive goals.

Under strong pressure from the government and from parliamentarians with experience in fiscal administration, Congress scaled down these favors. The law adopted in mid-1990 guaranteed the full readjustment of benefits for inflation but without a real increase. Yet it left the time-of-service pension intact, added several new benefits for better-off categories, and stipulated generous rules for the calculation and readjustment of benefits (Mensagem N° 151, 1990, 3962–64). As the only measures directly favoring the poor, the law raised the threshold value of benefits to the level of the minimum wage and lowered the pension age for rural beneficiaries. It also allowed rural workers to join the contributive system, but kept most ruralites, who were unable to do so, in a special scheme with restricted benefits (Mensagem N° 151, 1990, 3963, art. 35).

Combating the state's fiscal crisis, President Collor followed the dire warnings of the economy ministry, vetoed the law in its entirety, and tried to impose more restrictive rules with emergency powers. As Congress revamped his decree-measure in line with the law it had passed, the president resorted to another veto, and an impasse resulted in late 1990 (interviews Carvalho 1992, Viegas 1992).

Collor's vetoes forced segmentalist associations to compromise in order to obtain any gains at all. The government knew, in turn, that in a politically sensitive area like social security it could not prevent the implementation of the new constitutional benefits indefinitely. CONTAG was already using legal means to ensure that the mandated reform of rural social insurance be enacted promptly. The delay also kept increasing government expenditures because the temporary constitutional provision (article 58) that all benefits be raised in real terms together with the minimum wage remained in force (interview Kandir 1992).

In mid-1991, the Ministry of Labor and Social Insurance (MTPS), the economy ministry, Congress, segmentalist organizations, particularly of pensioners, and CONTAG hammered out a compromise. The new laws finally put into practice the constitutional mandates on the raise in the minimum benefit value, the lower pension age for rural workers, and the protection of benefit calculation and readjustment against inflationary losses. They provided additional favors, especially for better-off categories, yet less than Congress had intended originally. In contrast, the new laws made little effort to expand coverage by lowering the social security tax for the less well-off, but they guaranteed the rural poor access to the improved minimum benefit (Lei N° 8.213; Alckmin 1991; interviews Alckmin 1992, Britto 1992, Urbano 1992, Viegas 1992).

An important equity-enhancing provision of the constitution, however, the extension of welfare pensions to the old and handicapped poor not covered by social insurance, was enacted only in a very restrictive way in late 1993. Since the potential recipients lack any organization and capacity to put pressure on the government, the finance ministry's insistence on resource constraints led to the stipulation of a tough means test, which will keep additional spending to a minimum (CD.PL 4.100/93, 12–13, 70; interviews Silva 1992, 1994; Macedo 1992). Thus, only the rural poor, represented by CONTAG, made real gains. The urban poor, who have no such encompassing association, benefited little and were even burdened by the new social security taxes. Since better-off sectors also reaped big favors, the new laws brought minimal, if any, redistribution. Once again, segmentalism undermined equity-enhancing change.

PROGRAM IMPLEMENTATION IN SOCIAL INSURANCE

Clientelism created additional impediments to redistributive reform in program implementation. The new democracy continued to use social security as a mass of patronage. The civilian alliance that took power in 1985 parceled out most administrative posts to its political supporters. It even devised an official formula according to which politicians nominated the "representatives" of the social security system in outlying regions (see chapter 4). When President Sarney pushed his personal agenda in the Constituent Assembly, he and his cronies, including MPAS minister Barbalho, changed the criteria for the nomination of these representatives in order to extract political concessions from parliamentarians. Even after President Collor extinguished the representation system in late 1990, the clientelist penetration of the social security administration has continued (interviews Carvalho 1992, Marques 1994, Araujo 1994).

Political appointees, particularly the representatives, channel benefits, at their discretion, to their patrons' supporters and withhold them from their adversaries. Due to this political misuse of social programs, which is enormously important to Brazil's clientelist politicians, patronage criteria take precedence over equity-enhancing principles. Clientelist interference in program implementation undermines the universalist goals guiding reform. Rather than being rights of citizenship, social benefits are granted as particular favors or denied for lack of personal connections.[10] Political expediency wins out over the needs of the poor. For example, Minister Antônio Britto (October 1992–December 1993) expanded the concession of social security benefits more rapidly in his well-developed home state,

Rio Grande do Sul, where he subsequently ran for governor, than in the destitute Northeast.

Since clientelist connections are based on reciprocity, they favor people who are better-off and harm the poor, who have little to offer in return for benefits. By reproducing social inequality, clientelism thus counteracts redistributive efforts. Since it undermines bureaucratic procedures, it also leads to tremendous corruption and waste. As political favors, people obtain benefits to which they are not entitled, and the evasion of controls and taxes is tolerated; the distributors of patronage demand a substantial "cut" on these favors. Widespread irregularities have aggravated the financial problems of the social security system and limited the resources available for equity-enhancing reform. Only the severe fiscal crisis of the 1990s induced the MPS to undertake investigations, which led to the cancellation or suspension of almost 9 percent of all benefits (MPS 1994, 22). In sum, clientelism has posed an important additional obstacle to equity-enhancing change in social insurance.

EMERGENCE OF A NEO-LIBERAL REFORM PROJECT

In recent years, the advance of neo-liberalism in Brazil has transformed the debate about social insurance. The new reform proposals have ambiguous implications for social equity. Some of them—such as to eliminate privileged benefits and extend (truly minimal) protection to all citizens—are similar to earlier equity-enhancing plans. Other proposed changes, however, would exacerbate social inequality. The reaffirmation of the contributive principle, especially in the form of pension privatization, would exclude the poor, who cannot afford the full price for quality social protection. Thus, the advance of neo-liberalism creates both opportunities and grave threats for equity-enhancing change. The diverse sociopolitical forces with an interest in social insurance have therefore fought fiercely over which, if any, of the new proposals to adopt.

The laws enacting the constitutional reform mandates were not even in force yet when, in early 1991, experts in the economy ministry, supported by some new specialists in the social security administration, designed a profound overhaul of social insurance along neo-liberal lines. In order to combat the fiscal crisis and comply with demands from the IMF, the project tried to reduce privileged benefits and rights enshrined in the new constitution and privatize parts of social insurance. It called for abolishing time-of-service pensions and reasserting the contributive principle, which would exclude most poor agricultural workers from social insurance. The public social security system should provide benefits only up to a low level (for example, five times the minimum wage). Social protection above this threshold, which was depicted as especially costly, would depend on private insurance. In compensation, social security taxes could be cut considerably (MEFP 1991; *Reforma da Previdência* 1992; interviews Rossi 1992, Mazzoli 1992, Carvalho 1992).

This proposal was attractive for business, which hoped to reduce the high burden of taxes, including social security taxes (chapter 5). Entrepreneurs supported the basic goals of the plan, and some neo-liberal groups demanded radical privatization (IL 1991). Even sectors of urban labor which had staunchly defended the established system started to question some of its features, such as the improvements in rural social protection, which did not favor them directly.[11]

Most urban unions, pensioner associations, and CONTAG, however, rejected the neo-liberal project and defended the gains they had made in the 1991 laws. Progressive experts in the MTPS disapproved of many neo-liberal proposals and mobilized opposition in society, using the contacts they had established in earlier consultations with interest groups. Politicians also refused to enact unpopular cuts in benefits and reduce patronage resources through privatization. For these reasons, Congress blew the whistle and blocked the overhaul in late 1991 (interviews Gabriel 1992, Viegas 1992).

But persistent financial problems and pressure from the IMF made the government insist on neo-liberal restructuring. In line with business demands, the tax reform commission convoked in early 1992 (chapter 5) proposed to slash social security contributions and expenditures. It wanted to abolish the taxes on firm profits and gross receipts, cut the payroll tax, and substitute part of the loss through the new tax on financial transactions. The government should reduce spending by phasing out the time-of-service pension, by excluding rural workers without contributive capacity from social insurance, by capping benefits at three times the minimum wage, and by reducing the value of welfare benefits to one-half the minimum wage (while extending this meager social protection to every citizen) (MEFP.Comissão 1992, 28–32, 43–44; Mattos 1993, 42–47, 230–39).

This project received praise from business but, as usual, little active support. Trade unions and pensioner organizations, however, were outraged at the proposed reversal of their gains (CUT 1992; interview Viegas 1992). Most parliamentarians opposed a cut in social benefits, which they used as electoral bait. Progressive commitments among experts and the organizational self-interest of the bureaucratic apparatus made the MPS also reject a drastic overhaul. As the government itself was divided, and strong interests in Congress and society rejected the plan, the neo-liberal project was shelved. Even the less radical proposals of the Congress and MPS (CD.Comissão Especial 1992; MPS 1992), which revived ideas like restrictions on time-of-service pensions, failed to pass.

Worsening financial problems induced the government of President Itamar Franco (1992–1994), installed after Collor's impeachment, to make further reform efforts. The implementation of the new benefit law as well as the threat of its reversal led to an explosion of requests for pensions from 1992 on. Since the new law also raised benefit values, spending skyrocketed compared to the depressed levels of the late 1980s and early 1990s. The MPS managed to finance this increase only by stopping its legally mandated transfers to the public health system. Changes clearly seemed in order. Yet experts disagreed strongly on the necessary adjustments. While some called mainly for tax raises, many others advocated different types of cuts in entitlements (MPS and CEPAL 1993/1994). Many of these plans combined neo-liberal and social-democratic proposals, such as partial pension privatization for better-off strata and universal protection for the poor; their net impact on social equity was difficult to foresee.

As in tax policy, the Franco government tried to use the constitutional revision beginning in late 1993 to revamp the social security system. In order to make reductions in spending possible, it wanted to tighten the rules for the calculation and readjustment of pension values. To prevent the premature concession of benefits, it advocated that a pension only be conceded if a person's age and years of contribution added up to ninety-five. In this way, poor people who started to work early and contributed for many years could retire at a younger age, whereas better-off people who started to contribute late would have to wait until a more advanced age. Reaffirming the contributive principle and trying to reduce spending, the MPS wanted to redefine rural social security benefits for which a direct wage contribution was not required as social welfare; welfare benefits would be de-linked from the minimum wage (esp. Lima 1993, N° 9490, 9495–97,

9513, 9515; interview Moraes 1994). While some of these proposals aimed to eliminate relative privileges of better-off strata, others threatened the chief gains made by the rural poor through the 1988 charter.

In a universalist vein, the government advocated including public employees who had their own, more generous pension system, in the general social security plan (Lima 1993, N° 9503–10). Congress had proposed this measure after the Collor government had started to divert general social security taxes for paying state employee pensions (CD. Comissão Especial 1992, sections II-D.5, III.10). The Franco government came to adopt the congressional proposal in order to reduce entitlements in the public sector pension plans, which had huge deficits. As the privileged benefits of state employees were subsidized through Brazil's regressive tax system, this project to restrict them had a redistributive character.

Interestingly, the government did not take a clear stance on privatizing pensions, for three reasons. First, bureaucratic self-interest made the MPS hesitate to advocate a reduction in its own responsibilities and patronage power. Second, radical privatization would create a grave transition problem that the Brazilian state, in the midst of a fiscal crisis, was unable to resolve. Privatization transfers social security taxes to private pension funds, saddling the public sector with the existing stock of benefits and the accumulated entitlements of pensioners-to-be. The Brazilian state was unable to sustain such a fiscal drain (interview Moraes 1994). Finally, partial privatization did not require constitutional reform (but simply a change in the income brackets delimiting coverage). Since privatization was a highly polemical issue, the government preferred postponing the debate.

Yet the other projects ran into fierce opposition. Public employees and their segmentalist associations, strongly represented in CUT, rejected an inclusion in the meager general social security system. The military flatly refused to accept this measure. CONTAG attacked the proposed de-linking of rural benefits from the minimum wage and their redefinition as social welfare, which was chronically underfunded. Urban unions and associations of pensioners bombarded the "95 point" formula and insisted on maintaining the time-of-service pension.[12] Together with CUT, CGT, and left-leaning parties, they rejected any constitutional revision of social rights. Given the upcoming elections of late 1994, patronage-hungry conservative and centrist parliamentarians, not disciplined by strong parties, were also unwilling to approve cuts in entitlements.

This widespread opposition blocked all reform efforts. Yet to make preparations for the administration of the government's presidential candidate, Fernando Henrique Cardoso, Congressman Nelson Jobim, who was in charge of drafting constitutional revisions, asked some parliamentarians and (former) government experts to elaborate a comprehensive project. This draft, never submitted to a vote, contained most of the government's proposals, such as including public employees in the general social security system and combining age and time of contribution in the concession of pensions; only the redefinition of rural benefits as social welfare was omitted (CN.*Parecer N° 78*, 23–38, 181; interviews Azevedo 1994, Moraes 1994). Whether President Cardoso, who has assigned priority to social security reform, will command enough political force to prevail on Congress to enact profound change is doubtful.

In sum, the advance of neo-liberalism has faced similar obstacles to those faced by earlier, unequivocally progressive plans. The segmentalist opposition of relatively privileged groups, the bureaucratic self-interest of established public agencies, the patronage calculations of electoral politicians, and the organizational weakness of political parties have so far impeded any lasting change. The organizational obstacles analyzed in this book protect the status quo in general. While they impede equity-enhancing reforms with particular force, they also make more regressive changes difficult to accomplish.

POLICY OUTPUTS IN SOCIAL INSURANCE

What has been the impact of all these reform efforts, especially the longstanding progressive attempts, on social equity? An analysis of policy outputs confirms that democracy has not brought about significant redistribution in social insurance.

Equity-enhancing change requires a *reallocation* of resources from the better-off to the poor. Yet a mere expansion of social insurance can also have a progressive impact if the established system redistributes some wealth. This may be the case in Brazil. Above all, the rural population, which is largely poor, receives ten times more in benefits than it directly pays in taxes (Capuano 1994, 13). Since rural social insurance is heavily subsidized by the better-off urban sector, the existing system seems to reallocate resources.[13] An increase in spending on social insurance could thus have an equity-enhancing impact.

Table 6.1   Spending on Social Insurance Benefits
(as percentage of GDP)

1980	1981	1982	1983	1984	1985	1986	1987
3.65	4.05	4.33	4.22	3.60	3.36	3.50	2.72

1988	1989	1990	1991	1992	1993	1994	
2.68	3.00	3.51	3.64	3.96	4.73	4.54	

Sources: PeD 5 (4) (October–December 1991), 63; IESP 1995, 19, 42.

Table 6.2   Percentage of the Economically Active Population
Paying Social Security Tax

1981	1982	1983	1984	1985	1986	1987	1988	1989	1990
49.9	48.0	47.7	46.8	47.2	49.9	49.4	50.7	50.6	50.1

Sources: PeD 4 (4) (October–December 1989), 40; IBGE 1990, 42; IBGE 1992, table 3.17.

Note: Data on the total number of people covered by public social security systems is unavailable. The table refers mostly to the general, contributive, urban social security system and excludes the special coverage of the rural poor.

As table 6.1 shows, however, expenditures as a percentage of GDP diminished after 1984 and recuperated only with the gradual implementation of the 1988 constitution, especially the laws of 1991. In fact, the large expansion of benefit concession from 1992 through 1994 raised spending barely above the level of the early 1980s. The main reason for this disappointing result was high inflation, which corroded benefit values and allowed the social security administration to contain spending. Thus, the new democracy has not improved equity by raising expenditures on social insurance.

If the existing system redistributes income, extending coverage could also enhance equity. Because many of the 28 percent of the economically active population who were still excluded from full social insurance in 1985 were marginals, this expansion would benefit poor people. Did reformist state officials succeed in their effort to bring such an extension about? While coverage did expand slightly from 1984 on (table 6.2), this was due not to democracy but to Brazil's emergence from the recession of the early 1980s, which had compressed employment and social security coverage.

Table 6.3   Social Distribution of Expenditures
(percentage of all spending with benefits)

	Below 1 SM[a]	1–2 SM	2–3 SM	3–7 SM	Above 7 SM
Early 1980s	———————— 55.50 ————————			31.81	12.62
April 1988	44.29	10.78	8.74	31.40	4.78
May 1989	27.87	9.59	9.70	30.56	22.29
December 1990	37.60	9.20	8.40	25.90	18.90
December 1991	58.80	9.40	7.90	21.10	2.80
December 1992	25.40	12.00	13.10	29.60	19.90
September 1993	0.80	48.60	7.20	26.90	16.50

Sources: Azevedo and Oliveira 1986, 136; DATAPREV 1989, 69–70; PeD 4 (3) (July–September 1989), 58; Capuano 1994, 28.

Note: In December 1993, benefits equal in value to one minimum wage took up 42.55 percent of all spending (IPS 6 [1] [January 1994]: 18).

a. SM = minimum wage.

The economic recovery after 1985 merely compensated for this contraction. As the similar numbers for 1981 and 1990 suggest, democratization did not make a difference.

Democratization could, finally, lead to a reallocation of monetary benefits to poorer strata. However, data on the social distribution of benefits shows that minimal, if any, redistribution has occurred (table 6.3). The expenditure shares received by different strata of beneficiaries—as identified by levels of benefit value—have changed very little since the early 1980s. As argued above, the 1988 constitution and the 1991 laws did not *re*distribute income; even the doubling of rural benefit values, finally implemented in 1992, did not lead to a significant reallocation of expenditures. While these rule changes raised spending over the depressed levels of the late 1980s, they benefited better-off sectors as much as the poor. Several of the rule changes mandated by the new charter particularly helped recip-

Table 6.4 Functional Distribution of Expenditures
(percentage of all spending with benefits)

	All Urban Benefits	All Rural Benefits	Time-of-Service and "Special" Pensions
1980	85.6	14.4	31.6
1984	84.4	15.6	33.5
1988	83.4	16.6	31.7
1990	86.8	13.2	36.7
1991	75.4	24.6	26.6
1992	77.2	22.8	32.7
1993	75.1	24.9	32.6

Source: MPS. AEPS 93, 680–81, 688–89.

ients who were already better-off. In 1989, the effect of past inflationary losses, which had eroded pensions of higher value especially, was eliminated (PeD 4 [2] [April–June 1989], 15). The 1991 laws made the rules for the calculation of benefit values more generous and instituted additional favors for time-of-service pensioners. As a result of these regressive changes, "privileged" benefits with their relatively high average value (MPS.AEPS 93, 50) have retained their expenditure share (table 6.4). The 1988 charter facilitated (rather than limited) their concession and raised their value. This favored almost entirely better-off workers and employees in the formal sector.

Certainly, the rural poor have also made important gains. The lower pension age and doubled benefit values instituted in the 1991 law led to a dramatic increase in spending for this disadvantaged sector from 1992 on (table 6.4). However, improvements for privileged urban groups and the rural poor have balanced out, leaving the overall social distribution of expenditures virtually unchanged.

In addition, the urban poor have gained very little. The 1988 constitution extended a welfare pension equal to the minimum wage "to the handicapped and to the elderly who prove their incapability of providing for their own support or having it provided for by their families" (Article 203, V). Yet the law regulating this benefit, still not implemented by late 1995, stipulated such a strict means test that, at least initially, only 400,000 people will qualify. This restriction will keep additional spending to 1 percent of all benefit expenditures (CD.PL 4.100/93, 12–13, 70). In fact, since "handicapped" is defined narrowly, the 1993 law may well restrict the circle of beneficiaries, compared to the welfare pension instituted under the Geisel government (interview Silva 1994). Thus, whereas the rural poor and better-off urban sectors have made gains, compared especially to the depressed benefit levels of the late 1980s, the urban poor have won little and suffered relative losses.

In fact, the new social security taxes instituted by the 1988 constitution most probably imposed absolute costs on the urban poor and limited the improvements for the rural poor and the working and middle class. The contributions on firms' profits and gross receipts, which the government raised and extended in later years, have—according to all the available evidence—had a regressive social impact. Like the corporate income tax, business seems to transfer both new contributions largely to prices.[14] As a result, a cross section of the population shoulders the additional tax burden. Effectively transformed into indirect taxes, which are quite regressive in Brazil (Eris and Eris 1983, 124), these levies impose a disproportionately high burden on the poor. Thus, the new social security contributions have most probably reduced social equity.

Altogether, these findings show that the new democracy has effected very little, if any, redistribution in and through social insurance. The constitutional changes did not particularly favor the poor. The better-off and the poor retained their shares in spending, and they all pay higher taxes as well. As one of the few equity-enhancing successes of the new democracy, the rural poor achieved a significant net gain in their income, a result of persistent pressure by an encompassing association. But the urban poor, who lack such an organization, have seen their share in benefits diminish and their tax burden rise. Whereas some of the poor won with the new constitution, others lost. In sum, the advent of democracy has not enhanced equity in social insurance.

CONCLUSION

In contrast to the continuity in direct taxation, the decision-making process in social security has changed considerably with democratization.[15] Technocrats have lost predominance, and a multitude of political forces and social categories have acquired influence. As policy making has become thoroughly politicized, center-left politicians and progressive experts who were nominated to top state positions obtained the chance to advance important redistributive projects.

However, these proposals have faced opposition from several sides. Old-time bureaucratic specialists defended established procedures and organizational interests. Other state agencies impeded reforms in bureaucratic rivalries. Business groups lobbied against equity-enhancing tax raises. Better-off segments of the popular sectors demanded and defended relative privileges and limited the resources available for the poor. Clientelist politicians rejected reforms that threatened their base of political sustenance and corroded the implementation of equity-enhancing measures. Facing all this opposition, the reform initiators could draw on little support from the potential beneficiaries, many of whom lacked strong organization. As a result, the new democracy has effected very little redistribution in and through social security.

The technocrats who controlled social security policy through the Geisel government lost much of their power. President Sarney appointed three center-left politicians as ministers, who in turn nominated new progressive experts as their aides. The ministers encouraged redistributive reforms that the experts designed on the basis of their universalist ideas and perception of state (and career) interests. While politicians were important in reform initiation, experts soon became decisive, especially in giving the progressive efforts continuity. The appointment of center-left politicians and experts who were uncommitted to the established social security system with its remaining corporatist features reinforced equity-enhancing impulses inside the state. The new state officials drew up important redistributive proposals to extend coverage, improve benefits for the poor, and impose the cost on better-off categories.

However, the lack of experience and special training made the new experts in social insurance dependent on advice from the bureaucratic apparatus and former IAPI technocrats. These old-time officials defended the established rules and procedures and the organizational interests of their agencies. Their technical arguments persuaded the reform-minded experts to moderate their plans considerably. Other state agencies also posed obstacles. The fiscal crisis induced MF and SEPLAN to limit social spending and gave them a pretext for trying to get the huge social security budget under their control. These economic constraints and inter-agency rivalries hindered equity-enhancing change.

A far wider range of social actors than under authoritarian rule became involved in social security policy. Excluded by the bifrontal corporatism of the military regime, labor was readmitted to consultation. Pensioners developed a very active and—despite their low power capabilities—surprisingly successful lobby. Congress gained importance and deeply altered many reform plans. Parliamentarians, often ceding to the pressures of segmentalist organizations, pursued their own electoral interests by passing "popular" measures and enhancing their control over patronage.

Reform-minded experts assumed that the wider distribution of power under democracy would favor their own projects. Different social categories would counteract each other's opposition, and the experts would mediate and engineer support for equity-enhancing reform. However, almost all organizations with effective demand-making capacity had a narrow segmentalist scope and defended the privileges of better-off categories. They refused to carry the burden of redistribution, and their demands for additional favors limited the resources available for programs favoring the poor.

Cooperation with parliament turned out to be a double-edged sword as well. Congressional backing for reform was essential, especially for extracting additional resources from society, which the MF and SEPLAN opposed. Congress indeed mandated a large increase in social spending (compared to the depressed levels of the late 1980s), but it also ceded to the demands of segmentalist interest associations. Since most political parties were weak in organization and program orientation, they could not guide and discipline parliamentarians (see in general Novaes 1994, 136), who were eager to appear "popular" and increase the mass of patronage at their disposal.

The clientelist tactics of many executive and legislative politicians posed additional obstacles to equity-enhancing change. To retain control over patronage, they interfered heavily in the implementation of social security programs, undermined universalist goals, and took away funds designated for the poor.

Many beneficiaries of redistributive reform, especially the urban marginals, did not become involved in these conflicts. They lacked an encompassing organization that could advance their interests in national politics. This organizational fragility deprived the reform initiators of allies. In contrast, the rural poor had CONTAG to voice their demands. This comparison shows the importance of encompassing organization for gaining political influence. As a result of CONTAG's incessant pressure, the rural poor obtained some equity-enhancing gains.

Altogether, the transition to democracy did not significantly improve the chances for redistributive reform in social insurance. Whereas experts with progressive plans got more access to state positions, they paid a price by getting drawn into bureaucratic politics. They also had to make concessions to segmentalist forces, which became stronger. Furthermore, clientelist politicians who saw redistributive reform as a threat to their electoral strategies gained influence.

As a result of these obstacles, most proposals to transfer income to the poor and impose the cost on more privileged strata were filtered out in the decision-making process. By granting new benefits to better-off categories, the Constituent Assembly and Congress undermined *redistribution* and raised the determination of MF and SEPLAN to limit spending by blocking improvements for the poor who had little demand-making power. These conflict patterns reflect institutional factors, especially the segmented structure of interest associations, pervasive clientelism, the weakness of political parties, and the lack of unity inside the state, which impeded redistribution even under democracy.

Due to the persistent fiscal crisis, economic constraints, reinforced by external pressures, have become ever tighter. Nevertheless, politicians depending on patronage enacted a large increase in social spending through the 1991 laws. Also, not economic constraints as such, but the differential power and organization of social categories has determined the distribution of gains and losses. These political-institutional factors are decisive for explaining why economic constraints have hindered redistributive change.

7

Politics of Health Care
in the New Democracy

HAS THE advent of democracy led to equity-enhancing change in health care? As immediate, basic needs of the poor are at stake, this area is the most likely case for bottom-up pressure to bring about redistribution. Social movements, in particular, may advance the interest of the large mass of disadvantaged people in obtaining access to quality health care. Political parties may reinforce these demands in order to win electoral support. As in social insurance, state officials may anticipate this bottom-up pressure and initiate equity-enhancing measures on their own.

During Brazil's lengthy transition to democracy, there was indeed some mobilization of popular groups and, especially, of medical experts and professionals in favor of profound health reform. How did this social pressure emerge? How did its protagonists advance their goals? Most important, how successful were these redistributive efforts? What obstacles did they face, and how much success did they achieve?

REFORM IMPULSES IN HEALTH CARE

Since the mid-1970s, medical professionals and experts demanded progressive health reform. They advocated universalizing the coverage of the public health care system, which gave only people enrolled in social insurance full entitlements. They wanted to extend preventive measures and basic services to the poor masses and thus reduce the need for expensive complicated treatments, which benefited few people. To reorient the system in these ways, they also proposed to subject the contracted private health care sector to greater state control.

This "sanitary movement" (Cohn 1989; Rodriguez 1988, chap. 2) sought broader support in society, especially among the popular sectors. In fact, from the late 1970s on, numerous social movements sprang up and demanded better medical services for their communities. They rarely pressed for national health care reform, however, but focused mainly on local problems, advancing distributive rather than redistributive demands (Almeida et al. 1988, 24; Capistrano and Pimenta 1988, 27; Stralen et al. 1983). Their frequent links to clientelist networks reinforced this narrow orientation. CONTAG contributed more to reform initiation by demanding that ruralites receive the same type of health care as urban residents (Stralen 1989). But even this more aggregate proposal fell short of a comprehensive reform plan.

Experts thus remained decisive in designing projects for redistributive health reform. They proposed a profound overhaul of medical care, rather than its mere extension, which financial constraints would have blocked. While social movements and CONTAG just wanted to guarantee their constituents access to health care services, experts also called for a reorientation from costly curative treatments to cheap preventive measures and basic services (*Saúde em Debate*, No. 17, 1985; Escritório Técnico do Presidente Tancredo Neves 1985, 18–38; MPAS 1986b, 732–52; Cordeiro 1985; 1988, 25–28, 105). Since, in their view, the private medical sector mainly fulfilled the existing demand from better-off strata for curative treatments, they advocated more planning and supervision by the state, which should satisfy the health needs of the poor and disadvantaged.

As in social insurance, a combination of equity-enhancing goals and financial concerns motivated these reform demands. By the mid-1980s, the established medical system was still failing to meet many of the basic needs of the urban informal sector and the rural poor while at the same time, better-off groups received costly and complicated treatments. Since spending seemed mistargeted, the progressive experts called for a redistribution of medical resources. Financial concerns also focused on the rising cost of curative treatments. The social security system spent enormous funds on hospital stays while neglecting inexpensive preventive measures and basic care. A shift in emphasis, they argued, would keep people from becoming sick in the first place and reduce overall expenditures. Furthermore, cooperation with medical business, which provided 66.5 percent of all hospital treatments and 32 percent of all doctors' visits in 1984, led to considerable waste.[1] In the recession of the early 1980s, INAMPS had compressed the remuneration of the private medical sector, which retaliated with fraud (Rezende et al. 1982). Reformist experts therefore wanted to strengthen state control over the private health care sector.

The sanitary movement hoped that this congruence of financial concerns and redistributive goals, of social demands and state interests, would make health reform appealing to a wide range of forces, both in society and inside the state. As mentioned earlier, however, bottom-up pressure for equity-enhancing change remained weak. The progressive experts therefore tried to gain positions inside the state apparatus (Campos 1988b, 181–91; Cohn 1989, 133; Rodriguez 1988, chap. 2). Interestingly, the fiscal problems of the early 1980s, which prompted criticism of the existing medical system with its rapidly rising cost, allowed the sanitary movement to win some posts in the public administration already at the end of military rule. But strong opposition from health care business interests, clientelist politicians, and the established bureaucratic apparatus of INAMPS quickly blocked their reform efforts (Oliveira and Teixeira 1986, 269–76, 291–301).

After the advent of democracy, the sanitary movement managed to occupy many more positions inside the state apparatus. Hésio Cordeiro, a leader of the movement, was appointed president of INAMPS, and other progressive experts assumed top posts in the MPAS and the Health Ministry (MS). The new state officials tried to use their bureaucratic powers to advance the equity-enhancing goals they had outlined during the regime transition (Escritório Técnico do Presidente Tancredo Neves 1985). The center-left politicians who headed the MPAS supported health care reform in order to increase the electoral appeal of their party, the PMDB. As in social insurance, a combination of party competition and state initiative thus propelled equity-enhancing efforts.

LEGAL EXTENSION AND EQUALIZATION OF COVERAGE

Expansion of coverage and the equalization of rural with urban health care were among the top priorities of the new, progressive state officials (Cordeiro 1985, 3). These goals were easy to realize through changes in administrative rules, which incited little public debate. Since 1987, every citizen has been entitled to medical treatment in public or contracted private facilities; proof of enrollment in the social security system is not required any more (INAMPS 1988, 8–9; MPAS 1988, 16). INAMPS also eliminated legal discriminations that had tightly restricted medical services in the countryside, especially in contracted private facilities (INAMPS 1988, 11; S. Vianna 1989, 13–17). This equalization granted an old CONTAG demand (Stralen 1989). Since the reforms had specific beneficiaries, whereas their costs were invisible to the multitude of those paying social security taxes, opposition from segmentalist interest associations did not arise.

This universalization and equalization of rights was a rare equity-enhancing success in Brazil's new democracy. It completed the gradual expansion of health care coverage that the Geisel government had promoted by extending to the whole population the right to receive publicly financed emergency treatment (see chapter 4). But the rule changes did not guarantee the poor effective access to health care. Vast areas, especially in the countryside, lacked medical facilities. To remedy this deficit, INAMPS planned to invest more resources in poor regions, mainly the Northeast. But at the end of his tenure, INAMPS president Cordeiro admitted that "the regional discrepancies in the provision of (medical) services and the extent of unsatisfied need for care in the poorest regions . . . were maintained" (INAMPS 1988, 10). What accounts for this failure?

EFFORTS TO REVAMP THE RELATIONSHIP WITH MEDICAL BUSINESS

The effective extension of health care to the poor depended on a shift in emphasis from expensive curative treatments to preventive measures and basic services. Such a reorientation faced powerful opposition from medical business and other conservative forces, as the failure of earlier efforts showed (Oliveira and Teixeira 1986, 269–76, 291–301). The private health care sector profited enormously from the established system because INAMPS guaranteed the demand for its costly services. It used its connections to INAMPS to safeguard its privileges, erode state controls, and even obtain illicit favors.

As a crucial step toward reorienting the health care system, the progressive experts called for stronger public control over medical business. MPAS and INAMPS should use state authority (and not just contractual rights) to make the private sector follow their guidelines. Yet, since INAMPS depended on medical business for providing health care, the reformers were willing to make economic concessions and pay fair remuneration to the contractees (Pires 1986, 49; Cordeiro 1988, 97–98, 169–85; INAMPS 1988, 8–9, 12–13).

In 1985, the progressive experts convoked a commission to redefine the rules of public-private cooperation. In order to weaken opposition, they pursued a divide-and-rule strategy. At the end of the military regime, INAMPS had consulted mainly with the Brazilian Hospital Federation (FBH), dominated by profit-seeking hospitals. The progressive experts now invited a variety of interest associations (INAMPS. Presidência 1985). Using the state's capacity to select its interlocutors for corporatist consultation, they included the Confederation of Philanthropic Hospitals (Confederação das Misericórdias do Brasil—CMB) in order to separate nonprofit from profit-seeking hospitals.

The for-profit hospitals strongly resisted the INAMPS proposal for enhanced state authority and control. They especially rejected a provision that allowed INAMPS to intervene in private facilities in order to guarantee medical service provision (INAMPS 1986; MPAS. Gabinete 1986, 19174; interviews Farhat 1989, Ferreira 1989). Trying to break this opposition, the progressive experts struck a deal with CMB. INAMPS granted philanthropic hospitals economic favors; in return they accepted the state's control rights (INAMPS 1988, 14–15; interviews Belaciano 1989, Felipe 1989). With this agreement, the progressive experts weakened their main enemy, the for-profit hospitals. They also advanced their goal to extend health care in Brazil's neglected interior, where charity hospitals were essential for guaranteeing medical services (profit-seeking hospitals were concentrated in well-provided urban areas).

Despite their isolation, the for-profit hospitals persisted in their opposition. Since they provided two-thirds of all publicly financed hospital treatments (NEPP 1989, 223), they had a strong bargaining position. When Minister Magalhães finally tried to impose the rule changes unilaterally, profit-seeking hospitals simply did not accept the new provisions, and the state could not enforce its will.[2] Public-private cooperation continued along the established lines. Despite their apt divide-and-rule strategy, progressive state officials could not reach their goals in a bilateral confrontation with medical business.

REORGANIZATION OF THE HEALTH CARE SYSTEM

To combat private sector resistance to health care reform, the progressive experts looked for allies. They found support in the sanitary movement and among state governments, which had gained political weight with the regime transition. However, the interests and ideas of these different actors were not fully congruent. The resulting conflicts weakened the reform effort.

The sanitary movement attacked the privileged position of medical business in Brazil's health care system. It backed the efforts of the progressive experts, but advocated more radical change. It turned the government-sponsored Eighth National Health Conference (March 1986) into a forum for its ideas. Thus, the conference called for a gradual "statization" of health care (MS 1986, 381–89). The sanitary movement also proposed a reorganization of the public health care sector. Authority and resources were concentrated at the federal level, where several agencies fought over attributions. The sanitary movement claimed that this centralization enabled health care business to focus its lobbying and gain great clout, while it kept medical service users from exercising influence through social movements, which were effective mainly at the local level. In order to weaken the private sector and advance the health care needs of the poor, the sanitary movement demanded decentralization (MS 1986, 381–89). At the local, state, and federal level, command over health care should be unified to facilitate planning and overcome the old dichotomy between curative and preventive medicine, which hindered basic health care for the poor. Thus, the sanitary movement saw reorganization of the health care system as necessary for profound redistributive reform.

MPAS and INAMPS officials shared many of these goals in a more moderate version (Cordeiro 1988; Felipe 1988b). But they rejected the unification of the health care system at the top, which required the MPAS to cede control over INAMPS to the MS—and lose an enormous amount of resources and power. Even the reform-minded experts in MPAS and INAMPS, who had called for this transfer before their appointment in 1985 (Escritório Técnico do Presidente Tancredo Neves 1985, 27–28), now opposed it. As this rapid shift suggests, they adopted the organizational interests of their agencies and showed loyalty to the MPAS ministers, who were among the most progressive members of the Sarney government.[3] But the sanitary movement found strong support for its transfer plan in the MS and in Congress. President Sarney favored the proposal in order to weaken the reform-minded MPAS minister and the center-left wing of the PMDB. This confluence of different political forces put tremendous pressure on Minister Magalhães, who took the initiative to reorganize the health care system in order to save his basic political and organizational interests (Rodriguez 1988, 76).

For this preemptive reform, Magalhães received support from state and municipal governments, which demanded decentralization in order to gain attributions and resources. The reorganization also shielded them from political pressure. President Sarney used his power over patronage to force politicians, including state governors, to support his personal goals in the Constituent Assembly.[4] In order to counteract this blackmail, the PMDB, which had elected almost all governors in 1986, needed to channel resources to state governments. This calculation probably played an important role in the hasty decision of Minister Magalhães, who was very close to the PMDB president, to decentralize health care.

In mid-1987, the MPAS launched the Unified and Decentralized Health System (Sistema Unificado e Descentralizado de Saúde—SUDS), which delegated INAMPS tasks and resources to the state governments. States and municipalities should run most public facilities and control the private sector. MPAS and INAMPS gave up many executive attributions in health care—an inevitable loss, given the pressure from state governments and the sanitary movement. But they kept considerable authority for policy making and financial control (MPAS 1989, 8, 12–14, 29–30, 45–46). For the MPAS, this outcome was preferable to a transfer of INAMPS to the MS. But the sanitary movement, especially its members in the MS, sharply criticized this maneuver (Rodriguez 1988, 77; see also Felipe 1988b). The resulting resentment and distrust among the reformist forces, a product of bureaucratic politics, weakened the pressure for redistributive change.

MPAS and INAMPS praised SUDS as an important equity-enhancing reform. Decentralization would bring health care closer to the poor and allow them to advance their needs through social movements of local scale. SUDS would thus make the universalization of health care effective (Cordeiro 1988, 77, 88–89, 94–95, 151–52). The old gulf between curative and preventive medicine would also be overcome. As municipal and state governments would realize that improvements in prevention reduced the high expenditures on curative treatments, they would rectify the traditional neglect of preventive measures (Cordeiro 1988, 79, 122, 151). Finally, decentralization would reduce the power of the private health care sector by cutting its links to INAMPS. Medical business would have to pulverize its influence, whereas the progressive experts could enlist state and municipal governments as allies in their struggle for health care reform, which they could not win alone (Cordeiro 1988, 151; Felipe 1988b, 70–71).

CONFLICTS OVER REORGANIZING THE HEALTH CARE SYSTEM

Minister Magalhães launched SUDS suddenly, without consultations with interest organizations. With this surprise strategy, he gained presidential approval for the reform before opposition in society and inside the state could mobilize. Soon, however, medical business, INAMPS bureaucrats, and clientelist politicians offered fierce resistance.

The private health care sector rejected the move toward decentralization in order to keep its close connections to INAMPS. Defending its chances for profit, it criticized a reorientation from curative to preventive medicine. Its segmentalist organizations, especially FBH, put pressure on the MPAS, the presidency, and Congress; challenged the legality of SUDS; and influenced reform implementation. They proved quite capable of creating connections to several state governments and gaining special favors. They also used established links to INAMPS to hinder decentralization. Thus, segmentalist associations obstructed SUDS through a variety of channels, especially direct connections to the state (ABH 1988; Toledo 1988; FBH 1989, 5–11; interviews Farhat 1989, Ferreira 1989).

The bureaucratic apparatus of INAMPS offered even stronger opposition. SUDS violated its basic organizational interests by handing over most of its attributions and resources to states and municipalities. INAMPS bureaucrats therefore tried to undermine decentralization. The hasty launching of SUDS gave them ample opportunity. Many reform provisions left much room for discretion. Thus, bureaucratic politics hindered equity-

enhancing reform (Marinho 1989; Temporão 1989, 50; interviews Belaciano 1989, Cordeiro 1990, Sá 1989, Teixeira 1990).

INAMPS service personnel, organized in trade unions with links to
CUT, feared that the decentralization would reduce their income to the
meager level that states and municipalities paid. State and municipal health
care employees, in turn, demanded the higher salaries that their new colleagues from INAMPS earned. In response to these pressures for parity in
remuneration *(isonomia)*, one of the central demands of public employees
under the new democracy, considerable resources went to raise salaries
rather than improve the medical system.[5] Thus, the demands of state employees and their segmentalist associations limited the extension of health
care to the poor.

In all these conflicts, the reform initiators could draw on little support.
Since more and more workers and middle-class people in the modern
sector were enrolled in purely private health insurance (Ferreira Neto
1992, 13) and stopped using medical services financed by INAMPS, they
did not pay much attention to SUDS. Trade unions from more backward
sectors were at best lukewarm about universal health care, which would
reduce the quality and availability of medical services to their members or
boost costs and lead to higher taxes (CD. Comissão de Saúde 1989a, 106–
07; MPAS 1986b, 369, 591–95). Since they lacked encompassing organizations, the poor and marginals hardly joined the fight. Organizational fragmentation left the progressive experts without social support and favored
the opponents of equity-enhancing change.

Yet the most effective opposition to SUDS came not from social forces
like medical business, but from clientelist politicians who feared for their
access to "pork" (interviews Cordeiro 1988, Teixeira 1990). President
Sarney himself came to condemn the decentralization as a PMDB trick to
undermine his patronage tactics vis-à-vis the Constituent Assembly by
channeling resources to his adversaries among state governors.[6] Many
other politicians also attacked SUDS because it wreaked havoc on a crucial
mechanism of electoral clientelism. They depended on social security as a
huge source of patronage for building their political base. Pandering to
these interests, the new democratic government had parceled out the spoils
among its supporters. Many politicians had nominated their cronies to
positions in the social security apparatus and in this way gained control
over numerous voters (see chapter 6).[7] By transferring rights of nomination to state governors, SUDS endangered these clientelist arrangements.

Since the PMDB had elected most governors in 1986, SUDS posed a special threat to politicians from the PFL, who protested vociferously (interviews Magalhães 1988, Maciel 1989).

Clientelist politicians also opposed a reorientation from curative to preventive medicine. While medical treatments benefit individuals, many preventive measures, such as assuring a clean water supply, target whole communities. But for patrons, "selective incentives" (Olson 1971) are more effective instruments than collective goods. Clients' fear of exclusion guarantees their political support for patrons. Thus, the logic of clientelism militated against a progressive reform of Brazil's health care system.

This clientelist opposition posed the biggest obstacle to SUDS. PFL politicians ceaselessly attacked Minister Magalhães and, after contributing to his ouster in October 1987, Minister Archer. In order to control the implementation of SUDS, President Sarney substituted in early 1988 INAMPS president Cordeiro by a conservative official and personal friend, José Serrão. The new INAMPS head brought old-time INAMPS bureaucrats back into top positions. Together they defended the established system and hindered decentralization. The strong opposition from INAMPS to a reform promoted by the MPAS, which formally directed INAMPS, is a striking case of state fragmentation (reinforced by clientelism) impeding redistributive reform.

In sum, health care reform became bogged down in continuous conflicts, especially over the administrative aspects of SUDS. The planned revamping of medical care, which would reduce the profit chances of the private sector in order to fulfill the basic needs of the poor, advanced very little. While decentralization proceeded haltingly, the multitude of opposition forces robbed it of its equity-enhancing impact.[8] The case of SUDS shows how clientelism, segmentalism, and bureaucratic politics created a spider's web of obstacles that stifled redistributive reform.

IMPLEMENTATION OF HEALTH CARE POLICIES

Despite many obstacles, the progressive experts reached a few redistributive decisions in health care, especially the legal universalization and equalization of coverage. But clientelism hindered the implementation of these measures and sharply limited their equity-enhancing impact. Personal connections, especially to politicians, have always been crucial for gaining access to health care, contrary to criteria of medical and social need.[9]

For these reasons, the reform-minded experts and politicians tried to combat clientelism (Cordeiro 1991, 53, 77; Magalhães 1988, 8–20; interviews Carvalho 1989, Cordeiro 1990, Pires 1989). Above all, Minister Magalhães called for the creation of community councils that should represent the citizenry before local social security offices and ensure rigorous policy execution and financial control (MPAS 1986a, 7–14). The reformers tried to enlist popular support, especially from the poor. They fostered participation in order to cooperate with social movements and stimulate their proliferation. Popular movements would counterbalance clientelist and segmentalist pressures (for example, from medical personnel) and give the beneficiaries of equity-enhancing reform a voice in program implementation.

Although the MPAS promoted participation, few councils were formed. By 1989, only 118 of them existed in Brazil's more than 4,000 municipalities (MPAS.SAS 1989b, 6). The reasons for this virtual failure were twofold. First, many social security bureaucrats and service personnel tried to obstruct the formation of councils that would supervise them and "interfere" in their activities (see MPAS 1987a, 9). Second, most of Brazil's local communities lacked the capacity and will for participation.[10] Even in São Paulo, which has the most highly organized and mobilized popular sectors in all of Brazil, the later efforts of the PT city administration (1989–1992) to promote participation in health care policy were often frustrated.[11] In the rest of Brazil, local communities and social movements faced even higher obstacles to effective participation, especially in rural areas pervaded by clientelism (MPAS.SAS 1989b, 3). As a result of this failure, health care remained vulnerable to clientelist interference. Politicians' hunger for patronage continued to hinder the implementation of any equity-enhancing change.

CONSTITUTIONAL REFORM MANDATES

The sanitary movement had more success in promoting health care reform in a broad, public arena, namely the Constituent Assembly (ANC), where narrow interests, which work best behind closed doors, operated less effectively than in the arcane labyrinths of Brazil's state apparatus. The movement had for a long time received support from some parliamentarians. Sectors of left and center-left parties, including the PMDB, criticized the neglect of the poor and hoped to win their support. Self-selection gave these progressive politicians, who were a clear minority in the ANC, strong representation on the committee in charge of social policy. The ANC also granted social forces open access through public hearings and the right to submit proposals ("popular amendments"). From inside and outside the state, the sanitary movement used these channels to advance its ideas (CNRS 1987; DANC.S # 96, 17 June 1987, 184–96; # 98, 19 June 1987, 108–16, 139–46).

Early constitutional drafts therefore embraced progressive health reform. They declared health a universal citizens' right that the state had to guarantee through medical care and welfare-oriented social and economic policies. The state should integrate curative and preventive measures and create a "unitary health system," in which public and nonprofit facilities would have priority while medical business would be contracted only as a last resort (Rodriguez 1988, 79–101, 233–75; NEPP 1989, 154–60).

Medical business, however, attacked these draft provisions and defended both its economic latitude and its guaranteed profit chances. The associations of profit-seeking hospitals denounced the proposed rules as a socialist threat to Brazil's health care system, tried to keep state control over their activities at a minimum, and wanted to preserve the established health care system with its emphasis on curative medicine (DANC.S # 97, 18 July 1987, 126–39). Conservative politicians were receptive to this lobby out of ideological aversion to the advances of the left. They also feared that equity-enhancing change would undermine their clientelist networks. The call for health care reform in the constitutional draft was therefore watered down.

To combat this reversal, the sanitary movement sought support in society and elaborated a "popular amendment." However, only 54,133 people in all of Brazil backed this proposal with their signatures (Arouca 1988, 42)—a minuscule number, given the large mass of poor people in desperate need of better health care. This failure strikingly shows the weakness of bottom-up pressure from social movements (Rodriguez 1988, 96–97). Even when mobilized by outside organizers for an important concern, the poor failed to provide strong support for equity-enhancing change. Opposed by medical business and conservative politicians, the popular amendment had little success.

The ANC therefore diluted the initial advance toward progressive health care reform. It restricted the attributions of the state and enhanced the latitude of the private sector, barring the gradual statization of health care demanded by the sanitary movement (Rodriguez 1988, 101–17; Rosas 1988). Nevertheless, the movement's pressure on the ANC from inside and outside the state achieved considerable success. The 1988 constitution proclaimed a universal right to health and reinforced public responsibility for its promotion. Going beyond SUDS, it called for the decentralization and unification of the health care system, strengthened the state's hand vis-à-vis the private sector, and demanded more attention to preventive measures (Articles 196–200).

However, the constitution enshrined only general principles. The ANC had purposefully left many provisions vague so as not to arouse strong ideological conflict. The new mandates needed to be transformed into specific laws. These deliberations gave medical business and other conservative forces another opportunity to safeguard their interests against redistributive efforts.

PARLIAMENTARY DELIBERATIONS ON CONSTITUTIONAL PROVISIONS

The new round of deliberations favored the opponents of equity-enhancing change. Medical business, INAMPS bureaucrats, and clientelist politicians had strong organizations, many resources, or direct access to Congress, which allowed them to engage in sustained lobbying and gain considerable influence. The sanitary movement, in contrast, lacked firm organization. Internal divisions had increased, especially as a result of bureaucratic politics. Due to clientelist pressures, the movement had lost many positions inside the state from which it could influence Congress. Its support base in society, belonging to a welter of segmentalist associations and social movements, could mobilize only for a limited time. After focusing on the Constituent Assembly as the seemingly decisive forum, it was unable to exert strong influence on the subsequent debates (Rodriguez 1988, 96–101; interview Lefcovitz 1990).

The government, where few progressive health care experts had survived conservative pressures, elaborated a draft bill that fell between the extreme positions of the sanitary movement (NESP 1989) and of medical business, INAMPS bureaucrats, and clientelist politicians.[12] It proposed to Congress to go beyond SUDS by fully unifying and decentralizing medical care (CD.PL 3110/89). However, the bill contained few specific rules and programs for substantive health care reform and for the cooperation between private and public sectors. The government would retain wide discretion.

Whereas states and municipalities supported the bill because they favored a decentralized health care system (CONASS 1989), medical business, INAMPS, and clientelist politicians resisted it fiercely. They wanted to re-centralize health care, strengthen INAMPS, limit the role of the state, and guarantee wide latitude and ample profit chances for medical business (FBH 1989, 11–22, 70–80; CD.PL 2358/89). They tried to block progressive reform and even revert the changes brought by SUDS. The charity hospitals also criticized important provisions, especially the effort to intensify public control over private medical facilities.

Profit-seeking hospitals, INAMPS bureaucrats, and clientelist politicians lobbied strongly and used obstruction to extract concessions from center-left politicians, who wanted to pass the new health care law. The sanitary movement was unable to counteract these conservative pressures. The skewed balance of influence led to a compromise that further watered down the mandate for health care reform. The new law, passed by Congress in mid-1990, guaranteed the profit-seeking and nonprofit hospitals wide latitude from state control and gave nonstate providers of medical services economic safeguards and direct participation in health care policy making through the National Health Council.[13] Despite an endorsement of decentralization, it assigned many important responsibilities to the federal government, such as the definition of the norms for contracting private providers, and preserved the remaining apparatus of INAMPS, which had been transferred to the MS (MS 1991, 13–14, 28). While the law unified and decentralized medical services, it did not revamp public-private cooperation nor reorient health care policy to favor the poor.

Segmentalist business sectors, clientelist politicians, and an autonomous state agency defeated most of the proposals for equity-enhancing health care reform. The opponents were better organized and could use their considerable resources more effectively than the heterogeneous sanitary movement, which had lost many positions inside the state and had never been able to organize firm support in society. Only conservative forces could engage in sustained lobbying and sway parliamentarians who were not guided by program-oriented, minimally disciplined parties. Organizational factors played a crucial role in skewing the balance of influence to the detriment of redistributive reform.

HEALTH POLICY OF THE COLLOR GOVERNMENT

President Collor blocked some of the few advances in the new law. In line with his conservative background, he nominated as health minister Alceni Guerra, a clientelist politician who had been an INAMPS official under the military regime. Eager to retain sources of patronage and unwilling to destroy his former agency, Guerra slowed down the decentralization of health care. Collor's own interest in patronage and the effort of the Economy Ministry to control public resources added to this obstruction and induced the president to veto numerous provisions of the new law. Above all, he undermined the automatic transfer of resources to the sub-national governments in order to retain discretion, which could be used to extract political favors (MS 1991, 27, 30). Pressed by Congress and states and municipalities, where the sanitary movement retained a foothold, the government reenacted some of these rules in a vague version (CD.PL 5.995/90; MS 1991, 33–35; interview Arouca 1992).

The pressures of state and municipal governments in favor of decentralization and the resistance of the federal government and INAMPS led to numerous conflicts. Competition among the different parties controlling the federal, state, and municipal governments—a result of democratization—exacerbated these fights. As INAMPS used administrative rules to retain attributions and resources (INAMPS 1991; MS.SNAS 1992; interview Sanfim 1992) and the sub-national governments challenged these efforts, little energy was left for improvements in health care. Bureaucratic politics undermined the remaining efforts at redistributive reform.

In addition, the fiscal crisis created ever tighter economic constraints. Since health care spending could be reduced more easily than expenditures for the quasi-contractual benefits in social insurance, medical services bore the brunt of the burden of austerity efforts in social security (Vianna 1992, 6–13; interview Mazzoli 1992). After the transfer of INAMPS from the purview of the MPS to the MS, it was in the MPS's organizational interest and the political self-interest of its minister to use the social security taxes collected by the MPS ever more exclusively for benefit payments and cut the mandatory resource transfers to the MS. The MPS's bureaucratic egotism thus aggravated the scarcity of resources for health care.

The Economy Ministry also diverted funds from the new social security taxes, which it was supposed to allocate to health care, to other purposes. Finally, upon President Collor's instigation and on his own initiative, Minister Guerra allocated ample resources to patronage projects, such as an enormous expansion of hospital construction. Clientelism and bureaucratic politics thus intensified the resource constraints on health care severely.

These economic limitations and political interests left barely any funds for extending preventive measures and basic services to the poor. INAMPS even compressed the remuneration for its private contractees, which had already fallen considerably in the late 1980s. This resulted in sharp conflicts with health care business, which reacted to the squeezing of its profits with an ever more drastic reduction in the quality and quantity of services. After Guerra was forced out of office by a corruption scandal, renowned surgeon Adib Jatene tried to rectify these problems (interview Jatene 1992) but achieved only limited success during his few months as health minister (March–September 1992).

The sanitary movement barely held any positions in the federal government during the Collor administration. It used its foothold in states and municipalities to prevent a reversal of the earlier, rather limited reform efforts. Yet decentralization led to a focus on local problems and dispersed the movement. Therefore, it was unable to put effective pressure on the federal government and sustain the impulse toward national health care reform.

HEALTH POLICY OF THE FRANCO GOVERNMENT

The crisis of the medical system worsened further under the Franco government, whose first health minister, Jamil Haddad (October 1992–August 1993), had little political weight and administrative competence. The MPS therefore managed to solve its own financial problems at the expense of health care. From mid-1993 on, it simply stopped the mandatory transfer of revenues from wage and payroll taxes to the MS (IPS 6[9] [September 1994], 10), which had to appeal to the Finance Ministry for resources. Since the MF tried hard to combat the state's fiscal crisis, funds for health care shrank further. In this setting of financial scarcity, bureaucratic politics, especially the MPS's organizational egotism, blocked any improvement in health care.

The MS tried to obtain a more solid source of funding through the constitutional revision beginning in late 1993. It proposed the earmarking of certain taxes or the allocation of a fixed percentage of social security revenues to health care spending (interview Carvalho 1994). This proposal found widespread support among interest groups, including a strange alliance of medical business and members of the sanitary movement (interview Azevedo 1994). But MF and SEPLAN tried to regain latitude in budgeting and therefore combated the earmarking of revenues for specific expenditures. Also, the whole effort at constitutional revision was doomed by leftist parties' obstruction and the lack of party discipline among centrist and rightist parliamentarians, who failed to guarantee the necessary quorum for changing the 1988 charter (see chapter 5). Therefore, the draft provision mandating the allocation of a fixed percentage of social security funds to health care (CN. *Parecer N° 24*, 29) never came up for a vote. The MS remained dependent on discretionary budget funds dispensed by the MF.

The MF and SEPLAN took this financial dependence and the evidence of rampant fraud in medical service provision as an excuse to interfere in the administration of President Franco's second health minister, Henrique Santillo (September 1993–December 1994). They demanded better controls on spending and cuts in costly hospital treatments (*Conclusões* 1994, 2–11). In the medium run, this intervention could actually enhance social equity. Resource scarcity may induce SEPLAN and MF to press for a reorientation of health care from expensive curative medicine to cheaper and more effective preventive measures and basic care—the goal the sanitary movement pursued for fifteen years with little success. Thus, the fiscal crisis is not an unequivocal obstacle to redistributive reform; it may even provide a positive impulse.

At this time of this writing (late 1994), however, Brazil's health care system was in deep crisis. Resource scarcities limited and interrupted the provision of services, whose quality plummeted. Widespread waste and fraud exacerbated the problem. Decentralization destroyed many aspects of the old health care system, including essential planning and control mechanisms; political infighting and lack of technical capacity, especially at the municipal level, blocked the emergence of a functioning new system. Every citizen was entitled to publicly financed health care, but the unequal distribution of facilities limited effective access for many poor people, especially in rural areas (*Conclusões* 1994, 4, 24–26). Clientelist connections with all their arbitrariness were often a prerequisite for receiving treatment (interview Araujo 1994). Thus, after fifteen years of intense effort, the sanitary movement had achieved only minimal success in reorienting Brazil's health care system to satisfy the basic needs of the poor.

POLICY OUTPUTS IN HEALTH CARE

An analysis of policy outputs confirms that the advent of democracy has entailed little redistribution in health care. Theoretically, changes in public health care spending could enhance equity in two ways. First, expenditures could be reallocated from the rich to the poor. Second, overall public spending could be raised on medical services, which are legally uniform: In Brazil's new democracy, all citizens are entitled to the same type of publicly financed health care, regardless of their income level (but effective access is much less egalitarian). Since better-off sectors pay—in absolute terms— higher social security taxes than the poor, health care spending seems to improve equity. Its increase could thus have a redistributive effect.[14]

As table 7.1 shows, however, health care spending rose only temporarily in the late 1980s; in the early 1990s, its per capita value fell back to the level of the early 1980s. This decline was due to the fiscal crisis and the bureaucratic egotism of the MPS; but the low value of health care spending in 1984 also resulted from economic factors, namely the recession plaguing Brazil between 1981 and 1984. Thus, democracy has so far brought little lasting improvement.

The temporary increase in the late 1980s, facilitated by the economic recovery of the mid-1980s, was meant to finance SUDS. As part of this redistributive reform effort, progressive experts and politicians allocated more funds to health care. The real impact of this expenditure raise was, however, much lower than table 7.1 suggests. The implementation of SUDS was deeply affected by political interests that cared little about health care. The conflict of clientelist politicians, led by President Sarney, with the center-left wing of the PMDB led to a diversion of SUDS resources. Hard pressed for funds, PMDB state governments used SUDS money for purposes other than health care. The conservative group that dominated INAMPS after early 1988 also misused funds for President Sarney's political goals. As a result, there were many irregularities in SUDS expendi-

Table 7.1   Public Spending on Health

	Aggregate Spending (in $U.S. millions, 1992)				Per Capita Spending (in $U.S., 1992)	
	Federal	State	Municipal	Total	Federal	Total
1980	7,356	1,666	687	9,710	61.82	81.59
1982	7,148	1,379	755	9,282	57.86	75.13
1984	5,957	1,470	729	8,155	46.44	63.58
1986	7,341	1,963	1,062	10,366	55.13	80.03
1987	10,624	906	982	12,513	78.31	92.23
1988	10,030	−59	1,535	11,506	72.56	83.24
1989	11,320	1,159	1,500	13,980	80.37	99.26
1990	9,452	1,621	1,430	12,503	65.86	87.13
1991	7,847	1,384	1,787	11,018	53.67	75.38
1992	6,571	1,343	1,783	9,697	44.11	65.11
1993	8,308	1,256	1,667	11,231	54.73	74.02

Source: Data prepared by MS. Secretaria de Assistência à Saúde, 1994.

tures, which have continued to the present day (TCU 1989; *Conclusões* 1994, 2–7).

In addition, medical service personnel in municipalities and states pressed hard for equal remuneration with the better-paid INAMPS employees. Considerable amounts of SUDS money were used to satisfy this demand rather than to extend health care to the poor.[15] Last, not least, many states reduced their own health care spending when they obtained more federal funds (TCU 1989, 7, 19; NEPP 1989, 211; Felipe 1988a, 248). For all these reasons, the impact of SUDS on improvements in medical services, particularly to the poor, was much lower than the data in table 7.1 suggest. The temporary increase in spending on medical services probably did have an equity-enhancing effect—but a fairly modest one.

Since 1990, public health care spending has fallen drastically. Whereas the MPS ceded in 1991 28 percent of its resources to INAMPS, this percentage dropped to 14.7 percent in 1992, and to zero in the second half of 1993 and in 1994 (IPS 6[9] [September 1994], 10). This reduction in transfers, driven by bureaucratic politics, reversed the earlier redistributive trend. The effort to improve equity by augmenting health care spending had only temporary success.

Table 7.2 Functional Distribution of Federal Health Care Spending
(in percent)

	1980	1982	1984	1986	1988	1889	1990
Curative	85.4	83.2	84.6	80.4	81.6	75.1	79.8
Preventive	2.5	2.3	2.2	5.4	4.2	6.4	4.1

Source: Data prepared by Sergio F. Piola, Sebastião Camargo, and Solon M. Vianna, Coordenadoria de Política Social, IPEA, Brasília.

Note: Curative medicine comprises medical and sanitary assistance; preventive programs comprise control and combat of transmissible diseases and sanitary control. Other programs and administrative expenditures are not reported in this table.

Has the new democracy reallocated expenditures from the rich to the poor? Unfortunately, data on the social distribution of public health care spending is not available. Data on its functional and regional distribution can, however, provide important hints, although they are limited due to the administrative disorder caused by the reorganization of the medical system.[16] A shift from costly curative treatments to cheaper preventive measures and basic services, or a reallocation of spending from the more developed Southeast and South of the country to the poor Northeast could enhance social equity.[17] Have such redistributive changes occurred since the early 1980s?

Table 7.2 shows great continuity in the functional distribution of health care spending. Contrary to the goals of the sanitary movement, curative medicine has maintained its overwhelming expenditure share, which has decreased only slightly since the end of military rule. Given the extremely low starting point, resources for prevention have grown by a large percentage but have remained at a very meager level. These changes hardly constitute a significant redistribution of health care services. The main reasons for the high level of continuity are the bureaucratic self-interest of INAMPS and MPAS/MPS and the profit interest of medical business in preserving the established emphasis on curative medicine.

As regards different types of medical services, reformers wanted to de-emphasize hospital treatments, which benefit relatively few people at a high cost, and concentrate more on basic medical care. Doctors' visits solve many simple health problems, especially of the poor. Yet the data in table 7.3 shows that at least in the late 1980s, there was no equity-enhancing reorientation toward simpler medical services. After gradually increasing through the early 1980s, the number of doctors' visits stagnated from 1984

Table 7.3 Medical Services Financed by INAMPS
(in millions)

	1982	1983	1984	1985	1986	1987	1988	1989
Doctors' visits	206	219	236	238	238	247	237	234
Hospital stays	13.1	12.1	12.7	12.1	11.4	11.8	13.2	13.6

Sources: Computed from PeD 2 (4) (October–December 1987), 47–48; PeD 5 (4) (October–December 1990), 57–58; PeD 6 (2) (April–June 1991), 78–79.

Note: The data from 1990 on is heavily distorted because of the transfer of INAMPS facilities to states and municipalities.

on, despite a continuously growing population and despite the temporary increase in health care spending. The number of hospital treatments dropped slightly at the beginning of the new democracy, but grew afterward. At the end of the Sarney government, the number of hospital stays was higher than during the military regime, whose emphasis on hospital treatments the progressive experts had sharply criticized. This data does not suggest any equity-enhancing reorientation in the type of medical services provided under the new democracy.

Has democracy changed the regional distribution of medical services? Have Brazil's poor areas, particularly the Northeast, received a larger share of health care benefits than under the military regime? The reformers regarded the extension of health care in the Northeast as a priority (INAMPS 1988, 4, 10–11). Did they succeed in their efforts?

The most striking finding (shown in table 7.4) is the high degree of stability in most regional shares.[18] Only slight fluctuations can be discerned in the number of doctors' visits, although the reform-minded experts had considered their expansion in the poor Northeast particularly important. Even in hospital stays, changes have been anything but drastic. Yet given the low point of departure, the increase in the Northeast's share looks significant. However, disaggregated data shows a striking anomaly. If one state, Maranhão, is left out, the increase in the Northeast's share in hospital stays disappears almost completely (table 7.5). Maranhão itself reported incredible gains. What made this state so special that its share in hospital stays almost quintupled under the Sarney government? Maranhão received preferential treatment because it was the president's political base. Relying heavily on clientelism, Sarney channeled huge amounts of public funds to his state.[19] The increase in health care spending most probably did not benefit the poor but Sarney's political cronies and busi-

Table 7.4 Regional Distribution of Medical Services Financed by INAMPS
(in percent)

	Doctors' Visits				Hospital Stays			
	SE	S	CW,N	NE	SE	S	CW,N	NE
1982	55.5	17.3	8.5	18.7	48.3	21.6	11.4	18.7
1983	57.5	16.1	8.3	18.1	48.8	21.8	10.9	18.6
1984	57.5	14.6	8.4	19.4	49.4	20.3	10.3	19.9
1985	55.6	14.8	8.6	20.9	48.9	18.9	10.5	21.7
1986	54.5	16.6	8.4	20.4	46.6	20.3	10.8	22.2
1987	58.2	15.8	7.9	18.0	47.6	19.8	10.9	21.7
1988	56.0	16.0	8.6	19.4	46.3	19.3	11.3	23.1
1989	56.1	16.9	9.4	17.6	44.6	18.4	12.1	24.8

Sources: Computed from PeD 2 (4) (October–December 1987), 47–48; PeD 5 (4) (October–December 1990), 57–58; PeD 6 (2) (April–June 1991), 78–79.

Note: The data from 1990 on is heavily distorted because many state and municipal governments finally took over INAMPS functions.

Key:
SE = Southeast (Espírito Santo, Minas Gerais, Rio de Janeiro, São Paulo)
S = South (Paraná, Rio Grande do Sul, Santa Catarina)
NE = Northeast (Alagoas, Bahia, Ceará, Maranhão, Paraíba, Pernambuco, Piauí, Rio Grande do Norte, Sergipe)
N = North (Acre, Amapá, Amazonas, Pará, Rondônia, Roraima)
CW = Center-West (Federal District, Goiás, Mato Grosso, Mato Grosso do Sul)

ness friends. A later investigation found that irregularities and fraud in hospital bills were especially high in Maranhão, reaching 60 percent compared to a national average of 28 percent.[20]

Thus, under closer scrutiny, the increase in medical services in the Northeast loses its equity-enhancing appearance. The new democracy made only minimal progress in extending medical services to the poor in this region—and this at a time when overall health care spending rose considerably. The stagnation in simpler services, such as doctors' visits, is noteworthy, given the enormous unsatisfied need. Overall, these data provide little, if any, evidence of equity-enhancing change favoring the poor in Brazil's backward regions.

These data also provide some hints for assessing the success of the progressive experts in extending health care to poor people who had been excluded before. Did the legal reforms of the new democracy improve the effective access of the poor to health care? In Brazil, medical facilities have

Table 7.5 INAMPS-Financed Hospital Stays in Maranhão, and in the
Northeast Without Maranhão
(as percentage of total)

	1982	1983	1984	1985	1986	1987	1988	1989
Maranhão	1.1	1.0	1.1	1.5	2.1	2.9	4.3	5.2
Northeast without Maranhão	17.6	17.6	18.8	20.2	20.1	18.8	18.8	19.6

Sources: Computed from PeD 2 (4) (October–December 1987), 47–48; PeD 5 (4) (October–December 1990), 57–58; PeD 6 (2) (April–June 1991), 78–79.

always had a very unequal geographic distribution. They are concentrated in urban middle-class areas and are missing in poor neighborhoods and rural regions (MPAS 1975b, 17–18; Rodrigues 1987; World Bank 1988; *Conclusões* 1994, 4, 25–26). Rule changes were therefore not sufficient to give the poor effective access to health care.

Whether the poor gained such access is hard to assess because an important confounding change occurred. During the 1980s, privately paid health insurance schemes expanded greatly, especially in the state of São Paulo. From 1979 to 1991, their coverage rose from 6.5 million to 28.5 million people (Ferreira Neto 1992, 13). Many people who joined these completely private schemes had before used government-financed medical services (provided by the public or contracted private sector), which they now stopped doing. The lack of drastic overall growth in health care provision (table 7.3, above) hides a shift of better-off patients from publicly financed to privately paid medical services. Compensating for this exit, some of the previously excluded poor have gained access to public or private medical services financed by the social security system (Favaret and Oliveira 1989, 20–36).

For lack of statistical data, a numerical estimate of this displacement is difficult. However, since Brazil's regions differ in their social composition, changes in the regional distribution of medical services can provide some hints. If universalization was effective, regions with a large number of poor people, yet a small working and middle class that could enroll in private health insurance, should experience an increase in medical service provision. These conditions apply in the Northeast. The Southeast, in contrast, had large numbers of non-insured urban poor but also a big working and middle class, which has come to rely on privately paid health care. Therefore, the universalization of publicly financed health care is unlikely to raise the absolute number of medical services in the Southeast.

Table 7.4 suggests, however, that the Northeast has not made gains in doctors' visits, which are most desperately needed in the region. Also, most of the reported increase in hospital treatments in the Northeast did not stem from universalizing reforms but from President Sarney's clientelism and his cronies' fraud. Thus, decisions to universalize health care seem not to have improved the effective access of the rural poor. This category, which has been most neglected, has gained little in medical attention. But significant integration of previously non-attended urban poor has probably occurred in the Southeast, whose regional shares would otherwise have fallen more, given the growth of purely private medical insurance. Based on this reasoning, I estimate that by 1991 newly integrated poor people received about 10 percent of government-financed medical services in public or contracted private facilities. This was one of the rare equity-enhancing changes that the new democracy effected.

This improvement must be seen in historical context, however. The military regime had also given many previously excluded poor people access to health care provided by the public or contracted private sector (Roriz 1980; see chapter 4). Viewed in comparative perspective, the difference that democratization made diminishes greatly.

Altogether, the new democracy has effected very little equity-enhancing change in health care. The sanitary movement has clearly fallen far short of attaining its redistributive goals. Given that the authoritarian regime also achieved some success in broadening medical service coverage, the impact of the regime change on policy outputs in this area seems minor.

CONCLUSION

The disappointing results of policy making in health care dashed particularly high hopes for equity-enhancing change under democracy. Although large numbers of poor citizens suffered from health problems and although they enjoyed ample rights of political participation in the new civilian regime, strong bottom-up pressure for national health care reform failed to emerge. Clientelism exacerbated the collective-action problems facing the disadvantaged and hindered the formation of solid, broad-based organizations. The social movements springing up in major cities mostly focused on local problems rather than demanding a comprehensive over-haul of Brazil's unjust medical system.

The medical experts and professionals spearheading the reform effort therefore pursued a state-centered strategy. In order to compensate for its deficient mass base, this sanitary movement tried to occupy positions in-side the state apparatus. With the advent of democracy, movement leaders indeed gained important bureaucratic posts, which they used to advance their equity-enhancing goals. While they achieved some improvements, especially the legal universalization and equalization of health care cover-age, their success remained very limited. As in social provision, a series of organizational obstacles blocked or corroded redistributive initiatives.

First, its state-centered strategy drew the sanitary movement into bu-reaucratic politics. Since progressive experts were nominated to different state agencies, whose organizational interests they increasingly adopted, they came to advance divergent proposals. The resulting tensions diverted attention away from health care reform and caused internal rifts, weaken-ing the movement's political force. In fact, the partial decentralization of the health care system dissipated the movement. Rather than working for national-level reform, many of its members have come to focus on local problems.

Among the bureaucratic conflicts plaguing the health care reform-ers, the longstanding rivalry between the Ministries of Social Insurance (MPAS/MPS) and of Health (MS) had a particularly deleterious impact. The MPAS's defense of its established attributions and its control over social security funds hindered the intended shift from curative to preven-tive medicine and kept the MS dependent on resource transfers, which the MPS cut in the early 1990s in order to solve its own financial problems. The far-reaching autonomy of INAMPS also helped to undermine health care reform, especially the implementation of SUDS. In order to defend its power, the agency's bureaucratic apparatus offered tenacious active and passive resistance to decentralization.

Segmentalist groups of medical business with their long-established links to INAMPS opposed profound health care reform as well. They defended the established centralized health care system, which gave them lobbying access, and attacked the proposed shift from curative to preven-tive medicine, which threatened their profits. Working more and more through Congress, the private health care sector succeeded in toning down the reform mandates of the 1988 constitution and in preserving the basic outlines of the existing system. Yet while medical business has clearly been a source of strong opposition to redistributive reform, it has not been as decisive an obstacle as parts of the sanitary movement have claimed. Political forces have arguably been more important in blocking equity-enhancing change.

The single most effective impediment to redistributive reform in health care arose from the clientelist machinations of politicians. President Sarney and his conservative cronies combated profound health care reform, especially administrative decentralization, because their electoral sustenance depended on the patronage dispensed through the established medical system. This clientelist counterattack cost most members of the sanitary movement their positions inside the state apparatus and thus blocked the strong impulse for health care reform in the late 1980s. Patronage calculations also motivated President Collor and his first health minister, Guerra, to defend important aspects of the established health care system against reform efforts. Finally, clientelist interference in program implementation has continued to limit the equity-enhancing impact of the few changes the sanitary movement succeeded in enacting.

In sum, organizational obstacles have been crucial in impeding redistributive health care reform in Brazil's new democracy. Financial constraints, another potential impediment, were clearly not important in the late 1980s, as the drastic temporary increase in health care spending shows. In the early 1990s, however, fiscal problems have become more severe, causing a decline in expenditures that has blocked equity-enhancing improvements. Yet the dramatic impact of this economic constraint on health care has resulted in part from bureaucratic politics, especially the MPS's egotism in monopolizing funds. Thus, while they are not alone decisive, organizational obstacles have greatly hindered equity-enhancing change in health care.

8

Theoretical and Comparative

Perspectives

THIS STUDY has elaborated an institutionalist explanation for the virtually complete failure of Brazil's new democracy to effect redistributive reform and bring about greater social equity. This chapter refines the main argument, based on the empirical findings, and elucidates its theoretical context. Then I place this single-country study into a broader comparative perspective, showing how its results shed light on the difficulties of democratic reformism in Latin America and in other countries, especially the world's two largest democracies, the United States and India. I also draw in depth the contrast with the redistributive successes of social-democratic Europe.

THEORETICAL PERSPECTIVES

This book argues that the organizational fragmentation of society and the state has posed crucial obstacles to equity-enhancing reform in Brazil's new democracy. Pervasive personalism and segmentalism have prevented the poor from advancing their interests effectively and have induced better-off strata to focus on their narrow self-interests and reject equity-enhancing benefits for the poor. Personalism and segmentalism have also undermined the internal unity of the state, which has been unable to impose reforms on its own initiative. For all these reasons, the new democracy has effected very little redistributive change—as little as the conservative military regime.

For the Brazilian case, my argument provides a theoretical explanation for the empirical finding that democracy in general has minimal impact on social equity (Jackman 1975, chap. 4; Weede and Tiefenbach 1981, 265–69). The fragmentation of society and state blocks both bottom-up pressure and top-down initiatives for redistributive reform. It obstructs the four mechanisms through which democracy could theoretically lead to equity-enhancing change, namely demand making by encompassing interest associations, broad-based social movements and organized political parties, and independent action by a strong state.

As regards bottom-up pressure, personalism and segmentalism keep social strata divided. This weakens the poor, who need to act in a united fashion in order to mobilize their large numbers and counterbalance the advantages of better-off strata in command of power capabilities. Fragmentation keeps the poor from forming wide-ranging interest associations or social movements, which could aggregate their specific needs into demands for equity-enhancing reform and put strong pressure on elites and the state. Personalism and segmentalism also undermine the organization and program orientation of political parties, whose competition could otherwise mobilize the poor and promote redistribution.

Organizational fragmentation also makes the better-off strata more intransigent. They define their self-interests in narrow ways and oppose concessions to the poor. Disregarding broad collective interests, their distributional coalitions seek direct connections to state agencies and officials. This privileged access allows better-off groups to defend their privileges and undermine redistributive efforts.

Thus, personalism and segmentalism are the organizational mechanisms that skew political participation in Brazil, greatly favoring better-off strata over the poor.[1] These institutional structures explain why Brazil's interest group system "sings with a strong upper-class accent" (Schattschneider 1975, 34–35) and why parties and social movements fail to rectify this bias.

As regards top-down reform, organizational fragmentation keeps the Brazilian state from enacting equity-enhancing change on its own. The state is internally divided and hamstrung by innumerable particularistic links to narrow social groupings. As bureaucratic politics rages, state agencies often act at cross purposes and lose sight of overarching state interests. The apex of the state cannot ensure central coordination and control. For these reasons, the Brazilian state has great difficulty in achieving its goals, despite its earlier importance as the motor of development and its continuing deep intervention in economy and society.

Rampant bureaucratic politics and multiple outside links pose particular obstacles to redistributive state action, which would require the cooperation of different agencies and impose costs on powerful strata (Rueschemeyer and Evans 1985, 53–54). State fragmentation skews policy making toward distribution (Lowi 1964, 690), that is, handouts to the most vocal groups, usually the better-off. In Brazil's deeply divided state, these privileged groups usually find some point of access to decision making to hinder equity-enhancing change. Also, the reform-initiating agency faces strong opposition from rival bureaus that defend their own administrative turf. For these reasons, there has been little top-down reform in the new democracy.[2]

Neo-Statist Approach of This Book

Despite my emphasis on the current weakness of the Brazilian state, the argument of this book is state-centered but with a paradoxical twist. The state has long had a strong impact on society as an authority structure but has become weaker and weaker as an actor.[3] Responding to vast state intervention in economy and society, all social forces have adjusted their demands to the state's structure, but through their pressures they have made it ever more difficult for the state to reach its goals.

On the one hand, the Brazilian state has set crucial parameters for the interest definition and organization of social actors (Schneider 1992, chap. 6). To this day, social groups often do not take the political initiative but respond in their demand making to state actions.[4] Particularly, they adjust their interest articulation to the structure of the state. Rather than confronting the state head-on, they establish close connections to specific agencies inside the divided state apparatus. For this purpose, they form narrow groupings. Thus, the state's structure heavily conditions how society is organized.

On the other hand, however, the state has increasingly lost the capacity to attain its own goals. For more than ten years, it has been incapable of resolving the severe fiscal crisis, which has undermined its ability to propel development. As Brazil's long history of runaway inflation shows, the state has failed to keep conflicts among powerful segments of society in check. The state's weakness has been a primary obstacle to much-needed redistributive reform.

Paradoxically, the state's diminishing capacity to act has been the unintended consequence of earlier strong state action. The state fragmented Brazilian society, but in a dialectical fashion, society's fragmentation ended up undermining the unity of the state. In its effort to push ahead industrialization while maintaining sociopolitical order, the Brazilian state assumed enormous power and autonomy in the 1930s and 1940s. It imposed state corporatism on the modern strata, especially business and labor, and reinforced clientelism to contain the backward sectors. It kept society fragmented so as to ensure its own domination. However, this divide-and-rule strategy soon backfired. Unable to press their broad-based interests, social groups focused on their narrow demands and advanced them by infiltrating the state. The increasing scope of state interventionism, which made internal command and control difficult, facilitated this penetration. As state agencies and officials acquired more and more outside links, the state's unity and capacity to pursue its goals were undermined.

With democratization, the fragmentation of state and society has deepened further. The dispersion of power in Brazil's polity has become ever more extreme. As the state has become weaker, social actors have gained increasing veto power. Since alternate mechanisms of political coordination, such as strong parties, have not emerged, a profound impasse has resulted. Thus, recent Brazilian politics has been characterized both by the crucial importance and the political incapacity of the state.

This "dialectical" argument provides a neo-statist explanation for the organizational fragmentation of Brazil's state and society. It takes the state seriously as an actor that *can* gain autonomy and strength; but these features can also diminish as state efforts to fragment society backfire by undermining the unity and capacity of the state. Thus, I have treated state autonomy and strength as variables not as inherent qualities of the state, as traditional state theory used to do.[5]

The current weakness of the Brazilian state provides the crucial institutional setting for redistributive efforts in the new democracy. In fact, these reform attempts have tried to strengthen the state and enhance its control over society. Advanced mainly by state officials, they have been efforts at state building. The many tax reform proposals were meant to reinforce the state by extracting more resources from society and by enhancing public supervision of powerful business sectors. Social security reforms tried to bypass clientelist intermediaries and establish direct links between the state and the poor, thus guaranteeing political stability and state domination. In sum, state interests were among the main motives of universalist equity-enhancing initiatives.[6]

But these efforts at state building have mostly failed. The narrow forces in society that the state itself had promoted or sustained successfully have defended their independence against attempts at strengthening state control. The conflict over redistributive change in Brazil's new democracy is thus one of the many struggles for predominance among the state and particularistic social actors that have raged in the Third World (Migdal 1988; Badie 1992, chaps. 2, 5). This neo-statist interpretation is crucial for understanding the constant failure of equity-enhancing efforts in post-authoritarian Brazil.

Institutional Constraints and Political Leadership

How much latitude does the neo-statist approach leave for political choice? Has weak leadership hindered redistributive efforts in the new democracy, or have institutional constraints been determinant? Faulty political tactics are often invoked as causes for the failure of redistributive reform in the Third World (Ascher 1984, 3–10; Grindle and Thomas 1991, 5–10, 32–37). What role has inept leadership played in Brazil?

In the country's top-heavy political system, the traits of presidents, in particular, may affect the chances of equity-enhancing reform. President Sarney easily gave in to segmentalist and personalist pressures and shelved many redistributive efforts. Early in his term, President Collor, in contrast, kept segmentalist and personalist influences at bay (Schneider 1991a, 324–31; Weyland 1993, 9–16) and imposed several equity-enhancing tax measures the Sarney government had in vain attempted to take.

As this comparison suggests, political leaders can override organizational constraints under certain conditions. Leaders are more or less daring and willing to confront opponents. Their political background and context can differ in crucial ways. In his long political career, Sarney has been closely linked to powerful segmentalist and personalist forces; whereas Collor, as a relative newcomer, had more autonomy (interview Collor 1995). As for differences in political context, the first civilian government was chosen indirectly by an electoral college that much of public opinion had repudiated in the "direct election" campaign of 1984 (Skidmore 1988, 240–44). Sarney assumed office due to an accident, Tancredo Neves's death. This further reduced his legitimacy as president. In contrast, Collor was the first president elected by direct popular vote in twenty-nine years. While Sarney was the guarantor of continuity on Neves's ticket, Collor won the election with his rhetorical rejection of old-style politics in Brazil. It is thus no wonder that Sarney readily gave in to segmentalist and personalist opposition, whereas Collor was more willing and able to insist on his plans.

The comparison between Presidents Sarney and Collor shows that under certain conditions—a strong political base and distance from established elites—political leaders can overcome the organizational obstacles that this book emphasizes. However, three important considerations bolster my emphasis on institutional constraints. First, the latitude for leadership is not a matter of personal decision but depends on the political context. President Collor attained his initial successes in an exceptional situation. He gained a strong mandate by receiving massive electoral support and defeating a socialist, much feared by business and clientelist politicians. Since he enjoyed backing (as the lesser evil) from the usual opponents of redistribution, he had a unique opportunity to enact some equity-enhancing measures. Such a situation, exceptionally propitious for reform, is unlikely to recur often.

Second, the impact of the political context on leaders' choices is conditioned by the organizational factors emphasized in this book. President Sarney's weak political base did not compel him to capitulate to the segmentalist and personalist opponents of equity-enhancing reform. On the contrary, he first tried to strengthen his position by winning mass support through the Cruzado Plan of 1986, which led to a short-lived redistribution of income (Camargo and Ramos 1988). This strategy failed in part because the popular sectors did not have enough organizational capacity to form a counterweight to business associations, ensure private sector compliance with state controls, and defend their gains in a negotiated incomes policy (Singer 1987, 111–14, 126–36). Only after this failure did Sarney side with the opponents of redistribution. He adjusted to the prevailing balance of political power, which reflected organizational factors, rather than shaping it through leadership.

Third, whereas President Collor acted more independently at the beginning of his term, his unique "window of opportunity" closed in late 1990. When he did not live up to his promise to save Brazil from its severe economic crisis, the segmentalist and personalist opponents of redistribution quickly reasserted their influence. In exchange for their support in parliament, clientelist politicians demanded increasing say in decision making and implementation. Defeated several times in Congress (partly on equity-enhancing projects), Collor made more and more concessions. After initially excluding segmentalist business associations from top-level consultations, the Collor government soon strengthened links to the private sector as well. The substitution of the first team of economic policy makers, led by the brash Zélia Cardoso de Mello, and the appointment of officials who had held important posts under the Sarney government reinforced this tendency toward accommodation with business. With the reassertion of segmentalist and personalist connections to the government, Collor's latitude for choice dwindled fast, and redistributive reform stopped.

The rapid closing of Collor's window of opportunity provides evidence for the resilience of organizational obstacles to equity-enhancing reform. Even leaders who can temporarily override these constraints can usually not eliminate them.[7] They are soon pulled back into the spider's web of segmentalist and personalist links. Thus, while my institutional constraint approach is not deterministic, it accounts for politics in Brazil most of the time.

During the few months since President Fernando Henrique Cardoso took office in January 1995, he has already experienced the strength of the impediments that plagued his predecessors. Although he achieved a stunning first-round victory in the presidential election of October 1994, and although the parties backing his government have a comfortable majority in Congress, many of his crucial constitutional reform projects have encountered enormous resistance. Rivalry among state agencies, demands of segmentalist interest groups, and pressures from clientelist politicians have made it very difficult for the new president to enact any reforms that go beyond economic modernization.

The government's plan for social-security reform (Mensagem No. 306) aroused the usual opposition from social groups and patronage-hungry politicians. Even Cardoso's official supporters in Congress were so lukewarm that they divided the project into four amendments so as to complicate deliberations. In order to have any change enacted, the government will have to make substantial additional concessions. Regarding tax reform, disagreements between MF and SEPLAN, anticipated opposition from state and municipal governments, and the divergence between the government's effort to overcome the fiscal crisis and business demands to lower the tax burden have so far blocked the very elaboration of an official reform proposal. Finally, Cardoso's health minister has tried unsuccessfully to combat the severe financial problems stemming from MPAS's cut of resource transfers. This struggle has left him with little opportunity to promote equity-enhancing change. Thus, at the time of this writing (July 1995), the Cardoso government appears unlikely to remove the organizational obstacles analyzed in this book and successfully effect redistributive reform.

Leadership and Structural Constraints in Regime Change

In de-emphasizing political leadership, the institutionalist approach differs from the first wave of writings on democratic transitions in Latin America. Much impressed by the indeterminacy of regime changes, authors stressed the role of elite choices (O'Donnell and Schmitter 1986, 3–5, 19–21; Di Palma 1990, chaps. 4–5). The structural approaches prevailing before could not account for the fall of authoritarian rule in countries with a wide variety of socioeconomic and political characteristics. The latitude for leadership seemed to be much broader than Marxist-inspired and institutionalist theories had assumed.

But as the focus of attention shifts from the origin and process of regime change to its impact, structural factors regain their importance. Regime consolidation[8] and the quality of democracy, measured by citizen participation and the accessibility, accountability, and responsiveness of political leaders (Schmitter 1983, 888–91; 1992, 426–30), depend largely on socioeconomic and particularly institutional factors that constrain the latitude for leadership. Contrary to early expectations, even the mode of transition seems to have limited long-run impact.[9]

Institutional continuities and their effect on Latin America's new democracies are particularly obvious in party systems. The structure of party systems changed little with authoritarian rule. Countries that had highly institutionalized party systems under earlier periods of democracy have retained this feature after the demise of military rule; continuity also prevails in most countries that had fluid party systems.[10] Where parties have retained a high level of institutionalization, as in Chile and Uruguay, democracy seems stable and its quality high. In contrast, where parties are, once again, very fluid, as in Brazil, citizens cannot advance their interests effectively and hold their leaders accountable (Mainwaring and Scully 1995, 6–21; see also Dix 1992). Thus, persistent institutional features of parties have a great impact on the new democracies.

My study extends this institutionalist argument to interest groups, social movements, and the state. Personalism, segmentalism, and state fragmentation have persisted, have kept the scope of these organizations low, and continue to limit the quality of democracy. Clientelism and segmentalism have had strong self-perpetuating tendencies because they create powerful incentives for individuals to focus on their particularistic and sectoral interests.[11] Similarly, except for neo-liberal measures to shrink the state in Chile, military rule did not enhance the unity of the state. On the contrary, it often expanded state interventionism and exacerbated command problems inside the state.

Such a fragmented institutional setting severely limits the quality of democracy. As explained earlier, personalism skews interest representation and undermines equality before the law. Segmentalism induces interest groups to establish direct links to the state and thus diminishes the importance of parties, which are central for modern democracy. Finally, state fragmentation makes policy making highly complex and reduces accountability.

By focusing on these institutional factors and their impact on Brazil's new democracy, this book sides with the adherents to "structure," rather than "choice," in the ongoing debate about regime formation (Kitschelt 1992). Leadership may affect the timing and process of a transition, but institutional factors are crucial for the character and quality of the new democracies.

Institutionalism versus Socioeconomic Approaches and Rational Choice

The institutionalist approach of this book differs from other structural theories, which invoke socioeconomic factors or rational incentive structures. These rival theories are insufficient in neglecting the organizational framework of the polity, but when placed inside institutional parameters, they do help elucidate redistributive policy making in Brazil.

This study has invoked socioeconomic factors. Brazil's heterogeneous class structure has posed obstacles to equity-enhancing reform. In particular, the gulf between the formal and informal economy has divided the popular sectors and hindered bottom-up pressure for social change. Also, external dependency has bolstered the clout of private business, which can use its exit options as a powerful threat. The debt crisis and the resulting fiscal problems created financial limitations that have hindered equity-enhancing reform, especially in the early 1990s. These socioeconomic factors have skewed the balance of power, limited resources, and thus made redistribution more difficult.

However, the influence and the very constitution of class forces depend on institutional factors. Chapter 3 shows how deeply the Brazilian state has shaped society. Socioeconomic factors cannot be considered as independent variables for explaining the dearth of redistribution in the new democracy. Indeed, class forces have not been the protagonists of conflicts over equity-enhancing change. Most reform efforts have been initiated by state officials and experts, not by subordinate classes. Dominant classes have not been the decisive opponents of equity-enhancing reform, at least in social security. Wherever patronage resources were at stake, clientelist politicians have offered the most important resistance.[12] Thus, political forces have been crucial in redistributive policy making, which is more a conflict over state building than a part of class struggle. Whereas socioeconomic approaches stress important factors, they need to be integrated into a political-institutional approach.

Political forces have also mediated the impact of Brazil's prolonged economic crisis on equity-enhancing reform. Whereas fiscal problems and chronic inflation have clearly hindered redistribution, mainly by limiting or eroding increases in social spending, their effect has been heavily conditioned by political factors. Politicians overrode financial constraints and brought about great increases in federal government spending in the late 1980s in order to further their patronage interests (Mussi, Ohana, and Guedes 1992, table III-d). That the poor did not benefit much from these expenditures was a result of their political and organizational weakness not of economic factors.

The case studies also show that economic constraints have frequently provided a strong impulse for equity-enhancing reform. The state's fiscal crisis has prompted determined efforts to cut tax privileges of the rich, and the financial difficulties of the social security system have led to many attempts to reduce regressively financed benefits for better-off sectors and to reorient health care from expensive curative medicine to more cost-efficient preventive measures favoring the poor. Financial constraints have thus stimulated redistributive plans. Their failure was due mainly to the political influence of better-off groups, which organizational fragmentation boosted greatly. In sum, Brazil's economic crisis has imposed costs on society, but the distribution of these costs has depended in crucial ways on political and organizational factors. Socioeconomic variables always operate in an institutional context.

Institutionalism also provides the indispensable framework for rational-choice arguments. Rational-choice theories leave actors' interests and the parameters of their actions unexplained or depict them as the product of rational calculations. Whereas the former strategy is insufficient for understanding historical continuity and change, the latter exaggerates the flexibility of institutions. As chapter 3 shows, organizational structures have a high propensity toward self-perpetuation. Because of this resilience, they are mainly lasting constraints on choices rather than adapting easily to changes in actor behavior or being available for purposive manipulation. These institutions shape actors much more than actors shape these institutions.

Organizational continuity in the midst of sociopolitical change is a central postulate of the institutionalist approach (Krasner 1984, 225; March and Olsen 1989, 54–56). Without invoking preexisting institutional parameters, it can hardly be claimed that changing constellations of actors and their interests would "produce" the same institutional outcome. Institutional persistence results, of course, from actors' interests and capabilities, but these interests and capabilities themselves are shaped by the prevailing institutional framework.

Yet while insufficient as a full explanation, rational-choice arguments are useful for understanding actions inside institutional parameters. This study draws heavily on Olson's theories (1971, 1982, 1986), incorporating insights from rational choice into an institutionalist framework. As organizational structures shape the constitution and interest definition of actors, rational choices execute institutional constraints.

This integration of rational-choice arguments into an institutionalist interpretation draws on the increasing convergence of these two approaches, which appear less and less as polar opposites (Dowding 1994). On the one hand, advanced applications of the rational-actor approach to politics have recognized insufficiencies in their individualistic paradigm and drawn on holistic factors, such as socioeconomic structures, culture, and, above all, institutions (Bates 1990, 47–54; Cook and Levi 1990, chaps. 1, 6, 9; North 1990, chaps. 5, 11; Ordeshook 1990, 17–30; Shepsle 1989). On the other hand, adherents to alternative approaches have used insights from rational choice, for example, Olson's analysis of collective-action dilemmas (1971).[13]

Indeed, recent contributions to rational choice have qualified earlier claims to universal validity and specified the conditions under which rational-choice models have most explanatory power. Rational action can be expected to prevail where institutional structures, such as markets, reward correct means-ends calculations and punish or eliminate actors whose decisions run counter to such calculations (Tsebelis 1990, 31–39). Thus, the very applicability of rational-choice arguments depends on institutional parameters.

Institutionalism, therefore, has logical priority in the integration of approaches this book proposes. It provides the basic framework for rational-actor models. Adherents to rational choice have often criticized rival theories for their lack of "micro-foundations" (Knight 1992, 14, 39; Lichbach 1990, 1049–51; Roemer 1986, 192–93). They have overlooked, however, that rational choice needs a *macro*-foundation. I argue that institutionalism provides this indispensable fundament and starting point.

COMPARATIVE PERSPECTIVES

Are the findings of this book unique to Brazil, or do they apply to other countries? Do organizational obstacles render equity-enhancing change as difficult to effect in other democracies? Whereas systematic comparative analysis would require research far beyond the scope of this study, some tentative answers to these important questions are in order. The assessment proceeds in two steps. Since the rest of Latin America shares many characteristics with Brazil, I first discuss the applicability of my findings to these nations. Then I extend my view to other democracies, particularly

India, the United States, and Western Europe. Interestingly, my institutionalist argument applies even to this heterogeneous set of nations.

The case studies analyzed the first ten years of Brazil's new democracy. The following comparisons therefore pay special attention to the initial decade after a democratic transition, and they focus in particular depth on the other major countries in Latin America that reestablished democracy during the 1980s, Argentina, Peru, and Chile. When examining older democracies, however, such as Costa Rica, Venezuela, Colombia, and Chile before 1973, I extend the discussion beyond the first decade. This subjects my argument to a more stringent comparative test, for the following reason. Democracy may, theoretically, erode the organizational obstacles to equity-enhancing reform over time; for instance, party competition may gradually undermine clientelism. The following discussion will assess whether older democracies therefore have a better equity-enhancing record than new civilian regimes.

Populism and Democratic Reformism in Latin America

Brazil's new democracy has so far achieved very little equity-enhancing reform. But there have been democratic governments in Latin America that did enact some redistributive measures, especially during the waves of populism from the 1930s to the 1950s and democratic reformism in the 1950s and 1960s. While the democratic credentials of many populists, such as Juan Perón in Argentina, are dubious at best, some democracies did effect equity-enhancing change, most prominently in Costa Rica. How can these accomplishments be squared with the institutional constraint approach advanced in this study?

Organizational obstacles to redistribution are not constants but variables. Variations in personalism (especially clientelism), segmentalism (arising often from state corporatism) and state fragmentation help explain the differences in redistributive performance among Latin American democracies.[14] Where these institutional constraints were firmly entrenched, as in Brazil and Colombia, equity-enhancing reform was unlikely; where they were less strong, as in Costa Rica and contemporary Chile, the chances for redistribution improved.

The strength of these organizational obstacles has also changed over time. In most of Latin America, clientelism's hold on the poor has slowly declined with "social mobilization" (Deutsch 1961). State fragmentation and bureaucratic politics, in contrast, intensified with the enormous expansion of state interventionism and the proliferation of public agencies from the 1930s to the 1980s (Martins 1985, chap. 2; Mols 1981, 343–47). Similarly, state corporatism was imposed from the 1930s on, usually by populist governments (Malloy 1977, 12–17). These rough trends help understand the equity-enhancing efforts and limited successes of populist and democratic-reformist governments.

Populist leaders of the 1930s to 1950s acted in an organizational setting that was exceptionally propitious for redistribution. Urbanization had weakened the hold of clientelism on part of the poor. It had created a politically available mass that provided populists with support, in exchange for equity-enhancing reforms (Germani 1978, 176–203; Weffort 1980, 74–75; Mouzelis 1985, 333–41). The modest size of the state allowed populist leaders to control and direct the public bureaucracy (Most 1980), keeping state fragmentation in check. Finally, state corporatism had not yet been established. The lack of institutional connections to state agencies made it harder for business sectors to block redistributive reform, and the emerging working class, excluded before in sociopolitical terms, supported equity-enhancing measures, which favored it directly.

Populist leaders thus encountered a unique window of opportunity (figure 8.1). Whereas one organizational obstacle to redistribution had partly declined, the other two had not yet risen to high levels. As a result of this favorable institutional configuration, populism managed to effect some equity-enhancing reform. Leadership was important, but only where the institutional setting provided it with space for action.

However, the amount of redistribution that populists brought about was often quite limited. Most populist reforms were less than radical. While favoring the working and middle class, they entailed indirect benefits for business sectors as well. For example, higher wages boosted demand and guaranteed profits. More important, populist reforms rarely benefited— indeed, they probably hurt—the poorest strata, especially in the countryside (Cardoso and Helwege 1991, 61–67). The poor often had to bear part of the cost of these reforms, which business sectors tried to transfer to society's weakest sectors. In order to give to the middle rungs of the social pyramid, populism often took from the worst-off—hardly a progressive procedure.

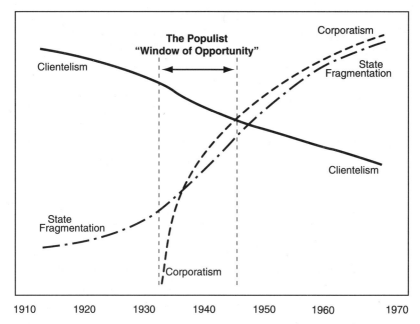

Figure 8.1 The Populist "Window of Opportunity"

The most successful case of populist redistribution took place under the government of Juan Perón in Argentina (1946–1955). Using the decline of clientelism and the emergence of an available urban mass to build his own power (Germani 1978, 176–203), Perón managed to achieve significant redistribution (Ascher 1984, 53–55, 65–68). For example, the years from 1946 to 1955 saw the single largest extension of social security coverage, which came to include even informals and rural workers (Mesa-Lago 1978, 164–65, 202). Urban workers, however, populism's strongest base of support, received especially generous benefits.

Perón's redistributive efforts were facilitated by Argentina's temporary accumulation of enormous economic resources during World War II. Also, since the country's class structure was distinguished from the rest of Latin America by having relatively few urban marginals and rural poor, his policies favoring the urban working class reached most of the poor. Because of Argentina's unique social structure, socioeconomic and organizational obstacles to equity-enhancing efforts were weak. Particularly, established elites could not draw on clientelism to command a mass following. Since the opponents of redistribution and of Perón's accumulation of power remained without adequate defenses, they resorted to a military coup to stop the populist experiment in 1955 (Waldmann 1974, 173–78).

Mexico's Lázaro Cárdenas (1934–1940) effected even more equity-enhancing reform than Perón but in an even less democratic setting. Unusually for Latin American populism, Cárdenas extended benefits to the rural poor through a radical land reform. But as the price for the favors they received, workers and peasants were coaxed into state-corporatist organizations and linked to the government party, which also used clientelism to guarantee its predominance. The popular sectors thus lost their capacity for autonomous demand making (Hamilton 1982, 242–44; Collier 1982, 71–77). As Mexico's political elite soon concentrated on rapid industrialization, state corporatism and clientelism allowed it to neglect social welfare.

For example, compared to countries at similar levels of development, Mexico was a laggard in extending social security coverage, which barely reached 25 percent of the economically active population by 1970 (Mesa-Lago 1978, 231). Since better-off groups received the benefits while the poorer strata indirectly helped finance them, the system had a regressive impact. Also, state efforts to raise tax revenues by reducing privileges of the rich, especially an important project advanced under the "late populist" presidency of Luis Echeverría (1970–1976) (Basurto 1982), were foiled by strong opposition from corporatist business associations and infighting among different state agencies (Purcell and Kaufman 1976; Elizondo 1994, 165–73). As a result, Mexico has had a highly skewed distribution of income. Thus, one-time redistribution under Cárdenas served as the basis for maintaining deep inequality afterward.

Populism in Brazil was restricted to urban areas, and its beneficiaries enjoyed much less demand-making power than in Argentina. Dictator Getúlio Vargas (1930–1945) integrated the working class into state-corporatist associations and placated it with social benefits. He based his return to power in 1950 on a second pillar of support, namely an extensive network of rural elites and their clientelist followers (Souza 1983, 109, 134). In addition, private business enjoyed favorable treatment because of its contribution to the main state goal, rapid economic development. Clientelism, segmentalism, and increasing state fragmentation kept the opportunities for equity-enhancing reform limited. Whereas organized labor gained some additional benefits, the urban marginals and rural poor remained excluded. For example, urban unions opposed the further extension of social security coverage and the elimination of inequalities in the existing system (Malloy 1979, chap. 4). The effort made by President Goulart (1961–1964) to overcome the organizational obstacles to redistribution, mobilize the poorer strata, and effect "basic reforms" aroused strong opposition and led to the 1964 military coup.

As these cases show, populist redistribution was restricted to a narrow time frame because its institutional preconditions disappeared fast. Populism itself helped to close this window of opportunity quickly by re-creating clientelism among the urban population and by boosting segmentalism and state fragmentation (see figure 8.1, above). First, populism was deeply personalistic, being based on (the illusion of) a personal connection between the leader and the masses (Drake 1982, 220–26). Populist leaders tried to consolidate their position by incorporating their followers into new clientelist networks, linked to populist parties.[15] The masses, recently released from traditional clientelism, were integrated into new personalist pyramids. This severely limited their capacity for advancing their interests autonomously.

Second, populism integrated many sectors of the working and middle class into segmentalist organizations. It had a great affinity with state corporatism (Malloy 1977, 12–17). Where the state was particularly strong, the new corporatist organizations had a narrow scope. Whereas Argentina's more powerful working class retained some autonomy and unity, state corporatism in Brazil and Mexico enforced deliberate organizational fragmentation (Schmitter 1971, 115–19; Reyna 1977, 161). By incorporating the working and middle class while leaving the urban marginals and rural poor excluded, populism also widened the cleavage inside the popular sectors. It gave the strata that it favored considerable capacity to defend their privileges and oppose the extension of benefits to the poor mass (Rosenberg and Malloy 1978, 159–63). By boosting segmentalism, populism thus created an important obstacle to further equity-enhancing reform.

Third, the populist promotion of state-led industrialization and the concession of social benefits greatly expanded the state apparatus. As public agencies mushroomed, many of them were penetrated by clientelist or segmentalist forces (Malloy 1987, 240–44). This reduced central control and coordination. Populist leaders faced ever greater difficulties in guaranteeing that the state apparatus would execute their plans. As bureaucratic politics intensified, their capacity for imposing reform through state action diminished (Most 1980; see also Basurto 1982, 105).

In these ways, populism reinforced organizational obstacles to equity-enhancing reform. It was difficult, above all, to extend to the urban marginals and rural poor the benefits that populism had conceded to the better-off segments of the popular sectors. Countries with important populist experiences, such as Brazil and Mexico, have therefore failed to reduce inequality in recent decades. Attempts at reviving populism faltered rapidly. For example, the reform efforts of Luis Echeverría in Mexico were defeated by opposition from inside a divided state apparatus (Purcell and Kaufman 1976), from segmentalist business and labor organizations, and from clientelist politicians (Basurto 1982, 105–10; Grindle 1977, chap. 6). Thus, whereas classical populism achieved some equity-enhancing successes, they remained very limited in amount and duration.

The democratic reformism of the 1950s and 1960s, whose prototypical examples are the governments of Costa Rica after 1949, the Acción Democrática (AD) administration in Venezuela (1959–1969), and the presidencies of Eduardo Frei in Chile (1964–1970) and Fernando Belaúnde in Peru (1963–1968), shared many characteristics with populism. These movements emerged and made equity-enhancing efforts in a similar window of opportunity as populism. Democratic reformism arose only where a significant part of the population was not enveloped in clientelism any more, and it achieved redistributive successes only where segmentalism and state fragmentation were at low to moderate levels.

Contrary to populism, however, individual leadership played less of a role. Parties that were well organized and program oriented by Latin American standards acted as the protagonists for redistributive initiatives (Levine 1978; Rosenberg 1979, 125–26; Peeler 1985, 123–30). Electoral competition induced them to try to gain a mass following by providing benefits to hitherto neglected segments of the population. Their commitment to democracy, which differed from the authoritarian leanings of populism, induced these parties to win broad electoral support. Therefore, their appeal was often wider than that of populism, extending to the urban marginals and rural poor.[16]

However, democratic-reformist parties also found it difficult to attain their equity-enhancing goals. As happened with populism, redistributive successes soon turned into obstacles. To consolidate support, reformist parties enveloped the poorest reform beneficiaries (for example, people receiving land through agrarian reform) in clientelist networks, reducing their capacity for further demand making. Better-off sectors, in contrast, were organized in segmentalist associations, which came to resist the extension of benefits to the poorest strata (Ascher 1984, 34). Democratic-reformist parties also arrived at greater accommodation with business associations, which they needed for economic growth. Finally, in order to promote development (and provide patronage), they expanded the state apparatus. As state fragmentation intensified, reform plans were obstructed by bureaucratic politics. For these reasons, the redistributive efforts of democratic reformism tended to diminish over time.

Democratic reformism had a lasting impact only in Costa Rica and Venezuela, where it emerged in the 1940s, when segmentalism and state fragmentation were still at low levels. In Venezuela, socioeconomic modernization had eroded clientelism (Karl 1986, 199–201) and the long dictatorship of Juan Vicente Gómez (1908–1935) had not incorporated the popular sectors into new organizations (Levine 1978, 85–89). This left them available for mobilization by a reformist party, Acción Democrática (AD), which quickly gained overwhelming support. After a short spate of radical reformism (1945–1948), which was stopped by a conservative coup, a more moderate AD came back to power in 1958 through a pact that guaranteed the basic interests of business, the military, and the church but left considerable room for reform (Levine 1978, 93–101, 105–07; more critical Karl 1986, 210–19).

In the 1960s, AD effected significant redistribution in Venezuela, compared to other Latin American countries (Kirby 1973; Peeler 1985, 127). However, it soon integrated the sectors it had favored into clientelist networks and thus kept the demand-making power of the poor low, especially in rural areas (Hanes de Acevedo 1991). AD also moved ever closer to business, whose peak association, FEDECAMARAS, moderated reformism (Gil 1977, 145–54). For example, FEDECAMARAS attacked the plan for a progressive overhaul of the tax system in 1966, inducing the government to water down the reform considerably (Kelley 1970; Combellas 1973). Finally, the mushrooming of state agencies and their clientelist penetration limited the opportunities for top-down reform. For these reasons, the social security system, for example, has developed slowly in Venezuela; it covers only 33 percent of the economically active population and has not redistributed income (Márquez 1992, 5–6, 27–41; Márquez and Acedo 1994, 157–61). As equity-enhancing efforts diminished over time, large-scale poverty has persisted in this oil-rich country.

Reformism in Costa Rica retained more equity-enhancing momentum.

In the 1940s, political leaders responded to incipient popular pressure for social change and preempted a perceived Communist challenge by instituting reforms from above. They facilitated the organization of workers, conceded social security and health benefits (Rosenberg 1981), and created a progressive income tax (Bell 1971, 75–79). Major redistributive reforms thus preceded the installation of full democracy in 1949. The new regime continued on this gradual reform path—more slowly in the 1950s, yet with increasing impetus in the 1960s and 1970s. Although redistribution has not assumed radical proportions (Ameringer 1982, chap. 6; Peeler 1985, 118–30), political competition has favored many lower-class people. Since both the major party, Liberación Nacional, and the coalition opposing it have not been beholden to segmentalist forces, they have appealed to Costa Rican voters from different categories and promoted universalist reforms. Thus, the 1960s and 1970s saw a big expansion of social insurance and health care, which created a safety net for most of the population.[17]

Costa Rica's unique state organization, which relies heavily on independent agencies, initially favored reformism. Since "public employees are protected against the spoils system, unlike virtually any other government in Latin America" (Ameringer 1982, 46; see Kearney 1988), these agencies acquired considerable competence and cohesion. Experts in these bureaus, such as the Social Insurance Fund, were crucial initiators of equity-enhancing reforms (Rosenberg 1979). Thus, Costa Rican reformism was driven both by party competition and by state initiatives.

However, while being shielded from personalist pressures, the independent agencies were difficult to coordinate and control. Several of them used their latitude to contract huge foreign debts, which contributed to Costa Rica's severe economic crisis in the early 1980s, thus helping to limit reformism (Del Aguila 1982). Also, redistributive efforts had never focused on the poorest 20 percent of the population, mainly landless rural workers. Persistent clientelism hindered their interest articulation. Whereas reforms raised their absolute standard of living, their relative income share diminished as the large middle of the social pyramid gained most from equity-enhancing efforts (Booth 1989, 404–07; González-Vega and Céspedes 1993, 44–58). Thus, democratic reformism in Costa Rica, the most successful case in Latin America, has developed slowly and has had important limits.

The Frei administration in Chile and the Belaúnde government in Peru effected even less equity-enhancing change. In these cases, democratic-reformist parties came to power in polities with a much denser network of segmentalist organizations and, in the Chilean case, with considerable state fragmentation (Cleaves 1974). Both Presidents Frei and Belaúnde faced opposition from rightist parties with a clientelist following in rural areas or urban squatter settlements and from populist or left-wing parties with a strong base among urban labor. Segmentalist trade unions demanded benefits for themselves and hindered universalist efforts to channel resources to the poor (Ascher 1984, 34, 213–15). For example, both Belaúnde's and Frei's efforts to reduce inequalities in the social security system and to unify social protection failed (Mesa-Lago 1978, 29, 33, 120, 126). Frei also had difficulty in controlling a fragmented state apparatus. These organizational obstacles made it hard to override the resistance of businesspeople and landowners. For these reasons, both presidents achieved little redistributive success, especially in the area of tax reform (Ascher 1984, 128–31, 167–72). They also failed politically, as the military overthrew democracy in Peru and the Marxist "Popular Unity" won the 1970 presidential election in Chile.

The effort of the Allende government in Chile (1970–1973) to bring about socialism triggered a rare instance of open class struggle in Latin America. While not even commanding a majority of the popular vote and while suffering from deep internal divisions, the "Popular Unity" encountered ever more strenuous opposition from domestic and foreign business, sectors of the middle class, the U.S. government, and, finally, the armed forces. Escalating polarization led to a military coup in 1973. The following harsh dictatorship reversed most of Allende's redistributive measures and imposed a neo-liberal development model that intensified social inequality. Thus, the radicalization of democratic reformism in Chile proved highly counterproductive.

Altogether, democratic reformism and populism achieved only limited equity-enhancing successes. Most democratic governments in Latin America effected very little progressive redistribution. Even the windows of opportunity that the decline of clientelism created—before segmentalism and state fragmentation emerged in full force—were rarely used to benefit urban marginals and rural poor. Populism mostly favored better-off strata, namely the middle and working classes, and democratic reformism encountered in the resistance of these sectors one obstacle to its efforts to extend benefits further down in the social pyramid. In fact, the limited equity-enhancing successes that were achieved often ended up reinforcing clien-

204 / *Democracy Without Equity*

telism and boosting segmentalism and state fragmentation. Thus, windows of opportunity for reform closed fast as organizational obstacles to redistribution quickly (re)asserted themselves.

These comparative considerations suggest that the chances and successes of redistributive reform in Latin America have depended to a large extent on variations in the organizational obstacles emphasized in this study.[18] Equity-enhancing reform was only possible during temporary erosions of organizational obstacles, and even then it remained quite limited. The universalization of the benefits conceded to better-off segments, that is, their extension to urban marginals and rural poor, proved particularly hard to effect. Thus, in most countries for most of the time, the organizational factors emphasized in this book have posed crucial obstacles to equity-enhancing efforts. Brazil has not been unique in this respect, although personalism, segmentalism, and state fragmentation have been particularly pronounced. Only in Argentina (after 1955) and in Chile (1970–1973), where social and institutional structures differed considerably from the rest of Latin America, was open conflict crucial. While my institutional framework cannot account well for these exceptional cases of confrontation, it helps explain why they have remained so rare in a continent plagued by deep inequity.

These conclusions about the organizational preconditions of equity-enhancing efforts are confirmed by the contrast case of Colombia, where persistent clientelism has obstructed populist or democratic-reformist redistribution. Repeated clashes among traditional parties froze clientelist loyalties into place and thus preserved hierarchical personalist pyramids. Clientelism, which has formed the backbone of the firmly entrenched, but organizationally weak, party system, has blocked populism (Urrutia 1991, 376) and kept the poor from making effective demands for the concession of rights and benefits (Archer 1995, 188–91, 48). Therefore, income inequality in Colombia was high even for Third World standards (Gillis and McLure 1980, 49).

Even when state interests were at stake, the opposition of conservative politicians and business associations to equity-enhancing measures could only be overcome by bypassing democratic rules. For example, in 1974 the government enacted a progressive tax reform through emergency powers.[19] Hemmed in by clientelism and besieged by segmentalist interests (Bailey 1977, 268, 288–89), it could not effect redistribution through democratic procedures. Organizational obstacles, particularly persistent clientelism, have thus greatly hindered equity-enhancing efforts in Colombia.

The preceding discussion suggests that longer established democracies do not have a much better equity-enhancing record than new civilian regimes. The theoretically possible erosion of fragmented organizational structures by democratic competition took place only in Chile but with disastrous final results; it has not proceeded much at all in Colombia; and the opposite tendency has prevailed in Venezuela as the beneficiaries of early reform were soon enveloped in clientelism, losing the capacity to press for further change. Only Costa Rica's democracy achieved lasting equity-enhancing success in its second and third decade. These mixed results indicate that old democracies do not have more redistributive capacity than new civilian regimes. Thus, the conclusions on the importance of organizational fragmentation that my analysis of Brazil's new democracy yields seem to apply to other democracies in Latin America, both old and new.

Redistribution in New Democracies?

Has exclusionary military rule, which many Latin American countries experienced in the 1960s to 1980s, created a new window of opportunity for equity-enhancing reform? The authoritarian regimes stimulated socioeconomic modernization, which further eroded clientelism. Reluctant or unable to establish inclusionary corporatism, military rulers left a large mass of urban marginals and rural poor available for political mobilization. In their effort to centralize power, they also tried to unify the state apparatus. Thus, have organizational obstacles to redistribution diminished and have revivals of populism and democratic reformism become possible in the new democracies?

Where state corporatism left behind a welter of segmentalist organizations and where political parties had always had low levels of institutionalization, as in Brazil and Peru, neo-populism did indeed emerge (Kaufman and Stallings 1991, 22–25). The weakness of organized channels of political participation and their inability to absorb the politically disposable mass gave personal leaders the chance to rise and draw a wide yet fluid following (O'Donnell 1994, 61–62, 65–68). In populist fashion, they bypassed established intermediary institutions and tried to guarantee support from poorer strata by promising to benefit them through redistributive policies. Alan García (1985–1990) revived populism in Peru, and even José Sarney of Brazil embarked on a brief neo-populist experiment with the Cruzado Plan.[20]

Populist rhetoric was, however, followed by even less equity-enhancing success than in the 1930s to 1950s. Neo-populist leaders lacked solid organized support. Even where an established party had helped them win power, such as the Alianza Popular Revolucionaria Americana (APRA) in Peru, they marginalized it from decision making and ruled in a personalistic fashion. As a result, their policy choices were erratic, their accountability was low, and they could not draw on firm backing when their initial popularity waned. For these reasons, the neo-populist leaders of the late 1980s were unable to enact a coherent, sustained reform plan.

García's ambitious policies to stabilize Peru's economy and stimulate growth simultaneously were especially haphazard. For instance, his government did not create a solid fiscal basis for the planned extension of state interventionism by extracting more tax revenues from the well-to-do. Instead, trying to court leading business groups, García conceded new fiscal incentives and lowered tax rates. As a result of these measures and of skyrocketing inflation, the share of tax revenues in GDP fell from a modest 14.5 percent in 1985 to a low 9.0 percent in 1987 and a dismal 6.5 percent in 1989 (Crabtree 1992, 60; Pita 1993, 61).

García also did not overhaul Peru's social security system, which had limited population coverage and insured only 38.1 percent of the economically active population in 1983 (Mesa-Lago 1989, 183). He did not try to universalize social protection and health care, as his predecessor, Fernando Belaúnde (1980–1985), had attempted in vain (Mesa-Lago 1989, 178–79). Given the resource limitations imposed by the debt crisis, such a progressive effort would have required curbing relative privileges enjoyed by the middle and organized working class. Since these better-off strata were represented in fairly strong segmentalist associations—while at the same time the poor had no firm national organization—García lacked support to embark on such a redistributive reform.

Instead, the president channeled benefits in a discretionary fashion to his main supporters, the urban marginals and rural poor. By disrupting local community organizations, undermining self-help efforts, and boosting clientelism, these programs may have done more harm than good

(Graham 1992, 180–99). Also, the deep crisis that García's imprudent economic policies caused after 1987 made the further distribution of benefits impossible. In fact, runaway inflation hurt especially the poorest sectors, reversing any gains they made in the early years of this neo-populist experiment (Lago 1991, 311–12; Wise 1989, 165, 175–78).

Thus, García's failure to enhance social equity had political-institutional roots in addition to the constraints imposed by economic problems. The urban marginals and rural poor to whom neo-populism mainly appealed had a low capacity for organization and were unable to provide solid mass backing for reform efforts. Also, redistribution faced opposition not only from business groups. Even segmentalist middle and working class associations resisted the extension of the benefits their members enjoyed to the poorest strata; they feared that favors for marginals would impose costs on them. The political need to satisfy a wide range of sectors, the low administrative capacity of the state, and the scarcity of fiscal resources pushed García's neo-populism rapidly into a profound economic crisis, which eliminated its early redistributive successes (Dornbusch and Edwards 1990; Lago 1991, 311–12; Wise 1989, 165, 175–78).

Like García's administration, the first government in Argentina's new democracy, led by Raúl Alfonsín (1983–1989), embraced heterodox policies designed to attain economic stabilization without hurting poorer strata. Contrary to García, however, the Alfonsín administration tried to raise revenues through a wide-ranging tax reform. But it encountered strong opposition from segmentalist business associations and party politicians.[21] After long debates, the government achieved some successes, such as the extension of the personal income tax to dividends and an increase in the excise tax on luxury goods (Atchabahian 1988, 69–73, 77). But these changes modified only slightly Argentina's "extremely low reliance on direct income taxation" (World Bank 1990, 21) and the regressive structure of its indirect taxes. Also, proliferating tax evasion and accelerating inflation eroded revenues from 1987 on, forcing the government to extract resources by any means, regardless of social equity. The increasing tax burden on energy, for instance, had a regressive impact. Thus, the Alfonsín government did not effect significant redistribution through the tax system.

The deleterious consequences of organizational fragmentation became obvious in social policy. Argentina's social security system suffered from a lack of institutional coordination (Isuani and Tenti 1989, 23–24) and had long been plagued by severe financial deficits, due to the overly generous benefits conceded to better-off segments of the organized working and middle class. As a result, the state accumulated a growing debt with pensioners, who responded with a wave of judicial injunctions.

The Alfonsín government lacked the political strength to go beyond some emergency measures and revamp the system. It failed to curb excessive privileges and extend minimal coverage to the poorest sectors, who were still excluded but lacked any organized capacity for demand making. Such a redistributive reform would have aroused fierce resistance from the trade union movement, which was deeply divided, despite the existence of a peak association, the Confederación General del Trabajo (McGuire 1992). Since the different union factions competed fiercely with each other and behaved like distributional coalitions, they were unwilling to make any concessions. Their Peronist allies in parliament defeated in 1984 a crucial government project for labor reform, and the more combative strands of labor constantly tried to undermine the government's economic policies. Alfonsín therefore considered it prudent not to provoke the unions into an all-out confrontation by reorganizing the pension system. He also refrained from overhauling health care, which was administered largely by the labor movement itself. Thus, anticipated resistance from powerful segmentalist forces precluded any serious effort at equity-enhancing social policies.

Unable to curb public spending in many areas and to raise taxes, besieged by hostile trade unions, and lacking the trust of many business sectors, Alfonsín did not manage to stabilize the economy. After a temporary reduction from mid-1985 through 1986, inflation soon started to accelerate again, reaching exorbitant levels from 1988 on. As inflation exploded and riots erupted in mid-1989, the president had to step down early, betraying the high hopes his government had inspired at its inception in 1983.

The failures in countries such as Argentina and Peru left a large mass of people available for mobilization and allowed a second generation of neopopulists to emerge. Carlos Menem in Argentina (1989–present), Alberto Fujimori in Peru (1990–present), and Fernando Collor in Brazil gained decisive electoral support by promising benefits to the poor. Yet upon reaching office, they imposed tough economic stabilization and market-oriented, "neo-liberal" restructuring. This turnabout was only feasible in societies that were highly fragmented and battered by prolonged crises; no sociopolitical force was strong enough to hold the new leaders accountable and limit their political latitude.

Although the harsh neo-liberal policies lowered the income of the poor, they encountered strong popular backing because they prevented a hyper-inflationary catastrophe, which would have hurt the destitute the most. Also, in order to maintain electoral support among the poorest strata, neo-populist presidents sooner or later created social emergency programs and distributed resources in a discretionary way. Therefore, neo-liberal neo-populism has proven remarkably viable (Weyland 1996).

The long-term impact of neo-liberal reform on social equity is difficult to predict. On the one hand, the installation of universalist market rules may remove privileges enjoyed by "special interests," undermine the distributional coalitions that have besieged the state and captured many public agencies, and thus weaken segmentalism. The diminution of state intervention may also reduce patronage resources that sustain clientelism and allow for greater coordination and control inside the public administration. In these ways, neo-liberalism may enfeeble organizational obstacles to redistribution and in the long run facilitate the emergence of broad-based organizations pressing for equity-enhancing reform.

On the other hand, discretionary social programs may reinforce clientelism among the poor; sectors of big business may capture privileged niches through haphazard privatization deals; and the state may lose much of its capacity for enacting policy change due to the neo-liberal attack on the public bureaucracy. Exposing domestic industry to foreign competition may boost unemployment and push more people into the informal sector, widening a gap that keeps the poor divided. The harsh austerity required for economic stabilization and the constraints resulting from an export-oriented development model may forever limit the resources available for social policies. Finally, the privatization of social programs may exclude sectors that cannot pay the full price for their social protection.

Given these counteracting tendencies, the distributional impact of the current wave of neo-liberal reforms is difficult to predict. At least, no major improvement in social equity is to be expected in the short and medium run, as the following analysis of reform initiatives in tax and social security policy suggests.

Neo-liberal tax policy has tried to raise much-needed revenue and stimulate economic effort and efficiency. Therefore, the governments of Carlos Menem and Alberto Fujimori have reduced the marginal rates of income taxes and raised and extended indirect taxes, especially the value-added tax (World Bank 1993, 40–45; Durand 1994, 5–6, 18–21). Yet, compensating for these regressive changes, stricter tax enforcement, which burdens better-off strata more heavily, has prompted an increase in income tax payments (Ministerio de Economía 1995, 12; SUNAT 1994, fig. 6).

Neo-liberal social policy wants to target public resources to the poorest strata who cannot succeed in the market place and leave protection of better-off groups to the private sector. The severe fiscal crisis, however, led especially Peru's President Fujimori to slash all social spending. The organizational weakness of the poor made these austerity measures politically feasible. As a result, areas such as health care have suffered substantial deterioration (Kruse 1992, 40–44; Salcedo 1992, 16–20). This has hurt especially the most destitute, who lack the funds to buy private health insurance and therefore have to rely on dilapidated public facilities.

The neo-liberal tendency to shift the responsibility for providing social protection from the state to the private sector has prevailed in social insurance. Both the Menem and Fujimori governments have promoted pension privatization, though in different forms. Argentina retained a public system guaranteeing a basic benefit and gave the insured a choice between the public and private sector for buying additional, earnings-related pension insurance; the Fujimori government, in contrast, pressured the insured to join fully private pension plans.[22]

These differences have resulted in good part from political-institutional factors. The political feasibility of radical neo-liberal reform has depended on the weakness of trade unions, the main organizations representing current and prospective beneficiaries in the established, fairly generous public schemes. While Peruvian unions have seen their influence destroyed by economic crisis and neo-liberal restructuring, Argentina's labor movement, though enfeebled, has retained some veto power (Balbi 1993; Kay 1995, 10–12). Democracy prevented President Menem from ignoring or squashing labor opposition. President Fujimori, in contrast, imposed his more drastic reform after assuming dictatorial powers in 1992.

The difference in reform approaches has also reflected the cost of pension privatization for the public sector. The state needs to finance the pension rights and the stock of benefits accumulated in the public sector while losing revenues from social security taxes that are transferred to private insurance companies. The deficit that would result from full privatization is prohibitive where the pension system has broad coverage and generous entitlements, as in Argentina.[23] The deficit is much lower in a country like Peru, where the social security system is limited in coverage and more modest in its benefits. Thus, the greater the amount of benefits provided in the existing system, the more restricted are the options for privatization.

The distributional consequences of these neo-liberal reforms are not yet clear. Radical pension privatization is exclusionary because it implants a strict contributive principle, which makes it difficult to extend protection to the poorest strata. Yet privatization can also have progressive effects by removing privileged benefits for better-off sectors that more destitute people helped finance directly or indirectly. Also, where reforms reduce or abolish employer contributions to social security, they lower labor costs; this may in the long run stimulate employment in the formal sector and thus include more workers into the social security system.

In conclusion, the impact of neo-liberal restructuring on social equity is not easy to foresee. Much will depend on the economic success of the new development model. Yet the argument of this book suggests that the organization of major social forces and the state will also be of crucial importance for the future of social equity. The organizational fragmentation that has long prevailed in countries such as Argentina and especially Peru does not bode well for progressive redistribution.

In contrast, some significant equity-enhancing progress has been achieved in Chile's new democracy (1990–present). In this country, more encompassing, cohesive organization has prevailed in society and inside the state.[24] Typically, these encompassing associations, broad-based party alliances, and the fairly unified state have focused their attention not on narrow, particularistic interests but on overarching goals. They have sought to consolidate the new democracy and legitimate the basic outlines of the ultimately successful market-oriented development model imposed by the Pinochet regime. For these purposes, the center-left governing coalition and the conservative opposition, as well as the peak associations of labor and business, have agreed on gradual equity-enhancing change, designed to reduce the sharp inequalities left behind by the dictatorship and help especially the poorest strata. One of the main goals of this prudent reformism has been to prevent an upsurge of populism, which ravaged the economies and threatened the fragile democracies of other Latin American countries in the 1980s (Foxley 1990, 117–22; interview Boeninger 1993). Thus, in the context of low organizational fragmentation, the return of democracy has led to significant redistributive reform. The economic stability and sustained growth that Chile has enjoyed in recent years has, of course, facilitated this achievement.

Chile's political parties have retained their organizational strength and programmatic orientation despite seventeen years of harsh authoritarian rule. The desire to overcome the polarization that led to the 1973 coup has induced parties of the center and the renovated left to forge a stable governing coalition, the Concertación de Partidos por la Democracia. This alliance, like the alliance of the rightist opposition, is solidified by an electoral system that rewards party coalitions. Given their encompassing reach, both party alliances have advanced overarching goals, including gradual redistribution designed to bolster sociopolitical stability.

This prudent reform course has received support from the peak associations of business, the Confederación de la Producción y del Comercio (CPC), and labor, the Central Unitaria de Trabajadores (CUT). Contrary to the organizational fragmentation prevailing in Brazil and other new democracies in the region, both of these classes have an encompassing organization that can advance their collective interests. Business has therefore been willing and able to make some equity-enhancing sacrifices in order to give greater legitimacy to the market model imposed by force under the dictatorship (CPC 1990, I.1–II.10; interview Feliú 1993). Labor, in turn, has moderated its demands in order not to endanger democratic consolidation (Díaz 1991). Also, to bolster its claim to represent the whole working class, CUT has focused on the needs of the weakly unionized poorer strata, not only on the "special interests" of the better-off segments predominating among its current membership.

Finally, as the main initiator and executor of reform in the new democracy, Chile's state has had a fairly high degree of internal cohesion. General Pinochet's centralization of authority and his neo-liberal policies, which cut many links between state agencies and social groups, have had a lasting unifying impact. Coordinating agencies, especially the General Secretariat of the Presidency and the Finance Ministry, have managed to design and execute a coherent reform program (Rehren 1993, 23–27). The absence of deep clientelist penetration of the public administration, due in part to the suspension of electoral politics during the dictatorship, has made the comparatively effective implementation of equity-enhancing measures possible.

Due to the predominance of encompassing, cohesive organization in society and inside the state, Chile's new democracy has achieved considerable success in enacting redistributive policies. A tax reform approved in 1990, grudgingly endorsed by the business peak association CPC and by a conservative opposition party, raised direct taxes on better-off strata and private enterprises and made the composition of tax revenues more progressive. Together with an increase in the value-added tax it provided the necessary resources for a major increase in social spending targeted to lower-income sectors of the population.[25] Health spending, for example, grew by a striking 70 percent in real terms between 1990 and 1994. The additional resources were used to improve emergency and basic medical services for the poorer strata and to save hospitals from the deterioration they suffered under the authoritarian regime (Ministerio de Hacienda 1993, 3–5, 8–9; 1994, 4–10; Jiménez 1992, 105–22).

The Chilean government also raised social security benefits in the public pension system, especially for poorer recipients, and doubled the meager welfare pensions for the most destitute (Cortázar 1993, 76). These measures expanded the limited redistributive components of the system of social insurance,[26] which the Pinochet regime had radically privatized. Although the parties of the Concertación had criticized the unsolidaristic features of the strictly contributive private system, which is based on individual retirement accounts, the new democratic government decided against an overhaul in order not to stir up right-wing opposition and fuel tensions in its own midst (interview Lagos 1993). Yet by augmenting the welfare benefits for indigent noncontributors and the minimum pension guaranteed to poor contributors both in the remaining public and the new private system, it did improve social equity.

Due in part to these and other redistributive measures, poverty and indigence diminished greatly under the government of Patricio Aylwin (1990–1994). Obviously, sustained growth, a belated result of the painful economic adjustment enforced by the Pinochet regime, facilitated this accomplishment and made redistribution more acceptable to established elites. However, per percentage point of economic growth, the number of poor people shrank three and a half times more under democracy in Chile than at the end of authoritarian rule (Gatica and Ruiz 1993, 2). This striking difference suggests that the above-mentioned equity-enhancing measures had a major independent impact.[27] Thus, in the rare case where encompassing, cohesive organization prevails, a new democracy can effect sustainable redistribution.

The case of Spain, which shares many characteristics with the new democracies in Latin America's Southern Cone, corroborates the impact of organizational factors on the chances for equity-enhancing reform. It also shows that despite a severe economic crisis and determined market-oriented restructuring—adverse conditions that many of Latin America's new democracies face as well—some meaningful redistributive reform is possible.

Spain ranks in between the extremes of Brazil and Chile in terms of organizational fragmentation. Due to the predominance of a fairly cohesive technocracy in the last two decades of the Franco regime, the state enjoyed a high degree of internal unity and considerable strength vis-à-vis society, especially at the beginning of the new democracy in 1977.[28] In contrast, society has been more fragmented. Private business has a number of associations, yet the Confederación Española de Organizaciones Empresariales has over time become most important. Organized labor is divided into two competing union peak associations, the Socialist Unión General de Trabajadores and the Communist Comisiones Obreras. Finally, the party system has been quite fluid and fragmented on the right. The effort to form a broad-based center-right party failed with the implosion of the Unión de Centro Democrático (UCD) in the early 1980s, and the consolidation of the conservative Partido Popular took the rest of the decade. On the center-left, however, the well-organized and programmatically oriented Partido Socialista Obrero Español (PSOE) turned from an ideological and class party into a broadly encompassing organization, winning an electoral majority in 1982.

Redistributive reform in Spain's new democracy has followed these organizational developments. Initially, the state was the main proponent of change. Focusing on its core interests, it promoted important tax reforms. As for social policy, the PSOE's assumption of power led to significant equity-enhancing change, meant to benefit its wide-ranging constituency.

Under General Franco, the public bureaucracy had already made efforts to modernize Spain's outdated tax system and turn it progressive by extracting more resources from the better-off. The old dictator, however, had vetoed these proposals. After his death in 1975, government technocrats—as in Brazil—used the boost that democratization gave to universalist principles to achieve their goal. They gained support from various sociopolitical forces, which were concerned about the fragility of the nascent democracy and therefore willing to cooperate in a social pact. The Moncloa Agreement of 1977 committed the government to a progressive tax reform and an overhaul of social policy in exchange for the opposition's support of budget austerity and wage restraint. Accordingly, the government created in 1978 a property tax, unified the income tax, made its rates more progressive, and took steps to tighten enforcement (Russin, Pastor, and Bralove 1978). As a result of this equity-enhancing reform, income tax revenues rose from 3.5 percent of GDP in 1977 to 5.8 percent in 1983 (OECD 1986, 372). Since the yield of indirect taxes increased less drastically, the revenue composition of the Spanish tax system turned more progressive.

In addition to this redistributive success, the UCD government greatly expanded public spending in areas such as social insurance and health care. Social expenditures had been rather low under the dictatorship, compared to the Western European countries that served Spain's new democracy as models. From 1975 to 1982, public spending on pensions, for instance, rose from 4.3 percent of GDP to 8.2 percent (Guillén 1992, 141). However, the UCD government was too divided and weak to enact structural reform and make the financing system or the entitlement conditions more progressive. Thus, the rise in spending probably did not have a *redistributive* effect but maintained the existing distributional patterns.

The PSOE government, however, sustained by a programmatic, well-organized, and broad-based party, enacted substantial redistributive reforms, especially in social insurance, health care, and education. While the government party had close links to organized labor, its encompassing reach and majoritarian mandate induced it to promote universalist goals benefiting a wide range of the population, even at the risk of conflicts with trade unions advancing segmentalist demands.[29] This focus on overarching needs, even to the detriment of the special interests of party-linked labor sectors, prevailed in the government's strategy of determined economic restructuring and in its social policy initiatives.

As regards social insurance, Spain's grave economic problems prompted an effort to stem the continuing spending increase but improve coverage for the poorest. The PSOE government therefore tried to revamp the existing occupationally based system, which mainly provided earnings-related pensions to workers who had paid social security taxes. The new system should concede a basic flat-rate pension to all citizens, even non-contributors; less generous earnings-related pensions would complement this universal benefit (González-Sancho and Durán 1985, 137–39).

Foreseeing losses for their constituents, trade unions opposed this redistributive proposal. Sustained by an encompassing party, the PSOE government insisted on its universalist initiative. After long negotiations, a compromise emerged. The government tightened the entitlement conditions for earnings-related pensions while greatly raising the value of the welfare pensions paid to noncontributors. This redistributive reform, enacted in 1985, was meant as the first step toward the universalist scheme outlined initially (Spain 1986).

The PSOE government also revamped the health-care system in order to rationalize the provision of services, focus more on prevention and primary care, and extend coverage to all citizens. The reform brought significant advances, especially by making effective coverage nearly universal. But it did not reach all of its goals. Resistance from segmentalist organizations, especially associations of doctors, impeded a decisive reorientation from curative to preventive medicine. Increased state fragmentation, caused by the decentralization of authority from the central government to the provinces, also hindered efforts at administrative integration and reduction of regional inequality. Despite these limitations, the health reform enhanced social equity considerably (De Miguel and Rodríguez 1993, 253–59).

The fact that the PSOE government attained these successes in the midst of a painful restructuring process suggests that economic constraints are not decisive obstacles to redistributive reform. While financial difficulties limit spending increases, they may stimulate a *reallocation* of resources, as in the case of social insurance. The chances for equity-enhancing change in Spain's new democracy have hinged less on economic constraints and more on the degree and development of organizational fragmentation in the state and in society.

This comparative analysis of Spain's and Latin America's new democracies shows that the chances for redistributive reform have depended to a considerable extent on whether encompassing and cohesive organization prevails in society and inside the state apparatus. Where the major interest associations have a narrow segmentalist scope; where political parties are weakly institutionalized and not program oriented; and where the state lacks internal unity—as in Brazil, Argentina, and Peru—equity-enhancing change is unlikely. Economic crisis and the advance of neo-liberalism have tightened the constraints on redistribution, but political-institutional factors have been crucial in the allocation of the resulting costs (and benefits). In contrast, only where parties are broad-based and well-organized; where major interest associations have an encompassing reach; and where the state is internally unified—as in Spain and especially in Chile—has gradual equity-enhancing reform been able to proceed.

Thus, the impact of democracy on social equity has varied with the strength of the organizational obstacles of personalism, segmentalism, and state fragmentation. In much of Latin America, these obstacles have usually existed at a high level.

Comparisons Outside Latin America

The preceding sections have shown that the institutionalist argument of my study applies broadly to Latin America. Can this argument also shed light on nations in other regions, which diverge in their socioeconomic, cultural, and political context from Brazil? Is it valid for democracy in general rather than being area specific? Only such broad applicability bears out my claim that institutional factors are decisive, analytically independent of skewed class structures and the constraints of dependency. The following discussion therefore focuses on vastly different cases, namely the longstanding democracies of India, the United States, and Western Europe.[30]

Disregarding a short interruption in the mid-1970s, India has had one of the oldest democracies in the Third World. Many of its early leaders hoped that democracy would allow the poor masses to advance their interests effectively, bring about profound social reform, and reduce widespread poverty (Frankel 1978, chap. 1). In fact, however, inequality has not diminished much since India won independence in 1947, and a large mass of people continue to live in misery. Why has Indian democracy not had more of an equity-enhancing impact? What role have organizational obstacles such as clientelism and segmentalism played for this disappointing outcome?

The hierarchical values sacramented in the caste system help account for the absence of strong bottom-up pressure for reform, but Kohli's (1987) finding of significant differences in the redistributive performance of various Indian states suggests that political-institutional variables also play an important role. As regards socioeconomic factors, the sharp "dualism" between India's pockets of industrializing growth and the vast, backward countryside has accentuated inequality. However, as in Latin America, this socioeconomic gulf has been conditioned by organizational differences. The government could only neglect the countryside in the 1950s and early 1960s because its control there was guaranteed by clientelism, and it focused on urban, industrial growth because of state interests and demands from segmentalist associations of business, middle class, and workers.

As regards clientelism, India's Congress Party, which has predominated since independence, deliberately allied with rural elites who could deliver the support of their peasant followers. In this way, it tried to guarantee solid electoral backing. But it also consolidated rural clientelism and became incapable of spearheading profound agrarian reform (Frankel 1978, 190–201). Commanding the support of the countryside, the government was able to concentrate resources on industrial development, which benefited only a small part of the rapidly growing population. These groups, however, were organized in narrow segmentalist associations, which induced them to focus on their own "special interests" and allowed them to articulate these demands successfully (Rudolph and Rudolph 1987, 272, 279–80). They gained considerable benefits, whereas much of the rural population remained poverty stricken.

The focus on industrial development also sprang from state interests and the development ideology held by political and bureaucratic elites. In order to safeguard its national integrity, India was to become a powerful nation, able to respond to any threat from its regional rivals, China and Pakistan. This military objective required accelerated industrial development. This growth strategy seemed validated by the accomplishments of the industrialized First World and the Soviet Union. Thus, state interests and elite ideas reinforced the pronounced inequality of India's development and helped maintain large-scale poverty.

Social inequality faced greater challenges from the late 1960s on. Socioeconomic modernization and gradual land reforms weakened (but did not eliminate) rural clientelism and produced a politically available, unorganized mass. In her battles with established Congress Party bosses, Prime Minister Indira Gandhi used this opportunity to strengthen her position through populist appeals to the poor. Yet these conflicts and Gandhi's drive for personal power reduced the organizational strength of the Congress Party and de-institutionalized the state (Rudolph and Rudolph 1987, 84–102, 132–44). Solid support for reform among the rural poor could not be mobilized, and the public bureaucracy, tied by multiple links to politicians and businesspeople (Wade 1985), was unable to execute central programs. Since the organizational capacity for reform implementation was missing, Gandhi's radical rhetoric was followed by few redistributive accomplishments (Frankel 1978, 505–06, 548–51; Kohli 1987, chap. 5). As in Latin America, populism had little equity-enhancing impact.

The organizational weakening of the Congress Party and the fragmentation of most of the opposition has kept the gradually rising popular mobilization from being aggregated and channeled. Recent Indian politics has thus been dominated by the proliferation of narrow "demand groups," that is, distributional coalitions striving for immediate benefits (Rudolph and Rudolph 1987, 20–35, 247–392). Mushrooming segmentalism has blocked the emergence of broad-based pressure for structural change and favored the strategically best-positioned sectors of business, middle class professionals, and urban labor. The poorest strata have continued to be largely neglected. Thus, as in Latin America, persistent, though declining, clientelism, rising segmentalism, and increasing state fragmentation have posed crucial impediments to redistributive reform in India. Sharpening clashes among the country's diverse ethnic, cultural, and religious forces have served as an additional important obstacle.

At a much lower level of inequality and poverty, the United States has also experienced surprisingly few efforts at redistributive reform, compared to much of Western Europe. "Socialism" has been notably absent (Sombart 1976; Hartz 1955, chap. 1), and even gradual equity-enhancing reform has proceeded much less far than in many European countries. For example, the American "welfare state" has scored low among First World nations in population coverage and redistributive effect (Kudrle and Marmor 1987; Stephens 1986, 149–56; Esping-Andersen 1990, 69–77). The extension of health insurance to all citizens, which most of Europe achieved decades ago, was blocked again in 1993–1994; narrow business sectors have been in the forefront of the opposition. Because of the lack of equity-enhancing reform, large numbers of people in this tremendously rich country have remained poor.

Analysts have invoked many factors to account for this anomaly, including the ethnic and cultural heterogeneity of this nation of immigrants, the exit options provided for a long time by an open frontier, and the ruthless use of business power (overview in Shalev and Korpi 1980). While these peculiar factors militated against redistributive efforts, the United States has shared important obstacles with the other countries discussed in this study. Given the enormous socioeconomic and cultural differences between the United States, on the one hand, and Latin America and India, on the other, these similarities stem from political-institutional characteristics. U.S. politics shares some crucial organizational features with these countries.

Compared to many European nations, U.S. parties are more weakly organized and lack a programmatic orientation. In turn, they have not promoted mass mobilization and have failed to enable the poorer strata to counterbalance through their large numbers the resource advantages of small better-off groups (Verba, Nie, and Kim 1978, chap. 7; Schattschneider 1975, chap. 6). Clientelism played a critical role as a cause of party weakness in the age of party machines in northern cities and "old-boy" networks in the South. By keeping the working class divided, these personalist networks helped impede the emergence of a strong left-leaning party (Katznelson 1985, 274; Amenta and Skocpol 1989, 317–18).

As clientelism eroded with socioeconomic modernization and the gradual integration of many ethnic minorities into mainstream society, more space opened up for segmentalist associations.[31] Contrary to many Third World countries, segmentalism was not imposed by the state, which for a long time remained weak. The pronounced pluralism in the United States reflects the diversity of a society that—given its large resource base and protected international position—has not faced much pressure or incentive for broad-based collective action and national cohesion. The fragmentation and decentralization of the American state, which provided multiple points of access for narrow groups, strongly reinforced this fragmentation of society (Wilson 1982, 224–30). When state intervention grew with the New Deal and the Great Society, many segmentalist associations established direct links to state agencies. These connections hindered equity-enhancing reforms (McConnell 1966; Lowi 1979, chap. 6).

This "interest-group liberalism" has further eroded the internal unity of the American state, which had always been highly decentralized. The spoils system, which only a country protected from external threats could afford, impeded the formation of a cohesive public bureaucracy and gave personalist networks or segmentalist associations the opportunity to influence public appointments. Even when industrialization, urbanization, and growing international involvement created demands for more state action, this fragmented institutional structure hindered administrative reform and kept the state's capacity low (Skowronek 1982). State interventionism grew in the twentieth century, but party politicians and segmentalist interest groups, eager to preserve their influence, continued to undermine central command and control inside the state apparatus (Amenta and Skocpol 1989). The American state therefore remains the prototypical case of rampant bureaucratic politics. By allowing narrow groups to advance their interests effectively, persistent state fragmentation has prevented top-down reform and provided incentives for maintaining low organizational scope in society.

Thus, despite enormous economic, social, and cultural differences, political organizations in the United States have had low levels of organizational scope, like their counterparts in Third World democracies. This institutional fragmentation has posed severe obstacles to redistributive reform in all these nations. Integrated into personalist networks or segmentalist associations, the poorer strata have been divided and mostly unable to mobilize bottom-up pressure for equity-enhancing change. The state has had too little internal unity and administrative capacity to enact reforms on its own.

In contrast, many Western European polities are characterized by much less organizational fragmentation, and strong bottom-up pressure or top-down state initiatives have led to important equity-enhancing reforms. In order to enhance their control over society, early-modern states had already taken steps to combat poverty through paternalistic social measures, such as workhouses. Since European states had a high level of cohesion and administrative capacity, public officials and experts were the main initiators of welfare programs in the nineteenth and early twentieth centuries (Heclo 1974). But in the course of Europe's slow and uneven transition to mass democracy, bottom-up pressure from broad-based lower-class organizations became more important. Depending on the strength of the state, this pressure posed challenges to which state officials felt compelled to react, or it directly brought about redistributive efforts.[32]

Where the state was particularly strong, as in Germany and France (Birnbaum 1980), it tried to preempt formidable leftist mobilization of the emerging working class in the late nineteenth and early twentieth centuries. To mitigate discontent and guarantee sociopolitical stability, it conceded social benefits to a wide range of categories but preserved the existing status hierarchy. The state attempted to put different categories in their place, yet give all of them a stake in the system. Therefore, it established on its own initiative social security systems that were stratified, but—in contrast to the United States—provided even the poorest strata with considerable social protection (Esping-Andersen 1990, 58–61).

Where the state was not as dominant, as in Great Britain and Scandinavia, bottom-up pressure became the driving force behind equity-enhancing efforts. Demands from encompassing associations and ever broader based, well-organized parties led to considerable redistribution (Stephens 1986, chaps. 4–5; Esping-Andersen 1990, 65–77). Facing states that limited political participation (for example, by restricting suffrage), workers and other lower-class people in the late nineteenth century organized in broad fronts and pressed for full political and social citizenship.[33] These struggles gave rise to encompassing labor movements and powerful social democratic parties, which tried to attract lower- or middle-class allies in order to win power. After decades of gradually increasing their support base, these well-organized center-left forces assumed the government and enacted important equity-enhancing reforms, most notably in Scandinavia.

In many Western European countries having different levels of state strength, the formation of catch-all parties contributed to the enormous expansion of welfare states after World War II. Most parties had been based on categorical cleavages—for example, of class and religion (Lipset and Rokkan 1967). As socioeconomic modernization and the disruptions caused by two world wars eroded these gulfs, electoral competition induced more and more parties to widen their appeal to embrace the whole population (Kirchheimer 1964, 184–97; Panebianco 1988, chap. 14) and therefore to promote universalist reform. In much of Western Europe, rivaling catch-all parties promoted the extension of social security to all citizens and considerable improvements in benefits (Alber 1987, 170–78; Pierson 1992, 125–32).

In conclusion, the existence of unified states with high administrative capacity and the formation of encompassing trade unions and well-organized parties with ever wider appeal were essential for the success of equity-enhancing change in Western Europe. In this institutional context, democracy did bring about social reform. Bottom-up pressure and top-down initiatives often complemented each other. Despite significant variation in process and outcome, the impetus that democracy has given to redistribution in a setting of low organizational fragmentation has been common to most of Western Europe. This equity-enhancing dynamic has set the region apart from the United States, Latin America, and India.

These considerations of similarities and contrasts suggest that organizational fragmentation has posed enormous obstacles to redistribution in a wide range of democracies outside of Western Europe. Institutional structures shared by Latin America, India, and even the United States seem to be crucial in impeding equity-enhancing reform, whereas the widely varying economic, social, and cultural context factors are not decisive.

CONCLUSION

As the preceding discussion shows, the institutionalist argument of this book directly applies to many Latin American and other extra-European countries, and it sheds light on the contrast cases of Western Europe. These wide-ranging comparisons corroborate the claim that organizational patterns, interacting with socioeconomic structures, condition the chances for redistributive reform under democracy. The more personalism, segmentalism, and state fragmentation are entrenched, the less likely that reforms to advance the cause of social equity will be made. In contrast, where broad-based, organized and program-oriented parties prevail, where interest associations have an encompassing scope, and where the state is fairly united, there is a higher probability that the poor are favored through public policy outputs.

Given the strength of these organizational obstacles in many non-European countries, the installation of democracy often contributes little to overcoming social inequality. In these regions, the link between political liberty and social equity seems tenuous at best. The expectation that democracy leads to redistribution, based mainly on experiences in Western Europe, does not apply to other areas.

If democracy has done little in these countries to ease the plight of the poor, are there alternatives? The findings of chapter 4 and the experiences of other Latin American countries make abundantly clear that authoritarian rule does not have a better record.[34] While socialist Cuba may claim greater accomplishments in reducing social inequality, it paid an enormous price by sacrificing political liberty. Also, social revolutionaries triumphed in the Third World only when challenging colonialism or personalist dictators. Decolonization and the growth of coercive state power make new revolutions very unlikely (Skocpol 1979, 287–92). Thus, there is no easy escape from the disappointments of democracy.

The only hope for reducing inequality while maintaining liberty lies in patient long-term efforts to "deepen" democracy itself by gradually extending effective citizenship rights to the poor (Weffort 1992a, 194–202; O'Donnell and Schmitter 1986, 11–14; Frankel 1978, 579–82). Party competition may erode the predominance of patrons by giving clients alternative sources of benefits. This may slowly transform clientelism into a more democratic form of representation.[35] The strengthening of the electoral arena and of parliament under democracy may induce segmentalist associations to look beyond the narrow confines of their specific interests and enter into broader alliances. Finally, increasing public accountability of the government and the state may curtail the close connections that business sectors have maintained with public officials and agencies and could raise the state's unity and capacity for enacting reform. In the long run, these processes, which deliberate political action can reinforce, may open up greater opportunities for equity-enhancing change.

Given the self-perpetuating and mutually reinforcing tendencies of personalism, segmentalism, and state fragmentation, it will take a long time to defeat these obstacles to redistribution. In fact, poverty itself helps preserve these impediments. Poor people enter into clientelist networks in order to guarantee their survival. Facing the potential aspirations of a poor mass, privileged sectors are especially intent upon preserving their direct access to the state, which cements segmentalism and state fragmentation. These vicious circles are difficult to overcome.

For these reasons, anybody embarking on democratizing and equity-enhancing efforts cannot expect rapid progress. As change will be glacial, stubborn persistence is essential. Max Weber's characterization of politics as "strong, slow boring of hard boards" (1971, 560) provides the motto for democratic reformism in Brazil, and in Latin America more broadly.

APPENDIX

———

NOTES

———

BIBLIOGRAPHY

———

INDEX

APPENDIX:
SELECTED INTERVIEWS

Alckmin Filho, Geraldo, Deputado Federal (PSDB—São Paulo), Brasília, 6 March 1990 and 17 June 1992.

Araújo, Luiz Gonzaga de, Assessor Jurídico, CONTAG, Brasília, 28 October 1994.

Arouca, Sergio, Deputado Federal (PPS—Rio de Janeiro), Brasília, 23 June 1992.

Azevedo, Maria Emília Mello de, former Secretária-Geral Adjunta, MPAS (1987–1988), Brasília, 8 June 1989, and Assessora Técnica da Liderança do PSDB, Brasília, 13 July 1992 and 24 October 1994.

Barbosa, Fábio, Secretaria de Política Econômica, MEFP, Brasília, 13 July 1992.

Bastos, Murillo Villela, former Assessor Especial do Sub-Secretário de Estudos Especiais, MPAS (1974–1979), Rio de Janeiro, 20 and 27 January 1990.

Belaciano, Mourad Ibrahim, Assessor da CIPLAN, MPAS, Brasília, 23 June 1989.

Belluzzo, Luiz Gonzaga, former Secretário Especial de Assuntos Econômicos, MF (August 1985–April 1987), São Paulo, 7 November 1989.

Boeninger, Edgardo, Ministro Secretario General de la Presidencia, Santiago, 16 July 1993.

Bogéa, Mauro Sérgio, Coordenador-Geral de Estudos Econômico-Tributários, SRF, MF, Brasília, 26 October 1994.

Bornhausen, Roberto Konder, former president of FEBRABAN, São Paulo, 6 December 1989 and 9 June 1992.

Branco, José Mário Paranhos do Rio, Departamento Jurídico, FIESP, São Paulo, 20 December 1989.

Bresser Pereira, Luiz Carlos, former finance minister (April–December 1987), São Paulo, 21 September 1988 and 10 November 1989.

Britto, Antônio, Deputado Federal (PMDB—Rio Grande do Sul), Brasília, 28 March 1990 and 26 June 1992.

Butori, Paulo Roberto, Coordenador do PNBE and entrepreneur, São Paulo, 21 December 1989 and 12 June 1992.

Calabi, Andrea, former Secretário do Tesouro Nacional, MF (1986–1988), São Paulo, 8 November 1989.

Carvalho, Gilson de Cássia Marques de, Secretário de Assistência à Saúde, Ministério da Saúde, Brasília, 21 October 1994.

Carvalho Filho, Celecino de, Secretário de Estudos Especiais, MPAS, Brasília, 11 August 1987, 18 July and 26 September 1989, and Diretor de Previdência Social, MPS, Brasília, 22 June 1992.

Coelho, José Washington, Chefe do Departamento Econômico, CNC, Rio de Janeiro, 18 January 1990 and 14 May 1992.

Collor de Mello, Fernando, former president (March 1990–October 1992), Brasília, 9 June 1995.

Cordeiro, Hésio, former president of INAMPS (May 1985–March 1988), Rio de Janeiro, 18 October 1988 and 30 January 1990.

Corrêa, Oiram, Diretor da Divisão de Estudos Econômicos, Superintendência Técnica, Federação de Comércio do Estado de São Paulo (FCESP), São Paulo, 22 November 1989.

Corrêa Sobrinho, José Dias, former Assessor do Ministro, MPAS (1974–1979), Teresópolis, 7 February 1990.

Coutinho, Gerson Sá, former president of INAMPS (1978–1979), Rio de Janeiro, 5 February 1990.

Cunha, Paulo Guilherme Aguiar, Diretor-Presidente, IEDI, São Paulo, 11 June 1992.

Dain, Sulamis, former Secretária-Geral Adjunta, MPAS (1986–1987), Rio de Janeiro, 22 July 1987 and 5 February 1990.

Delfim Netto, Antônio, Deputado Federal (PDS—São Paulo), Brasília, 2 August 1989 and 24 June 1992.

Dellape, Francisco Ubiratán, president of FENAESS, São Paulo, 12 June 1992.

Dias Neto, João, former Técnico, SRF, Brasília, 19 April 1989.

Eris, Ibrahim, former president of Banco Central (March 1990–May 1991), São Paulo, 27 May 1992.

Farhat, Chafic, Secretário Geral, FENAESS, São Paulo, 14 December 1989.

Felipe, José Saraiva, former Secretário de Serviços Médicos, MPAS (1985–July 1988), Brasília, 23 June 1989.

Feliú Justiniano, Manuel, former president of Confederación de la Producción y del Comercio (1986–1990), Santiago, 19 July 1993.

Fernandes, José Augusto Coelho, Secretário Executivo, CNI, Rio de Janeiro, 13 May and 29 July 1992.

Ferreira, Carlos Eduardo, president of FBH, Brasília, 5 October 1989 and 2 July 1992.

Freire, José Carlos Soares, former Secretário-Geral, MF (1974–1979), Rio de Janeiro, 12 February 1990.

Gabriel, Almir, Senador Federal (PSDB—Pará), Brasília, 27 June 1989 and 17 June 1992.

Giffoni, Francisco de Paula C., former member of the Comissão de Reforma Tributária e Descentralização Administrativa, Brasília, 2 May 1989.

Hülse, José Rodolfo, Secretário Adjunto, SRF, Brasília, 13 April 1989.

Jatene, Adib Domingos, health minister, Brasília, 9 July 1992.

Jefferson, Roberto, Deputado Federal (PTB—Rio de Janeiro), Brasília, 27 June 1989.

Kandir, Antônio, former Secretário de Política Econômica (March 1990–May 1991), MEFP, São Paulo, 8 June 1992.

Kapaz, Emerson, Coordenador do PNBE, São Paulo, 19 December 1989.

Lagos, Ricardo, former president of Partido por la Democracia, Santiago, 26 July 1993.

Lefcovitz, Eduardo, Superintendente de Planejamento da Secretaria Estadual de Saúde, Rio de Janeiro, 29 January 1990, and Diretor de Acompanhamento do Sistema Único de Saúde (SUS), INAMPS, Brasília, 2 July 1992.

Levin, Jacques, DATASUS, Ministério da Saúde, Rio de Janeiro, 27 July 1992.

Lício, Antônio, Chefe do Departamento Econômico, CNA, Brasília, 14 September 1989.

Lima, Antônio Milão Rodrigues, former Secretário Adjunto, SRF (under President Geisel), Rio de Janeiro, 9 February 1990.

Longo, Carlos Alberto, tax expert and member of Comissão Executiva de Reforma Fiscal, MEFP, São Paulo, 8 June 1992.

Lopes Filho, Osiris de Azevedo, former Coordenador do Sistema de Fiscalização, SRF (1987), Brasília, 16 June 1989.

Luna, Francisco Vidal, former Assessor do Ministro-Chefe da SEPLAN (March 1985–March 1987), São Paulo, 17 November 1989.

Macedo, Roberto Bras Matos, Secretário de Política Econômica, MEFP, Brasília, 2 July 1992.

Maciel, Marco, former Ministro-Chefe do Gabinete Civil (1986–1987), Brasília, 6 July 1989.

Magalhães, Raphael de Almeida, former minister of MPAS (February 1986–October 1987), Rio de Janeiro, 20 October 1988.

Mansur, Mansur José, vice-president of FBH, Rio de Janeiro, 5 February 1990.

Marques, Maria Cassiana Costa, Chefe de Divisão de Concessão de Benefícios, INSS, MPS, Brasília, 24 October 1994.

Mattos Filho, Ary Oswaldo, head of Comissão Executiva de Reforma Fiscal, MEFP, Brasília, 1 July 1992.

Mazzoli, Márcia Bassit da Costa, Secretária-Geral Adjunta, MPAS, Brasília, 17 October 1989, and Secretária Nacional de Previdência Social, MPS, Brasília, 6 July 1992.

Medeiros, Luiz Antônio de, president of Força Sindical, São Paulo, 5 June 1992.

Mesquita Neto, Antônio Augusto de, former Secretário da Receita Federal (May 1987–January 1988) and Coordenador do Sistema de Tributação, SRF (under President Geisel), São Paulo, 29 September 1988 and 9 November 1989.

Miranda Souza, Raimundo José, former Secretário-Geral Adjunto, MPAS (March 1985–February 1986), Brasília, 30 August 1989.

Moraes, Marcelo Viana Estevão de, Diretor do Departamento Nacional de Relações de Trabalho, Ministério do Trabalho, Brasília, 7 July 1992, and Secretário de Previdência Social, MPS, Brasília, 19 October 1994.

Moreira, Marcílio Marques, former minister of the economy, finance, and planning (May 1991–October 1992), Brasília, 9 July 1992, and Rio de Janeiro, 7 July 1995.

Mulin, Márcia, Assessora do Secretário Municipal de Saúde, São Paulo, 12 December 1989.

Nakano, Yoshiaki, former Secretário Especial de Assuntos Econômicos, MF (May 1987–December 1987), São Paulo, 28 November 1989.

Nascimento e Silva, Luiz Gonzaga do, former minister of MPAS (1974–1979), Rio de Janeiro, 17 January 1990.

Oliveira, Adilson Gomes de, former Secretário da Receita Federal (1974–1979), Rio de Janeiro, 6 February 1990.

Oliveira, Francisco Luiz Torres de, former Sub-Secretário de Estudos Especiais, MPAS (1974–1979), Rio de Janeiro, 31 January 1990.

Oliveira, Moacyr Velloso C. de, former Secretário de Previdência Social, MPAS (1983–1988), Rio de Janeiro, 12 February 1990.

Patury, Luiz Romero, former Secretário da Receita Federal (March 1985–April 1986), Brasília, 14 April 1989.

Piola, Sérgio, former administrator of PIASS under President Geisel, Brasília, 26 June 1989.

Pires, Waldir, former minister of MPAS (March 1985–February 1986), Brasília, 23 August 1989.

Ramos, Paulo, Coordenação do Sistema de Arrecadação, SRF, Brasília, 3 May 1989.

Rebouças, Osmundo, Deputado Federal (PMDB—Ceará), Brasília, 4 May 1989.

Rêgo, Reynaldo Jorge Pereira, Secretário Adjunto, SRF, Brasília, 10 August 1989.

Reis, José Guilherme Almeida dos, Sub-Chefe do Departamento Econômico, CNI, Rio de Janeiro, 31 October 1994.

Rezende da Silva, Fernando, former Secretário Executivo da Comissão de Reforma Tributária e Descentralização Administrativa (1986–1987), Rio de Janeiro, 19 October 1988.

Rodrigues, Jorge Victor, Secretário Adjunto, SRF, Brasília, 5 June 1989.

Rosa, José Rui Gonçalves, former Técnico and Assessor do Secretário Adjunto, SRF (during the Geisel government), Brasília, 18 April and 11 October 1989.

Rosar, Soraya Saavedra, Assessora do Presidente da Associação do Comércio Exterior do Brasil, Rio de Janeiro, 26 January 1990.

Rossi, José Arnaldo, former president of INSS (1990–1992), Rio de Janeiro, 30 July 1992.

Sá, Orlando Maranhão Gomes de, Diretor de Controle e Avaliação, INAMPS, Brasília, 31 July and 20 September 1989.

Salaro, Romeu, Secretário Adjunto, SRF, Brasília, 24 April 1989.

Sanfim, Clemilce, Diretora de Administração e Finanças, INAMPS, Brasília, 16 June 1992.

Scalco, Euclides, Deputado Federal (PSDB—Paraná), Brasília, 15 May 1989.

Schöntag, José Antônio, Coordenação do Sistema de Informações Econômico-Fiscais, SRF, Rio de Janeiro, 15 January 1990.

Silva, Eivany Antônio da, Secretário-Substituto da SRF, Brasília, 18 September 1989.

Silva, Joana Maria Braga da, Departamento de Promoção Humana, Ministério do Bem-Estar Social, Brasília, 23 June 1992 and 20 October 1994.

Silva, José Francisco da, former president of CONTAG (1968–1989), Brasília, 21 March 1990.

Silva, Pedro Luiz Barros, Assessor do Secretário de Planejamento, INAMPS, Rio de Janeiro, 2 September 1987.

Simonsen, Mário Henrique, former finance minister (1974–1979), Rio de Janeiro, 21 October 1988.

Solimeo, Marcel Domingos, Diretor do Instituto de Economia Gastão Vidigal, Associação Comercial de São Paulo, São Paulo, 30 November 1989 and 29 May 1992.

Stephanes, Reinhold, former president of INPS (1974–1978), São Paulo, 23 November 1989, and minister of MPS, Brasília, 29 June 1992.

Szajman, Abraham, president of Federação de Comércio do Estado de São Paulo (FCESP), São Paulo, 2 June 1992.

Teixeira, Aloísio, former Secretário-Geral, MPAS (October 1987–July 1988), Rio de Janeiro, 19 February 1990.

Temporal, Amaury, former president of Confederação das Associações Comerciais do Brasil, Rio de Janeiro, 6 February 1990 and 20 July 1992.

Urbano Filho, Francisco, president of CONTAG, Brasília, 29 June 1992.

Vasconcelos, Maurício, Chefe da Assessoria Econômica, Gabinete Civil, Brasília, 3 October 1989.

Velloso, João Paulo dos Reis, former Ministro-Chefe da SEPLAN, (1974–1979), Rio de Janeiro, 15 February 1990.

Velloso, Luiz Assumpção Paranhos, former Secretário-Geral, MPAS (1974–1979), Rio de Janeiro, 24 January 1990.

Viegas, Luiz, COBAP, Rio de Janeiro, 27 February 1990 and 15 May 1992.

Wellisch, Luiz Fernando Gusmão, Diretor do Departamento da Receita Federal, MEFP, Brasília, 24 June 1992.

Werneck, Dorothéa, Secretária Nacional de Economia, MEFP, Brasília, 6 July 1992.

Zockun, Maria Helena, Departamento Econômico, FIESP, São Paulo, 9 June 1992.

NOTES

Chapter 1. Introduction

1. John Stuart Mill, for example, advocated graduated voting rights (1975, 282–90).

2. See among many examples Lipset 1981, chaps. 7–8; Lenski 1966, 83–84; 428–30; Huntington and Nelson 1976, 23–24, 72–78 (on more advanced developing countries, such as Brazil); Kohli et al. 1984, 305–08; Oszlak 1984; Przeworski 1985, 35–38.

3. Jackman 1975, 79–89; Weede and Tiefenbach 1981; Bollen and Jackman 1985. One reason for the divergence may be that the above-mentioned theorists focus mainly on political processes and policy *outputs*, whereas the statistical analyses use data on a policy *outcome*, namely societal income distribution.

4. On taxation, social insurance, and health care, see chaps. 5–7 in this book; on land reform, see "Reforma agrária do governo não chega a 10 percent da meta," *Jornal do Brasil*, 19 February 1990, 3; on public housing, M.O. Silva 1989, chaps. 3–4; on income distribution, IBGE 1990, 75.

5. The expectation that the Brazilian military would retain tutelage over the new democracy (Stepan 1988) has not come true, as Hunter's thorough investigation (1992) shows.

6. These arguments owe much to Malloy (1979). O'Donnell's recent work (1988, 1993) advances similar ideas, yet over-emphasizes the impact of Brazil's economic crisis; see also Hagopian (1990) on the political impact of clientelism.

7. According to Weber (1973, 263–84 (political) science cannot determine ultimate value choices, but it can arrive at conditional imperatives by taking an ultimate value as given and using scholarly knowledge to derive specific strategies from it.

8. Sixty-three percent of the 450 members of Brazil's sociopolitical elite whom Lamounier and Souza (1990, 8) interviewed considered as highly likely a "chronic state of social convulsion," resulting from the country's deep socioeconomic inequalities.

9. Tocqueville argued that reform may promote revolution because it is based on criticism of the status quo and in this way delegitimates the established system (1955, 180–92).

10. See especially Mainwaring 1988; Eckstein 1989; Alvarez 1990; Keck 1992; Foweraker and Craig 1990.

11. Rare exceptions are Malloy 1987; Reis 1988; O'Donnell 1993.

12. I follow especially Evans et al. 1985; March and Olsen 1984; Stepan 1978; Skocpol 1979; Badie and Birnbaum 1983; Krasner 1984; Grafstein 1992; Thelen and Steinmo 1992. See already Weber 1976; Hintze 1981; Heller 1983.

13. This definition is inspired especially by Schmitter and Karl (1991, 76–82).

14. The presidency is quite important in Brazilian politics, but its influence has diminished considerably with democratization, which has empowered parliament, law courts, state and municipal governments, public opinion, interest associations, and so on.

15. Since then, however, most parliamentarians have used their budgetary prerogatives not for influencing substantive policy decisions but simply for channeling particularistic benefits ("pork") to their voters (Ames and Nixon 1993, 18–19).

16. This definition includes the provision of public services, such as medical care. By defining redistribution as change in the *relative* shares of societal categories in national wealth, this book applies a broader concept than other authors. Fagen (1978, 185), for example, restricts the notion to reforms that take away from the rich in absolute terms. This ties the concept by definition to one of several criteria for measuring (in)equality (compare Rae and Fessler 1981, 205–18). The broader concept used here follows the strategy for making the different criteria congruent. They all converge if "redistribution" is defined in terms of relative shares; conceptual complications are avoided. Based on this broad definition, I use interchangeably the terms *redistributive* and *equity-enhancing*, which authors like Fagen distinguish.

17. The term *(social) category* is used broadly as any number of people delimited by a common characteristic (including common interests). Such categories include social classes and groups, but also the vegetarians and the brown-eyed people. *Stratum*, applied below, is a category defined in socioeconomic terms, that is, by its position in the production process (social class and sector) or in the sphere of consumption (status group).

18. Organization members usually retain considerable personal independence and self-interest orientation. Therefore, it is leaders' decisive task to make individual behavior compatible with organizational goals (see recently Miller 1993).

19. Of course, individuals are usually better integrated than institutions; therefore, it makes particular sense to impute interests to them.

20. Weber 1976, 29. The basic interests of the state derive directly from this institutional definition, namely external defense, domestic stability, and, as a means, financial capacity. For the identification of state interests beyond these core goals, see Krasner (1978, chap. 2).

21. The political-institutional definition of the state encompasses the different "branches of government." In addition to this broad concept of the state as the repository of public authority, there is the more narrow notion of the state apparatus. This core of the state encompasses the administrative hierarchy of the executive branch. Using this narrow notion, the book refers to the state apparatus as "the state."

22. For the distinction between needs and interests and the process of interest formation, see Schmitter (1981, 20–47); Easton (1979, 70–84); Dahl (1971, 95).

23. In light of the plethora of unfulfilled needs stemming from extreme poverty and inequality in a stagnating economy, the very fact that there is not even more expression of redistributive interests in Brazil cannot be taken as given, but requires explanation. See the general theoretical discussions in Bachrach and Baratz (1970, chaps. 1, 3) and Frey (1971) and the application of these ideas to Brazil in Cohen (1989, chap. 4).

24. Contrary to its narrow meaning in the United States, this book uses *social security* as an overarching term covering old-age, disability, and survivors' pensions (called *previdência* in Brazil, that is, social insurance), health care, and social welfare.

25. This is especially true where the rule of law is precarious, as in Brazil. A well-informed public official told me confidentially that the Sarney government deliberately publicized a case of alleged tax evasion in order to silence an outspoken business critic.

26. This calculation already prevailed in ancient Rome (Meier 1980, 128–44).

27. For a classification of issue areas along these lines, see Wilson (1980, 366–72).

28. From 1990 to 1992, the MF was united with the ministries of planning and of industry and commerce as the *Ministério da Economia, Fazenda e Planejamento* (MEFP).

29. From 1990 to 1992, the MPAS was united with the labor ministry as *Ministério do Trabalho e da Previdência Social* (MTPS). In early 1992, President Collor divided the MTPS and created the *Ministério da Previdência Social* (MPS), which regained its responsibilities for social welfare in early 1995 and was therefore named MPAS again. The term *previdência* is difficult to translate. Neither one of the terms Malloy (1979) uses (*social security* and *insurance)* is perfect. *Social security* is used in Brazil as a broad term encompassing *previdência*, health care, and welfare. *Insurance* omits the paternalistic connotation of *previdência* as the provision of social benefits by a benevolent state, but in its denotation, it is the most adequate term available.

Chapter 2. Explaining the Dearth of Redistribution Under Democracy

1. Scholars of different theoretical persuasion have advanced this claim, esp. Lipset 1981, chaps. 7–8; Lenski 1966, 83–84, 428–30; Huntington and Nelson 1976, 23–24, 72–78; Offe 1984, 103–04, 121, 195; Przeworski 1985, 35–38, 140–56; Oszlak 1984, 15, 23.

2. Stephens (1986, chaps. 4–5) and Przeworski (1985, chap. 1) explain in this way the emergence of social democracy in Europe.

3. For a general discussion of a democratic order based on interest associations, see Streeck and Schmitter (1985).

4. For an interesting model of participatory democracy, which accepts the importance of representative institutions but proposes to complement them with direct-democratic mechanisms, see Barber (1984).

5. On the basic logic, see Downs (1957, 198–204). Geddes (1994, 36) uses this argument to analyze Latin American land reforms. From a different theoretical perspective, Lipset depicts elections as "the expression of the democratic class struggle" (1981, chaps. 7–8).

6. Focusing on Europe and the United States, Leibholz (1974, 78–131) argues that parties have become the central agents in modern democracy and that this has furthered the advance of social rights.

7. Elements of this top-down mechanism are outlined in Kohli et al. (1984, 303–04); Chenery (1974, 69–71); Skocpol (1985, 11–15).

8. For examples of social reforms initiated by principle-driven state officials, see Heclo (1974, 301–22); Malloy (1979, chap. 4; 1993); on the tendency of state officials to advance universalist goals that differ from elite interests, see also Rueschemeyer and Evans (1985, 47, 53, 61).

9. Lichbach's (1990) claim that it is irrational for people to "rebel against inequality" is based on a flawed premise. The author neglects that poorer people may intend and

expect a reallocation of resources to improve their own situation (1074, note 9); in this case, "rebellion against inequality" is rational. Chong (1991) provides an interesting rational-choice account of a nonviolent "rebellion against inequality," the U.S. civil-rights movement (but he draws heavily on social incentives, reputational concerns, and expressive benefits [chaps. 3–4] that "soften" strict rational-choice principles).

10. From a class-theoretical perspective, Offe and Wiesenthal (1985) reinforce this argument by claiming that business, the most important elite in modern societies, does not even need collective action as much as workers (and other underprivileged strata). Whereas workers have to rely on collective action for defining and advancing their common interests, business has clear interests and can advance them in ways other than collective action, for example, by individual disinvestment. Doubly privileged by having a higher capacity and a lower need for collective action, business can squelch equity-enhancing efforts. For an incisive critique of these arguments, see Streeck (1992).

11. Thus, Olson (1982, chaps. 3–4) convincingly explains the impact of distributional coalitions, but not their emergence, and Bates accounts for the activities of state agencies but not for their formation (1981, 12–13, 122).

12. Shepsle 1986; North 1981, chaps. 2–4; Geddes 1994, chaps. 4–5. For a critical discussion of this argument, as applied to Brazil's new democracy, see Mainwaring 1994. Rational-choice theorists who depict institutions as efficient solutions to coordination problems (Williamson 1985; review in Moe 1984) come close to functionalist arguments that violate the individualistic premises of rational choice (Granovetter 1985, 503, 505).

13. Many rational-choice predictions are indeterminate because their antecedent conditions are hard to ascertain. For example, it is difficult to assess whether actors had sufficient interest in a collective good to provide it on their own, even without any contribution from others—a possibility stressed by Olson (1971, 34–35). Obviously, if interests are inferred from actions themselves, rational-choice explanations turn tautological.

14. This line of argument is outlined in general terms, for example, in Arrighi (1990, 26–35). While focusing on the military regime, Evans (1979, 287–88) advanced an especially sophisticated version.

15. If the income brackets set by the government are not fully readjusted for inflation, nominal income increases put many taxpayers into higher tax brackets and make them subject to higher rates of the progressive income tax.

16. Although these increases in spending did not benefit the poor and effect progressive redistribution (chapters 6 and 7), they contradicted dependency expectations by exacerbating fiscal problems, disregarding the IMF's insistence on austerity, and countering business interests.

17. Cacciamali 1991, 138–41; Portes and Schauffler 1993, 45, 51, 53; see also Infante and Klein 1991, 132–34. I use *marginal* as a synonym of *informal* mainly for stylistic reasons. Despite strong criticism of its dualistic implications (Perlman 1976), *marginal* is widely applied in Latin American social science (for example, Tironi 1990; Weffort 1992b, 22–26).

18. This term, applied by O'Donnell (1979), comprises the urban and rural working class in the formal sector of the economy and the urban marginals and the rural poor in the informal sector.

19. For a comparison of Latin America and the United States, see Portes (1985, 28–30).

20. In their analysis of Latin American social security policy, Rosenberg and Malloy (1978, 159–63) point to such self-interested behavior by trade unions.

21. See the critical discussion in Stepan (1978, chap. 1); Skocpol (1985, 5–6).

22. "In the Brazilian case, . . . there is ample evidence that the decentralization [that is, fragmentation] constituted a deliberate means [of Getúlio Vargas' government (1930–1945)] to dilute the clout both of business and labor and to facilitate the imposition of state tutelage" (Almeida 1994, 7–8; my translation).

23. Rueschemeyer and Evans (1985, 53–55) argue convincingly that the state's "effective bureaucratic organization . . . required for intervention [is] perhaps nowhere more put to the test than in attempts at income redistribution."

24. For the impact of institutional structures on the use of power capabilities, see in general March and Olsen (1989, 13–14).

25. Does the fragmentation of the elite, the likely opponent of equity-enhancing change, not favor reform, rather than impede it, as the main argument of my institutionalist explanation implies? Do divisions inside the elite not make it possible to play different factions off against each other and thus engineer redistribution through "reform-mongering" (Hirschman 1973)?

Equity-enhancing reform is, indeed, easier if the elite is not completely united but split into few segments, as in Argentina in the 1940s. Competing against each other, such elite segments vie for lower-class support and make redistributive concessions in return. But this strategy is worth the price only for broad, cohesive elite segments. If the elite is fragmented into numerous small factions, none of them may be willing to incur the necessary cost of redistribution. None of them has an interest in caring for overarching goals that may require equity-enhancing reforms, such as development of the internal market, or systemic legitimacy. Knowing that their own actions have little impact on such overarching concerns, that is, facing a collective-action problem, they concentrate on gaining special benefits for themselves. If such small factions seek allies among the popular sectors, they prefer to co-opt only a narrow sector, such as workers in their own firms, and pass on the cost of any concessions to society at large. This burden shift hurts the poor, who have low power and are least able to defend their interests.

Medium to high levels of elite fragmentation thus tend to increase social inequality and do not favor redistribution but make it more difficult. The central argument of my institutionalist explanation applies to the elite with only one exception: complete elite unity may impede equity-enhancing reform. But the complex cleavages of modern societies make this case rare.

26. Focusing on constitutional structures in Europe, Immergut (1990) and Tsebelis (1994) advance similar arguments.

27. This distinction is inspired by Badie 1992; Migdal 1988; Nunes 1984; O'Donnell 1988, 1993; Olson 1982, 1986; Santos 1987.

28. For example, where the rule of law is guaranteed, the police ticket only those drivers who exceed the speed limit. But they are not allowed to overlook traffic violations committed by their personal friends or by other public employees.

29. Obviously, this notion of the universalist state is an ideal-type that is never fully realized. But it is useful as a reference point for highlighting the characteristics of

existing states and for assessing differences among them. Thus, the French state approximates the universalist ideal-type much more (Badie and Birnbaum 1983, chap. 7; Suleiman 1974) than the Brazilian state with its welter of independent agencies, weak central control, and rampant bureaucratic politics.

30. As an interesting example, a Brazilian senator from the socialist Workers' Party has propagated a minimal-income guarantee scheme (Suplicy 1992) that is similar to Friedman's project of a negative income tax (1962, 191–94).

31. Landé 1977, xxix; Scott 1977, 125–26, 137; Silverman 1977, 299. In urban areas, clientelism is less encompassing and monolithic, and individuals can belong to different clientelist networks in their workplace and their residential site.

32. See Jaguaribe (1989) and Goñi (1990) for important other reasons.

33. For competing explanations for the striking differences among European countries, see Stephens 1986, 40–46; Wallerstein 1989.

34. In Latin America, working-class pressure was also less important for the establishment of democracy than in Europe (Rueschemeyer, Stephens and Stephens 1992, 182–86), where long struggles for political citizenship often induced the labor movement to form a broad front and even extend its appeal to other strata, thus laying the basis for encompassing organization (for example, Pontusson 1988, 43–44; Katznelson 1985, 272–78).

35. By stressing the role of states, this explanation differs from dependency theory, which points to external *economic* forces.

36. See esp. Purcell and Purcell (1977, 203–20) on Mexico.

37. Many members of other social strata are also integrated in clientelist networks. But, in addition, they use other forms of organization and interest representation (such as segmentalist associations) that allow and induce them to engage in broader-based collective action. This counterbalances the fragmenting effect of clientelism, to which most marginals are fully subject because they cannot rely on alternative patterns of organization.

38. Dix 1989; Chalmers 1977a, 411–13. Even Archer's challenge to this claim admits that most Latin American parties are weak as organizational structures and as vehicles for societal interest representation (1991, 9, 14–16). For the following, see McDonald and Ruhl 1989, 7–9, 341–44; Mols 1985, 124–42.

39. These characteristics are especially pronounced in Brazil (Mainwaring 1992–93). They are not as extreme in other Latin American countries but clearly present (except for Chile and, until recently, Venezuela). See especially Chalmers 1977a; Kaufman 1977; Archer 1991.

40. Clientelism has increasingly depended on state resources (Scott 1977, 140; Silverman 1977, 294, 298–303; for Brazil, see Hagopian 1986, chap. 5).

41. See the case of Chile under President Frei (Ascher 1984, chap. 7) and the beginning of President Collor's term in Brazil (chapter 5).

Chapter 3. Organizational Fragmentation in Brazil

1. Since many organizational features have persisted, I often use the present perfect tense.

2. Hirschman's (1971) concept focuses on import-substitution industrialization. East Asian countries, in contrast, soon switched from this model to export-led development (Gereffi and Wyman 1990).

3. In 1988, only 17.3 percent of rural laborers had official labor registration (IBGE 1990, 45).

4. Schmitter 1974, 115–25; Erickson 1977. This fragmented variant of corporatism differed greatly from the encompassing societal corporatism prevailing in social-democratic Europe.

5. One important cleavage has *not* led to associational divisions, namely the aversion that many Brazilian businesspeople harbor against the numerous transnational corporations (TNCs) operating in the country (Domínguez 1982, 53–58). TNCs have been fully integrated into the system of business associations. Together with domestic firms, they have advanced their interests through corporatist associations, autonomous organizations, and personal links. TNC-specific associations, such as the American Chamber of Commerce, have acted on issues that concern only TNCs.

6. Therefore, affiliation to interest associations differs strikingly from membership in political parties, the main conduits of clientelism in Brazil. While affiliation to interest associations increases strongly and steadily with income level (from 5.9 percent of the poorest stratum to 37.6 percent of the richest), membership in parties is highest among the second and third poorest stratum (19.3 percent) and then gradually diminishes with rising income level (10.4 percent among the richest) (Santos 1992, 65, 74).

7. See Diniz and Boschi (1987, 80–101) on price controls, and Cordeiro (1991, 77) on combat of fraud in public health care.

8. Schneider (1987, 43–44); Bank of Boston (1990, 3) mentions "an estimated 500 central government offices / agencies" and "at least 488 federal state enterprises."

9. "O Estado burocrático," *Gazeta Mercantil,* 6 January 1989, 3.

10. Lima and Abranches 1987. In stressing bureaucratic politics, I diverge from Schneider (1991b, chap. 2). Invoking the high mobility of "elite bureaucrats" among state agencies, Schneider claims that top officials do not identify with any agency's organizational interest. He therefore rejects a bureaucratic politics interpretation (32–35). I doubt that this claim has general validity. Schneider focuses on public enterprises executing economic development projects, that is, entrepreneurial agencies of the state (257), where one would expect Weberian principles of bureaucratic careers to be exceptionally weak. At least in the sectors of the direct administration I studied, many bureaucrats in important (though not top) positions stay in their agency for many years. These long-term officials elaborate many of the projects their agency pursues. Even highly mobile top officials often rely on these projects, precisely because their short tenure and lack of prior experience keeps them from elaborating their own proposals. In this way, they advance the organizational interests of the established bureaucratic apparatus. Even in the sectors he analyzed, Schneider's focus on "elite bureaucrats" may simply have overlooked this underlying stability and continuity.

Indeed, my research found several instances of new officials quickly adopting the organizational interests of the agencies to which they were appointed. For example, experts who demanded a transfer of INAMPS from the purview of the MPAS to the MS in early 1985 reversed their position a few weeks later, after assuming posts in MPAS or INAMPS; an MPS official who bargained hard in the early 1990s to increase the MPS' share of the "social budget" at the expense of the MS came to criticize the MPS' strong-armed tactics after accepting a post in INAMPS, now subordinated to the MS. Thus, at least in the state agencies I studied, bureaucratic politics clearly was at work.

11. Diniz and Boschi (1988, 18) even claim that the corporatist structure has been "revitalized" in the 1980s.

12. CNA, CNC, and CNI kept their presidents for more than ten years during the transition to democracy. After a rare revolt against a long-term leader in 1980, FIESP agreed on a six-year limit for its president. But this did not break continuity. Mário Amato was a vice-president of FIESP from the mid-1970s until 1986 when he became president; in 1992, his first vice-president was elected his successor.

13. See "Chapa única é característica de eleição empresarial," *Jornal do Brasil*, 2 July 1989, 31; *Istoé Senhor*, 23 August 1989, 45. On the conflicts inside FIESP, see PNBE 1989, 12–18; *Isto É*, 5 August 1992, 60–63; interviews Kapaz 1989, Butori 1992. On the corporatist mechanisms for perpetuating the existing leadership, see Schmitter 1971, 232–33; interview Butori 1989.

14. Confidential author interview with a FIESP official, 1989.

15. See, for example, "Banco Mundial revela que BNDES favorece 'panelinha,'" *Jornal do Brasil*, 2 January 1990, 13; *Istoé Senhor*, 10 January 1990, 37.

16. The name of this movement in literal translation is "National Thinking of the Entrepreneurial Bases."

17. PNBE 1989; "Uma geração pede passagem," *Folha de São Paulo, Caderno d'*, 5 November 1989, 22–29; interview Kapaz 1989; on political activism among other small businesspeople, see Nylen (1990).

18. Viola 1987, 8, 36–38; Alvarez 1990, 26, 138, 231. Feminine movements, how-ever, which make gender-related demands, but without a strong ideological orientation, have found considerable support among poor women (Alvarez 1990, chaps. 4–5).

19. The Collor government tried to eliminate this linchpin of corporatism, but ran into strong opposition in Congress and among established confederations of workers and businesspeople. Even if it had succeeded, the "voluntary" contributions that the constitution permits unions to institute would have provided a substitute. The rules for creating such contributions give associational leaders ample latitude for manipulation and members little chance to escape from this levy (interview Moraes 1992; Gomes and D'Araújo 1993, 334–37, 341–46).

20. During the abortive constitutional revision of late 1993 and early 1994, a num-ber of parliamentarians proposed to abolish these remnants of state corporatism (CN. *Parecer Nº 50)* but without success. The frontal opposition of many trade unions to any constitutional revision and their defense of corporatist features contributed to this failure. However, several of the corporatist restrictions on associational competition have been enforced less and less in recent years.

21. Almeida 1988, 352–62. According to rumors, behind closed doors even more radical labor leaders supported certain corporatist features, like the obligatory union dues. Voluntarist organization can severely weaken the labor movement, especially in more backward areas and sectors (Schmitter 1992, 432–33). Business associations also pressed for the preservation of corporatist features out of fear of increasing union militancy (Diniz and Boschi 1989, 129–33).

22. Compare CUT 1986, 15–16, 45–57 with CGT 1986, 5–6; see "Medida já divide

os sindicalistas," *Jornal do Brasil,* 26 March 1989, 30; confidential author interviews with officials from trade unions and the Ministry of Labor, 1989 and 1992.

23. See CUT 1991, 29–32. In fact, there have been important divisions inside CUT, the strongest peak association ("CUT expõe suas divergências," *Gazeta Mercantil,* 16 August 1989, 7; *Istoé Senhor,* 26 September 1990, 20–23).

24. Interview Viegas 1992. In 1991, 65 percent of the organizations participating in COBAP's national meeting came from three of the most highly developed of Brazil's 27 states, and most of the delegates came from better-off sectors (COBAP 1991, 11, 15–24).

25. For the hold of clientelism even on urban marginals, see Mainwaring 1987, 146–47, 151–53; Gay 1988, chaps. 4, 8; "Clientelismo agrava crise," *Jornal do Brasil, Cidade,* 12 November 1988, 6; "Clientelismo garante eleição," *Jornal do Brasil,* 9 July 1989, 4.

26. Associational affiliation among the poor has remained low, reaching 5.9 percent of those earning up to one-half the minimum wage in 1988 and 8.7 percent of the next-higher income level (up to one minimum wage), compared to 37.6 percent among the richest, who earn more than ten times the minimum wage (Santos 1992, 65).

27. In 1979, the military government abolished the artificial two-party system in order to split the MDB. Several new parties emerged, especially the Democratic Labor Party (Partido Democrático Trabalhista—PDT), the Workers' Party (Partido dos Trabalhadores—PT), and, in 1988, the Party of Brazilian Social Democracy (Partido da Social Democracia Brasileira—PSDB). The second government party after 1985, the Party of the Liberal Front (Partido da Frente Liberal—PFL), broke in 1984 away from the ARENA-successor, the Democratic-Social Party (Partido Democrático Social—PDS), now called the Progressive Reform Party (Partido Progressista Reformador—PPR).

28. "Pires dá ao PMDB segundo escalão da Previdência," *Globo,* 17 May 1985, 6; *Senhor,* 25 February 1986, 30–32; "Previdência dá emprego por computador a políticos," *Jornal do Brasil,* 28 June 1987, 5; "PFL cobra sua cota nos cargos que Raphael entrega ao PMDB," *Jornal do Brasil,* 10 September 1987, 4.

29. Many decisions to run in elections were based on individual considerations and not part of a coordinated effort by business to increase its influence. In fact, important business associations dislike the deep involvement of entrepreneurs in party politics. FIESP, for example, sharply criticized the double role of the CNI president, who was also an active congressman ("Fiesp sugere a Albano que renuncie," *Estado de São Paulo,* 13 November 1987, 5; interview Branco 1989).

30. See, for example, "Embaixador é o contato com empresários," *Jornal do Brasil,* 27 January 1990, A-8; *Istoé Senhor,* 11 April 1990, 31; interview Temporal 1992.

31. "Políticos tradicionais voltam ao Congresso," *Jornal do Brasil,* 16 October 1994, 3.

32. Budget unification was induced not only by democratization but even more so by the fiscal and debt crisis and insistent IMF demands that the Brazilian state control its public deficit. On this gradual reform, see Teixeira 1986, 67–70; Serra 1989; "Ministro da Fazenda perde velhos poderes," *Correio Braziliense,* 20 August 1989, 7.

33. See, for example, Varsano 1988, 9; "Pacote já está capenga," *Jornal do Brasil, Economia,* 12 December 1988, 1.

34. Confidential author interviews with many public officials, Brasília, April–October 1989, March 1990, June–July 1992, October 1994.

35. For example, top positions in the MPAS, which had been commanded by technocrats under the Geisel government, have been filled by patronage appointments

since then (Faleiros 1986, 137). Similarly, new political appointees undermined recruitment procedures in the state development bank (Schneider 1991, 36–37).

36. In 1985, a broad alliance of political forces took power, distributed the spoils of office among their regional groupings, and gave top state posts even to leftist parties (confidential author interviews with numerous politicians and state officials; "Políticos correm atrás dos cargos da Previdência," *Folha de São Paulo,* 17 April 1985, 7; "Uma crise maior que a de 1985," *Estado de São Paulo,* 29 June 1986; "Instituto pode passar ao Ministério da Saúde," *Folha de São Paulo,* 9 March 1988, 12).

37. See for an example "Estados vão a Ulysses e unem-se contra o orçamento da União," *Gazeta Mercantil,* 14 October 1988, 5; "Governo desarticulado sofreu derrota no Congresso," *Jornal do Brasil,* 11 December 1988, 5.

38. Confidential author interviews in the *Secretaria de Administração Federal,* Brasília, July 1992.

39. Boccanera 1981. Often, the president, not the minister, selected the heads of these para-state agencies. The minister therefore had little control over them. See, for example, "Raphael já reclama do fisiologismo político," *Jornal do Brasil,* 23 May 1987, 4; "Sarney demite Cordeiro do Inamps e Archer aceita," *Jornal do Brasil,* 8 March 1988, 4.

40. This is obvious in budget decisions ("Pressões deformam orçamento," *Jornal do Brasil,* 17 December 1989, 38; Hunter 1992, chap. 5). Since President Collor's austerity policy reduced salaries in the bureaucracy, many *técnicos* tried to leave the executive branch for higher-paying jobs as legislative aides (confidential author interviews with several state officials, Brasília, July 1992). This movement reduced the executive's advantage in technical knowledge.

Chapter 4. Redistributive Policy Making Under Authoritarian Rule

1. Focusing on the last fully authoritarian government minimizes problems of documentation. Written material becomes ever more deficient and the memories of interview partners turn ever less reliable the more the researcher goes back in time.

2. As several of the former SRF officials among my interview partners claimed confidentially, the middle-class background of most SRF officials intensified this resentment.

3. Before taking office, Simonsen had been vice-president of a private investment bank.

4. Many SRF officials remained in "their" agency for a long time and therefore identified their own career goals with the SRF's organizational interests (interviews Dias 1989; Rosa 1989). This differs from Schneider's findings (1991b, 26–35).

5. Tax exemptions and deductions and the strictness of tax enforcement are also important, but for reasons of simplicity, they are not discussed here.

6. Since nominal incomes rose faster than the income brackets to which the progressive tax rates applied, many people slid into higher tax brackets and had to pay more tax, although their real income had not changed.

7. Interviews A. Oliveira 1990, Hülse 1989; "Novo sistema reduzirá burocracia," *Gazeta Mercantil,* 5 June 1974; "I. de Renda pode alterar regime de abatimentos," *Globo,* 14 July 1974, 25.

8. "A nova lei do imposto de renda," *Estado de São Paulo,* 27 November 1977. For MF

consultation with business, interviews Coelho 1990, Freire 1990, Lima 1990, A. Oliveira 1990, Solimeo 1989. For examples of suggestions, see Arthur Andersen 1977.

9. Interviews A. Oliveira 1990, Mesquita 1989, Rosa 1989; "Extinção da tributação conjunta é 'contradição injustificável,'" *Gazeta Mercantil*, 20 December 1978.

10. Interviews Freire 1990, Lima 1990, Coelho 1990, Solimeo 1989. A former top SRF official told me confidentially that the Geisel "government was not authoritarian for business."

11. MF. SRF, *AEF* 1975, 196–203, 208–09; AEF 1980, 410–11. For different income types, information is only available on the amount reported to the SRF, not on the actual tax paid.

12. For the regressive impact of indirect taxes in Brazil in the 1970s, see Eris et al. (1983, 124).

13. MF. SRF, *ATF* 1973 e 1974, 19–20; ATF 1979, 11. The calculations for 1979 are not precise because the data source does not clearly distinguish the share of firms and individuals in tax payments on capital gains.

14. Nascimento e Silva 1974, 155–59; "Geisel quer Previdência para marginalizados," *Estado de São Paulo*, 5 July 1974; MPAS 1979, 10.

15. "Assistência social," *Estado de São Paulo*, 31 August 1976, 22; INPS 1980, 27.

16. Interview L. Velloso 1990; MPAS 1979, 31–32; "Previdência: técnico propõe a unificação," *Folha de São Paulo*, 13 November 1975.

17. Montenegro 1978, 44; "Não confirmado o limite mínimo da aposentadoria," *Estado de São Paulo*, 6 April 1978; Leite 1978, 328.

18. Interview Corrêa 1990; "Nascimento: Previdência não dividirá verba," *Estado de São Paulo*, 5 August 1977; J. Oliveira 1983, 41–47.

19. "Presidente do INPS quer mudar a mentalidade," *Diário de São Paulo*, 26 September 1974; "Ineficiência do INPS irrita seu presidente," *Folha de São Paulo*, 13 August 1976, 7.

20. "Previdência mudará fórmula para requisição de hospitais," *Estado de São Paulo*, 7 July 1977, 18; "Ministro anuncia que só o Presidente da República poderá requisitar hospital," *Jornal do Brasil*, 20 August 1977; interview Ferreira 1989.

21. Interviews F. Oliveira 1990, L. Velloso 1990. ARENA members advanced many amendments for maintaining FUNRURAL (MPAS 1978).

22. "Ministro: Setor médico-hospitalar precisa de atenção exclusiva," *Globo*, 20 February 1977; "Nascimento: Previdência não dividirá verba," *Estado de São Paulo*, 5 August 1977; interviews Coutinho 1989, Piola 1989.

23. PIASS. GEIN (1979, II 20) puts this number at 7.2 million. This estimate is probably inflated because clientelism effectively excluded many of the formally entitled beneficiaries.

Chapter 5. Politics of Taxation in the New Democracy

1. Confidential author interviews with tax experts and MF officials, Rio de Janeiro and Brasília, 1989–1990.

2. Cruz 1988, 267–71; Bresser 1988, 8–10; Maílson da Nóbrega, "Rever a Constituição," *Gazeta Mercantil*, 9 May 1989, 5.

3. However, Funaro was not indicated by a business association. In fact, his policies, driven in part by his political ambitions, soon antagonized the most powerful sectors of business, led by FIESP. An important FIESP official told me in a confidential interview that under Funaro the cordial relationship between São Paulo business and the MF deteriorated greatly. Thus, Funaro did not act as the agent of business.

4. The SRF could have withheld tax on capital gains at the top progressive rate and granted refunds to people whose annual income fell into lower tax brackets. This scheme would not have relied on the reporting of capital gains in the annual tax return, which was, indeed, hard to enforce.

5. When established bureaucrats' technical arguments invariably coincide with the defense of organizational attributions and resources and of standard operating procedures, and especially when the technical arguments are unconvincing, "it makes pragmatic theoretical sense to impute" organizational self-"interests" (March and Olsen 1989, 18), in congruence with a basic principle of bureaucratic politics, "Where you stand depends on where you sit" (Allison 1971, 176).

6. In a similar vein, SRF bureaucrats strenuously opposed the progressive taxation of capital gains and other equity-enhancing proposals that experts from SEPLAN's think tank advanced in a government commission on tax reform (interviews Rezende 1988, Giffoni 1989, Dain 1990; see Lopes 1987). Because of this resistance, which reflected resentment over the "interference" of SEPLAN in tax policy, the commission never agreed on a set of recommendations. The SEPLAN experts therefore submitted their proposal (Rezende 1987b) directly to the Constituent Assembly.

7. Individuals had an incentive to over-report the purchase value of their property in order to minimize their profits in case of sale and, thus, reduce their capital gains tax. Bresser's aides assumed that a tax on property would stop such cheating.

8. "Pacote fiscal deve alterar tributação na agropecuária," *Folha de São Paulo*, 4 December 1987, A-23; "Novo quadro político prejudica reformas," *Gazeta Mercantil*, 4 December 1987. However, the proposal to differentiate taxes on profits that firms did and did not reinvest was directly blocked by resistance from inside the SRF (interview Nakano 1989).

9. Interviews Rodrigues 1989, E. Silva 1989, Schöntag 1990. Despite Brazil's unequal income distribution, which could justify high taxes on the rich, this plan cut tax rates more drastically than reforms in the First World (analyzed in Peters 1991, 277).

10. IEDI 1991; FCESP 1992; Ponte 1992; Rezende 1992; interviews Fernandes 1992, Zockun 1992. The strong aversion in Brazilian society and Congress to any increase in the personal income tax made FIESP's proposal infeasible (interview Wellisch 1992).

11. As a FIESP official proudly told me in a confidential interview, three of the six members of this commission had worked as consultants for this powerful association. See also interviews Mattos 1992, Moreira 1992.

12. *Propostas* 1993, 16–33, esp. 21; FIPE 1994; interview Reis 1994; Abram Szajman, "Contra o Truque do IVV, a Transparência do IVA," *Folha de São Paulo*, 15 March 1994, 2–2.

13. CN. *Parecer Nº 24*, 2–10; "Congresso vai aprovar os aumentos de impostos," *Jornal do Brasil, Negócios e Finanças*, 20 January 1994, 1; "Fundo poupa estados e taxa bancos," *Correio Braziliense*, 31 January 1994, 2; "Concessões não afetam o plano,"

Jornal do Brasil, 9 February 1994, 3; "Governo negocia aprovação do Fundo Social," *Jornal do Brasil,* 22 February 1994, 4.

14. Interview Bogéa 1994; "IR de 35% é inócuo, diz tributarista," *Folha de São Paulo,* 2 February 1994.

15. The last empirical study shows that indirect taxes in Brazil were highly regressive in the mid-1970s (Eris et al. 1983, 124). Subsequent reforms tried to improve equity by reducing indirect taxes on primary necessities. But alcoholic beverages and tobacco products, which are widely consumed by the poor, still are among the biggest revenue sources from federal indirect taxes (Varsano 1987, 5–6).

16. The last empirical analysis (Contador 1976, 153–65) shows that in the early 1970s, 88 percent of the corporate income tax was passed on to consumers via prices. The factors that allow business firms such a shift of the tax burden (Allan 1971, 53–60) have not changed drastically since then. See also Eris et al. (1983, 98–100). For announcements by businesspeople to shift corporate income taxes to consumers, see "Pesquisa revela as opiniões dos executivos," *Folha de São Paulo,* 21 December 1985, 8; "Mais IR para financiar investimentos," *Gazeta Mercantil,* 6 August 1987; "Efeito bumerangue," *Diário Comércio e Indústria,* 1 August 1988, 3.

17. Therefore, it is methodologically problematic to define effective tax rates as the fraction of tax liabilities officially assessed in the annual tax return *(imposto líquido devido)* over gross taxable income, as Giambiagi and Villela (1989) do.

18. I proceeded in the following way. I computed the effective rate of the withholding tax by income level by dividing the amount of tax withheld by the amount of gross taxable income. I added (subtracted) the effective rate of the tax paid (refunded) with the annual tax return, computed in the following way. I divided tax payments (subtracting refunds) by gross taxable income, which I corrected for inflation. For this correction, I computed an index, based on figures for monthly inflation. Since most taxpayers are dependently employed and receive a thirteenth monthly salary per year, I added, $2/13 + 1/13$ x (100 + inflation rate in December)/100 + 1/13 x {(100 + inflation Nov.)/100 x (100 + inflation Dec.)/100)} + ... (Monthly inflation rates for 1984 from CE 39, 1 [January 1985], 60). This correction index was 1.75 for 1984. Such a correction does not eliminate all distortions (for example, irregular flux of income), but it is as far as one can go on the basis of the available information. The 1988 reform introduced such a correction in tax declarations so that no adjustment was necessary for 1989.

19. None of the many officials I interviewed ever claimed they were inspired by a party program. In fact, the PMDB's "program" on taxation was designed by a specialist and former official of a governmental tax reform commission (PMDB 1987, 39–47, 82). Experts influenced the party, not the other way around. See also Sardenberg 1987; Sola 1988, 37–43.

20. Rezende 1992; interviews Szajman 1992; Zockun 1992. The same is true of Força Sindical 1993, 169–81.

21. Interviews Rêgo 1989, Rodrigues 1989, Silva 1989, Lício 1989. An important FIESP official confidentially told me in 1989 that "FIESP is always consulted; when it is not consulted [by the government], it makes itself consulted."

22. Confidential author interview with a top SRF official, 1989.

23. Many former SRF officials now work as consultants, "Ex-fiscais da Receita assessoram empresas," *Jornal do Brasil, Negócios e Finanças,* 24 May 1992, 2.

Chapter 6. Politics of Social Insurance in the New Democracy

1. Reliable data on total social security coverage, including the protection of dependents and the welfare system, does not exist. Mesa-Lago (1991, 50) estimates it as 96.3 percent of the population, assuming extensive protection of dependents. But only people who paid direct social security taxes—47.2 percent of the economically active population in 1985 (IBGE 1990, 42)—enjoyed full entitlements; another 1 percent was covered by special pension systems for state officials. If FUNRURAL is—generously—assumed to cover all the rural poor (24 percent of the EAP), 28 percent of the EAP remained outside full social insurance, entitled at best to a limited gamut of benefits, especially survivors' pensions. For similar estimates, see World Bank 1989a, 2; MPAS 1986b, 853–54.

2. Dain 1989, 2–14; for corporatist versus universalist principles guiding different welfare states in the First World, see Esping-Andersen (1990, chap. 3).

3. This figure includes the 1 percent of the EAP covered by special pension systems for state officials.

4. MPAS 1986b, 307, 406, 691, 864; Dain 1988, 154–61; Cordeiro 1988, 99–100; Rezende and Silva 1987, 46–48. Above all, however, a diversification of social security taxes should protect the system from fluctuations in economic conjuncture.

5. MPAS 1986b, 13, 455–56, 685–86. In the early 1980s, the authoritarian regime had imposed a scheme for the inflationary readjustment of wages and pensions that raised the remuneration of better-off categories by less than the official inflation rate. The higher the income level, the bigger the loss. A correction of this loss would benefit better-off pensioners disproportionately.

6. "Previdência não altera alíquotas com a reforma," *Estado de São Paulo*, 18 November 1986; MPAS. SEE 1987, 35–42.

7. On the impact of patronage calculations on voting in the ANC, see in general Ames and Nixon (1993, 14–15, 24–25).

8. Arguing that welfare pensions of equal value as the minimal benefits of social insurance would remove the incentive for people to join the system and pay social security taxes, the MPAS opposed this generous measure (MPAS. SGA 1987, 8–9), but the ANC passed it anyway.

9. Fernandes 1989, 63–64; FIPREV 1989; author's observations at the "I Simpósio Nacional sobre Previdência Social," held in the federal Chamber of Deputies, Brasília, May 16–18, 1989.

10. *Veja*, 22 July 1987, 31–32; "RPS troca benefícios por votos," *Estado de São Paulo*, 23 August 1988; Magalhães 1988, 10–14; interview Araujo 1994.

11. Confidential author interviews with a labor leader and social security officials, 1992; see also Força Sindical 1993, 183–202.

12. COBAP 1994; "Interesse corporativo tenta bloquear revisão," *Jornal do Brasil*, 13 February 1994, 3.

13. It is extremely difficult to assess the distributional impact of social security systems; the effective incidence of social security taxes is particularly unclear (Musgrove 1985, 190–92).

14. Contador 1976, 153–65; Eris et al. 1983, 98–100; see in general Allan 1971, 52–53; Pechman and Okner 1974, 31. Brazilian businesspeople and state officials confirmed

this burden shift, "Empresários fazem críticas," *Folha de São Paulo,* 13 October 1989, C-10; "Empresários criticam alteração do Finsocial," *Gazeta Mercantil,* 14 October 1989, 35; "Governo analisa cortes para segurar o déficit," *Folha de São Paulo,* 1 September 1989, C-3.

15. There is much similarity to Brazil's first democratic period (1945–1964); see above all Malloy 1979, chap. 4 (and, for other Latin American countries, Rosenberg and Malloy 1978). But while many obstacles to reform have persisted, organized labor— excluded by the military regime from participation in social security administration— now plays a less important role.

Chapter 7. Politics of Health Care in the New Democracy

1. INAMPS 1985, 46–47. Since later reforms incorporated already existing public facilities into INAMPS' accounting system, valid data for assessing changes in the relative shares of public and private facilities in service provision is not available.

2. MPAS. Gabinete 1986, 19174; Netto 1988, 165–68; interview Ferreira 1989. This conflict persisted (CIPLAN 1989; interview Dellape 1992).

3. Felipe 1988b, 67; Rodriguez 1988, 46–47; confidential author interviews with former social security officials, 1989–1990.

4. See, for example, "Cinco anos de Sarney já valem CZ$ 183 bilhões," *Jornal do Brasil,* 23 May 1987, 3; "Deputado critica métodos da 'ciência política maranhense,'" *Folha de São Paulo,* 23 May 1987; "PMDB crê que afirmação sobre cargos seria resposta a Ulysses," *Globo,* 26 May 1987.

5. Cordeiro 1988, 152; Chonny and Noronha 1988, 237; "Equiparação salarial impede melhoria na Previdência Social," *Estado de São Paulo,* 8 December 1987.

6. "Ministro da Previdência 'deu golpe', diz Sarney," *Folha de São Paulo,* 9 September 1987; "PFL cobra sua cota nos cargos que Raphael entrega ao PMDB," *Jornal do Brasil,* 10 September 1987, 4.

7. Magalhães 1988, 8–20; Cordeiro 1991, 53, 77; interviews Miranda 1989, Pires 1989; confidential author interview with the MPAS official administering this patronage, March 1990.

8. For problems in the implementation of SUDS, see Chonny and Noronha 1988, 235–39; Felipe 1988a, 246–53; Dantas et al. 1988, 271–72; Netto 1988, 158–63.

9. See for instance, "'Pistolão' dribla precariedade na saúde," *Estado de São Paulo,* 3 October 1994, A-17; interview Araujo 1994.

10. M. Vianna 1989, 26–31, 56–60; see several articles in *Saúde em Debate* no. 21 (June 1988), 10–32.

11. SP. SMS. CMS 1989, 3; interview Mulin 1989; see Cohn et al. 1992 and, in general, the frequent complaints at the "1° Encontro Paulista de Conselheiros e Movimentos de Saúde," São José dos Campos, São Paulo, 23 May 1992; interview Arouca 1992.

12. This conservative counter-proposal, which remained secret, is reflected in Marinho (1989, 2) and CD. PL 2358/89, 12–13.

13. CD. Comissão de Saúde 1989c, 9, 18–19; MS 1991, 16–17; interviews Jefferson 1989, Ferreira 1989, Alckmin 1990. The private health sector celebrated its "victory in

the majority of the points defended" (FENAESS 1989, 1), while CUT (1989, 3) noted a "sense of defeat for the labor and popular movement."

14. Malloy 1979, 137; Roriz 1980, 34–36, 61; Mesa-Lago 1991, 105–08; see, however, Musgrove's (1985, 201–02) analysis of the difficulty of determining the value of health benefits.

15. TCU 1989, 8–9, 21, 30–34; "Orçamento de 90 tem rombo de 6,4 bilhões," *Jornal do Brasil,* 27 August 1989, 29.

16. In the early 1990s, the accounting system for simple medical services changed, and the accounting system for private hospital treatments was extended to public hospitals. Consistent time series for the whole period under investigation are therefore not available (interview Levin 1992). The figures reported below cover only the first few years of the new democracy, when the most important reform efforts took place. For the same reason, it is impossible to compare the relative shares of public and private facilities in the provision of health care over time.

17. However, findings must be interpreted with caution in order to avoid the "ecological fallacy." The income share of a poor *region* may increase because the few rich *people* living there get richer, not because the many poor people make gains. Therefore, the following conclusions are tentative. Interestingly, the regional distribution of Brazil's population barely changed between 1980 and 1991 (IBGE. AEB 1992, 206).

18. Data on INAMPS spending, which include expenditures on investments, show only minor changes in regional shares between 1984 and 1988. For 1989, most expenditures (probably especially SUDS funds) were attributed to the "administrative headquarters" so that a comparable regional distribution cannot be computed (PeD 5[4] [October–December 1990], 34, 49).

19. "Recursos mudaram o perfil do MA," *Folha de São Paulo, Especial: Era Collor,* 5 March 1990, 4. The use of medical services for purposes of patronage is common in Brazil. For example, during Jáder Barbalho's tenure as MPAS minister (1988–1990), the number of medical services in his clientelist base, the state of Pará, suddenly rose drastically.

20. "Auditoria em 952 hospitais descobre rombo de CR$ 1,7 bi," *Globo,* 18 May 1994, 8.

Chapter 8. Theoretical and Comparative Perspectives

1. For the impact of institutional structures on the propensity of different social strata to engage in political participation, see in general Verba, Nie, and Kim (1978, chap. 5).

2. The conclusions of this book claim validity for noncrisis situations. The redistribution of property directly challenges elites and usually leads to fierce conflict. In this open class struggle, actors and resources not analyzed here, such as the military and its coercive power, become essential. Yet whereas the organizational structures emphasized in this book may not be decisive in moments of acute, profound conflict, they are crucial for explaining why such confrontation has occurred rarely in Brazil. They diffuse tension and prevent the outbreak of class struggle by deflecting attention to narrow concerns and keeping social forces fragmented. Thus, this book concentrates

on the rule, rather than the exception in Brazil; its institutionalist approach explains why—despite tremendous inequalities—all-out confrontation is so exceptional in the country.

3. For this distinction, see Skocpol (1985, 21).

4. For example, most business sectors have assumed a reactive posture toward the state's recent push for economic liberalization.

5. Hegel 1972, 213–65; Schmitt 1987, 38–45. Migdal's (1994, 8–18) attack on state-centered theories overlooks this crucial difference between neo-statism and classical state theory.

6. Given the fragmentation of society, which obstructed bottom-up pressure for equity, even experts in society who saw redistribution as their primary goal worked through the state and promoted state interests in order to reach their aim.

7. For the conditions under which system-transforming leaders can emerge and attain political success, see Weyland (1995).

8. The debate on democratic consolidation (Valenzuela 1992) is plagued by a strong tendency toward tautology because the postulated causes of consolidation, such as "legitimacy," are hard to measure independently of their effects.

9. See especially Karl (1990); and Hunter's (1992) compelling criticism of this literature. Whether the experience of harsh authoritarian rule, as in Argentina and Chile, will have more of a lasting impact and guarantee a willingness to compromise (O'Donnell 1986, 15–17) remains to be seen.

10. Dix 1992; Mainwaring and Scully 1995. Remmer (1989, chap. 3) stresses the changes that military rule brought about for individual parties, but her analysis confirms the institutional continuities in party systems.

11. O'Donnell (1988, 62–64) stresses the persistence of clientelism in Brazil but attributes it to the mode of the democratic transition, not to the self-perpetuating institutional dynamic emphasized in this book.

12. This is also true for other time periods and countries (Geddes 1994, 82; Grindle 1977, chaps. 6–7).

13. Schmitter 1981, 91–129, esp. 109–21; Przeworski 1991, chap. 1; Keohane 1984, chap. 5. For a comprehensive integration of rational choice into an institutionalist framework, see Grafstein (1992).

14. Obviously, other factors, such as international constraints and incentives, also played an important role. The rise of populism was favored by the disruptions in the international system stemming from the Depression and World War II, and democratic reformists obtained inspiration and support from the "Alliance for Progress" spearheaded by the United States.

15. For Mexico and Brazil, Purcell 1981; Schwartzman 1982, 122. This is also true of Peronism in rural areas (Snow 1979, 42).

16. Dix (1985, 35–39) makes this point for AD, which he—incorrectly, in my view—labels "populist." On the Frei government in Chile, see Valenzuela (1978, 27–33).

17. Mesa-Lago 1989, chap. 2. On the importance of party competition for the expansion of coverage, see Rosenberg 1979, 125–26. Bossert's interesting essay is marred by conceptual confusion, for example, a lack of distinction between "state" and "regime" (1983, 425–35).

18. Other factors, such as domestic socioeconomic structures and international

constraints and pressures also played important roles, often in interaction with organizational patterns.

19. Gillis and McLure 1980, 53–66, esp. 66. In 1988, another tax reform was adopted through emergency powers (McLure 1990, 223).

20. Kaufman and Stallings (1991, 16–18) overestimate President Sarney's populist leanings. They apply a questionable definition of populism via economic policies, inspired by Sachs (1989), which neglects the political bases and dynamics of populism.

21. On organizational fragmentation among Argentine business, see Acuña (1992, 21–24); Waisman (1992, 235).

22. Campbell 1993; Mesa-Lago 1994, 133–35, 149–55; "Argentina. The Race Is on for the Pension Funds," *Latin American Weekly Report*, 2 June 1994, 2–3.

23. Although privatization in Argentina was less radical than in Chile, it has caused substantial financial problems ("Pide Economía una emergencia previsional," *La Nación*, 29 October 1994, 1).

24. The following discussion is based on Weyland 1997.

25. Ministerio de Hacienda 1993. A new agreement among the government, opposition, and business extended the most important of these changes (Acuerdo Tributario 1993), which were scheduled to expire in late 1993. The resulting tax system is more progressive than before 1990. Above all, the government insisted on maintaining the raise in the corporate income tax, which in Chile's open economy has a progressive impact because it cannot easily be transferred to prices.

26. On the redistributive impact of the minimum pension in Chile, see Diamond and Valdés-Prieto (1994, 261–64).

27. Larrañaga (1994, 17) shows that the modest reduction in income inequality between late 1990 and late 1992 accounts for 17.5 percent of the decrease in the number of poor households and 36.6 percent of the reduction in the poverty gap, that is, in the amount of resources required for lifting every Chilean above the poverty line.

28. Spain is best classified as democratic from mid-1977 on, when the first general elections were held and a popularly legitimated government assumed office.

29. My interpretation diverges from the emphasis many scholars put on the limitations and failures of Spain's new democracy, especially under the PSOE government, which ran into considerable conflict with labor unions (Gillespie 1990; Wozniak 1992–93). These authors neglect the fact that the working class is not the most disadvantaged sector in Spain. For instance, real wages rose throughout the severe economic crisis of the late 1970s and 1980s, while up to 25 percent of the workforce, especially young people, were unemployed (Pérez-Díaz 1993, 221–22, 226–30). Given the resource limitations stemming from the crisis, special attention to the needs of the worst-off groups may require some disregard for the interests of organized labor.

30. Obviously, given constraints of time and space, this discussion is not meant as a full-fledged "most different systems" analysis, but as a heuristic suggestion. Also, I paint with very broad strokes and neglect important differences among countries, especially in Western Europe.

31. For example, ethnic minorities created their own organizations, defined by their national origin.

32. Stephens 1986, chaps. 4–5; Alber 1987, 171–77; Esping-Andersen 1990, chaps. 1–3. A social structure in which poor people gradually joined the formal, urban econ-

omy and marginality remained small bolstered the cohesion of the popular sectors, strengthened bottom-up pressure, and helped make equity-enhancing efforts successful by guaranteeing that benefits for the working class reached most of the poor. For example, the contributive principle of social insurance could be applied to most of the poor, in contrast to a country with a large informal sector, such as Brazil. But the comparison with the United States, which had a similarly favorable social structure, yet enacted much less equity-enhancing reform, shows that this socioeconomic factor—while important—is by no means decisive.

33. See for Great Britain, Katznelson 1985, 272–78; for Sweden, Pontusson 1988, 43–44.

34. See, for example, Sloan and Tedin 1987, 116–21; Pluta 1979, 470–78; Bossert 1983. This evaluation includes Peru's reformist military regime (Ascher 1984, chap. 12).

35. For an interesting case study, see Fox (1994).

BIBLIOGRAPHY

ABH (Associação Brasileira de Hospitais). 1988. Telex by Wilson Aude Freua, president of ABH, to Ronaldo Costa Couto, Gabinete Civil da Presidência da República, 16 May. n.p.

Abranches, Sérgio Henrique. 1978. The Divided Leviathan. Ph.D. Dissertation, Cornell University.

———. 1985. *Os Despossuídos*. Rio de Janeiro: Jorge Zahar.

Acuerdo Tributario. 1993. Santiago, n.p.

Acuña, Carlos H. 1992. Lucha Política y Organizaciones Empresariales de Cúpula. Paper for XVII International Congress, Latin American Studies Association, Los Angeles, September 24–27.

Afonso, José Roberto, et al. 1988. A Reforma do Imposto de Renda, Comentários ao Projeto de Lei Nº 1.064/88. Rio de Janeiro: IPEA/INPES.

Alavi, Hamza. 1972. The State in Post-Colonial Societies, *New Left Review* 74 (July–August): 59–82.

Alber, Jens. 1987. Government Responses to the Challenge of Unemployment. In *The Development of Welfare States in Europe and America*, 3d ed., ed. Peter Flora and Arnold J. Heidenheimer, 151–83. New Brunswick, NJ: Transaction.

Albuquerque, Marcos Cintra Cavalcanti de. 1991. *O Imposto Único Sobre Transações (IUT)*. São Paulo: Fundação Getúlio Vargas.

Alckmin Filho, Geraldo. 1991. *A Nova Previdência Social*. Brasília: Câmara dos Deputados.

Allan, Charles M. 1971. The Incidence of Taxation. Chap. in *The Theory of Taxation*, 45–60. Harmondsworth: Penguin.

Allison, Graham T. 1971. *Essence of Decision*. Boston: Little, Brown.

Almeida, Márcio, et al. 1988. O Município e as AIS no Paraná. *Saúde em Debate* 21 (June): 18–24.

Almeida, Maria Hermínia Tavares de. 1988. Difícil Caminho. In *A Democracia no Brasil*, ed. Fábio Wanderley Reis and Guillermo O'Donnell, 327–67. São Paulo: Vértice.

———. 1994. Além do Corporativismo. Paper for XVIII International Congress, Latin American Studies Association, Atlanta, March 10–13.

Alt, James E., and Kenneth A. Shepsle. 1990. Editors' Introduction. In *Perspectives on Positive Political Economy*, ed. Alt and Shepsle, 1–5. Cambridge: Cambridge University Press.

Alvarez, Sonia. 1990. *Engendering Democracy in Brazil.* Princeton: Princeton University Press.

Alves, Maria Helena Moreira. 1985. *State and Opposition in Military Brazil.* Austin: University of Texas Press.

——. 1988. Dilemmas of Consolidation of Democracy from the Top in Brazil. *Latin American Perspectives* 15 (3) (Summer): 47–63.

Alves, Sílvio Rodrigues. 1987. O Desafio do Déficit Público. Brasília, Banco Central do Brasil, Departamento Econômico.

Amenta, Edwin, and Theda Skocpol. 1989. Taking Exception. In *The Comparative History of Public Policy,* ed. Francis G. Castles, 292–333. New York: Oxford University Press.

Ameringer, Charles D. 1982. *Democracy in Costa Rica.* New York: Praeger.

Ames, Barry. 1987. *Political Survival.* Berkeley and Los Angeles: University of California Press.

——. 1994. The Reverse Coattails Effect. *American Political Science Review* 88 (1) (March): 95–111.

Ames, Barry, and David Nixon. 1993. *Understanding New Legislatures?* Paper no. 215. Political Science Department, Washington University.

Anderson, Charles W. 1967. *Politics and Economic Change in Latin America.* New York: Van Nostrand Reinhold.

Archer, Ronald P. 1991. Comparative Party Strength and Weakness in Latin America. Paper for XVI International Congress, Latin American Studies Association, April 4–6, Washington, D.C.

——. 1995. Party Strength and Weakness in Colombia's Besieged Democracy. In *Building Democratic Institutions,* ed. Scott Mainwaring and Timothy R. Scully, 164–99. Stanford: Stanford University Press.

Aristotle. 1976. *Die Politik.* München: Deutscher Taschenbuch Verlag.

Arouca, Sérgio. 1988. Saúde na Constituinte: A Defesa da Emenda Popular. *Saúde em Debate* 20 (April): 39–46.

Arrighi, Giovanni. 1990. The Developmentalist Illusion. In *Semiperipheral States in the World Economy,* ed. William G. Martin, 11–42. New York: Greenwood.

Arrow, Kenneth J. 1963. *Social Choice and Individual Values,* 2d ed. New Haven: Yale University Press.

Arthur Andersen. 1977. Sugestões ao Anteprojeto de Decreto-Lei Sobre o Imposto de Renda das Pessoas Jurídicas. Rio de Janeiro: Arthur Andersen.

Ascher, William. 1984. *Scheming for the Poor.* Cambridge: Harvard University Press.

——. 1989. Risk, Politics, and Tax Reform. In *Tax Reform in Developing Countries,* ed. Malcolm Gillis, 417–72. Durham, NC: Duke University Press.

Assies, Willem. 1994. Urban Social Movements in Brazil. *Latin American Perspectives* 21 (2) (Spring): 81–105.

Atchabahian, Adolfo. 1988. Argentina: Tax Reform Process, 1983–1987. *Bulletin for International Fiscal Documentation* 42 (2) (February): 65–73, 77.

Azeredo, Beatriz. 1987. *As Contribuições Sociais no Projeto de Constituição.* Texto para Discussão Interna no. 124. Rio de Janeiro: IPEA/INPES.

Azevedo, Maria Emília Rocha Mello de. 1984. *Subsídios à Reflexão sobre a Previdência Social no Brasil.* CNRH. Documento de Trabalho no. 27. Brasília: IPEA/IPLAN.

Azevedo, Maria Emília Rocha Mello de, and Francisco E. Barreto de Oliveira. 1986. Previdência Social. In *Rumos da Nova Previdência,* Ministério da Previdência e Assistência Social (MPAS), 115–70. Brasília: MPAS.

Bacha, Edmar, Milton da Mata and Rui Lyrio Modenesi. 1972. *Encargos Trabalhistas e Absorção de Mão-de-Obra.* Rio de Janeiro: IPEA/INPES.

Bachrach, Peter, and Morton S. Baratz. 1970. *Power and Poverty.* New York: Oxford University Press.

Badie, Bertrand. 1992. *L'État Importé.* Paris: Arthème Fayard.

Badie, Bertrand, and Pierre Birnbaum. 1983. *The Sociology of the State.* Chicago: University of Chicago Press.

Baer, Werner, and Paul Beckerman. 1989. The Decline and Fall of Brazil's Cruzado. *Latin American Research Review* 24 (1): 35–64.

Bailey, John J. 1977. Pluralist and Corporatist Dimensions of Interest Representation in Colombia. In *Authoritarianism and Corporatism in Latin America,* ed. James M. Malloy, 259–302. Pittsburgh: University of Pittsburgh Press.

Balbi, Carmen. 1993. El Desaparecido Poder del Sindicalismo. In *El Podor en el Perú,* ed. Augusto Álvarez Rodrich, 97–104. Lima: Editorial APOYO.

Bank of Boston. 1990. Plano Brasil Novo. *Newsletter Brazil* 28 (8) (March 26): 1–4.

Barber, Benjamin. 1984. *Strong Democracy.* Berkeley and Los Angeles: University of California Press.

Barzelay, Michael. 1986. *The Politicized Market Economy.* Berkeley and Los Angeles: University of California Press.

Basurto, Jorge. 1982. The Late Populism of Luis Echeverría. In *Latin American Populism in Comparative Perspective,* ed. Michael L. Conniff, 93–111. Albuquerque: University of New Mexico Press.

Bates, Robert H. 1981. *Markets and States in Tropical Africa.* Berkeley and Los Angeles: University of California Press.

——. 1990. Macropolitical Economy in the Field of Development. In *Perspectives on Positive Political Economy,* ed. James E. Alt and Kenneth A. Shepsle, 31–54. Cambridge: Cambridge University Press.

Becker, David G. 1990. Business Associations in Latin America. *Comparative Political Studies* 23 (1) (April): 114–38.

Bell, John P. 1971. *Crisis in Costa Rica.* Austin: University of Texas Press.

Bernstein, Eduard. 1991. *Die Voraussetzungen des Sozialismus und die Aufgaben der Sozialdemokratie.* Berlin: Dietz.

Birnbaum, Pierre. 1980. States, Ideologies, and Collective Action in Western Europe. *International Social Science Journal* 32 (4): 671–86.

Blay, Eva. 1993. *Proposta Revisional, Nº 13869 a 13936.* Brasília: Congresso Nacional, Revisão da Constituição Federal.

Block, Fred. 1977. The Ruling Class Does Not Rule. *Socialist Revolution* 7 (3) (May–June): 6–28.

Boccanera, Ney da Fontoura. 1981. O Estado e as Autarquias de Serviços. *Revista de Informação Legislativa* 18 (69) (January–March): 153–64.

Boito Jr., Armando. 1991. *O Sindicalismo de Estado no Brasil.* Campinas: Editora da UNICAMP.

Bollen, Kenneth A., and Robert W. Jackman. 1985. Political Democracy and the Size Distribution of Income. *American Sociological Review* 50 (3) (September): 438–57.

Booth, John A. 1989. Costa Rica: The Roots of Democratic Stability. In *Democracy in Developing Countries.* Vol.4, *Latin America,* ed. Larry Diamond, Juan J. Linz, and Seymour Martin Lipset, 387–422. Boulder, CO: Lynne Rienner.

Boschi, Renato Raul. 1979. *Elites Industriais e Democracia.* Rio de Janeiro: Graal.

——. 1987. *A Arte da Associação.* São Paulo: Vértice.

——. 1990. Social Movements: Party System and Democratic Consolidation. In *Democratic Transition and Consolidation in Southern Europe, Latin America, and Southeast Asia,* ed. Diane Ethier, 214–34. Houndmills: Macmillan.

Bossert, Thomas J. 1983. Can We Return to the Regime for Comparative Policy Analysis? *Comparative Politics* 15 (4) (July): 419–41.

Braga, José Carlos de Souza, and Sergio Góes de Paula. 1986. *Saúde e Previdência,* 2d ed. São Paulo: HUCITEC.

Bresser Pereira, Luiz Carlos. 1988. *Experiências de um Governo.* Cadernos de Conjuntura no. 16. Rio de Janeiro: IUPERJ.

Bulhões, Augusto de. 1948. A Reforma da Legislação do Impôsto de Renda de 1947. *Revista do Serviço Público* 11 (3–4) (November–December): 5–12.

Cacciamali, Maria C. 1991. As Economias Informal e Submersa. In *Distribuição de Renda no Brasil,* ed. José Márcio Camargo and Fabio Giambiagi, 121–43. Rio de Janeiro: Paz e Terra.

Camargo, José Márcio, and Carlos Alberto Ramos. 1988. *A Revolução Indesejada.* Rio de Janeiro: Campus.

Campbell, G. Ricardo. 1993. Argentina Approves a Privatization Option for Social Security. *Social Security Bulletin* 56 (4) (Winter): 99–100.

Cammack, Paul. 1982. Clientelism and Military Government in Brazil. In *Private Patronage and Public Power,* ed. Christopher Clapham, 53–75. New York: St. Martin's Press.

Campos, Gastão Wagner de Souza. 1988. *Os Médicos e a Política de Saúde.* São Paulo: HUCITEC.

——. 1988. A Reforma Sanitária Necessária. In *Reforma Sanitária.* Giovanni Berlinguer et al., 179–94. São Paulo: HUCITEC/CEBES.

Capistrano Filho, David, and Aparecida L. Pimenta. 1988. Bauru, A Experiência que Deu Certo. *Saúde em Debate* 21 (June): 25–28.

Capuano, Ethel Airton. 1994. Por Dentro da Previdência Social. *Conjuntura Social* 5 (8) (August): 11–44.

Cardoso, Eliana, and Ann Helwege. 1991. Populism, Profligacy, and Redistribution. In *The Macroeconomics of Populism in Latin America*, ed. Rüdiger Dornbusch and Sebastian Edwards, 45–70. Chicago: University of Chicago Press.

Cardoso, Fernando Henrique. 1964. *Empresário Industrial e Desenvolvimento Econômico no Brasil.* São Paulo: DIFEL.

——. 1975. *Autoritarismo e Democratização,* 3d ed. Rio de Janeiro: Paz e Terra.

——. 1979. On the Characterization of Authoritarian Regimes in Latin America. In *The New Authoritarianism in Latin America*, ed. David Collier, 33–57. Princeton: Princeton University Press.

——. 1986. Entrepreneurs and the Transition Process: The Brazilian Case. In *Transitions from Authoritarian Rule. Comparative Perspectives*, ed. Guillermo O'Donnell, Philippe C. Schmitter, and Laurence Whitehead, 137–53. Baltimore: Johns Hopkins University Press.

Cardoso, Fernando Henrique, and Enzo Faletto. 1979. *Dependency and Development in Latin America.* Berkeley and Los Angeles: University of California Press.

Cardoso, Ruth Corrêa Leite. 1988. Os Movimentos Populares no Contexto da Consolidação da Democracia. In *A Democracia no Brasil,* ed. Fábio Wanderley Reis and Guillermo O'Donnell, 368–82. São Paulo: Vértice.

Castro, Paulo Rabello de. 1987. O "Dízimo" e a Constituinte. n.p.

CD (Câmara dos Deputados). 1988. *Projeto de Lei N 1.064-B de 1988. Emendas Oferecidas em Plenário.* Brasília: CD.

——. 1989. *Projeto de Lei Nº 2.358, de 1989.* Brasília: CD.

——. 1989. *Projeto de Lei Nº 2.570, de 1989.* Brasília: CD.

——. 1989. *Projeto de Lei Nº 3.110, de 1989.* Brasília: CD.

——. 1990. *Projeto de Lei Nº 5.995, de 1990.* Brasília: CD.

——. 1992. *Proposta de Emenda à Constituição Nº 55, de 1991. Relatório.* Brasília: CD.

——. 1993. *Projeto de Lei Nº 4.100, de 1993.* Brasília: CD.

CD (Câmara dos Deputados). Comissão Especial para Estudo do Sistema Previdenciário. 1992. *Relatório Final.* Brasília: CD.

CD (Câmara dos Deputados). Comissão de Saúde, Previdência e Assistência Social. 1989. *Anais do I Simpósio Nacional sobre Previdência Social.* Brasília: CD.

——. 1989. *Projeto de Lei Nº 2.570, de 1989. Relatório.* Brasília: CD.

——. 1989. *Projeto de Lei Nº 3.110, de 1989. Substitutivo Adotado pela Comissão.* Brasília: CD.

CE (Conjuntura Econômica), ed. Fundação Getúlio Vargas.

CEC (Comissão Empresarial de Competitividade). 1992. *Comitê Papel e Custo do Estado. Dossiê.* n.p. CEC.

CGT (Central Geral dos Trabalhadores). 1986. *CONCLAT 86. A Força da Unidade do Campo e da Cidade.* São Paulo: CGT.

CGT (Confederação Geral dos Trabalhadores). 1989. Brasil 1989. Elementos de la Situación Sindical. São Paulo: CGT.

Chalmers, Douglas A. 1977. Parties and Society in Latin America. In *Friends, Followers, and Factions,* ed. Steffen W. Schmidt et al., 401–21. Berkeley and Los Angeles: University of California Press.

———. 1977. The Politicized State in Latin America. In *Authoritarianism and Corporatism in Latin America,* ed. James M. Malloy, 23–45. Pittsburgh: University of Pittsburgh Press.

Chenery, Hollis, et al. 1974. *Redistribution with Growth.* New York: Oxford University Press.

Chong, Dennis. 1991. *Collective Action and the Civil Rights Movement.* Chicago: University of Chicago Press.

Chonny, Adolfo Horácio, and José Carvalho Noronha. 1988. SUDS/RJ, Presente e Futuro. In *Seminário sobre Financiamento do Sistema Unificado e Descentralizado de Saúde,* ed. Governo do Estado de São Paulo, Secretaria de Saúde, 231–41. São Paulo: Governo do Estado de São Paulo, Secretaria de Saúde.

CIPLAN (Comissão Interministerial de Planejamento e Coordenação). 1989. Estudo Comparativo Item a Item e por Tema, entre os Novos Contratos Administrativos Propostos pelos Contratantes (SES) e pelos Contratados (FBH e FENAESS). Brasília: MPAS.

Cleaves, Peter S. 1974. *Bureaucratic Politics and Administration in Chile.* Berkeley and Los Angeles: University of California Press.

CN (Congresso Nacional). Revisão da Constituição Federal. 1994. *Parecer N° 24, de 1994-RCF.* Brasília: CN.

———. 1994. *Parecer N° 50, de 1994-RCF.* Brasília: CN.

———. 1994. *Parecer N° 78, de 1994-RCF.* Brasília: CN.

CNI (Confederação Nacional da Indústria). 1984. *Encontro Nacional da Indústria— ENIND.* Tema II. Documento 5. *Previdência e Assistência Social.* Rio de Janeiro: CNI.

CNI (Confederação Nacional da Indústria) and CNC (Confederação Nacional do Comércio). 1987. Lei de Diretrizes e Bases de Seguridade Social. Rio de Janeiro: CNI/CNC.

CNRS (Comissão Nacional da Reforma Sanitária). 1987. *Documentos.* 3 vols. Rio de Janeiro: CNRS.

COBAP (Confederação Brasileira de Aposentados e Pensionistas). 1991. *XII Congresso Nacional dos Aposentados e Pensionistas.* n.p.

———. 1994. Posicionamento da "COBAP" sobre o Conteúdo Programático do Ciclo de Estudos sobre Seguridade Social Promovido pela "ANFIP." n.p.

Cohen, Youssef. 1989. *The Manipulation of Consent.* Pittsburgh: University of Pittsburgh Press.

Cohn, Amélia. 1989. Caminhos da Reforma Sanitária. *Lua Nova* 19 (November): 123–40.

Cohn, Amélia, et al. 1992. Participação na Gestão da Saúde. *Participação e Saúde*, ed. CEDEC, no. 4 (February): 3–4.

Collier, David, and Ruth Berins Collier. 1979. Inducements versus Constraints. *American Political Science Review* 73 (4) (December): 967–86.

Collier, Ruth Berins. 1982. Popular Sector Incorporation and Political Supremacy. In *Brazil and Mexico*, ed. Sylvia Ann Hewlett and Richard S. Weinert, 57–109. Philadelphia: Institute for the Study of Human Issues.

Collor, Fernando. 1991. *Brasil: Um Projeto de Reconstrução Nacional*. Brasília: Presidência da República.

Combellas, Ricardo. 1973. La Actuación de FEDECAMARAS y de la CTV ante la Reforma Tributaria de 1966. *Politeia* 2: 301–23.

Comissão para o Plano de Governo. 1985. Subsídios para a Política de Previdência e Assistência Social. n.p.

Conaghan, Catherine M., James M. Malloy, and Luis Abugattás. 1990. Business and the "Boys." *Latin American Research Review* 25 (2): 3–30.

CONASS (Conselho Nacional de Secretários de Saúde). 1989. A Lei Orgânica da Saúde. n.p.

Conclusões do Grupo de Trabalho Interministerial para Racionalização dos Gastos com Saúde e Melhoria do Atendimento a População. 1994. Brasília: n.p.

Conniff, Michael L. 1982. Toward a Comparative Definition of Populism. In *Latin American Populism in Comparative Perspective*, ed. Michael L. Conniff, 3–30. Albuquerque: University of New Mexico Press.

Constitution of the Federative Republic of Brazil 1988. n.d. Brasília: Senado Federal.

Contador, Claudio Roberto. 1976. *A Transferência do Imposto de Renda e Incentivos Fiscais no Brasil*. Rio de Janeiro: IPEA.

CONTAG (Confederação Nacional dos Trabalhadores na Agricultura). 1979. Contribuição da CONTAG ao Grupo Interministerial de Trabalho que Estuda a Reformulação da Previdência e Assistência Social Rural. Brasília: CONTAG.

———. 1984. Anteprojeto de Lei Complementar. Brasília: CONTAG.

———. 1988. Previdência Social Rural. Brasília: CONTAG.

———. 1989. Estudo Preliminar sobre Projeto de Lei da Previdência Social. Brasília: CONTAG.

Cook, Karen S., and Margaret Levi, eds. 1990. *The Limits of Rationality*. Chicago: University of Chicago Press.

Coppedge, Michael. 1992. (De)institutionalization of Latin American Party Systems. Paper for XVII International Congress, Latin American Studies Association, September 24–27, Los Angeles.

Cordeiro, Hésio. 1985. *O INAMPS na Nova República*. Rio de Janeiro: INAMPS.

———, ed. 1988. A Reforma Sanitária. *Cadernos do IMS* (Instituto de Medicina Social) 2 (1) (April–May). Rio de Janeiro: UERJ, IMS.

——. 1991. *Sistema Único de Saúde.* Rio de Janeiro: Ayuri.

Cornelius, Wayne A. 1977. Leaders, Followers, and Official Patrons in Urban Mexico. In *Friends, Followers, and Factions,* ed. Steffen W. Schmidt et al., 337–53. Berkeley and Los Angeles: University of California Press.

Cortázar Sanz, René. 1993. *Política Laboral en el Chile Democrático.* Santiago: Ediciones Dolmen.

Coutinho, Maurício C. 1986. A Previdência Social em Xeque. *Revista de Economia Política* 6 (4) (October–December): 116–24.

CPC (Confederación de la Producción y del Comercio). 1990. *Cuenta de la Presidencia de Don Manuel Feliú Justiniano.* Santiago: CPC.

Crenson, Matthew A. 1971. *The Un-Politics of Air Pollution.* Baltimore: Johns Hopkins University Press.

Cruz, Sebastião Velasco e. 1984. Empresários e o Regime no Brasil. Ph.D. Dissertation, Universidade de São Paulo.

——. 1988. Empresários, Economistas e Perspectivas da Democratização no Brasil. In *A Democracia no Brasil,* ed. Fábio Wanderley Reis and Guillermo O'Donnell, 256–81. São Paulo: Vértice.

CUT (Central Única dos Trabalhadores). 1986. *Resoluções do 2° Congresso Nacional.* São Paulo: CUT.

——. 1989. *Em Luta—Seguridade Social* 1 (1) (November–December).

——. 1991. A Crise Brasileira e os Trabalhadores. *Debate Sindical* 5 (12) (September).

——. 1992. Seguridade Social, Direito do Cidadão, Dever do Estado. 13 Pontos em Defesa da Previdência Social. São Paulo: CUT, Secretaria Nacional de Políticas Sociais.

Dahl, Robert A. 1971. *Polyarchy.* New Haven: Yale University Press.

Dain, Sulamis. 1988. Crise Fiscal e Dilema Distributivo. Ph.D. Dissertation, Faculdade de Economia e Administração, UFRJ.

——. 1989. Elementos para a Formulação de uma Política de Previdência Social no Brasil até o Ano 2010. n.p.

Daland, Robert. 1981. *Exploring Brazilian Bureaucracy.* Washington, D.C.: University Press of America.

Da Matta, Roberto. 1985. *A Casa e a Rua.* Rio de Janeiro: Guanabara.

DANC.S (Diário da Assembléia Nacional Constituinte. Suplemento), ed. Assembléia Nacional Constituinte.

Dantas, Paulo, et al. 1988. O SUDS em Pernambuco. In *Seminário sobre Financiamento do Sistema Unificado e Descentralizado de Saúde,* ed. Governo do Estado de São Paulo, Secretaria de Saúde, 267–77. São Paulo: Governo do Estado de São Paulo, Secretaria de Saúde.

DATAPREV (Empresa de Processamento de Dados da Previdência Social). 1989. Benefícios Utilizados no Estudo da Paridade. Rio de Janeiro: DATAPREV.

De Janvry, Alain. 1981. *The Agrarian Question and Reformism in Latin America.* Baltimore: Johns Hopkins University Press.

Del Aguila, Juan M. 1982. The Limits of Reform Development in Contemporary Costa Rica. *Journal of Interamerican Studies and World Affairs* 24 (3) (August): 355–74.

De Miguel, Jesús, and Josep A. Rodríguez. 1993. The Politics of Health Policy Reform in Spain. In *Politics, Society, and Democracy. The Case of Spain*, ed. Richard Gunther, 246–59. Boulder, CO: Westview.

De Nigris, Theobaldo. 1975. Quais as Vantagens da Pesada Carga Tributária. *Tendência* 3 (25) (October): 76–77.

Deutsch, Karl. 1961. Social Mobilization and Political Development. *American Political Science Review* 55 (3) (September): 493–514.

Diamond, Larry, Juan J. Linz, and Seymour Martin Lipset, eds. 1989. *Democracy in Developing Countries*. 4 vols. Boulder, CO: Lynne Rienner.

Diamond, Peter, and Salvador Valdés-Prieto. 1994. Social Security Reforms. In *The Chilean Economy*, ed. Barry P. Bosworth, Rüdiger Dornbusch, and Raúl Labán, 257–328. Washington, D.C.: Brookings.

Dias Neto, João. 1984. *Um Estudo do Grau de Progressividade do Imposto de Renda-Pessoa Física no Brasil*. Coleção Teses de Mestrado no. 10. Brasília: Escola de Administração Fazendária.

———. 1986. Imposto de Renda—Pessoa Física no Brasil. *Revista de Finanças Públicas* 46 (366) (April–June): 51–77.

Díaz, Eugenio. 1991. *Hacia un Nuevo Proyecto del Sindicalismo*. Santiago: Centro de Investigación y Asesoría Sindical.

DIEESE (Departamento Intersindical de Estatística e Estudos Socio-Econômicos). 1987. Uma Proposta para o Sistema Tributário. *Boletim DIEESE* 6 (August): 6–16.

Diniz, Eli. 1989. The Post-1930 Industrial Elite. In *Modern Brazil*, ed. Michael L. Conniff and Frank D. McCann, 103–20. Lincoln: University of Nebraska Press.

Diniz, Eli, and Renato Raul Boschi. 1979. Autonomia e Dependência na Representação de Interesses Industriais. *Dados* 22, 25–48.

———. 1987. Burocracia, Clientelismo e Oligopólio. In *As Origens da Crise*, ed. Olavo Brasil de Lima Jr. and Sérgio Henrique Abranches, 57–101. São Paulo: Vértice.

———. 1988. Interesses Industriais e Democratização. Paper for Working Group of CLACSO on "Businessmen and State in Latin America," November, Buenos Aires.

———. 1989. Empresários e Constituinte. In *Continuidade e Mudança no Brasil da Nova República*, ed. Aspásia Camargo and Eli Diniz, 116–36. São Paulo: Vértice.

Di Palma, Giuseppe. 1990. *To Craft Democracies*. Berkeley and Los Angeles: University of California Press.

Dix, Robert. 1985. Populism: Authoritarian and Democratic. *Latin American Research Review* 20 (2): 29–52.

———. 1989. Cleavage Structures and Party Systems in Latin America. *Comparative Politics* 22 (1) (October): 23–38.

———. 1992. Democratization and the Institutionalization of Latin American Political Parties. *Comparative Political Studies* 24 (4) (January): 488–511.

Domínguez, Jorge I. 1982. Business Nationalism. In *Economic Issues and Political Conflict*, ed. Domínguez, 16–67. London: Butterworth.

Dornbusch, Rüdiger, and Sebastian Edwards. 1990. Macroeconomic Populism. *Journal of Development Economics* 32: 247–77.

Dowding, Keith. 1994. The Compatibility of Behaviouralism, Rational Choice, and "New Institutionalism". *Journal of Theoretical Politics* 6 (1) (January): 105–17.

Downs, Anthony. 1957. *An Economic Theory of Democracy*. New York: Harper & Row.

Drake, Paul. 1982. Requiem for Populism? In *Latin American Populism in Comparative Perspective*, ed. Michael L. Conniff, 217–45. Albuquerque: University of New Mexico Press.

Dreifuss, René Armand. 1989. *O Jogo da Direita na Nova República*. Petrópolis: Vozes.

Durand, Francisco. 1993. *Business and Politics in Peru*. Boulder, CO: Westview.

———. 1994. The Politics of Tax Revolutions in Peru, Bolivia and Argentina. Paper for XVIII International Congress, Latin American Studies Association, March 10–13, Atlanta.

Durham, Eunice Ribeiro. 1984. Movimentos Sociais. *Novos Estudos CEBRAP* 10 (October): 24–30.

Dyson, Kenneth H.F. 1980. *The State Tradition in Western Europe*. Oxford: Martin Robertson.

Easton, David. 1979. *A Systems Analysis of Political Life*. Chicago: University of Chicago Press.

Eckstein, Susan, ed. 1989. *Power and Popular Protest*. Berkeley and Los Angeles: University of California Press.

Elizondo, Carlos. 1994. In Search of Revenue. *Journal of Latin American Studies* 26 (1) (February): 159–90.

Erickson, Kenneth Paul. 1977. *The Brazilian Corporatist State and Working-Class Politics*. Berkeley and Los Angeles: University of California Press.

Eris, Ibrahim, et al. 1983. A Distribuição de Renda e o Sistema Tributário no Brasil. In *Finanças Públicas*, Cláudia Cunha Campos Eris et al., 95–151. São Paulo: Pioneira/FIPE.

Escritório Técnico do Presidente Tancredo Neves. 1985. Programa de Ação do Governo. Setor: Saúde. n.p.

Esping-Andersen, Gøsta. 1990. *The Three Worlds of Welfare Capitalism*. Princeton: Princeton University Press.

Evans, Peter B. 1979. *Dependent Development*. Princeton: Princeton University Press.

———. 1982. Reinventing the Bourgeoisie. *American Journal of Sociology* 88 (Supplement): 210–47.

Evans, Peter B., Dietrich Rueschemeyer, and Theda Skocpol, eds. *Bringing the State Back In*. Cambridge: Cambridge University Press.

Fagen, Richard. 1978. Equity in the South in the Context of North-South Relations. In

Rich and Poor Nations in the World Economy, Albert Fishlow et al., 163–214. New York: McGraw-Hill.

Faleiros, Vicente de Paula. 1986. Previdência Social e Sociedade em Período de Crise. In *Cidadão, Estado e Políticas no Brasil Contemporâneo,* ed. Wilma de M. Figueiredo, 121–76. Brasília: Editorial da UnB.

Favaret Filho, Paulo, and Pedro Jorge de Oliveira. 1989. *A Universalização Excludente.* Texto para Discussão no. 216. Rio de Janeiro: UFRJ, Instituto de Economia Industrial.

FBH (Federação Brasileira de Hospitais). 1989. Saúde, Projetos de Lei. n.p.

FCESP (Federação do Comércio do Estado de São Paulo). 1992. Reforma Constitucional Tributária (Emendas Constitucionais). São Paulo: FCESP.

Felipe, José Saraiva. 1988. Alguns Aspectos sobre a Gestão do Sistema Unificado e Descentralizado de Saúde. In *Seminário sobre Financiamento do Sistema Unificado e Descentralizado de Saúde,* ed. Governo do Estado de São Paulo, Secretaria de Saúde, 243–66. São Paulo: Governo do Estado de São Paulo, Secretaria de Saúde.

———. 1988. MPAS—O Vilão da Reforma Sanitária? *Saúde em Debate* 20 (April): 65–73.

Feliú Justiniano, Manuel. 1988. *La Empresa de la Libertad.* Santiago: Zig-Zag.

FENAESS (Federação Nacional dos Estabelecimentos de Serviços de Saúde). 1989. Circular N° 85/89. São Paulo: FENAESS.

Fernandes, Anníbal. 1989. *Guía dos Aflitos da Previdência.* São Paulo: Oboré.

Ferreira Neto, Waldemar. 1992. O Mercado de Assistência Médica Supletiva em São Paulo e no Brasil. São Paulo: Associação de Medicina de Grupo do Estado de São Paulo.

FIESP (Federação das Indústrias do Estado de São Paulo) and CIESP (Centro das Indústrias do Estado de São Paulo). 1975. *Carga Tributária no Brasil.* Cadernos Econômicos no. 25. São Paulo: FIESP/CIESP.

Finnemore, Martha. 1992. Science, the State, and International Society. Ph.D. Dissertation, Stanford University.

FIPE (Fundação Instituto de Pesquisas Econômicas). 1994. *Proposta FIPE.* São Paulo: FIPE.

FIPREV (Forum Intersindical Permanente em Defesa da Previdência Social). 1989. Substitutivo ao Projeto-de-Lei N° 2.570, de 1989. Rio de Janeiro: FIPREV.

Força Sindical. 1993. *Um Projeto para o Brasil.* São Paulo: Geração Editorial.

Foweraker, Joe, and Ann L. Craig, eds. 1990. *Popular Movements and Political Change in Mexico.* Boulder, CO: Lynne Rienner.

Fox, M. Louise. 1990. *Poverty Alleviation in Brazil, 1970–1987.* Report no. IDP-072. Washington, D.C.: World Bank.

Foxley, Alejandro. 1990. La Política Económica para la Transición. In *Transición a la Democracia,* ed. Oscar Muñoz, 101–36. Santiago: CIEPLAN.

Frankel, Francine R. 1978. *India's Political Economy: 1947–1977.* Princeton: Princeton University Press.

Frey, Frederick W. 1971. On Issues and Nonissues in the Study of Power. *American Political Science Review* 65 (4) (December): 1081–1101.

Frías F., Patricio. 1993. *Construcción del Sindicalismo Chileno como Actor Nacional.* Vol.2, *1989–1992.* Santiago: Programa de Economía del Trabajo.

Frieden, Jeffry A. 1991. *Debt, Development, and Democracy.* Princeton: Princeton University Press.

Friedman, Milton. 1962. *Capitalism and Freedom.* Chicago: University of Chicago Press.

Fundação Getúlio Vargas. Comissão de Reforma do Ministério da Fazenda. 1966. *Evolução do Impôsto de Renda no Brasil.* Rio de Janeiro: Ministério da Fazenda.

Gatica B., Jaime, and Reinaldo Ruiz V. 1993. La Reducción de la Pobreza Durante el Gobierno de la Concertación. n.p.

Gay, Robert. 1988. Political Clientelism and Urban Social Movements in Rio de Janeiro. Ph.D. Dissertation, Brown University.

Geddes, Barbara. 1986. Economic Development as a Collective Action Problem. Ph.D. Dissertation, University of California, Berkeley.

———. 1994. *Politician's Dilemma.* Berkeley and Los Angeles: University of California Press.

Gereffi, Gary, and Donald L. Wyman, eds. 1990. *Manufacturing Miracles.* Princeton: Princeton University Press.

Gerheim, Renato Luiz R. 1982. Inflação e Incidência do Imposto sobre a Renda de Pessoa Física no Brasil, 1970–1980. M.A. Thesis, Departamento de Economia, PUC-Rio de Janeiro.

Germani, Gino. 1978. *Authoritarianism, Fascism, and National Populism.* New Brunswick, NJ: Transaction.

Giambiagi, Fabio, and Renato Villela. 1989. Uma Abordagem Crítica das Recentes Propostas de Reformulação do Imposto de Renda da Pessoa Física. In *XVI Encontro Nacional de Economia. Anais.* Vol. 3, ed. Associação Nacional de Centros de Pós-Graduação em Economia (ANPEC), 51–75. n.p.

Giffoni, Francisco de Paula C., and Luiz A. Villela. 1987. *Estudos para a Reforma Tributária.* Vol. 2, *Tributação da Renda e do Patrimônio.* Texto para Discussão Interna no. 105. Rio de Janeiro: IPEA/INPES.

Gil, José Antonio. 1977. Entrepreneurs and Regime Consolidation. In *Venezuela: The Democratic Experience,* ed. John D. Martz and David J. Myers, 215–34. New York: Praeger.

Gillespie, Richard. 1990. The Break-up of the "Socialist Family." *West European Politics* 13 (1) (January): 47–62.

Gillis, Malcolm, and Charles E. McLure, Jr. 1980. The 1974 Colombian Tax Reform and Income Distribution. In *Economic Policy and Income Distribution in Colombia,* ed. R. Albert Berry and Ronald Soligo, 47–68. Boulder, CO: Westview.

Gomes, Angela de Castro, and Maria Celina D'Araújo. 1993. A Extinção do Imposto Sindical. *Dados* 36 (2): 317–52.

Goñi, José, ed. 1990. *Democracia, Desarrollo y Equidad.* Caracas: Editorial Nueva Sociedad.

González-Sancho López, Emilio, and Almudena Durán Heras. 1985. La Sécurité Sociale Espagnole. *Futuribles* (October–November): 127–40.

González-Vega, Claudio, and Víctor Hugo Céspedes. 1993. Costa Rica. In *Costa Rica and Uruguay*, ed. Simon Rottenberg, 1–183. Oxford: Oxford University Press/ World Bank.

Grafstein, Robert. 1992. *Institutional Realism.* New Haven: Yale University Press.

Granovetter, Mark. 1985. Economic Action and Social Structure. *American Journal of Sociology* 91 (3) (November): 481–510.

Grindle, Merilee S. 1977. *Bureaucrats, Politicians, and Peasants in Mexico.* Berkeley and Los Angeles: University of California Press.

Grindle, Merilee S., and John W. Thomas. 1991. *Public Choices and Policy Change.* Baltimore: Johns Hopkins University Press.

Guillén, Ana M. 1992. Social Policy in Spain. In *Social Policy in a Changing Europe*, ed. Zsuzsa Ferge and Jon E. Kolberg, 119–42. Frankfurt am Main: Campus.

Guimarães, Cesar. 1977. Empresariado, Tipos de Capitalismo e Ordem Política. In *Estado e Capitalismo no Brasil*, ed. Carlos Estevam Martins, 191–204. São Paulo: HUCITEC.

Haggard, Stephan, and Robert R. Kaufman, eds. 1992. *The Politics of Economic Adjustment.* Princeton: Princeton University Press.

Hagopian, Frances. 1986. The Politics of Oligarchy. Ph.D. Dissertation, MIT.

———. 1990. "Democracy by Undemocratic Means"? *Comparative Political Studies* 23 (2) (July): 147–70.

Hamilton, Nora. 1982. *The Limits of State Autonomy.* Princeton: Princeton University Press.

Hanes de Acevedo, Rexene. 1991. El Control Político en Tiempos de Crisis. Paper for XVI International Congress, Latin American Studies Association, April 4–6, Washington, D.C.

Hartlyn, Jonathan. 1988. *The Politics of Coalition Rule in Colombia.* Cambridge: Cambridge University Press.

Hartz, Louis. 1955. *The Liberal Tradition in America.* New York: Harcourt Brace Jovanovich.

Hasenbalg, Carlos A., and Nelson do Valle Silva. 1987. Industrialization, Employment and Stratification in Brazil. In *State and Society in Brazil*, ed. John D. Wirth et al., 59–102. Boulder, CO: Westview.

Hayek, Friedrich August von. 1944. *The Road to Serfdom.* Chicago: University of Chicago Press.

Heclo, Hugh. 1974. *Modern Social Politics in Britain and Sweden.* New Haven: Yale University Press.

Hegel, Georg Wilhelm Friedrich. 1972. *Grundlinien der Philosophie des Rechts.* Frankfurt am Main: Ullstein.

Heimann, Eduard. 1980. *Soziale Theorie des Kapitalismus.* Frankfurt am Main: Suhrkamp.

Heller, Hermann. 1983. *Staatslehre.* Tübingen: J.C.B. Mohr.

Hellman, Judith Adler. 1994. Mexican Popular Movements, Clientelism, and the Process of Democratization. *Latin American Perspectives* 21 (2) (Spring): 124–42.

Hintze, Otto. 1975. *The Historical Essays of Otto Hintze,* ed. Felix Gilbert. New York: Oxford University Press.

———. 1981. *Beamtentum und Bürokratie.* Göttingen: Vandenhoeck & Ruprecht.

Hirschman, Albert O. 1970. *Exit, Voice, and Loyalty.* Cambridge: Harvard University Press.

———. 1971. The Political Economy of Import-Substituting Industrialization in Latin America. Chap. in *A Bias for Hope,* 85–123. New Haven: Yale University Press.

———. 1973. *Journeys Toward Progress.* New York: W.W. Norton.

Huber, Evelyne, Charles Ragin, and John D. Stephens. 1993. Social Democracy, Christian Democracy, Constitutional Structure, and the Welfare State. *American Journal of Sociology* 99 (3) (November): 711–49.

Hunter, Wendy A. 1992. Back to the Barracks? The Military in Post-Authoritarian Brazil. Ph.D. Dissertation, University of California, Berkeley.

Huntington, Samuel P. 1968. *Political Order in Changing Societies.* New Haven: Yale University Press.

———. 1991. *The Third Wave.* Norman, OK: University of Oklahoma Press.

Huntington, Samuel P., and Joan M. Nelson. 1976. *No Easy Choice.* Cambridge: Harvard University Press.

IAPAS (Instituto de Administração Financeira da Previdência e Assistência Social). 1990. Relatório de Arrecadação do IAPAS. n.p.

IBGE (Instituto Brasileiro de Geografia e Estatística). *Anuário Estatístico do Brasil (AEB).* Rio de Janeiro: IBGE.

———. 1990. *Pesquisa Nacional por Amostra de Domicílios (PNAD). Síntese de Indicadores da Pesquisa Básica da PNAD de 1981–1989.* Rio de Janeiro: IBGE.

———. 1992. Pesquisa Nacional por Amostra de Domicílios (PNAD) 1990. Brasil. n.p.

IEDI (Instituto de Estudos para o Desenvolvimento Industrial). 1991. *Carga Fiscal, Competitividade Industrial e Potencial de Crescimento Econômico.* São Paulo: IEDI.

IESP (Instituto de Economia do Setor Público). 1995. *Indicadores IESP* 41 (June).

IL (Instituto Liberal). 1991. *Previdência Social no Brasil: Uma Proposta de Reforma.* Rio de Janeiro: IL.

Immergut, Ellen M. 1990. Institutions, Veto Points, and Policy Results. *Journal of Public Policy* 10 (4) (October–December): 391–416.

INAMPS (Instituto Nacional de Assistência Médica da Previdência Social). 1979. *Atividades do INAMPS em 1978. Séries Históricas—1971 a 1978.* Rio de Janeiro: INAMPS.

———. 1979. *INAMPS em Dados. Número Especial 1978.* Rio de Janeiro: INAMPS.

———. 1986. Minuta de Contrato-Padrão. Quadro Comparativo. Pontos de Divergência na Comissão de Alto Nível. n.p.

———. 1988. *Relatório de Atividades 1986–1987*. Rio de Janeiro: INAMPS.

———. 1991. Norma Operacional Básica / SUS N° 01 / 91. n.p.

INAMPS (Instituto Nacional de Assistência Médica da Previdência Social). Presidência. 1985. *Portaria INAMPS / Presidência N° 2892 / 85, de 06 de Setembro de 1985*. Rio de Janeiro: INAMPS.

Infante, Ricardo, and Emilio Klein. 1991. The Latin American Labour Market, 1950–1990. *CEPAL Review* no. 45 (December): 121–35.

Informe de Previdência Social, ed. Ministério da Previdência Social. Secretaria da Previdência Social.

INPS (Instituto Nacional de Previdência Social). 1975. *Mensário Estatístico. Número Especial-1974*. Rio de Janeiro: INPS.

———. 1975. *O Plano de Pronta Ação / P.P.A. Portaria 39, 78, 79 e Normas Complementares*. Rio de Janeiro: INPS.

———. 1980. *Análise Institucional e Plano de Ação 1979 / 1985*. Rio de Janeiro: INPS.

Isuani, Ernesto A. 1985. Social Security and Public Assistance. In *The Crisis of Social Security and Health Care*, ed. Carmelo Mesa-Lago, 90–102. Pittsburgh: Center for Latin American Studies, University of Pittsburgh.

Isuani, Ernesto, and Emilio Tenti. 1989. Una Interpretación Global. In *Estado Democrático y Política Social*, ed. Ernesto Isuani and Emilio Tenti, 11–42. Buenos Aires: Editorial Universitaria de Buenos Aires.

Jackman, Robert W. 1975. *Politics and Social Equality*. New York: John Wiley.

Jacobi, Pedro. 1989. *Movimentos Sociais e Políticas Públicas*. São Paulo: Cortez.

Jaguaribe, Hélio, ed. 1989. *A Proposta Social-Democrata*. Rio de Janeiro: José Olympio.

Jaguaribe, Hélio, et al. 1986. *Brasil: 2.000*. Rio de Janeiro: Paz e Terra.

Jaguaribe, Hélio, et al. 1989. *Brasil: Reforma ou Caos*. Rio de Janeiro: Paz e Terra.

Jiménez de la Jara, Jorge. 1992. Gestión del Desarrollo Social Chileno, El Sector Salud. In *Gestión del Desarrollo Social Chileno, El Primer Año del Gobierno Democrático*, ed. Mercedes Aubá, 105–47. Santiago: Corporación de Promoción Universitaria.

Karl, Terry Lynn. 1986. Petroleum and Political Pacts. In *Transitions from Authoritarian Rule. Latin America*, ed. Guillermo O'Donnell, Philippe C. Schmitter, and Laurence Whitehead, 196–219. Baltimore: Johns Hopkins University Press.

———. 1990. Dilemmas of Democratization in Latin America. *Comparative Politics* 23 (1) (October): 1–21.

Katznelson, Ira. 1985. Working-Class Formation and the State. In *Bringing the State Back In*, ed. Peter B. Evans, Dietrich Rueschemeyer, and Theda Skocpol, 257–84. Cambridge: Cambridge University Press.

Kaufman, Robert R. 1977. Corporatism, Clientelism, and Partisan Conflict. In *Authoritarianism and Corporatism in Latin America*, ed. James M. Malloy, 109–48. Pittsburgh: University of Pittsburgh Press.

Kaufman, Robert R., and Barbara Stallings. 1991. The Political Economy of Latin American Populism. In *The Macroeconomics of Populism in Latin America*, ed.

Rüdiger Dornbusch and Sebastian Edwards, 15–43. Chicago: University of Chicago Press.

Kay, Stephen. 1995. The Political Determinants of Old Age Pension Insurance Reform in Argentina and Uruguay. Paper prepared for Conference on Poverty and Urban Violence, North-South Center, University of Miami, February.

Kearney, Richard C. 1988. Political Responsiveness and Neutral Competence in the Developing Countries. *Review of Public Personnel Administration* 8 (2) (Spring): 66–80.

Keck, Margaret. 1989. The New Unionism in the Brazilian Transition. In *Democratizing Brazil*, ed. Alfred Stepan, 252–96. New York: Oxford University Press.

———. 1992. *The Workers' Party and Democratization in Brazil*. New Haven: Yale University Press.

Kelley, R. Lynn. 1970. The 1966 Venezuelan Tax Reform. *Inter-American Economic Affairs* 24 (1) (Summer): 77–92.

Keohane, Robert. 1984. *After Hegemony*. Princeton: Princeton University Press.

Kirby, John. 1973. Venezuela's Land Reform. *Journal of Interamerican Studies and World Affairs* 15 (2): 205–20.

Kirchheimer, Otto. 1964. The Transformation of the Western European Party Systems. In *Political Parties and Political Development*, ed. Joseph LaPalombara and Myron Weiner, 177–200. Princeton: Princeton University Press.

Kitschelt, Herbert. 1992. Political Regime Change. *American Political Science Review* 86 (4) (December): 1028–34.

Knight, Jack. 1992. *Institutions and Social Conflict*. Cambridge: Cambridge University Press.

Kohli, Atul. 1987. *The State and Poverty in India.* Cambridge: Cambridge University Press.

Kohli, Atul, et al. 1984. Inequality in the Third World. *Comparative Political Studies* 17 (3) (April): 283–318.

Krasner, Stephen D. 1978. *Defending the National Interest*. Princeton: Princeton University Press.

———. 1984. Approaches to the State. *Comparative Politics* 16 (2) (January): 223–45.

Kraus, Franz. 1987. The Historical Development of Income Inequality in Western Europe and the United States. In *The Development of Welfare States in Europe and America*, 3d ed., ed. Peter Flora and Arnold Heidenheimer, 187–236. New Brunswick, NJ: Transaction.

Kreps, David M. 1990. *Game Theory and Economic Modelling*. Oxford: Clarendon Press.

Kruse, Sabine. 1992. Peru: Anpassungspolitik und "autogolpe." *Lateinamerika*, Supplement 11 (August): 1–58.

Kudrle, Robert T., and Theodore R. Marmor. 1987. The Development of Welfare States in North America. In *The Development of Welfare States in Europe and America*, 3d ed., ed. Peter Flora and Arnold Heidenheimer, 81–121. New Brunswick, NJ: Transaction.

Lago, Ricardo. 1991. The Illusion of Pursuing Redistribution Through Macropolicy. In *The Macroeconomics of Populism in Latin America*, ed. Rüdiger Dornbusch and Sebastian Edwards, 263–323. Chicago: University of Chicago Press.

Lamounier, Bolívar. 1989. *Partidos e Utopias*. São Paulo: Edições Loyola.

Lamounier, Bolívar, and Amaury de Souza. 1990. *As Elites Brasileiras e a Modernização do Setor Público*. São Paulo: Instituto de Estudos Sociais, Econômicos e Políticos de São Paulo.

Landé, Carl H. 1977. The Dyadic Basis of Clientelism. In *Friends, Followers, and Factions*, ed. Steffen W. Schmidt et al., xiii–xxxvii. Berkeley and Los Angeles: University of California Press.

Larrañaga, Osvaldo. 1994. *Pobreza, Crecimiento y Desigualdad: Chile 1987–92*. Serie Investigación I-77. Santiago: ILADES/Georgetown University.

Leff, Nathaniel H. 1968. *Economic Policy Making and Development in Brazil, 1947–1964*. New York: John Wiley.

Lehmbruch, Gerhard. 1977. Liberal Corporatism and Party Government. *Comparative Political Studies* 10 (1) (April): 91–126.

Lei Nº 8.213, de 24 de Julho de 1991. *Previdência em Dados* 6 (4) (October–December): 20–36.

Lei Nº 8.848, de 28 de Janeiro de 1994. *Diário Oficial* 132 (20-A) (29 January): 1383.

Leibholz, Gerhard. 1974. Der Strukturwandel der modernen Demokratie. Chap. in *Strukturprobleme der modernen Demokratie*, 78–131. Frankfurt am Main: Athenäum Fischer.

Leite, Celso Barroso. 1973. *Previdência Social*. São Paulo: Edições LTr.

———. 1978. Social Security in Brazil. *International Social Security Review* 31 (3): 318–29.

———. 1981. *A Crise da Previdência Social*. Rio de Janeiro: Zahar Editores.

Lenski, Gerhard. 1966. *Power and Privilege*. New York: McGraw-Hill.

Levi, Margaret. 1988. *Of Rule and Revenue*. Berkeley and Los Angeles: University of California Press.

Levine, Daniel H. 1978. Venezuela Since 1958. In *The Breakdown of Democratic Regimes. Latin America*, ed. Juan J. Linz and Alfred Stepan, 82–109. Baltimore: Johns Hopkins University Press.

Lichbach, Mark Irving. 1990. Will Rational People Rebel Against Inequality? *American Journal of Political Science* 34 (4) (November): 1049–76.

Lima, Maurílio Ferreira. 1993. *Proposta Revisional, Nº 9489 a 9515*. Brasília: Congresso Nacional. Revisão da Constituição Federal.

Lima Jr., Olavo Brasil de, and Sérgio Henrique Abranches, eds. 1987. *As Origens da Crise*. São Paulo: Vértice.

Lindblom, Charles E. 1977. *Politics and Markets*. New York: Basic Books.

Linz, Juan J. 1970. An Authoritarian Regime: Spain. In *Mass Politics*, ed. Erik Allardt and Stein Rokkan, 251–83. New York: Free Press.

Linz, Juan J., and Arturo Valenzuela, eds. 1994. *The Failure of Presidential Democracy*. 2 vols. Baltimore: Johns Hopkins University Press.

Lipset, Seymour Martin. 1981. *Political Man*. Baltimore: Johns Hopkins University Press.

Lipset, Seymour Martin, and Stein Rokkan. 1967. Cleavage Structures, Party Systems, and Voter Alignments. In *Party Systems and Voter Alignments*, ed. Lipset and Rokkan, 1–62. New York: Free Press.

Lipton, Michael. 1977. *Why Poor People Stay Poor*. Cambridge: Harvard University Press.

Longo, Carlos Alberto. 1984. *Em Defesa de um Imposto de Renda Abrangente*. São Paulo: FIPE/Pioneira.

——. 1986. *Caminhos para a Reforma Tributária*. São Paulo: FIPE/Pioneira.

Lopes, Leandro A. 1981. Relatório de Avaliação do Programa de Interiorização de Ações de Saúde e Saneamento-PIASS. Brasília: IPEA. CNRH.

Lopes Filho, Osiris de Azevedo. 1987. O Sistema Tributário na Nova Constituição. *Revista de Finanças Públicas* 47 (369) (January–March): 5–15.

Lowi, Theodore J. 1964. American Business, Public Policy, Case-Studies, and Political Theory. *World Politics* 16 (4) (July): 677–715.

——. 1979. *The End of Liberalism*, 2d ed. New York: W.W. Norton.

Luxemburg, Rosa. 1970. Sozialreform oder Revolution. Chap. in *Schriften zur Theorie der Spontaneität*, 7–67. Reinbek bei Hamburg: Rowohlt.

McConnell, Grant. 1966. *Private Power and American Democracy*. New York: Alfred Knopf.

McCoy, Jennifer. 1989. Labor and the State in a Party-Mediated Democracy. *Latin American Research Review* 24 (2): 35–67.

McDonald, Ronald H., and J. Mark Ruhl. 1989. *Party Politics and Elections in Latin America*. Boulder, CO: Westview.

McGuire, James W. 1992. Union Political Tactics and Democratic Consolidation in Alfonsín's Argentina, 1983–1989. *Latin American Research Review* 27 (1): 37–74.

McLure, Charles E., Jr. 1990. Tax Reform in an Inflationary Environment. In *World Tax Reform*, ed. Michael J. Boskin and Charles E. McLure, Jr., 205–26. San Francisco: International Center for Contemporary Studies.

Magalhães, Raphael de Almeida. 1988. *Obstáculos à Modernização do Estado*. Cadernos de Conjuntura no. 14. Rio de Janeiro: IUPERJ.

Mainwaring, Scott. 1987. Urban Popular Movements, Identity, and Democratization in Brazil. *Comparative Political Studies* 20 (2) (July): 131–59.

——. 1988. Political Parties and Democratization in Brazil and the Southern Cone. *Comparative Politics* 21 (1) (October): 91–120.

——. 1989. Grassroots Popular Movements and the Struggle for Democracy. In *Democratizing Brazil*, ed. Alfred Stepan, 168–204. New York: Oxford University Press.

——. 1991. Politicians, Parties, and Electoral Systems. *Comparative Politics* 24 (1) (October): 21–43.

——. 1992–93. Brazilian Party Underdevelopment in Comparative Perspective. *Political Science Quarterly* 107 (4) (Winter): 677–707.

——. 1994. Explaining Choices of Political Institutions. Paper for 90th Annual Meeting, American Political Science Association, September 1–4, New York.

Mainwaring, Scott, and Timothy R. Scully. 1995. Introduction: Party Systems in Latin America. In *Building Democratic Institutions*, ed. Scott Mainwaring and Timothy R. Scully, 1–34. Stanford: Stanford University Press.

Malloy, James M. 1977. Authoritarianism and Corporatism in Latin America. In *Authoritarianism and Corporatism in Latin America*, ed. James M. Malloy, 3–19. Pittsburgh: University of Pittsburgh Press.

——. 1979. *The Politics of Social Security in Brazil*. Pittsburgh: University of Pittsburgh Press.

——. 1987. The Politics of Transition in Latin America. In *Authoritarians and Democrats*, ed. James M. Malloy and Mitchell A. Seligson, 235–58. Pittsburgh: University of Pittsburgh Press.

——. 1993. Statecraft, Social Policy, and Governance in Latin America. *Governance* 6 (2) (April): 220–74.

Maravall, José María. 1993. Politics and Policy. In *Economic Reforms in New Democracies*, Luiz Carlos Bresser Pereira, José María Maravall, and Adam Przeworski, 77–131. Cambridge: Cambridge University Press.

March, James G., and Johan P. Olsen. 1984. The New Institutionalism. *American Political Science Review* 78 (3) (September): 734–49.

——. 1989. *Rediscovering Institutions*. New York: Free Press.

Marinho, Apparício. 1989. Projeto de Reconstrução do Sistema Nacional de Saúde. n.p.

Márquez, Gustavo. 1992. *El Seguro Social en Venezuela*. Serie de Monografías 8. Washington, D.C.: IDB.

Márquez, Gustavo, and Clementina Acedo. 1994. El Sistema de Seguros Sociales en Venezuela. In *Sistemas de Seguridad Social en la Región*, ed. Francisco E. Barreto de Oliveira, 155–96. Rio de Janeiro: IPEA/IDB.

Marshall, Thomas H. 1963. Citizenship and Social Class. Chap. in *Class, Citizenship, and Social Development*, 65–122. Westport, CT: Greenwood.

Martins, Luciano. 1985. *Estado Capitalista e Burocracia no Brasil Pós-64*. Rio de Janeiro: Paz e Terra.

Marx, Karl. 1971. *Die Frühschriften*. Stuttgart: Alfred Kröner.

Mattos Filho, Ary Oswaldo, ed. 1993. *Reforma Fiscal*. Vol.1: *Relatório da Comissão Executiva de Reforma Fiscal*. São Paulo: Dórea Books and Art.

Maybury-Lewis, Biorn. 1990. *The Agrarian Reform Debate in Brazil*. Working Paper no. 14. New York: Institute of Latin American and Iberian Studies, Columbia University.

——. 1991. The Politics of the Possible. Ph.D. Dissertation, Columbia University.

MEFP (Ministério da Economia, Fazenda e Planejamento). 1991. Programa de Saneamento Financeiro e Ajuste Fiscal. Reprinted in *Gazeta Mercantil* (23 August): 11–14.

——. Comissão Executiva de Reforma Fiscal. 1992. *Projeto de Emenda à Constituição (Versão atual-26/06/92)*. Brasília: MEFP.

MEFP.SEPE (Ministério da Economia, Fazenda e Planejamento. Secretaria Especial de Política Econômica). 1991. *Propostas de Emendas à Constituição, Agrupadas Segundo Blocos ou Tópicos.* Brasília: MEFP. SEPE.

Meier, Christian. 1980. *Res publica amissa.* Frankfurt am Main: Suhrkamp.

Mello, Carlos Gentile de. 1977. *Saúde e Assistência Médica no Brasil.* São Paulo: CEBES-HUCITEC.

———. 1981. *O Sistema de Saúde em Crise,* 2d ed. São Paulo: CEBES-HUCITEC.

Meneguello, Rachel. 1989. *PT: A Formação de um Partido, 1979–1982.* Rio de Janeiro: Paz e Terra.

Mensagem N° 151, de 1990-CN. 1990. *Diário do Congresso Nacional* (10 October): 3958–68.

Mensagem N° 306, de 1995. Brasília: n.p.

Mericle, Kenneth S. 1977. Corporatist Control of the Working Class. In *Authoritarianism and Corporatism in Latin America,* ed. James M. Malloy, 303–38. Pittsburgh: University of Pittsburgh Press.

Mesa-Lago, Carmelo. 1978. *Social Security in Latin America.* Pittsburgh: University of Pittsburgh Press.

———. 1989. *Ascent to Bankruptcy.* Pittsburgh: University of Pittsburgh Press.

———. 1991. *Social Security and Prospects for Equity in Latin America.* Discussion Paper no. 140. Washington, D.C.: World Bank.

———. 1994. *Changing Social Security in Latin America.* Boulder, CO: Lynne Rienner.

Mettenheim, Kurt von. 1990. The Brazilian Voter in Democratic Transition. *Comparative Politics* 23 (1) (October): 23–44.

MF (Ministério da Fazenda). 1987. *Plano de Controle Macroeconômico.* Brasília: MF.

MF. SRF (Ministério da Fazenda. Secretaria da Receita Federal). *Anuário Econômico-Fiscal (AEF).* Brasília: MF. SRF.

———. *Arrecadação dos Tributos Federais (ATF).* Brasília: MF. SRF.

———. *Imposto de Renda Pessoa Física (IRPF).* Brasília: MF. SRF.

———. 1985. *Esclarecendo Dúvidas sobre o Projeto de Reforma do Imposto de Renda.* Brasília: MF. SRF.

———. 1992. *Síntese da Reforma Proposta.* Brasília: MF. SRF. Coordenação Geral de Estudos Econômico-Tributários.

———. 1993. *Avaliação Quantitativa da Carga Tributária, 1984–1992.* Brasília: MF. SRF.

Migdal, Joel S. 1988. *Strong Societies and Weak States.* Princeton: Princeton University Press.

———. 1994. The State in Society. In *State Power and Social Forces,* ed. Migdal, Atul Kohli, and Vivienne Shue, 7–34. Cambridge: Cambridge University Press.

Migdal, Joel S., Atul Kohli, and Vivienne Shue, eds. 1994. *State Power and Social Forces.* Cambridge: Cambridge University Press.

Mill, John Stuart. 1975. *Three Essays on Liberty, Representative Government, the Subjection of Women.* Oxford: Oxford University Press.

Miller, Gary J. 1993. *Managerial Dilemmas.* Cambridge: Cambridge University Press.

Ministério de Economía. 1995. *La Recaudación Tributaria en el Cuarto Trimestre de 1994.* Buenos Aires: Ministério de Economía. Secretaría de Ingresos Públicos. Dirección Nacional de Investigaciones y Análisis Fiscal.

Ministerio de Hacienda. 1993. *Gastos Financiados con la Reforma Tributaria.* Santiago: Ministerio de Hacienda. Dirección de Presupuestos.

———. 1994. Inversión en las Personas: Recursos y Políticas para el Desarrollo con Equidad en Chile. Santiago: Ministério de Hacienda.

Moe, Terry M. 1984. The New Economics of Organization. *American Journal of Political Science* 28 (4) (November): 739–77.

Mols, Manfred. 1981. *Mexiko im 20. Jahrhundert.* Paderborn: Schöningh.

———. 1985. *Demokratie in Lateinamerika.* Stuttgart: Kohlhammer.

Montenegro, Severino. 1978. A Aposentadoria por Tempo de Serviço. *Conjuntura Social* 1 (4) (July–September): 42–46.

Moore, Barrington. 1967. *Social Origins of Dictatorship and Democracy.* Boston: Beacon.

Moreira, Roberto, et al. 1984. Correntes e Tendências da Reforma Tributária. *Revista de Administração Pública* 18 (4)(October–December): 125–54.

Most, Benjamin A. 1980. Authoritarianism and the Growth of the State in Latin America. *Comparative Political Studies* 13 (2) (July): 173–203.

Mouzelis, Nicos. 1985. On the Concept of Populism. *Politics and Society* 14 (3) 329–48.

MPAS (Ministério da Previdência e Assistência Social). 1975. FUNAMES. n.p.: MPAS.

———. 1975. *Sistema Nacional de Saúde. Contribuição para a Discussão do Tema Oficial "Sistema Nacional de Saúde" da V Conferência Nacional de Saúde.* Brasília: MPAS.

———. 1978. Relatório de 1977. Brasília: MPAS.

———. 1978. *A Reorganização e a Racionalização da Previdência Social. SINPAS.* Rio de Janeiro: MPAS.

———. 1979. *Dossiê sobre o MPAS.* Rio de Janeiro: MPAS.

———. 1984. *Projeto de Revisão da Previdência e Assistência Social.* Brasília: MPAS.

———. 1986. *Conselhos Comunitários da Previdência Social.* Brasília: MPAS.

———. 1986. *Rumos da Nova Previdência. Anais do Grupo de Trabalho para Reestruturação da Previdência Social, 1986.* 3 vols. Brasília: MPAS.

———. 1987. *Conselhos Comunitários da Previdência Social.* Brasília: MPAS.

———. 1987. Lei de Diretrizes e Bases de Seguridade Social. n.p.

———. 1988. Convênio-SUDS-01/88. n.p.

———. 1989. *Coletânea da Legislação Básica. SUDS.* Brasília: MPAS.

MPAS. CSPAS (Ministério da Previdência e Assistência Social. Conselho Superior da Previdência e Assistência Social). 1987. Lei de Diretrizes e Bases da Previdência Social. Sugestões e Propostas Apresentadas por Membros do Conselho Superior da Previdência e Assistência Social. Brasília: MPAS. CSPAS.

———. 1987. Memória do CSPAS. n.p.

MPAS. FUNRURAL (Ministério da Previdência e Assistência Social. Fundo de Assistência ao Trabalhador Rural). 1978. *Boletim Estatístico 1977.* Brasília: MPAS. FUNRURAL.

MPAS (Ministério da Previdência e Assistência Social). Gabinete do Ministro. 1986. Portaria N° 3.893, de 11 de dezembro de 1986. *Diário Oficial da União* (18 December): 19171–74.

MPAS. SAS (Ministério da Previdência e Assistência Social. Secretaria de Assistência Social). 1989. Equivalência dos Benefícios e Serviços às Populações Urbanas e Rurais. Brasília: MPAS. SAS.

——. 1989. A Participação Popular na Previdência Social. Brasília: MPAS. SAS.

MPAS. SEE (Ministério da Previdência e Assistência Social. Sub-Secretaria de Estudos Especiais). 1975. Organização do Setor Saúde para o Desenvolvimento Social. Brasília: MPAS. SEE.

MPAS. SEE (Ministério da Previdência e Assistência Social. Secretaria de Estudos Especiais). 1987. Previdência e Assistência Social Rural no Brasil. Diagnóstico, Propostas de Mudanças. Brasília: MPAS. SEE.

——. 1988. Anteprojeto de Lei da Previdência Social, 1st version. Brasília: MPAS. SEE.

——. 1988. A Seguridade Social na Nova Constituição. Previdência Social. Brasília: MPAS. SEE.

MPAS. SG (Ministério da Previdência e Assistência Social. Secretaria-Geral). 1986. Revisão da Previdência Social Rural. Anteprojetos de Lei do Regime do Empregador Rural e do Trabalhador Rural, Ofício N° 63. Brasília: MPAS. SG.

MPAS. SGA (Ministério da Previdência e Assistência Social. Secretaria-Geral Adjunta). 1987. Nota sobre o Anteprojeto da Comissão de Sistematização—Seguridade Social. Brasília: MPAS. SGA.

MPAS. SPO (Ministério da Previdência e Assistência Social. Secretaria de Planejamento e Orçamento). 1985. *I PND da Nova República. Plano Setorial da Previdência.* Brasília: MPAS. SPO.

——. 1986. *Plano de Metas. Exercício / 86.* Brasília: MPAS. SPO.

MPS (Ministério da Previdência Social). *Anuário Estatístico da Previdência Social (AEPS).* Brasília: MPS.

——. 1992. Registro sobre as "Recomendações da Comissão Especial para a Reforma da Previdência." Brasília: MPS.

——. 1994. *Previdência Social no Brasil. (Conferência proferida pelo ministro Sérgio Cutolo na Escola Superior de Guerra-ESG).* Brasília: MPS.

MPS (Ministério da Previdência Social) and CEPAL (Comissão Econômica para América Latina). 1993–1994. *A Previdência Social e a Revisão Constitucional.* 7 vols. Brasília: MPS / CEPAL.

MS (Ministério da Saúde). 1986. *Anais da 8ª Conferência Nacional de Saúde, 1986.* Brasília: MS.

——. 1989. *Lei Orgânica da Saúde. Projeto de Lei.* Brasília: MS.

——. 1991. *Lei Orgânica da Saúde.* Brasília: MS.

MS. SNAS (Ministério da Saúde. Secretaria Nacional de Assistência à Saúde). 1992. Norma Operacional Básica-SUS/1992. *Diário Oficial* (10 February): 1584–88.

Musgrove, Philip. 1985. The Impact of Social Security on Income Distribution. In *The Crisis of Social Security and Health Care*, ed. Carmelo Mesa-Lago, 186–208. Pittsburgh: Center for Latin American Studies, University of Pittsburgh.

Mussi, Carlos, Eduardo F. Ohana, and José Rildo Guedes. 1992. *Análise da Estrutura Funcional do Gasto Público no Brasil 1985–1990*. Texto para Discussão no. 249. Brasília: IPEA.

Myerson, Roger B. 1992. On the Value of Game Theory in Social Science. *Rationality and Society* 4 (1) (January): 62–73.

Nascimento e Silva, Luiz Gonzaga do. 1974. Política Nacional de Previdência Social. *Segurança e Desenvolvimento* 23 (157): 151–61.

———. 1975. Política de Previdência e Assisténcia Social. *Segurança e Desenvolvimento* 24 (160): 147–59.

Nelson, Joan M., ed. 1990. *Economic Crisis and Policy Choice*. Princeton: Princeton University Press.

NEPP (Núcleo de Estudos de Políticas Públicas). 1989. *Brasil 1987. Relatório sobre a Situação Social do País*. Campinas: UNICAMP.

NESP (Núcleo de Estudos em Saúde Pública). 1989. *Anteprojeto: Lei Orgânica do Sistema Único de Saúde*. Brasília: NESP. UnB.

Netto, Francisco Costa. 1988. Comentários sobre a Institucionalização do SUDS. In *A Reforma Sanitária*, ed. Hésio Cordeiro = *Cadernos do IMS* (Instituto de Medicina Social) 2 (1) (April–May): 155–68. Rio de Janeiro: UERJ. IMS.

Nordlinger, Eric A. 1981. *On the Autonomy of the Democratic State*. Cambridge: Harvard University Press.

North, Douglass C. 1981. *Structure and Change in Economic History*. New York: W.W. Norton.

———. 1990. *Institutions, Institutional Change and Economic Performance*. Cambridge: Cambridge University Press.

Novaes, Carlos A. Marques. 1994. Dinâmica Institucional de Representação. *Novos Estudos CEBRAP* 38 (March): 99–147.

Nunes, Edson de Oliveira. 1984. Bureaucratic Insulation and Clientelism in Contemporary Brazil. Ph.D. Dissertation, University of California, Berkeley.

Nylen, William Russell. 1990. Liberalismo para Tudo Mundo, Menos Eu. Conference Paper no. 25. Department of Political Science, Columbia University.

O'Donnell, Guillermo A. 1977. Corporatism and the Question of the State. In *Authoritarianism and Corporatism in Latin America*, ed. James M. Malloy, 47–87. Pittsburgh: University of Pittsburgh Press.

———. 1978. Reflections on the Pattern of Change in the Bureaucratic-Authoritarian State. *Latin American Research Review* 13 (1): 3–38.

———. 1979. *Modernization and Bureaucratic-Authoritarianism*, 2d ed. Berkeley: Institute of International Studies, University of California.

——. 1994. Delegative Democracy. *Journal of Democracy* 5 (1) (January): 55–69.

——. 1986. Introduction to the Latin American Cases. In *Transitions from Authoritarian Rule. Latin America*, ed. Guillermo O'Donnell, Philippe C. Schmitter, and Laurence Whitehead, 3–18. Baltimore: Johns Hopkins University Press.

——. 1988. Transições, Continuidades e Alguns Paradoxos, and Hiatos, Instituições e Perspectivas Democráticas. In *A Democracia no Brasil*, ed. Fábio Wanderley Reis and Guillermo O'Donnell, 41–90. São Paulo: Vértice.

——. 1993. On the State, Democratization, and Some Conceptual Problems. *World Development* 21 (8) (August): 1355–69.

O'Donnell, Guillermo A., and Philippe C. Schmitter. 1986. *Transitions from Authoritarian Rule. Tentative Conclusions about Uncertain Democracies*. Baltimore: Johns Hopkins University Press.

O'Donnell, Guillermo A., Philippe C. Schmitter, and Laurence Whitehead, eds. 1986. *Transitions from Authoritarian Rule*. Baltimore: Johns Hopkins University Press.

OECD (Organisation for Economic Co-operation and Development). 1986. *Personal Income Tax Systems Under Changing Economic Conditions*. Paris: OECD.

Offe, Claus. 1984. *Contradictions of the Welfare State*. Cambridge: MIT Press.

Offe, Claus, and Helmut Wiesenthal. 1985. Two Logics of Collective Action. In Claus Offe, *Disorganized Capitalism*, 170–220. Cambridge: MIT Press.

Oliveira, Fabrício A. de. 1981. *A Reforma Tributária de 1966 e a Acumulação de Capital no Brasil*. São Paulo: Brasil Debates.

Oliveira, Francisco E. Barreto de. 1987. Reforma Previdenciária. *Revista de Administração Pública* 21 (4) (October–December): 62–93.

Oliveira, Francisco E. Barreto de, Kaizô I. Beltrão, and Leandro Maniero. 1993. Aposentadoria por Tempo de Serviço. In *A Previdência Social e a Revisão Constitucional. Pesquisas*. Vol. 2, ed. MPS (Ministério da Previdência Social) and CEPAL (Comissão Econômica para América Latina), 197–263. Brasília: MPS/CEPAL.

Oliveira, Francisco E. Barreto de, et al. 1985. *Tendências a Médio Prazo da Previdência Social Brasileira*. Texto para Discussão Interna no. 73. Rio de Janeiro: IPEA/INPES.

Oliveira, Francisco Luiz Torres de. 1978. A Aposentadoria por Tempo de Serviço e os Tecnocratas. *Conjuntura Social* 2 (5) (October–December): 47–50.

Oliveira, Jaime A. de Araújo. 1983. Interesses Sociais e Mecanismos de Representação: A Política de Saúde no Brasil Pós-64. Rio de Janeiro: Escola Nacional de Saúde Pública, Fundação Oswaldo Cruz.

Oliveira, Jaime A. de Araújo, and Sonia Maria Fleury Teixeira. 1986. *(Im)Previdência Social*. Petrópolis: Vozes.

Oliveira, Jane Souto de. 1993. *O Traço da Desigualdade Social no Brasil*. Rio de Janeiro: IBGE.

Olsen, Johan P. 1983. *Organized Democracy*. Bergen: Universitetsforlaget.

Olson, Mancur. 1971. *The Logic of Collective Action*. Cambridge: Harvard University Press.

———. 1982. *The Rise and Decline of Nations.* New Haven: Yale University Press.

———. 1986. A Theory of the Incentives Facing Political Organizations. *International Political Science Review* 7 (2) (April): 165–89.

Ordeshook, Peter. 1990. The Emerging Discipline of Political Economy. In *Perspectives on Positive Political Economy*, ed. James E. Alt and Kenneth A. Shepsle, 9–30. Cambridge: Cambridge University Press.

Oszlak, Oscar. 1984. *Public Policies and Political Regimes in Latin America.* Working Paper no. 139. Washington, D.C.: Wilson Center.

Oxhorn, Philip. 1994. Where Did All the Protesters Go? *Latin American Perspectives* 21 (3) (Summer): 49–68.

Panebianco, Angelo. 1988. *Political Parties.* Cambridge: Cambridge University Press.

Payne, Leigh A. 1994. *Brazilian Industrialists and Democratic Change.* Baltimore: Johns Hopkins University Press.

Pechman, Joseph A., and Benjamin A. Okner. 1974. *Who Bears the Tax Burden?* Washington, D.C.: Brookings Institution.

PeD (Previdência em Dados), ed. DATAPREV.

Peeler, John A. 1985. *Latin American Democracies.* Chapel Hill: University of North Carolina Press.

Pellegrini Filho, Alberto, et al. 1979. PIASS: O Relato e a Análise de uma Experiência. n.p.

Pérez-Díaz, Víctor M. 1993. Region, Economy, and the Scale of Governance. Chap. in *The Return of Civil Society*, 184–235. Cambridge: Harvard University Press.

Perlman, Janice E. 1976. *The Myth of Marginality.* Berkeley and Los Angeles: University of California Press.

Peters, Guy. 1991. *The Politics of Taxation.* Cambridge: Blackwell.

Petras, James, and Morris Morley. 1992. *Latin America in the Time of Cholera.* New York: Routledge.

Pierson, Christopher. 1992. *Beyond the Welfare State?* University Park: Pennsylvania State University Press.

Pinto, Luiz Fernando Teixeira. 1989. Brazilian Tax Treatment of Foreign Investments. *Bulletin for International Fiscal Documentation* 43 (8–9) (August–September): 376–78.

Pires, Waldir. 1986. A Previdência Social é Viável. In *A Previdência Social é Viável*, Ministério da Previdência e Assistência Social (MPAS), 29–60. Brasília: MPAS.

———. 1989. A Social-Democracia nas Condições do Brasil. In *A Proposta Social-Democrata*, ed. Hélio Jaguaribe, 245–59. Rio de Janeiro: José Olympio.

Piscitelli, Roberto Bocaccio. 1988. Estudo Analítico dos Novos Dispositivos Constitucionais Tributários. In *O Sistema Tributário na Nova Constituição*, Roberto Bocaccio Piscitelli et al., 59–82. Brasília: Editora da UnB.

Pita, Claudino. 1993. *La Reforma Tributária en América Latina en la Década de los Años 80.* Documento de Trabajo no. 164. Washington, D.C.: IDB.

Pluta, Joseph. 1979. The Performance of South American Civilian and Military Governments from a Socio-Economic Perspective. *Development and Change* 10 (3) (July): 461–83.

PMDB (Partido do Movimento Democrático Brasileiro). 1982. Esperança e Mudança. *Revista do PMDB* 4 (October–November).

———. 1987. Primeiro Congresso. Teses e Resoluções. Vol. 2. *Revista do PMDB* 10 (July).

PNBE (Pensamento Nacional das Bases Empresariais). 1989. Relatório de Atividades do PNBE. São Paulo: PNBE.

———. 1992. Proposta do PNBE sobre Reforma Tributária. São Paulo: PNBE.

Ponte, Luis Roberto. 1992. Estudos para uma Reforma Tributária. Brasília: n.p.

———. 1993. *Proposta Revisional, N° 8227.* Brasília: Congresso Nacional. Revisão da Constituição Federal.

Pontusson, Jonas. 1988. *Swedish Social Democracy and British Labour.* Occasional Paper no. 19. Western Societies Program, Cornell University.

Portes, Alejandro. 1985. Latin American Class Structures. *Latin American Research Review* 20 (3): 7–39.

Portes, Alejandro, and Richard Schauffler. 1993. Competing Perspectives on the Latin American Informal Sector. *Population and Development Review* 19 (1) (March): 33–60.

Poulantzas, Nicos. 1980. *State-Power-Socialism.* London: Verso.

Power, Timothy J. 1991. Politicized Democracy. *Journal of Interamerican Studies and World Affairs* 33 (3) (Fall): 75–112.

PIASS. GEIN (Programa de Interiorização das Ações de Saúde e Saneamento. Grupo Executivo Interministerial). Secretaria Técnica. 1979. *PIASS-Programa de Interiorização das Ações de Saúde e Saneamento.* Brasília: PIASS. GEIN.

Propostas de Revisão Constitucional. 1993. n.p.

Przeworski, Adam. 1985. *Capitalism and Social Democracy.* Cambridge: Cambridge University Press.

———. 1991. *Democracy and the Market.* Cambridge: Cambridge University Press.

Przeworski, Adam, and John Sprague. 1986. *Paper Stones.* Chicago: University of Chicago Press.

Purcell, John F.H., and Susan Kaufman. 1976. El Estado y la Empresa Privada. *Nueva Política* 1 (2) (April–June): 229–50.

———. 1977. Mexican Business and Public Policy. In *Authoritarianism and Corporatism in Latin America,* ed. James M. Malloy, 191–226. Pittsburgh: University of Pittsburgh Press.

Purcell, Susan Kaufman. 1981. Mexico: Clientelism, Corporatism and Political Stability. In *Political Clientelism, Patronage and Development,* ed. S.N. Eisenstadt and René Lemarchand, 191–216. Beverly Hills: Sage.

Rae, Douglas, and Carol Fessler. 1981. The Varieties of Equality. In *Value Judgement and Income Distribution,* ed. Robert A. Solo and Charles W. Anderson, 201–26. New York: Praeger.

Rebouças, Osmundo. 1984. Sistema Tributário e Justiça Fiscal. *Revista Econômica do Nordeste* 15 (4) (October–December): 633–52.

Reforma da Previdência. 1992. Brasília? n.p.

Rehren, Alfredo. 1993. La Presidencia en el Gobierno de la Concertación. *Estudios Sociales* 75 (January–March): 15–38.

Reis, Fábio Wanderley. 1988. Consolidação Democrática e Construção do Estado. In *A Democracia no Brasil*, ed. Fábio Wanderley Reis and Guillermo O'Donnell, 13–40. São Paulo: Vértice.

Remmer, Karen. 1989. *Military Rule in Latin America*. Boston: Unwin Hyman.

Resende, Valmir José de. 1986. A Tributação dos Ganhos de Capital. *Revista de Finanças Públicas* 46 (368) (October–December): 28–46.

Reyna, José Luis. 1977. Redefining the Authoritarian Regime. In *Authoritarianism in Mexico*, ed. José Luis Reyna and Richard S. Weinert, 155–71. Philadelphia: Institute for the Study of Human Issues.

Rezende da Silva, Fernando A. 1976. Redistribuição de Renda Através da Previdência Social. *Revista de Administração Pública* 10 (4) (October–December): 7–19.

——. 1984. A Imprevidência da Previdência. *Revista de Economia Política* 4 (2) (April–June): 51–67.

——. 1987. O Crescimento (Descontrolado) da Intervenção Governamental na Economia Brasileira. In *As Origens da Crise*, ed. Olavo Brasil de Lima Jr. and Sérgio Henrique Abranches, 214–52. São Paulo: Vértice.

——, ed. 1987. *Estudos para a Reforma Tributária*. Vol. 1. *Proposta de Reforma do Sistema Tributário Brasileiro*. Texto para Discussão Interna no. 104. Rio de Janeiro: IPEA/INPES.

——. 1992. Papel e Custo do Estado. n.p.

Rezende da Silva, Fernando A., and Beatriz Azeredo Silva. 1987. *Estudos para a Reforma Tributária*. Vol. 4: *Contribuições Sociais*. Texto para Discussão Interna no. 107. Rio de Janeiro: IPEA/INPES.

Rezende da Silva, Fernando A., et al. 1982. Os Custos da Assistência Médica e a Crise Financeira da Previdência Social. *Dados* 25 (1): 25–43.

Roberts, Bryan. 1978. *Cities of Peasants*. Beverly Hills: Sage.

Rocha, Flávio. 1992. Imposto Único. Um Por Todos. Todos Por Um. Brasília: n.p.

Rochon, Thomas R., and Michael J. Mitchell. 1989. Social Bases of the Transition to Democracy in Brazil. *Comparative Politics* 21 (3) (April): 307–22.

Rodrigues, Leôncio Martins. 1990. *CUT: Os Militantes e a Ideologia*. Rio de Janeiro: Paz e Terra.

——. 1990. *Partidos e Sindicatos*. São Paulo: Atica.

——. 1991. As Tendências Políticas na Formação das Centrais Sindicais. In *O Sindicalismo Brasileiro nos Anos 80*, ed. Armando Boito Jr., 11–42. Rio de Janeiro: Paz e Terra.

Rodrigues, Leôncio Martins, and Adalberto Moreira Cardoso. 1993. *Força Sindical*. São Paulo: Paz e Terra.

Rodrigues Filho, José. 1987. A Distribuição dos Recursos de Saúde no Brasil. *Revista de Administração de Empresas* 27 (3) (July–September): 52–57.

Rodriguez Neto, Eleutério. 1988. Saúde: Promessas e Limites da Constituição. Ph.D. Dissertation, Faculdade de Medicina, Universidade de São Paulo.

Roemer, John. 1986. "Rational Choice" Marxism. In *Analytical Marxism*, ed. John Roemer, 191–201. Cambridge: Cambridge University Press.

Rokkan, Stein. 1966. Norway: Numerical Democracy and Corporate Pluralism. In *Political Oppositions in Western Democracies*, ed. Robert A. Dahl, 70–115. New Haven: Yale University Press.

Roriz, Ubirajara Sá. 1980. Uma Análise da Distribuição dos Benefícios da Assistência Médico-Hospitalar Urbana da Previdência Social. M.A. Thesis, Fundação Getúlio Vargas, Rio de Janeiro.

Rosa, José Rui Gonçalves. 1986. O Sistema Integrado de Tributação de Empresas e Acionistas. *Revista de Finanças Públicas* 46 (368) (October–December): 5–27.

Rosas, Carlos W. Chaves. 1978. A Matéria Financeira e a Matéria Tributária no Direito Constitucional Brasileiro. *Revista de Informação Legislativa* 15 (57) (January–March): 45–54.

Rosas, Eric Jener. 1988. Os Inimigos da Reforma Sanitária. *Saúde em Debate* 22 (October): 13–19.

Rosenberg, Mark B. 1979. Social Security Policymaking in Costa Rica. *Latin American Research Review* 14 (1): 116–33.

——. 1981. Social Reform in Costa Rica. *Hispanic American Historical Review* 61 (2) (May): 278–96.

Rosenberg, Mark, and James M. Malloy. 1978. Indirect Participation versus Social Equity in the Evolution of Latin American Social Security Policy. In *Political Participation in Latin America*. Vol.1. *Citizen and State*, ed. John Booth and Mitchell A. Seligson, 157–71. New York: Holmes & Meier.

Rudolph, Lloyd I., and Susanne Hoeber Rudolph. 1987. *In Pursuit of Lakshmi*. Chicago: University of Chicago Press.

Rueschemeyer, Dietrich, and Peter B. Evans. 1985. The State and Economic Transformation. In *Bringing the State Back In*, ed. Peter B. Evans, Dietrich Rueschemeyer, and Theda Scocpol, 44–77. Cambridge: Cambridge University Press.

Rueschemeyer, Dietrich, Evelyne Huber Stephens, and John D. Stephens. 1992. *Capitalist Development and Democracy*. Chicago: University of Chicago Press.

Russin, Jonathan, Enrique Pastor Vinardell, and David H. Bralove. 1978. Spain: New Personal Income Tax Law. *Tax Management International Journal* 78 (12) (December): 3–6.

Sachs, Jeffrey D. 1989. *Social Conflict and Populist Policies in Latin America*. Working Paper no. 2897. Cambridge, MA: National Bureau of Economic Research.

Salcedo, José María. 1992. Sí Hay Alternativas. *Quehacer* 79 (September–October): 11–23.

Salgado, René. 1987. Economic Pressure Groups and Policy-Making in Venezuela. *Latin American Research Review* 22 (3): 91–121.

Sandbrook, Richard. 1985. *The Politics of Africa's Economic Stagnation*. Cambridge: Cambridge University Press.

Sandoval, Salvador A. M. 1993. *Social Change and Labor Unrest in Brazil Since 1945*. Boulder, CO: Westview.

Santos, Maria Helena de Castro, and Antonio Luiz Paixão. 1989. O Álcool Combustível e a Pecuária de Corte. In *O Estado e as Políticas Públicas na Transição Democrática*, ed. Alexandrina Sobreira de Moura, 221–46. São Paulo: Vértice.

Santos, Wanderley Guilherme dos. 1985. A Pós-'Revolução' Brasileira. In *Brasil, Sociedade Democrática*, Hélio Jaguaribe et al., 223–335. Rio de Janeiro: José Olympio.

——. 1986. *Crise e Castigo*. São Paulo: Vértice.

——. 1987. *Cidadania e Justiça*, 2d ed. Rio de Janeiro: Campus.

——. 1992. Fronteiras do Estado Mínimo. In *O Brasil e as Reformas Políticas*, ed. João Paulo dos Reis Velloso, 49–94. Rio de Janeiro: José Olympio.

Sardenberg, Carlos Alberto. 1987. *Aventura e Agonia*. São Paulo: Companhia das Letras.

Saúde em Debate. 1985. Ed. Centro Brasileiro de Estudos de Saúde, no. 17.

Schattschneider, Elmer E. 1975. *The Semisovereign People*. Hinsdale, IL: Dryden.

Schmidt, Steffen W., et al., eds. 1977. *Friends, Followers, and Factions*. Berkeley and Los Angeles: University of California Press.

Schmitt, Carl. 1987. *Der Begriff des Politischen*. Berlin: Duncker & Humblot.

Schmitter, Philippe C. 1971. *Interest Conflict and Political Change in Brazil*. Stanford: Stanford University Press.

——. 1973. The "Portugalization" of Brazil? In *Authoritarian Brazil*, ed. Alfred Stepan, 179–232. New Haven: Yale University Press.

——. 1974. Still the Century of Corporatism? In *The New Corporatism*, ed. Fredrick B. Pike and Thomas Stritch, 85–131. Notre Dame, IN: University of Notre Dame Press.

——. 1981. *Needs, Interests, Concerns, Actions, Associations and Modes of Intermediation*. Chicago: University of Chicago.

——. 1983. Democratic Theory and Neo-Corporatist Practice. *Social Research* 50 (4) (Winter): 885–928.

——. 1992. The Consolidation of Democracy and Representation of Social Groups. *American Behavioral Scientist* 35 (4–5) (March–June): 422–49.

Schmitter, Philippe C., and Terry Lynn Karl. 1991. What Democracy Is . . . and Is Not. *Journal of Democracy* 2 (3) (Summer): 75–88.

Schneider, Ben Ross. 1987. Politics Within the State. Ph.D. Dissertation, University of California, Berkeley.

——. 1991. Brazil Under Collor. *World Policy Journal* 8 (2) (Spring): 321–47.

——. 1991. *Politics Within the State*. Pittsburgh: University of Pittsburgh Press.

——. 1992. The Rise and Collapse of the Developmental State in Brazil and Mexico. Princeton: Princeton University.

Schwartzman, Simon. 1982. *Bases do Autoritarismo Brasileiro*, 2d ed. Rio de Janeiro: Campus.

Scott, James C. 1977. Patron-Client Politics and Political Change in Southeast Asia. In *Friends, Followers, and Factions*, ed. Steffen W. Schmidt et al., 123–46. Berkeley and Los Angeles: University of California Press.

Scott, James C., and Benedict J. Kerkvliet. 1977. How Traditional Rural Patrons Lose Legitimacy. In *Friends, Followers, and Factions*, ed. Steffen W. Schmidt et al., 439–58. Berkeley and Los Angeles: University of California Press.

SEPLAN (Secretaria de Planejamento da Presidência da República). 1985. Programa de Prioridades Sociais. Exposições de Motivos e Anteprojetos. Brasília: SEPLAN.

SEPLAN (Secretaria de Planejamento da Presidência da República). GT Interministerial dos Encargos Sociais (SEPLAN-MPAS). 1979. Encargos Sociais e PIS-PASEP: Proposta de Nova Base de Incidência. Brasília: SEPLAN.

SEPLAN. SRH (Secretaria de Planejamento da Presidência da República. Secretaria de Recursos Humanos). 1989. Quadro de Antecedentes dos Recursos Humanos. Brasília: SEPLAN. SRH.

Serra, José. 1983. O Sistema Tributário. *Revista de Economia Política* 3 (1) (January–March): 5–29.

——. 1989. A Crise Fiscal e as Diretrizes Orçamentárias. *Revista de Economia Política* 9 (4) (October–December): 137–55.

Shalev, Michael, and Walter Korpi. 1980. Working Class Mobilization and American Exceptionalism. *Economic and Industrial Democracy* 1 (1) (February): 31–61.

Shepsle, Kenneth A. 1986. Institutional Equilibrium and Equilibrium Institutions. In *Political Science*, ed. Herbert F. Weisberg, 51–81. New York: Agathon Press.

——. 1989. Studying Institutions. *Journal of Theoretical Politics* 1 (2) (April): 131–47.

Shoup, Carl S. 1965. *O Sistema Tributário Brasileiro*. Rio de Janeiro: Fundação Getúlio Vargas, Comissão de Reforma do Ministério da Fazenda.

Silva, Eduardo. 1992. Capitalist Coalitions, Neoliberal Restructuring, and Redemocratization: Chile 1973–1991. Paper for 88th Annual Meeting, American Political Science Association, September 3–6, Chicago.

Silva, Lytha Spíndola. 1986. O Impasse da Tributação da Renda Agrícola. *Revista de Finanças Públicas* 46 (368) (October–December): 47–63.

Silva, Maria Ozanira da Silva e. 1989. *Política Habitacional Brasileira*. São Paulo: Cortez.

Silva, Mário Tinoco da. 1988. O Novo Sistema Tributário e a Crise Fiscal. In *O Sistema Tributário na Nova Constituição*, Roberto Bocaccio Piscitelli et al., 11–28. Brasília: Editora da UnB.

Silverman, Sydel F. 1977. Patronage and Community-Nation Relationships in Central Italy. In *Friends, Followers, and Factions*, ed. Steffen W. Schmidt et al., 293–304. Berkeley and Los Angeles: University of California Press.

Simonsen, Mário Henrique. 1975. A Política Tributária como Instrumento de Desenvolvimento Econômico. *Projeção* 5: 6–11.

———. 1977. *A Política Financeira do Atual Governo.* Brasília: Ministério da Fazenda. Gabinete do Ministro.

Singer, André. 1990. Collor na Periferia. In *De Geisel a Collor,* ed. Bolívar Lamounier, 135–52. São Paulo: Editora Sumaré.

Singer, Paul. 1987. *O Dia da Lagarta.* São Paulo: Brasiliense.

Sirowy, Larry, and Alex Inkeles. 1990. The Effects of Democracy on Economic Growth and Inequality. *Studies in Comparative International Development* 25 (1) (Spring): 126–57.

Skidmore, Thomas E. 1988. *The Politics of Military Rule in Brazil, 1964–1985.* London: Oxford University Press.

Skocpol, Theda. 1979. *States and Social Revolutions.* Cambridge: Cambridge University Press.

———. 1985. Bringing the State Back In. In *Bringing the State Back In,* ed. Peter B. Evans, Dietrich Rueschemeyer, and Theda Skocpol, 3–37. Cambridge: Cambridge University Press.

Skowronek, Stephen. 1982. *Building a New American State.* Cambridge: Cambridge University Press.

Sloan, John W. 1984. *Public Policy in Latin America.* Pittsburgh: University of Pittsburgh Press.

Sloan, John W., and Kent Tedin. 1987. The Consequences of Regime Type for Public-Policy Outputs. *Comparative Political Studies* 20 (1) (April): 98–124.

Snow, Peter G. 1979. *Political Forces in Argentina,* revised ed. New York: Praeger.

Sola, Lourdes. 1988. Choque Heterodoxo e Transição Democrática sem Ruptura. In *O Estado da Transição,* ed. Sola, 13–62. São Paulo: Vértice.

Sombart, Werner. 1976. *Why Is There No Socialism in the United States?* White Plains, NY: International Arts and Sciences Press.

Souza, Maria do Carmo Campello de. 1983. *Estado e Partidos Políticos no Brasil (1930 a 1964),* 2d ed. São Paulo: Alfa-Omega.

SP. SMS. CMS (São Paulo. Secretaria Municipal de Saúde. Conselho Municipal de Saúde). 1989. Informativo do Conselho Municipal de Saúde, Novembro/89. São Paulo: SMS.

Spain. First Stage in Social Security Reform. 1986. *Social and Labour Bulletin* 86 (1): 163–65.

Spalding, Rose J. 1994. *Capitalists and Revolution in Nicaragua.* Chapel Hill: University of North Carolina Press.

Stallings, Barbara, and Robert Kaufman, eds. 1989. *Debt and Democracy in Latin America.* Boulder, CO: Westview.

Stepan, Alfred. 1978. *The State and Society.* Princeton: Princeton University Press.

——. 1988. *Rethinking Military Politics.* Princeton: Princeton University Press.

——, ed. 1989. *Democratizing Brazil.* New York: Oxford University Press.

Stephens, Evelyne Huber. 1983. The Peruvian Military Government, Labor Mobilization, and the Political Strength of the Left. *Latin American Research Review* 18 (2): 57–93.

Stephens, John D. 1986. *The Transition from Capitalism to Socialism.* Urbana: University of Illinois Press.

Stokes, Susan C. 1991. Politics and Latin America's Urban Poor. *Latin American Research Review* 26 (2): 75–101.

Stralen, Cornelis van. 1989. A Luta do Movimento Sindical dos Trabalhadores Rurais pela Equiparação da Assistência Médica Rural à Assistência Médica Urbana. *Saúde em Debate* 24 (March): 28–36.

Stralen, Cornelis van, et al. 1983. Movimentos Sociais Urbanos e a Democratização dos Serviços de Saúde. *Revista de Administração Pública* 17 (3) (July–September): 38–60.

Streeck, Wolfgang. 1992. Interest Heterogeneity and Organizing Capacity. Chap. in *Social Institutions and Economic Performance,* 76–104. London: Sage.

Streeck, Wolfgang, and Philippe C. Schmitter. 1985. Community, Market, State—and Associations? In *Private Interest Government,* ed. Streeck and Schmitter, 1–29. London: Sage.

Suleiman, Ezra N. 1974. *Politics, Power, and Bureaucracy in France.* Princeton: Princeton University Press.

SUNAT (Superintendencia Nacional de Administración Tributaria). 1994. *Nota Tributaria* 3 (9) (September).

Sunkel, Osvaldo. 1972. Big Business and "Dependencia." *Foreign Affairs* 50 (3) (April): 517–31.

Suplicy, Eduardo Matarazzo. 1992. *Programa de Garantia de Renda Mínima.* Brasília: Senado Federal.

TCU (Tribunal de Contas da União). 1989. SUDS—Sistema Unificado e Descentralizado de Saúde nos Estados. TC N° 007.598/88–2. Brasília: TCU.

Teixeira, Aloisio. 1986. A Aposentadoria da Conta Movimento. *Presença* 7 (March): 61–70.

Teixeira, Carmen Fontes, Aníbal M. Silvany Neto, and Mari Saho. 1979. PIASS: Uma Alternativa para a Crise? M.A. Thesis, Universidade Federal da Bahia.

Teixeira, Sonia Maria Fleury. 1988. O Dilema da Reforma Sanitária Brasileira. In *Reforma Sanitária,* Giovanni Berlinguer et al., 195–207. São Paulo: HUCITEC/CEBES.

Temporão, José Gomes. 1989. Notas sobre o SUDS. In *A Experiência SUDS e os Desafios Atuais da Reforma Sanitária,* ed. ABRASCO, 49–53. Manguinhos: ABRASCO.

Thelen, Kathleen, and Sven Steinmo. 1992. Historical Institutionalism in Comparative Politics. In *Structuring Politics,* ed. Steinmo, Thelen, and Frank Longstreth, 1–32. Cambridge: Cambridge University Press.

Tilly, Charles, ed. 1975. *The Formation of National States in Western Europe.* Princeton: Princeton University Press.

——. 1992. *Coercion, Capital, and European States, AD 990–1992.* Cambridge: Basil Blackwell.

Tirado, Ricardo. 1992. Asociaciones Empresariales de Cúpula en México. Paper for XVII International Congress, Latin American Studies Association, September 24–27, Los Angeles.

Tironi, Eugenio. 1990. *Autoritarismo, Modernización y Marginalidad.* Santiago: Sur.

Tocqueville, Alexis de. 1955. *The Old Régime and the French Revolution.* Garden City, N.Y.: Doubleday.

Toledo, Luiz Plínio Moraes de. 1988. Considerações Gerais. In *Seminário sobre Financiamento do Sistema Unificado e Descentralizado de Saúde,* ed. Governo do Estado de São Paulo, Secretaria de Saúde, 227–30. São Paulo: Governo do Estado de São Paulo, Secretaria de Saúde.

Trimberger, Ellen Kay. 1978. *Revolution from Above.* New Brunswick, NJ: Transaction.

Tsebelis, George. 1990. *Nested Games.* Berkeley and Los Angeles: University of California Press.

——. 1994. Decision-Making in Political Systems. Paper for 90th Annual Meeting, American Political Science Association, September 1–4, New York.

Urrutia, Miguel. 1991. On the Absence of Economic Populism in Colombia. In *The Macroeconomics of Populism in Latin America,* ed. Rüdiger Dornbusch and Sebastian Edwards, 369–87. Chicago: University of Chicago Press.

Valenzuela, J. Samuel. 1992. Democratic Consolidation in Post-Transitional Settings. In *Issues in Democratic Consolidation,* ed. Scott Mainwaring, Guillermo O'Donnell, and Valenzuela, 57–104. Notre Dame, IN: University of Notre Dame Press.

Varsano, Ricardo. 1982. Os Incentivos Fiscais do Imposto de Renda das Empresas. *Revista Brasileira de Economia* 36 (2) (April–June): 107–27.

——. 1987. *Estudos para a Reforma Tributária.* Vol.3. *Tributação de Mercadorias e Serviços.* Texto para Discussão Interna no. 106. Rio de Janeiro: IPEA/INPES.

——. 1988. *De Como a Metamorfose do Pacote Preserveu o Déficit Público e uma Proposta para Mitigá-lo.* Informe Conjuntural no. 1/88. Rio de Janeiro: IPEA/INPES.

Verba, Sidney, Norman H. Nie, and Jae-on Kim. 1978. *Participation and Political Equality.* Chicago: University of Chicago Press.

Vianna, Maria Lucia Teixeira Werneck. 1989. *Política Social e Transição Democrática.* Texto para Discussão no. 226. Rio de Janeiro: UFRJ. Instituto de Economia Industrial.

Vianna, Solon Magalhães. 1989. *Eqüidade nos Serviços de Saúde,* Texto para Discussão no. 24. Brasília: IPEA/IPLAN.

——. 1992. A Seguridade Social, o Sistema Único de Saúde e a Partilha dos Recursos. n.p.

Villela, Luiz Arruda. 1989. *A Identificação dos Gastos Tributários no Brasil.* Estudos sobre Economia do Setor Público no. 3. Rio de Janeiro: IPEA/INPES.

Viola, Eduardo J. 1987. *O Movimento Ecológico no Brasil (1974–1986)*. Working Paper no. 93. Notre Dame, IN: Kellogg Institute, University of Notre Dame.

Wade, Robert. 1985. The Market for Public Office. *World Development* 13 (4) (April): 467–97.

Waisman, Carlos H. 1992. Argentina's Revolution from Above. In *The New Argentine Democracy*, ed. Edward Epstein, 228–43. Westport, CT: Praeger.

Waldmann, Peter. 1974. *Der Peronismus 1943–1955*. Hamburg: Hoffmann & Campe.

Wallerstein, Michael. 1989. Union Organization in Advanced Industrial Democracies. *American Political Science Review* 83 (2) (June): 481–501.

Weber, Max. 1971. *Gesammelte Politische Schriften*, 3d ed. Tübingen: J.C.B. Mohr.

——. 1973. *Soziologie, Universalgeschichtliche Analysen, Politik*. Stuttgart: Alfred Kröner.

——. 1976. *Wirtschaft und Gesellschaft*, 5th ed. Tübingen: J.C.B. Mohr.

Weede, Erich, and Horst Tiefenbach. 1981. Some Recent Explanations of Income Inequality. *International Studies Quarterly* 25 (2): 255–82.

Weffort, Francisco C. 1980. *O Populismo na Política Brasileira*. Rio de Janeiro: Paz e Terra.

——. 1992. Brasil: Condenado à Modernização. In *Brasileiro: Cidadão?* Roberto Da Matta et al., 185–215. São Paulo: Cultura.

——. 1992. *Qual Democracia?* São Paulo: Companhia das Letras.

Weir, Margaret, and Theda Skocpol. 1985. State Structures and the Possibilities for "Keynesian" Responses to the Great Depression in Sweden, Britain, and the United States. In *Bringing the State Back In*, ed. Peter B. Evans, Dietrich Rueschemeyer, and Theda Skocpol, 107–63. Cambridge: Cambridge University Press.

Weyland, Kurt. 1993. The Rise and Fall of President Collor and Its Impact on Brazilian Democracy. *Journal of Interamerican Studies and World Affairs* 35 (1): 1–37.

——. 1997. "Growth With Equity" in Chile's New Democracy? *Latin American Research Review* 32 (1), forthcoming.

——. 1996. Neo-Populism and Neo-Liberalism in Latin America. *Studies in Comparative International Development*, forthcoming.

——. 1995. Preliminary Thoughts on a Theory of Leadership. Paper for 91st Annual Meeting, American Political Science Association, Chicago, August 31–September 3.

Williamson, Oliver. 1985. *The Economic Institutions of Capitalism*. New York: Free Press.

Wilson, Graham K. 1982. Why Is There No Corporatism in the United States? In *Patterns of Corporatist Policy Making*, ed. Gerhard Lehmbruch and Philippe C. Schmitter, 219–36. Beverly Hills: Sage.

Wilson, James Q. 1980. The Politics of Regulation. In *The Politics of Regulation*, ed. Wilson, 357–94. New York: Basic Books.

Wise, Carol. 1989. Democratization, Crisis, and the APRA's Modernization Project in Peru. In *Debt and Democracy in Latin America*, ed. Barbara Stallings and Robert Kaufman, 163–80. Boulder, CO: Westview.

World Bank. *World Development Report (WDR)*. New York: Oxford University Press.

———. 1988. *Brazil: Public Spending on Social Programs*. Vol. 1. Report No. 7086-BR. Washington, D.C.: World Bank.

———. 1989. *Brazil: The Macroeconomics of Social Security*. Report No. 7800-BR. Washington, D.C.: World Bank.

———. 1989. Brazil. Tax Reform Proposals. Preliminary Report. Washington, D.C.: World Bank.

———. 1990. *Argentina. Tax Policy for Stabilization and Economic Recovery*. Washington, D.C.: World Bank.

———. 1993. *Argentina. From Insolvency to Growth*. Washington, D.C.: World Bank.

Wozniak, Lynne. 1992–1993. The Dissolution of Party-Union Relations in Spain. *International Journal of Political Economy* 22 (4) (Winter): 73–90.

INDEX